OLYMPUS INC.

OLYMPUS INC.

‘Just occasionally, a book stuns you with its freshness and wisdom. Olympus Inc. is the best thing on corporate culture I’ve read. Go get it.’

Guy Claxton – University of Bristol
Author of *The Wayward Mind*

‘Excellent . . . scholarly . . . well-researched . . . They analyze organizations as self-organizing, living systems filled with deep archetypal patterns . . . Their creative approach provides richness and color to our insights about complexities of organizational culture.’

Richard N. Knowles
Author of *The Leadership Dance: Pathways to Extraordinary Organizational Effectiveness*

‘. . . an impressive case for redefining the role of executives, consultants and change agents in organizational transformation. This book goes from ‘soup to nuts’ in its deep exploration of culture and Greco-Roman mythology, to real hands-on assessment tools and facilitation strategies. A wonderful and valued addition to the practitioner’s tool bag.’

Steve Zuieback – International Management Consultant
President of Synectics: Creative Management Strategies

This book is a treat for cognitive-oriented readers. The bibliography serves as a compendium n the field. I personally await a whole book on just the material in the Appendix.’

Michael Grinder – International Management Consultant
Author of *Patterns of Permission: The Science of Group Dynamics*

. . . extraordinary; as remarkable for its wisdom and practicality as for the depth and readth of its scholarship . . . Neville and Dalmau throw light into the dark places of rganizations – revealing why things are the way they are . . . Invaluable, ‘divinely inspired’ uidance for those seriously interested in the dynamics of organizations life and change.’

Peter Waterhouse
Managing Director, Workplace Learning Initiatives

ernie Neville and Tim Dalmau are the right people to introduce you to archetypes. addition they have the experience to explain the application of the archetypes for rganizational diagnosis and intervention. As a bonus you also learn about their DNAI, e Dalmau-Neville Archetypology Indicator, and how it might be used.’

Bob Dick – Southern Cross University
Author of *Jung for Sceptics*

Also by Bernie Neville

Educating Psyche – Flat Chat Press (2005)

Qualitative Research In Adult Education – CREW (1994)

Qualitative Research Practice In Adult Education – David Lovell Publishing (1996)

New Learning Technologies: A Challenge For Teachers – Graduate School of Education, Melbourne (1999)

Towards Re-Enchantment: Education, Imagination and the Search for Meaning – Post Pressed Publishers (2005)

As Others See Us: The Values Debate in Australia – Australian Scholarly Publishing (2008)

Also by Tim Dalmau

From The Profane To The Sacred: Small Groups As Vehicles For Cultural Change – Interchange Publications (1990)

Managing Transitions: A Key To Creating Effective Learning Environments – Interchange Publications (1990)

To Tame A Unicorn . . .: Recipes for Cultural Intervention – Abridged Version Revised – Interchange Publications (1989)

Values In Action: Applying the Ideas of Argyris and Schon – Second Edition – Interchange Publications (1999)

OLYMPUS INC.

Intervening for Cultural Change in Organizations

Bernie Neville Tim Dalmau

First published as e-book - Contemporary Arts Media 2004
Published by Flat Chat Press 2008

This edition published in 2010 by

Karnac Books Ltd
118 Finchley Road
London NW3 5HT

British Library Cataloguing in Publication Data
A C.I.P. for this book is available from the British Library

ISBN: 978-1-85575-804-9

Printed in Great Britain
www.karnacbooks.com

About the Authors

Bernie Neville

Bernie Neville is Associate Professor of Education at La Trobe University. He has taught, researched, written and consulted widely on educational practice, communication and organizational change for over 30 years. Neville's *Educating Psyche*, a companion volume to *Olympus Inc.*, has received extensive praise from educators and critics.

Tim Dalmau

Tim Dalmau is regarded as one of Australia's foremost management consultants. He has consulted for private and public institutions all over the world for more than 25 years. He is the author or co-author of an extensive range of publications on action research, management and organizational change.

PREFACE

In July 1991, we found ourselves in Copenhagen presenting papers at the annual meeting of the Standing Conference on Organizational Symbolism. Our papers both dealt with organizational culture and how cultural change can be initiated. We were both interested in exploring the nature of what we were calling 'the postmodern organization' and we had both brought a Jungian orientation to our work. When we looked closely at the market-driven, opportunistic, ethically bereft, image-obsessed, structurally slippery corporations and bureaucracies that had flourished in the eighties, we imagined we saw an ancient, deeply embedded pattern – Jungians would call it archetypal – in which the classical Greeks would recognized the god Hermes at work.

Talk about Hermes-inflated organizations led to talk about Zeus organizations, Eros organizations, and the like – all of which were familiar to us. Further late-night, wine-enhanced conversation led to the light-hearted experiment of designing a diagnostic instrument, called – with appropriate hubris – the Dalmau-Neville Archetypology Indicator, to provide consultants with a tool for distinguishing one god-inflated culture from another.

As you can see, the DNAI began its life as a joke. However, it seems significant that it has had a life. It has been used as a consulting tool and as a research instrument by ourselves and others for more than a decade. It has been subjected to statistical analysis and made the basis of strategic interventions. Ongoing experience and feedback (statistical as well as professional) have led to various modifications and its eventual electronic incarnation as an appendix to this book.

The book itself can be read as background information for consultants, change agents, students, or the simply curious who want to use the DNAI. Or it can stand as one of the very few serious attempts to bring depth psychology to the discussion of organizational change. One of us (Tim) is a management consultant who likes to write a bit. The other (Bernie) is an academic who does a bit of consulting when his teaching and research allow him time for it.

The thinking in Olympus Inc. has been shaped through innumerable conversations with friends and colleagues; the text itself has been shaped through the editing skills of Helen Neville. We are deeply grateful to all who have contributed.

Bernie Neville

Tim Dalmau

OLYMPUS INC.

CONTENTS

OLYMPUS INC.

INTRODUCTION

Every piece of human behavior, whatever its manifest and literal content, is always also a psychological statement.[1]
James Hillman

An old Zen koan points to the dilemma: How can a man riding on an ox, looking for an ox, ever find an ox.[2]
Sam Keen

The past two decades have seen an enormous increase in interest in the notion of organizational culture. During the same period we have seen a rise and fall of interest in the notion of the learning organization and the notion of quality in organizations.

At the heart of these movements is the very reasonable assumption that it is possible for an organization or other social system to reflect on its own behavior as a system and to adjust accordingly. But just who is supposed to do this reflection, and what are they supposed to reflect upon and subsequently adjust? The two quotations at the start of this introduction point to our particular perspective on these questions. It has been our experience that much of what goes on in organizations is hidden and tacit, deeply patterned into the behavior of the people who constitute the organization, so much so that it is largely beyond their awareness and often beyond their influence.

Those who study organizations and the challenges facing their leaders tell us that success in the next decade or more will depend ultimately on leaders' ability to engage all the members of their systems in continuous regeneration. Such insights represent a significant shift away from the individualistic psychology that has pervaded so much of the literature on management and leadership in the last two decades. They signify an increasing recognition and appreciation of the role of the large group in organizational transformation and improvement. But how to think about, manage, and intervene in the large group as an entity in its own right is not something in which your average executive, manager, or consultant usually has had much experience or training; nor have they developed much know-how. This is especially the case with those dynamics and forces at work in a group which are largely unconscious, recurrent, and stable over time; many of these can be grouped under the label *organizational culture*.

This book does not aim to provide the reader with a comprehensive model that explains everything that should be considered in trying to build a self-reflective and self-improving organization. Rather, we explore three specific doorways of understanding through which it is possible to enter the room of organizational and systemic behavior and gain greater insight into, and influence over, the tacit and unconscious aspects of the behavior of large groups of people in organizations. These three doorways are organizational culture, archetypal psychology, and group process intervention methodologies. These have captured our interest and demanded much of our energy over the past two decades. Nevertheless, as the Zen koan to which Keen refers suggests, entry through these doorways is fraught with contradictions, paradoxes, and dilemmas that minds who seek quick fixes or believe that all matters can be solved by rational inquiry will find frustrating.

We attempt to provide the reader with an increased appreciation of these complexities, and provide a means whereby the senior executive, manager, or change agent can bring greater reliability and intentionality to his or her attempts to influence such organizational forces as culture and values. Good working models provide a bridge between theory and action. Like all working models, ours is in a state of flux, so we would value comments from readers; your reactions will help us modify the model and make it more useful. Above all, this book represents a reflection on those things that intrigue us about people and the way they behave in groups and organizations, and it documents some of the insights and techniques that we have found useful in understanding and intervening in these phenomena.

There is considerable risk in a brief study of organizational culture – especially a study that aims at practical application in organizational change – of oversimplifying the notion of culture. Organizational culture cannot really be dealt with simply. As Gareth Morgan explains, during the 1970s and 1980s the metaphor of organization as culture replaced the earlier metaphors of organization as machine, as organism and as brain. However, these earlier metaphors still pervade the thinking of many managers and leaders in private and public sector organizations. Many organizations still treat their people as cogs in a machine, a consequence of the mechanical metaphor. Now, as the environment of organizations changes at an ever faster rate, the usefulness of this image decreases. Yet it is surprisingly persistent. Accompanying the later metaphor of organization as living organism, it coexists with such organismic developments as systems theory, contingency theory, socio-technical analysis, work redesign, systems redesign, and the like.

In this discussion of organizational culture we are not setting up the metaphor of culture as an alternative metaphor to the machine and the organism, competing with them in a contest to determine which model most adequately expresses the real nature of organizations. We do not believe that any of these images needs to be privileged over the others. In talking about organizations from within the metaphor of culture we are imagining organizations in a particular way, but it is a way that allows the meanings embedded in the other metaphors to be heard. Using the language of archetypal psychology to explore organizational culture enables us to acknowledge the metaphor in whatever we say about organizations; it enables us to acknowledge that organizations are both machines and organisms, and many other things besides; and it enables us to reflect on the images that shape our own reflections. It also gives us a way of discriminating between organizational cultures, with a view to designing intervention strategies that are specifically adapted to specific organizations in specific contexts.

Our approach to organizations is determined not so much by what we think about them as by how we imagine them. In this book there are three key metaphors framing our discussion. One is a vertical metaphor. We imagine an organization through a metaphor of height and depth. Our reflections on this image are strongly influenced by the ideas of Edgar Schein, Carl Lundberg; and others who see organizational culture as manifested in layers or levels, from the hidden and unconscious to the obvious and conscious, and also on the work of Jean Gebser who distinguishes several structures of consciousness ranging from the least aware to the most aware. The second key image is a horizontal one. We see the culture of any organization manifesting a number of strands or dimensions set side by side, all of them having both conscious and unconscious elements. Our thinking about this leans heavily on the archetypal psychology of Carl Jung and James Hillman. Our third image is an evolutionary one. We imagine organizations, like all living forms, to have an innate tendency to move towards greater differentiation and greater complexity in spite of the many factors that inhibit or negate this tendency. In imagining organizations in this way we have been influenced by a wide range of thinkers, among whom we are most aware of Carl Rogers and Alfred North Whitehead.

Finally, our experience supports the argument that it is possible to intervene in the culture of an organization in ways that change it, for better or for worse. We hope that what we have to say will provide some guidance for those who want to make organizations more creative, more productive, and more satisfying for those who dwell in them.

---

1. J Hillman (1983) *Archetypal Psychology*, p. 18.
2. S Keen (1994) *Hymns to an Unknown God*, p. 35.

OLYMPUS INC.

1

GUIDING IDEAS

My attempt to simplify, by means of the concepts I have adumbrated, will prove to be very misleading unless the reader bears in mind that the group situation is mostly perplexing and confused; operations of what I call the group mentality, or the group culture, only occasionally emerge in any strikingly clear way.[1]

– Wilfred Bion –

We wish to say something useful about organizational process and organizational culture, but we must balance the desire to make a clear, simple, and useful statement of theory against the confusion and complexity of experience. The statement we make comes out of reflections on our own experience of being in organizations and of consulting to organizations, reflections that are shaped by particular images and ideas. Borrowing a term from Peter Senge and his colleagues, we seek in this chapter to outline some of the *guiding ideas* on which this discussion rests. These notions will be explored and expanded throughout the book, but are outlined here so that the reader may glimpse the key elements in our thinking as they unfold in the text.

Five guiding ideas

There are five *guiding ideas* that pervade much of our thinking and our responses when we act in a consultant capacity to client organizations.

Firstly there is a background awareness that the changes going on in organizations and the ongoing changes in the way we and others understand such phenomena are reflections of some very large changes occurring in society at large; specifically changes in people's understanding of the world, their ways of thinking and their images of what it is to be a human in a social context. Whether we want to refer to this contemporary consciousness as 'postmodern', 'late capitalist', or 'post-industrial', or by some other label, we would argue that people in 'developed' Western cultures make different assumptions about the world and respond to it in different ways than their grandparents did. Contemporary organizations reflect this different way of thinking.

Secondly, we follow Freud and Jung in proposing that all of the behavior in which humans engage has unconscious components to it: elements, forces, needs, or dynamics of which the individual or group are totally or partly unaware. Moreover, we have come to appreciate just how potent these unconscious elements are in organizational life, and how excruciatingly difficult intentional organizational change can be when it does not acknowledge them – and even when it does!

Thirdly, we are persuaded that organizational behavior, like individual behavior, is archetypally patterned. In Jungian psychology, archetypal patterns are understood as manifestations of collective unconscious processes. Jung variously referred to archetypes as 'organizing factors in the unconscious', 'dominants of the collective unconscious', 'living dispositions', 'nodal points of psychic energy', 'primordial images', 'systems of readiness for action', 'modes of comprehension', and 'patterns of instinctual behavior'. We are struck by the evidence of recurring patterns of thinking, feeling, and behaving that are evident in the behavior of organizations, and find that Jung's notion of archetype gives us a rich language for discussing them.

Fourthly, we have come to appreciate the reality and significance of the whole, especially when it comes to dealing with the unconscious dimensions of organizational life. Many of those who seek to make organizations more effective or more profitable seem to imagine the organization as an aggregate of individuals, often missing the fact that there are some things at work in organizations that are independent of the individuals and reside in the group, almost as if the group were a person in its own right. To us, this seems truer of the unconscious components of social systems than of the more surface, more visible, more obvious aspects.

Finally, we have come to appreciate just how unpredictable is the true nature of organizational change, especially cultural change. We do believe it is possible to achieve some intentional and purposeful shifts in the culture of social systems, but we recognize that this possibility exists in far more bounded situations and with far more limited results than some academics would have their readers believe and many consultants would have their clients believe.

Contemporary Organizations Exist in a Postmodern World

In the early 1980s there was a gradual but marked transformation in the literature on organizational culture. There was a movement away from describing organizations as having a single culture to explorations of the many sub-cultures that may constitute an organization. Similarly, literature on organizational behavior moved away from the attempt to simplify the discussion by focusing on one aspect of organizational behavior to a position that considered the many interacting variables and forces that make up organizational reality. These shifts were similar in nature to a much wider set of transformations occurring in society at large, a shift from unitary models to pluralistic models, from a belief in one truth to an acceptance of many truths.

Unitary theories of culture are an expression of a way of experiencing the world that no longer rings true for many people. European culture (which includes the culture of many former European colonies) has for some centuries functioned on the basic assumption that there was one truth about the nature of reality. There were many arguments, and even wars, about which version of the truth was the correct one, but nobody doubted that there was one truth.

While there are still religious, political, and scientific fundamentalists about, it has become increasingly common for people to be more relativistic and ambiguous in their notion of truth. This seems especially true for those living in the information-rich and more affluent parts of the Western world. There is a tendency for people to think of their beliefs as partial truths rather than as absolute truths, and to appreciate that there is more than one way of seeing things. Even people who are religious in the conventional sense are inclined to see their religious beliefs as relative, to acknowledge that other people may have different religious beliefs, and that these also have a claim to truth. They may understand that there is a core and absolute divine truth that human minds cannot grasp, so that different religious systems are simply more or less adequate attempts to express it. Or they may take a more radical stance, and see all truth as personally constructed, subjective, and relative. Whichever way they think about this, they are thinking in a way very different from the way religious believers used to think about religious truth even fifty years ago.

The French philosopher Jacques Lyotard sees this relativization of belief as a symptom of a major change in consciousness that has been taking place. He talks about the decline of the grand narratives, such as Christianity, Rationalism, and Marxism, which provided their followers with a set of beliefs that they could assume were widely held by others. He claims that it is no longer possible to assume that there are universally held beliefs, ethics, or values in the developed societies.

In describing this new way of being in the world, which he referred to as 'the postmodern condition', he has noted a number of other specific characteristics. Lyotard suggests that postmodernity is an inevitable consequence of the information revolution. Our society is characterized by a constant flow of information, which has become essential to the maintenance of that society, regardless of what the information is actually about. The boundary between important information and trivial information has largely disappeared. This uninterrupted exchange of information is carried on the back of a runaway computer technology, which appears to be taking knowledge out of people's minds and storing it elsewhere.

In Lyotard's analysis the information society is governed by a fantasy of the marketplace, in which exchange is an end in itself – a fantasy of deregulation and free interchange that has led to a situation in which knowledge, wisdom, health, pleasure, law, religion, and relationship are now regarded as commodities, to be bought, sold, or traded. The consciousness of the marketplace now permeates all areas of life.

Postmodern thinking is characterized also by the abandonment of the heroic fantasy of controlling and possessing nature. Modern science, which set out to understand and control the world through the exercise of reason, is being supplanted by a postmodern science characterized by incomplete information, catastrophe and chaos, indeterminacy, paradox, discontinuity, and a tendency to uncover new questions rather than new answers. One of the defining features of the new science is its attempt to know by looking at the whole rather than the parts, and to understand phenomena from multiple and sometimes competing perspectives. Postmodern science does not expect to simplify things; it assumes that the more we know about things the more complex they will appear to be. It has abandoned the idea that it can discover the totally objective, unchallengeable facts about the universe, and has acknowledged that we cannot escape from our subjectivity. Postmodern writers like Michel Foucault argue that the rational, objective way of understanding the world that we associate with science is only one way of looking at the world, and that it has no right to be regarded as more 'true' than another way.

Another feature of the postmodern world is the significance of images. In fact images appear to be more influential than ideas. We are floating in a sea of images, which are no longer expected to represent any reality or truth. The notion of common or shared meanings seems to be in the process of disappearing. Trivial events and ideas get just as much attention as significant ones (if we still accept the notion that some things are more significant than others). Postmodern art and architecture reflect a world in which anything goes. There seems to be nothing fixed and enduring. Our understandings of the world have been destabilized and deconstructed. The ground has disappeared, and reality has become very slippery.

The broader culture in which our organizations exist is increasingly a culture of doubt. There are fewer and fewer universally accepted ways of behaving. There are fewer and fewer universally accepted beliefs. There are challenges even to society's basic assumptions. We can frame this pessimistically and see in this a threat to the stability and permanence of our social institutions and a sign of the imminent collapse of civilization. Or we can take a more optimistic view, and see ourselves living in a liminal phase, in a new and better way of being as the world struggles to emerge. Or we can put aside both of these fantasies and simply accept that this condition of doubt or liminality is the way things are for the time being, whatever the future may bring.

There has been a lot of discussion of postmodernity since Lyotard wrote about it some twenty-five years ago. Some see it as marking a decisive change in human consciousness, so that we will never be the same again. Some claim that it is a temporary condition, and that we will eventually get back to a world of shared meanings. Some, of course, deny that there has been any dramatic shift at all.

Against this background of disagreement it appears to us that organizations exist now in a world very different from the world in which conventional organizational structures were designed. When societies could be assumed to be based on shared beliefs, values, and meanings, it made sense to assume that the culture of a particular organization would be a unitary one. It is no longer possible to assume this. Gone also is the fantasy of permanence: that what has existed in the past will continue in its present form into the foreseeable future. Some of the most (apparently) stable and permanent institutions – the Soviet Union, the established churches, the nuclear family – crumbled and fragmented before our very eyes in the second half of the twentieth century. From our observations of attempts at deep change in organizations, it appears that those who now attempt to impose a unitary culture on an organization often unwittingly damage both the organization and the individuals who comprise it. And we would argue further that theories of organizational culture that assume without reflection that a unitary and cohesive culture is an indisputably good thing will not be adequate tools for dealing with contemporary challenges, with contemporary organizational pathology or with intentional organizational change.

Some organizations embrace a postmodern consciousness. Others resist it, and cling to what they see as 'traditional values'. In either case they have to survive within it, and are influenced by it whether they will or not.

The pervasive postmodern consciousness also influences those who theorize about organizations. For instance, Jeffrey Goldstein challenges the 'rational' assumptions on which conventional organizations are built, and the models of organizational change that have been conventionally followed. His theory of organizational change emerges from chaos theory and system dynamics. He abandons the conventional model of the organization as some sort of rationally structured machine, and abandons the notion that desirable change comes from imposing order on chaos. For him, change is order emerging out of chaos, self-generated and not imposed. It comes about through the enhancement of random, accidental, unpredictable events. The transformative process relies on the non-linear, far-from-equilibrium dimensions of organizational life. He argues, contrary to the conventional organizational wisdom, that the disturbance of equilibrium does not necessarily make a system more disoriented or turbulent:

> Far-from-equilibrium conditions challenge a nonlinear system to come up with a new way of functioning. A system that predominantly seeks equilibrium is a system that resists change. Such systems allow neither creative development nor innovative response to their environments.[2]

Gareth Morgan is another organizational theorist who reflects a postmodern consciousness. He relativizes the conventional image of the organization as a machine. He points out that when we talk about an organization in terms of its structure, its cause-and- effect relationships, its efficiencies, its productivity, we are not stating 'facts' about the organization, but rather expanding a metaphor. It is not uncommon to hear in the modern corporate corridors phrases such as 'driving the change', 'leveraging the effect' and 'engineering a solution'. Morgan would say that the statements we are making about the organization are closer to poetry than they are to science. An organization is a machine, it is true, but it is not only a machine. It is also an organism, a brain, a psychic prison, a political system and a culture. Each of these metaphors contains a partial truth about an organization, and each of them helps us understand how to work in organizations. However, none of them contains the whole truth, and to imprison ourselves in a single image is to be blind to a great deal of the organization's potential and to lose our flexibility of action.

Peter Senge confronts the dilemmas that the managers of organizations face in a postmodern world: overwhelming complexity, constant change, excess of information, conflicting demands, and the confusion and loss of purpose that are likely to accompany them. His solution is to learn to see organizations as organic systems rather than machines, to see the whole system rather than be obsessed with its parts. He argues that the perception of the manager as an omniscient planner is fundamentally out of step with the nature of the world to which organizations must now adjust. There is simply too much complexity in the demands on organizations and their responses to these for the fantasy of control-from-the-top to be indulged. His thinking about organizations parallels the way many contemporary psychologists in the Jungian-Freudian tradition talk about personality. They no longer think of the personality being governed by a rational ego. The ego (the part of our personality that we identify as 'I') is relativized as just one of the elements that go to make up the total personality system. They are inclined to see people as having many personalities or identities rather than a single one. Senge appears to be making a similar statement about organizational 'personality'. This pluralism of identity and values is characteristic of postmodern thought in every field.

We can find a postmodern consciousness behind the tendency of many current writers in this field not only to acknowledge the significance of irrational elements in organizational life, but also to challenge the conventional idea that rational interpretations and rational interventions can adequately deal with them. Mitroff[3] challenges the assumptions of the rational/scientific approach to organizational phenomena and argues that the reality of organizations is as validly manifested in organizational stories as it is in universal principles and clear and distinct concepts. Denhardt[4] likewise challenges the absolutist claims of conventional science, arguing that reality is socially constructed and essentially 'fictional', and that the scientific 'fiction' of objectivity, understanding, prediction, and control is now revealed to be filled with contradictions, surviving only because it serves the interests of the organizationally powerful. He argues that the rational model of organization fails to fully comprehend human meaning, rationalizes existing patterns of social domination, and assaults human values. Both Mitroff and Denhardt place their reflections on organizations in the context of a world in which change is the only constant and complexity is unending. Ralph Stacey[5] and Margaret

Wheatley[6] take up similar themes, writing about organizations in a way that reflects an understanding of the universe as creative process – a far cry from the image of a nechanical universe that once framed the thinking of management theorists.

Our own perspective on organizational phenomena is strongly influenced by a ostmodern consciousness. It is a perspective that aligns itself with those contemporary hinkers in the arts and sciences who see their own understandings as representing artial truths rather than absolute truths, and who acknowledge the validity of other erspectives. It is worth noting here that many of the most quoted postmodern theorists for example Foucault and Derrida) are radical skeptics who want to 'deconstruct' all elief systems and have argued that there is no valid basis for believing or valuing nything at all. That is not our stance. We take a much less pessimistic approach. We rgue that we should honor what is valuable in every perspective, while acknowledging hat all will be flawed. We can deny every perspective's claim to absolute 'truth' without sserting that nothing is true. We find ourselves aligned with what David Ray Griffin[7] alls 'constructive postmodernism', which accepts the evidence that we are undergoing profound revolution in the way we think but finds in the apparent collapse of all he absolutes of the 'modern' age, the possibility of transcending its limitations. This erspective is influenced by the cosmology of Alfred North Whitehead who argued, ke the ancient Greek guru-philosopher Heraklitus, that the universe is composed not f 'things' but of 'events'. From the human point of view, individually and collectively, fe is a series of 'moments of experience' in each of which we can either repeat the past r invent a future.

or us, organizations of people are extremely complex and subtle and it seems both rrogant and presumptuous to think that there is a single truth about them, let alone ne that we know and understand. Consequently we seek to discover many and diverse indows of understanding through which we can view organizational dynamics, and e many doors through which we may enter the life of organizations in order to fluence them. In so doing, we suspect that we have a lot in common with those who romote the concepts and technologies of 'the learning organization'. Like them, we ew organizations as living systems capable of emergent forms of self-organization. heir focus on organizations as learning systems seems to reflect, as does our own inking, the pluralistic, multi-perspectival approach to the world that has come to be called postmodern. Where our thinking differs from theirs, as we see it, is in our greater willingness to explore and intervene directly in the unconscious dynamics of corporate life and in a greater willingness to accept that there are more ways of knowing than can be attained by rational analysis alone. We find ourselves closely aligned with those who see an organization as a self-organizing entity in continual adaptive exchange both internally and externally, and whose primary deep drive is to come to know itself. In exploring the ways of the corporate unconscious from the perspectives of organizational culture, archetypal psychology, and group intervention methodologies, we have attempted in our work to develop a language that can cope with the pluralistic nature of organizational phenomena. We have attempted also to develop a methodology that acknowledges that organizational phenomena are multi-layered and need to be explored by imaginal, intuitive, and indirect methods as well as through rational, sensate, and direct analysis.

Organizational Behavior has Unconscious Components

Our understanding of unconscious processes and how they influence human behavior owes much to the research and thinking of Freud and Jung. They pointed to the ways in which our thoughts and actions are shaped by energies that are totally outside our awareness. Freud's interest was in how each person is dominated by the energy of desires and needs that have been repressed by upbringing and education, and by civilization itself. Jung was most impressed by the evidence he found that our unconscious motives and images are not simply personal, that we are psychically connected with other people, past and present, that unconscious processes are essentially collective rather than individual. They both emphasized the importance of the imaginal life, and they both pointed to the power of particular images in shaping the way we live. Between them and their colleagues, they left us a language for talking about unconscious processes: ego, id and superego, complex, archetype, persona, shadow and self, personal and collective unconscious, introversion and extraversion, anima and animus, individuation. They gave us labels for the numerous ways we deal with our unconscious drives: denial, projection, transference, counter-transference, reaction, formation, displacement, repression, sublimation, idealization, projective identification, transitional objects, rationalization, resistance and regression.

Freud, Jung and their followers in the psychoanalytic tradition have had a lot to say about the ways in which unconscious dynamics shape the behavior of individuals. When they talk about group behavior, they are inclined to describe the ways unconscious dynamics influence the way individuals behave in groups. This can provide very useful insights into the way a group is functioning. Jung's personality typology, for instance, is commonly used as a way of explaining the effectiveness or ineffectiveness of an organization's use of human resources. However it is conventionally focused on amplifying the individual contribution each member of the organization can make, and the greater effectiveness that can come about with the recognition of the differences in people's abilities and approaches. Likewise, psychoanalytic notions like complex, shadow, and projection come in very handy when explaining how things are going wrong between the people in organizations. However, neither Freudians nor Jungians have had much to say about the ways unconscious dynamics operate in groups as groups, rather than as collections of individuals.

A notable exception is Wilfred Bion, whose theory of group relations manages to maintain a sense of the group as a whole, while focusing on the unconscious and sometimes invisible dimensions of group life.

Bion argued that in every group, assembled for whatever purpose, there really exist two groups. One he called the *work group*. This is the group that has tasks to perform, information to consider and decisions to make. It goes about its work rationally and may fulfill its purposes effectively or ineffectively. The second group, consisting of the same people, he called the *basic assumptions group*. This group is irrational and inconsistent in its behavior, and quite incapable of making rational decisions. It is dominated by powerful emotional forces and by a powerful fantasy, which its members are caught up in. The two groups fill the same space and carry on simultaneously, interfering with each other's activities, with one or the other being dominant at any particular moment.

In Bion's view, the particular fantasy that basic group assumptions are caught up in is the fantasy of the mother-child relationship. He suggests that, as members of groups, people tend to regress to infantile behavior and they handle their experience of the group the way an infant is alleged to handle what it experiences as inconsistent behavior from its mother. The child splits its mother into two: the good mother who feeds and comforts it on demand, and the bad mother who denies it satisfaction and causes it pain. Bion here is following Melanie Klein's theory of child development. She argues that, in normal development, the child manages to integrate these two mothers, and accept that people can be both loving and imperfect. However, she asserts that we all carry some residue of this infantile dilemma, ready to be reactivated under the right conditions. Bion suggests that this is what is happening when a group is manifesting basic assumptions behavior. Whatever we may think we are doing and however we may rationalize it, part of us is identifying the group as mother and yearning to be united with her and nourished by her. When the group does not give us what we demand, we fight or sulk or withdraw.

Accordingly, if we want to understand what is going on in an organization we should look both at the surface behavior (both the rational, cooperative behavior of the work group and the anxious, impulse-driven behavior of the basic assumptions group) and the group purpose, which is to relive the union with mother. Group relations consultants, following Bion's theory, consult to organizations by closely observing the organization's basic assumptions behavior and then interpreting it to the organization. This approach follows Freudian psychoanalysis, on the grounds that the work group and the basic assumptions group in the organization are related the same way that conscious and unconscious behaviors are related in the individual. Individual psychoanalysis sets out to interpret the patient's behavior so that the client can see how his repressed and unconscious energies are controlling him. When the patient sees and understands this, he should be able to exercise some control over the behavior that is causing him anxiety or pain. He is able to shift control from his impulse-driven 'id' to his rational 'ego'. Similarly, when the work group, which is the 'ego' of the organization, is led to understand what is going on at the basic assumptions or 'id' level, it can supposedly take charge of it. The effective group is one in which the activity of the work group proceeds rationally and objectively without much interference from the basic assumptions group.

Freud was determined that he would uncover the facts about the human unconscious and the laws that governed its behavior. It seems to us now that he was not so much uncovering 'the facts' as creating powerful images of the way the unconscious functions. We may wish to challenge whether it is a fact that people in groups regress to a critical phase of their infancy, but we may well be satisfied with the evidence of Bion and others that we behave as though this is what is happening. The two powerful images around which Bion's group relations theory revolves are the image of the group as mother, and the image of the rational ego as the hero who gains independence of the mother and control over the blind forces of (mother) nature. It is clear that in this particular fantasy (whether in Freud's version or Bion's) it is the rational, work-oriented element in humanity that is the 'good guy' and the non-rational, emotive element that is the 'bad guy'.

Good theory is useful theory, and Bion's theory has proved very productive for groups and organizations where it has been applied. However, we need to see its truth as partial, and stay alive to other partial truths. In particular we need to remain aware that whatever we say about individuals and groups will be said through images. Jung did not share Freud's fantasy of the 'good guy' ego in constant conflict with the 'bad guy' id. Freud was convinced that the ego was the center of personality. For him, the drives that make up the unconscious were chaotic, senseless, irrational, anti-social, needing to be brought under the control of the ego. Jung, on the other hand, was convinced that the unconscious was not chaotic and directionless. While he acknowledged the importance of the ego in organizing our behavior in a purposeful manner, he was convinced that our personality is much bigger than the conscious part we identify with. For him, the center of personality was not the ego but the 'self', which includes both conscious and unconscious. The 'self' moves to combine all the mental contents of our personality, positive and negative, destructive and creative, private and public. It shapes the relationship of the various parts of the personality to each other. Where Freud's image of the mature person is of someone who is in control of him or herself, Jung's image is of someone who is whole, someone whose whole personality is available and whose maturity involves the continual integration of both conscious and unconscious elements.

If we approach organizational change with Jungian concepts the way Bion does with Freudian, we will take a more positive approach to the phenomena that Bion associates with the basic assumptions group. The chaos, irrationality, and emotionality will not appear as something that needs to be brought under strict rational control. On the contrary, it will appear as the source of the organization's energy, creativity, and potential for change. In the mature and effective organization, conscious identity and organizational purpose are in harmony with the organization's instinctual, emotional and imaginative life.

In the Jungian image of personality, there is no 'good guy' and 'bad guy'. Good and bad are completely tangled together. This is even true of Jung's notion of the shadow. Jung used this image to express those parts of our personality of which we are not aware. There are certain things that we prefer not to know about ourselves, certain things that we refuse to admit to ourselves, certain things we have never discovered. Some of these things are in our shadow because we have learned to define them as 'bad' and do not want to own them. But there are also parts of ourselves – needs, drives, values, abilities – that we do not admit to, even though we might define them as 'good'. We may be unable to acknowledge our own creativity, or altruism, or spirituality, so they remain in shadow alongside our sadism, racism, sexism, and violence. The person we think we are, the ego, represents only a fraction of our potential for good and evil. The public face we present to the world, our persona, is likely to represent even less.

These images can readily be applied to organizations. Every organization has a public face, an organizational persona, that reveals only what the organization wants the rest of the world to know. The persona may be a deliberately misleading mask, or it may be a mask that the organization is not aware of wearing. Every organization has an organizational ego, a center of control and identity (which may be narrow and defined, or broad and undefined) but which, in either case, knows what the organization is and decides what it does. Every organization has an organizational ego, a center of control and identity. This organizational ego may be narrow and defined, or it may be broad and undefined; in either case, it knows what the organization is and decides what it does. It may be a strong and flexible ego, or it may be a weak and defensive ego.

Likewise, every organization has an organizational shadow, which contains the best and worst of what it is, and which the organizational ego is usually determined not to know about. Every organization has an organizational self that, potentially at least, shapes all these parts of the organization into one purposeful and energized whole.

Jung's image of the shadow has been usefully employed in the analysis of organizational behavior.[8] When an individual refuses to acknowledge something in herself, she sets up a tension in which the repressed shadow energy strives for expression, while the ego fights to maintain its self-image. The repressed energy has to find some outlet. It may do so in impulsive or emotional behavior that the person can disown with statements like 'I was not really myself!', or 'I don't know what came over me'. It can express itself in physical tension or illness. It can be projected on to someone else. The aggressive person who cannot acknowledge her own aggression is likely to find herself surrounded by aggressive people, as if she is saying: 'I can sense that someone around here is aggressive. It certainly can't be me, so it must be you!' Organizations appear to behave in all of these ways.

Many organizations have a self-image that is strongly tied to images of rationality and objectivity. They denigrate the expression of emotion as being contrary to good organizational practice. Yet this shadow emotionality ends up being a very significant factor in the way the organization operates. Instead of having a balanced and harmonious emotional life, the organization is driven by the pathological forms of the repressed emotions. Vindictiveness, greed, rage, and panic may dominate organizational politics and decision-making. Major decisions may be generated by such emotions, and managers may effectively ignore the information on which they pretend to base their decisions. And yet the organization may continue to proudly maintain its picture of itself as rational. It uses all the devices that Freud found individuals using to defend themselves against knowledge of themselves.

We like to think of ourselves as conscious, reflecting beings, who are essentially in control of what we do. Freud and Jung challenged this notion. Freud argued that much of what we do is determined by motivations of which we are totally unaware. Jung argued that some of this unconscious motivation comes from our enmeshment in the psyche of the species, not just from our personal history.

Jean Gebser, an associate of Jung, made a significant contribution to our understanding of the relationship of consciousness to culture. He developed the notion of 'structures of consciousness' that are in dynamic interaction within us individually and within the culture at large. Gebser did not talk about an 'unconscious' as distinct from consciousness, but rather of different 'intensities' of consciousness ranging from the very dim 'archaic' consciousness of the earliest humans to the 'integral' consciousness of the aware, self-reflexive individual. Gebser did not write about organizations any more than Freud and Jung did, but his explorations of the characteristics of the different structures of consciousness add significantly to our understanding of the collective behavior of contemporary organizations.

Patterns of Behavior in Organizations are Archetypal

Archetypal psychology as a contemporary way of thinking about culture and behavior is largely based on Jung's work, but it actually goes back to the Greek philosopher Plato. Jung regarded himself as an empirical scientist, and in that role he devoted himself to documenting the patterns he found in human behavior, both individual and collective. He was fascinated by the way particular patterns of images kept recurring in people's imaginal lives: in their dreams, in their poetry, in art, and in mythology. When it came to understanding these patterns he was not satisfied with the explanations given by mainstream science, or by the explanations of his colleague Freud. So he went back to the ancient philosophers and found a more satisfactory explanation in Plato's notion of archetype.

Jung, following Plato, was inclined to understand archetypes as pre-existent forms that are replicated again and again in nature and in our experience. However, he was not very consistent in his way of defining archetype. On the one hand, he called the archetypes 'primordial images', but he also wrote of them as 'instinctual patterns of behavior' that are genetically inherited, as 'dominants of the collective unconscious', 'nodal points of psychic energy', and as 'modes of apprehension' that shape our encounter with reality. He spoke of them as 'systems of readiness for action'; that is to say, they exist as potentials that only become manifest when we act. He believed that the tendency to imagine the world in particular ways is 'hard-wired' in us. The archetypes were for him both the guiding patterns of evolution and its product. For Jung, all behavior is structured by these potentials, which we experience as archetypal images of great meaning and power. He made what he considered an essential distinction between th archetype *per se* (which is form without content and cannot be directly observed) and the archetypal image – its manifestation in culture and human personality.

The word archetype is now used in so many different and inconsistent ways that we could argue that it is useless as a scientific term. Nevertheless, we do recognize patterns in individual and group behavior. We recognize that many of the patterns that we observe today are the same as those recorded in ancient mythologies and associated with the personalities of the gods. And we now find that the sciences of brain and behavior seem to point to something hard-wired in our brains which, for want of a better word, we can continue to call archetype.[9]

The term *archetypal psychology* refers in a general way to the ideas of Jung and the school of analytical psychology he founded. However, it refers more specifically to the thinking of a group of contemporary Jungian psychologists who focus in a particular way on this aspect of Jung's theory. The central figure in this school of thought is James Hillman, who has a much less essentialist view of archetype than Jung. That is to say, he does not talk about the archetypes as 'things'. Jung says that the archetype exists of itself as form without content,[10] and is known to us only through its manifestation in an image; Hillman points out that if we cannot observe the archetype directly, as Jung maintains, there is no point in assuming its existence. What we know of the world, we know as image. Images don't 'stand' for anything, but are our basic experience of the world. For Hillman, every image is an archetypal image, and these archetypal images structure all our experience and behavior. For Hillman, the proper work of psychology is seeing through our personal and collective experience to the archetypal image behind it. He wants us to see the world metaphorically. He argues, in fact, that we have no other way of seeing it. Images are all we know.

In Hillman's understanding, all consciousness depends on fantasy images. All we know about the world, about the mind, the body, about anything whatsoever, comes through images and is organized by fantasies into one pattern or another. These patterns are archetypal, so we are always in one or another archetypal pattern, one or another archetypal fantasy.

Archetypal theory, as Hillman and his colleagues present it, is clearly a postmodern theory. Not only does it insist that image is all we know, but it is relativistic in its view of truth. Hillman argues that we cannot privilege one archetypal image over all the others by saying that it is 'truer' or 'better' than all the others. 'Truth' and 'goodness' reside equally in all the archetypal images, even when they appear to contradict each other. Hillman's argument takes him inevitably into a multi-perspectivist understanding of reality. It is a 'polytheistic' psychology, which honors many truths, not a 'monotheistic' psychology which declares that there is one truth. Like other postmodern theories it delights in paradox, acknowledging that in making a declaration like this it is stating a 'truth' that must itself be recognized as just one 'truth' among many conflicting 'truths'. When Hillman tells us that we are always in one archetypal fantasy or another, he is acknowledging that he is in an archetypal fantasy even as he makes this statement (and consequently is stating only a partial truth). Postmodern theorists don't have much problem with stating ideas that logically contradict themselves. They claim that this is what reality is like!

As a framework for his multi-perspectivism Hillman takes the gods of the Greco-Roman pantheon. Each of the gods personifies an archetypal image and energy, a 'mode of apprehension', 'an instinctual pattern', which gives a distinct and observable shape to our encounter with the world. They are distinct, but not discrete, for the archetypal patterns interpenetrate in complex ways that are represented by the relationships between the gods. Hillman takes the classical Greek pantheon as his preferred set of images because these images are embedded in European culture – even in the culture of modern science. The stories of the gods and their relationships are the way ancient cultures dealt with psychological and cultural issues. Archetypal psychologists suggest that human nature has not changed in any essential way since then, so the psychological understandings of classical civilizations are still relevant for us.[11]

Hillman suggests that the aim of archetypal psychology is to see through the events of our lives to the archetypal images that shape them. If we want to see through the behavior of an organization we will start by asking 'What is going on here?', 'What pattern can we see?' In asking 'What?', archetypal psychology is looking for an image, not following the lead of science and asking 'Why?' or 'How?'. Which image is behind this behavior? How is the world being imagined? What pattern can we observe here? In the archetypal perspective, the next question is 'Who?', that is, 'Which of the gods is at work here, in this organization?'[12]

Plato argued that the universe is ordered by first principles, which transcend personal and concrete experience, principles that he called Ideas, Forms, or Archetypes. He recognized that these principles were the stuff of the ancient myths, where they were represented as immortal gods and goddesses. Talking of archetypal images as though they are divine persons made sense to the Greeks of Plato's time, and it makes sense to contemporary archetypal psychologists, not because they worship many gods, but because the personalities and stories of the gods are an extremely rich and complex statement of how we experience the world. And also because archetypal psychologists are inclined to think that we comprehend the world better through images than we do through concepts. Indeed, many of them would argue that ideas are essentially images in disguise.

Jung and Hillman argue that archetypes are not only manifested in personal behavior. They are also manifest in the physical, social, linguistic, aesthetic, and spiritual modes by which groups of people function. They are bi-polar, that is to say they have a 'good', 'positive', or 'healthy' manifestation and a 'bad', 'negative', or 'pathological' manifestation.

If we are sensitized to them, we will see them not only in the study of psychology, but also in many, many aspects of our day-to-day (ordinary and not-so-ordinary) existence: politics, philosophy, science, social structures, the arts, management. For Hillman, as for Jung, the pre-eminent language of archetypal psychology is the language of myths; the great myths represent the most fundamental patterns of human existence. Hillman suggests that in order to understand human nature at its most basic level, we need to turn to culture (mythology, religion, art, architecture, epic, drama, ritual) where the patterns in the discourse of myths are portrayed. To venture into the realm of archetypal psychology is to move into a field that is essentially imaginal.

The term archetype has found its way into mainstream organizational literature through the work of Peter Senge and his colleagues. In view of the widespread currency of the term in the learning organization literature, it is perhaps worth pointing to some similarities and distinctions between their apparent use of the term and the way it is used in the Jungian tradition. Peter Senge suggests that certain patterns of structure occur again and again in organizations. By structure he means the basic inter-relationships that control behavior and the pattern of interrelationships among key components of a system. This might include the hierarchy and the process flows, but it also includes the attitudes and perceptions, the quality of products, the ways in which decisions are made and hundreds of other factors. Senge uses the term 'systems archetype' to refer to those patterns that seem to occur and recur in the structure of systems. In so doing, he points out that these archetypes not only recur regularly within a specific organization but are common to many organizational contexts, and that they are often not seen, but rather felt. Sometimes they produce a sense of deja vu, a hunch that you have seen this constellation of forces before. He suggests that systems archetypes provide a language that enables us to discuss these deep patterns and allows us to recondition our perceptions so that we can see the deeper structures at play. He and his colleagues also suggest that they are powerful tools for understanding systemic issues.

Before Jung began to speculate about archetypes, he developed the idea of the complex. We are all familiar with the notion of the 'inferiority complex', the 'martyr complex', the 'power complex', and so on. Jung explored the evidence that people's behavior is largely governed by these 'clusters of unconscious contents' that are 'strongly accented emotionally', and that are actually 'incompatible with the habitual attitude of consciousness.'[13] He found that these complexes appear to act autonomously, independently of our rational ego. In a sense we do not 'have' them at all. Rather, they 'have' us. Later, he began to think of these patterns of images, emotion, and behavior as having their source outside the individual, in what he called the collective unconscious. He came to see complexes as expressions in the individual of universal patterns that he later called archetypes. When Senge writes about systems archetypes functioning in groups – constellations of ideas, images, feelings, and behaviors that appear to act automatically and autonomously – he comes closer to Jung's use of the notion of complexes functioning in individuals, rather than to Jung's speculations about universal archetypes.

Jung, Hillman, and other archetypal psychologists clearly have a different focus of attention to Senge. They are trying to say something about the nature of reality, whereas Senge has very pragmatic intentions in focusing on organizations. Nevertheless, Jungian writing provides a rich background against which Senge's notions of innate systemic patterning can be viewed, and the theory of systems archetypes may readily be seen as an application of more general archetypal theory in a particular context. Senge's focus is not on the individual psyche, and Jung gave little attention to understanding group processes; yet Senge's ideas on organic transformation in the learning organization essentially parallel Jung's theory of individuation and the emergence of the self in the individual human being. Senge talks about organizations as complex systems the way Jungians, though they use a very different language for it, talk about individuals as complex systems. Moreover, he and an increasing number of management theorists[14] talk about organizations as self-organizing systems, analogous to persons, which grow from within rather than being constructed from without. An organization, reflecting on its own processes and allowing its own unconscious potentials to emerge, is analogous to the individuating human, becoming fully all he or she can be.

The word archetype has a broader and richer set of associations to the archetypal psychologist than it seems to have to the systems dynamicist of the 'learning organization' movement. Nevertheless, the two fields share the notion that organizational dynamics have unconscious and deep patterns within them and these patterns seem to recur in many contexts.

An archetypal psychologist working in the context of organizational culture and organizational change will be attempting to see through the behaviors, values, and assumptions of the organization to the archetypal image that is shaping them. He or she might ask:

- How do the people in this organization imagine the world?
- What is the image that best fits the phenomena with which we are dealing?
- Is this recognizable as a universal image?
- Does the god have a name?
- Does an exploration of this image release and develop further images?
- How can we stay with the image and use it as the basis for our learnings and insights about where we are going and where we want to go?

Such questions can be merely diagnostic. They can generate a label for a dysfunctional condition that is being experienced by the organization and that has not been brought to full awareness, but they do not necessarily have any impact.

Furthermore, it is fairly easy to categorize, correlate, and collect information about images and symbols that may be more appropriate to this particular phase in the organization's life-cycle, and to fancy that understanding the diagnosis and naming the medicine is enough to effect a cure. Freud and Jung entertained the idea that if we knew our unconscious motivations, if we knew why we keep acting in such crazy or hurtful ways, we would be in control of our behavior and stop acting crazily. Experience has not borne out this fantasy. Understanding our neurosis is rarely sufficient to put an end to individual pathology. Group pathology is even more resistant to healing.

Besides, archetypal psychology has rather more to offer. Archetypal psychology can go beyond mere analysis and take images seriously as bearers of our multiple meanings. The images we play with are the prime basis for our 'knowing' and our 'understanding'. They are carriers of human knowledge and experience, both collective and personal. It became increasingly clear to Jung in his work as a psychotherapist that the more intensely personal the exploration of his patients, the more their images resonated with a sense of the universal. By corollary, we find that the universalizing statements of great art and literature touch us deeply at a uniquely personal level. A change agent cannot work authentically and consistently within an archetypal framework without being prepared to be personally transformed by the experience.

The Whole Organization is more than the Sum of its Parts

Systems thinking, which has been influential in organizational theory for four decades, began in biology, though it was soon adopted by thinkers in other disciplines. Senge, Goldstein, Wheatley, Stacey, and other recent writers on organizational change tend to imagine organizations as self-organizing systems like plants rather than as externally controlled systems like machines.

The biological metaphor became increasingly powerful in our thinking in the late twentieth century, as the image of the machine has proved inadequate to represent the world as we find it. Nineteenth century and early twentieth century scientists were sure that they could demonstrate that the earth is a machine, that human beings are machines, that human societies are machines, constructed of a lot of separate parts related in a cause-and-effect fashion, following known mechanical laws, and ultimately predictable and controllable. Contemporary scientists are much less confident of this. They are increasingly likely to imagine the world as a living organism, as Lovelock does with his 'Gaia hypothesis'.[15] The old-fashioned distinction between dead and living matter appears to be breaking down, and we now find ourselves talking about the next 'generation' of machines as being self-organizing systems like animals and plants.

Most writing on groups and organizations during the twentieth century was grounded in the mechanical metaphor. It was also grounded in the assumption that human beings are essentially self-contained individuals. Groups, therefore, have been imagined as collections of individuals, interacting according to precise laws, which social psychologists are in the business of describing. However, there has been a movement away from this assumption in recent years, towards a view of the group as an organism with a life of its own. Senge, Capra, and Stacey represent this way of thinking now, but this shift of understanding (and of metaphor) has been going on for some time.

Wilfred Bion and other writers associated with the Tavistock Institute of Human Relations in the UK have had a major impact in helping us think of a collection of individuals as having some characteristics and processes in common, characteristics and processes that seem independent of the specific individuals who constitute the collective. The writers of the Tavistock School in the 1960s and 1970s gave us a very rich language with which to understand groups in many different settings. In doing so, they made us focus on a number of forces that existed in (and arose out of) the fact of the group's existence, and that could not be influenced simply by thinking and strategizing about how to influence a number of individuals. During this same period, on the other side of the Atlantic, Warren Bennis began to explore similar phenomena, focusing on sub-groups and the dynamics among them. Throughout his work, and that of his colleagues, we find a similar assumption: they are seeking to describe phenomena that exist independently of the specific individuals who comprise the group or sub-group. It is as reasonable to see the group as a web of relationships connected by individuals as it is to see it as a web of individuals connected by relationships. This tendency to see the whole as made up of interacting parts has continued into the study of organizational culture with the work of Meryl Louis,[16] who has maintained that organizations are more appropriately thought of as culture-bearing milieus: arenas in which one will find sites of sub-cultures, and through which sub-cultures may develop.

Those who focus on organizations as living systems maintain that we do not have to create interrelatedness. The world is already interrelated. We cannot understand what a clock is by examining each wheel and cog. We cannot grasp what it is to be human by looking at each bone and sinew and gland. We cannot grasp the nature of a group by only looking at the individuals who comprise it. There is a 'clockness' and 'humanness' and 'groupness' that transcends the aggregation of parts, and exists rather in the relationships and interactions between the parts.

This points to a fundamental perspective that we bring to this discussion. For us the deeper, less visible, more unconscious, less tangible aspects of organizational behavior are manifestations of a whole that we seek to understand, but this whole is made up of interrelated parts in dynamic interaction. Inquiring into matters both corporate and unconscious is like seeking to understand the interaction of tides, eddies, and currents below the surface of the sea. None of these things can exist independently of the whole (the sea); each arises from very different forces (gravitation, weather, etc); each has interactive effects on the others and all are below the surface of that which we would immediately notice.

One of Jung's key ideas is the idea of the collective unconscious. He argued that our sense of ourselves as separate and distinct individuals is illusory, that the personal ego is not the central psychological reality, that there is a common psychic reality that operates prior to and independently of our individual conscious functioning. According to Jung, our experience of 'I' is a secondary phenomenon, a particular expression in time and space of what he called the 'objective' psyche. This was not a new idea, of course. Several ancient religious and philosophical systems have had similar things to say about our place in the universe. Where Jung differs is that he located himself in the tradition of European science and came to his conclusions on the basis of carefully documented evidence. However, conventional science was not receptive to Jung's ideas, and the notion of humanity, or nations or groups having some sort of 'group mind' was regarded as fanciful. That is changing.

The ego is no longer assumed to be the central psychological reality, and it is no longer unfashionable to think of individuals as elements of a larger system, and individual consciousness as an expression of a larger consciousness. We seem to be abandoning the idea that we wander around the world in separate capsules passing messages to one another, and beginning to entertain the notion that the boundaries we imagine between 'self' and 'other' are fairly arbitrary. We acknowledge that our physical selves are continuous with the physical world, and are coming to accept not only that our mental selves are continuous with the mental world but even that the physical and mental worlds are continuous with each other. This shifting perception has considerable consequences for the way we talk about groups and for the way we think about organizations.

The organism is proving a useful metaphor in discussions of organizations and organizational change. We wish to push this metaphor a little further and talk about organizations in the language that belongs to a specific type of organism – the person. But first, some reflections about a simpler organism.

Termites seem to be a very rewarding object of study. One interesting fact about them is how fussy they are about temperature. They build their mounds with ventilator shafts and tunnels all carefully designed to maintain the mound at a steady temperature. As the outside temperature rises and falls they keep busy, opening a shaft here, closing one there, in order to keep the internal temperature constant. If you knock a piece off their mound they will rebuild it immediately, accurately, and without need for trial and error, in order to maintain its proper temperature. If you throw a sheet of plastic over the mound so as to artificially raise its temperature, they will immediately set to work and totally redesign it to keep to its original internal temperature. This is an extremely complex bit of engineering that, in our way of doing things, would demand fairly sophisticated mathematics, advanced computer technology, extensive planning, good communication and management, and, above all, time. Termites seem to need none of these things. They just do it. Immediately. They don't even have meetings or send memos about it.

When you knock the top off a termite mound, the poor things have to repair it by building an arch, which they do by working from both ends and meeting in the middle. This would not be remarkable, except that termites are blind and, to our eyes, they seem to do all these amazing things simply by bumping into one another. If you challenge their ingenuity by pushing a large sheet of steel through the mound to cut it in two so that no communication is possible between the two halves, the termites proceed as usual and repair the mound. All arches and tunnels meet exactly, with only the sheet of steel preventing them from joining.

If we think of all the thousands of termites in the mound as individuals, the way we think of human beings, all busy problem-solving, communicating with each other, giving and taking orders, each carrying out a specific task as part of a huge and complex project, it is difficult to explain such achievements. At the very least, we will have to admit that termites are much smarter than we are. On the other hand, if we think of the whole moundful of termites as the individual, the termite-organism, we are not forced to this conclusion. We know nothing about the consciousness of individual termites, though we can guess it does not extend to a grasp of mathematics and engineering. When we look at a termite-nest, however, we have to admit that it seems to behave like a conscious being, with a talent for solving particular kinds of problems relating to its survival.[17]

It seems we are studying more than one organism here. First, there is the very simple organism: the individual termite. Second, there is the larger, more complex organism: the termite colony, which (in its turn) may be perceived as part of an even larger organism, the species.

If we were able to communicate with an individual termite, we would not expect it to have much notion of the purposive behavior of the larger organism of which it is a part. Conversely, if we could look at humanity from an adequate distance, we would see our own species behaving as a collective unity, rather than as a collection of individuals making individual choices about their individual behavior.

Our experience in observing and working with groups and organizations is that they often behave collectively in ways that their individual members seem to have little awareness of. We do not think it fanciful to talk about 'group mind' as being something different from the individual awarenesses of all the group members. We think that, for all the distance between humans and termites on the evolutionary scale, the 'termite factor' is still residually at work in us. Groups act like organisms, like persons even, but unfortunately not always like intelligent ones.[18]

Intentional Cultural Change is Unpredictable

An influential textbook on organizational change, published in the early 1960s, made what was then considered an obvious and commonsense statement about intentional organizational change.

> In *From Trial and Error to Planning*, Mannheim discusses the interrelations between the forms of social organization and the mentalities, the modes of thinking, required by men [sic] to fulfill their life functions in a particular social organization. He argues that 'chance discovery' through 'trial and error' yielded in modern history to 'invention' as a way of introducing changes into the practices of society. The mode of thinking characteristic of the latter is now yielding progressively to a 'planning' mentality as our society depends less upon 'Edisons' and more upon 'Manhattan projects' and 'research and development departments' as ways of 'manufacturing' innovations in significant areas of social practice. As 'planning' thus makes its way in crucial areas of social experience, less adaptive mentalities must yield precedence to 'planning' mentalities in other, interdependent areas of human life, though these mentalities need not and probably will not lose all place in the new society.[19]

Bennis, Benne, and Chin were writing in an intellectual climate where the image of the corporation as machine was still dominant. However, they wrote with a strong sense that society is not static, that organizations cannot simply be wound up (or fuelled) and relied on to run smoothly and continuously as long as a manager has a hand on the throttle and an eye on the controls. They argued that organizations must continually adapt and adjust to changing pressures and contexts. They argued that these adaptive and adjustive processes can be brought largely under rational control. Effective planning develops effective mechanisms for adaptation and adjustment and builds them into the system. 'Systems thinking', with its notions of feedback, equilibrium, resistance, leverage, and boundary, was being applied to many fields for the first time, and was being embraced with enthusiasm because it seemed to provide a language and a set of concepts that were just as useful in talking about personality, economics, society, or culture as they were for talking about physics or chemistry.

It can be very productive to talk about the organizations in the kind of systems language Bennis and his colleagues used. We may still be dominated by the image of the machine, but it is a much more complex and sophisticated machine than the engine of levers and pulleys and gears that was characteristic of the industrial age. The image of the ideal corporation as a machine with multiple inbuilt feedback mechanisms, controlled by a clear-sighted, objective, realistic, and purposeful management, provides a vision and guidelines for action.

However, some aspects of organizational change are not acknowledged in such an image. One such aspect is the unpredictability of organizational behavior. Bennis and his colleagues found themselves moving towards an organic metaphor, as they discovered that there is something going on in organizations that is more like a plant growing or decaying, than it is like a machine running. Current applications of systems theory to organizations, such as Senge's 'fifth discipline' are much more strongly influenced by the metaphor of organization as living organism than Bennis and his colleagues could afford to be.

Systems theory has itself changed since the sixties. We can now distinguish 'nonlinear' systems from 'linear' systems, and challenge the traditional notion in organizational development that change consists in a shift from one state of equilibrium to another. The development of chaos theory and nonlinear mathematics has given scientific legitimacy to the commonsense observations that change in plants, animals, and organizations often involves a transformation into something quite different, even the creation of a new organism entirely, that growth and decay are continuous and dynamic phenomena, not shifts from one static condition to another. We are able to acknowledge that change often comes about in an unpredictable fashion, through unplannable, random events, that change emerges somehow from the 'self' of the organism or organization, rather than being the result of manageable external causes with predictable effects.

A central notion in systems thinking is feedback. Senge argues that there are a limited number of specific feedback processes at work in an organization. He sees these systems archetypes as basic patterns of organizational behavior that occur in all organizations again and again. They seem to be autonomous, automatic processes that resist any attempt by managers to manage them. What managers need to do is to learn how to see through the complexity to the underlying structures that generate change. Once we understand the system, Senge argues, we may find that an appropriate, small, but well-focused action can produce a significant and enduring change in it. The learning organization is sensitized to feedback and responds to it quickly and sensitively.

We must be wary, however, of viewing an organization as a system of simple feedback loops. An organization is a complex system of interacting feedback loops. Jay Forrester warns us not to expect to find simple cause and effect relationships:

> ... [I]n a complex system such as an organization, the cause of a difficulty may lie far back in time from the symptoms, or in a completely different or remote part of the system. In fact, causes are usually found, not in prior events, but in the structure and policies of the system.
>
> To make matters still worse, the complex system is even more deceptive than merely hiding causes. In the complex system, when we look for a cause near in time and space to a symptom, we usually find what appears to be a plausible cause. But it is usually not the cause. The complex system presents causes that are in fact coincident symptoms. The high degree of time correlation between variables in complex systems can lead us to make cause and effect associations between variables that are simply moving together as part of the total dynamic behavior of the system. Conditioned by our training in simple systems, we apply the same intuition to complex systems. As a result we are led into error. We treat symptoms, not causes. The outcome lies between ineffective and detrimental.[20]

Without a valid assumption of cause and effect we cannot predict the outcome of any intervention. Worse, basing an intervention on a wrongly assumed cause and effect relationship is likely to produce an outcome very different from what we intend.

Jeffrey Goldstein, in his radical application of nonlinear systems thinking to organizational change, argues that 'organizations can be understood as nonlinear systems whose inherent growth potential is being held in check by equilibrium-seeking processes'.[21] In this way of imagining organizational change, the evolutionary potential of an organization is to be found in its nonlinear aspects. Accordingly, the appropriate role for a change agent is to generate 'far-from-equilibrium' conditions, to disturb the unreflected assumptions, the self-fulfilling prophecies, and barriers to information that keep the organization in equilibrium. The self-organization and self-transformation that ensue may not be smooth or painless. Neither will they be entirely predictable. There are others such as Ralph Stacey[22] who have taken this notion of unpredictability even further and argued that planned intentional change is essentially impossible due to the positive feedback loops, non-linear dynamics, and the sensitivity to initial conditions that characterize all human organizations. In contrast, most approaches to planning are based on a simplistic notion of cause and effect that no longer has much credibility.

An element of unpredictability characterizes self-organization. A system can use random departures from self-organization to create and facilitate a new structure. Therefore, information in organizations can reside in organizational 'noise' or random, mostly neglected, departures from an organization's equilibrium. Far-from-equilibrium methods allow the organization or work group to notice, use, and amplify this noise, and thereby turn it into new information. What noise will prove useful, and how this noise is used, however, are largely matters of chance. Successful organizational transformation is frequently the serendipitous transformation of noise into useful information.

The notion of the organization as constantly 'emerging', shedding inappropriate habits, and re-organizing itself to adapt to a continually changing environment, always engaged in or resisting the project of becoming all that it is innately capable of becoming, has a lot in common with Jung's notion of the emerging self in the individual. Goldstein's picture of the consultant helping the organization reflect on the 'noise' in the system, to detect how it represents the organization's struggle to become its true self, seems to parallel the work of the Jungian therapist, exploring with her client the latter's 'noise', (apparently random images, dreams, compulsions, projections, 'deviant' behavior) in an attempt to understand what the client's whole 'self' is trying to be.

This is far from the conventional change agent's fantasy of 'managing' change rationally and the traditional Freudian psychoanalytic fantasy of enabling the rational ego to 'manage' the unconscious. Senge and complexity theorists like Stacey warn us not to identify the organization with its management and not to see the organization as a simple whole that can be controlled from an identifiable 'nerve center'. Contemporary organizations are simply too complex to be controlled from any one point. They are not self-contained, 'closed' systems, but 'open' systems, continually exchanging information and energy with their environment. They comprise interlocking systems within systems, all of them constantly adapting and adjusting to circumstances, and all of them capable of initiating an apparently minor change of purpose or procedure that may have enormous impact on the organization as a whole. It is usually much easier to map such changes after the event than to predict them, much less to initiate them.

It is indeed possible to intervene in the life of an organization in a way that brings about change. Executives, managers, consultants, and employees do it every day. Sometimes they do it knowingly and sometimes ignorantly or arbitrarily. Sometimes the change is constructive and sometimes not. Our view is that it is better to do it knowingly and constructively.

In our discussion of deep change in organizations we are indebted to a number of theorists who have contributed to our understanding of complex human systems. However, while acknowledging the insights of writers such as Wheatley, Capra, Stacey, Bennis, Senge, and Goldstein, we will be using a different language from theirs. This discussion rests on three supports: studies in archetypal psychology, studies in organizational culture, and experience in group process intervention. We have turned to archetypal psychology for a language that enables us to deal with the non-rational aspects of organizational behavior, because we are convinced that concentration on the 'merely rational' is a very poor basis for either understanding or action. We believe that an understanding of the deep dynamics of organizational culture will help the potential change agent to make some choices about what is important and what is not so important to deal with in an organization and how it might be approached or resolved. A working knowledge and wide experience in group process interventions (both large and small) gives the change agent specific tools and technologies to initiate and maintain the change.

In regard to the facilitation of cultural change, we must acknowledge that much more has been promised in the last two decades than has actually been delivered. The script has been written, with variations, over and over again. (Manager decides culture is inappropriate; manager intervenes to change culture; culture changes; manager is happy.) The performance rarely comes up to expectations. We have witnessed, in the last few years, many senior managers who have sought to spell out a new culture hoping that commitment would follow. They soon discovered that cultural change by proclamation and manipulation is not as easily accomplished as first thought.

It sounds straightforward enough. The decisions are made. Compliance is sought and expected. They proceed to the next step, as they see it: giving employees care and attention, resources and assurances. Workshops are held, discussion groups established (often for the first time), conferences are conducted (sometimes in quite elaborate settings). This approach can be called cultural change by seduction.

The approach ultimately fails for four quite fundamental reasons. Firstly, it does not address the culture at 'all its levels' and consequently only surface manifestations change for a short time while the deep underlying patterns remain untouched. Secondly, the managers involved do not realize that they themselves usually exhibit the very behavior patterns that they would have their employees change. The employees perceive this and consequently pay far more attention to what their leaders do than to what they say. Thirdly, the behavior that the senior managers seek to change is, in fact, an artifact of the existing organizational identity and, as such, will often be defended with a stunning ferocity. Some of the strongest and most entrenched opposition to change arises when the corporate identity of a group of people is at stake. This is a particularly poignant consequence, since resistance is not a necessary or natural companion to change providing the deep identity of the group is honored and validated. Fourthly and finally, it must be recognized that when one is dealing with cultural phenomena one is playing in the fields of the non-rational. And in these fields, rational processes, strategies, and decisions have limited utility. Yet, as we will explore in a number of ways throughout this book, rational ways and means are often the first recourse of executives, managers, and consultants.

These are difficulties that we too have faced many times and they have demonstrated the limitations of our understanding and of our methods. Yet we have found some conditions under which it is possible to effect planned change and some techniques, ools and methodologies that seem more effective than others. One aim of this book is o explore an approach to intervention for cultural change. But, lest the reader expect nore than we can deliver, we return to the words of Wilfred Bion at the start of this hapter. We suggest that, more often than not, the response of a group to intentional nd planned cultural change is perplexing and confusing – though it may also be xciting and fascinating! We will now turn to the exploration of a model that attempts o bring together a number of organizational phenomena with which executives, nanagers and consultants have to deal, and relates these to organizational culture.

W Bion (1969) *Experiences in Groups*, p. 23.

J Goldstein (1994) *The Unshackled Organization*, p. 15.

See I Mitroff (1983) *Stakeholders of the Organizational Mind.*

See DT Denhardt (1981) *In the Shadow of the Organization.*

See R Stacey (2001) *Complex Responsive Processes in Organizations.*

See M Wheatley (1999) *Leadership and the New Science.*

See DR Griffin 'Introduction to the SUNY Series on Constructive Postmodern Thought' in DW Orr (1992) *Ecological Literacy.*

See DT Denhardt (1981) *In the Shadow of the Organization*; MJ Bowles (1990) Recognising Deep Structures in Organizations, *Organization Studies*, 11(3).

For discussion of archetype from the perspective of neurobiology and evolutionary psychology, see A Stevens (1998) *Ariadne's Clue* and J Knox (2003) *Archetype, Attachment, Analysis: Jungian Psychology and the Emergent Mind.*

'Of course they do not exist, any more than a biological system exists in nature. But will any one deny the occurrence and continual repetition of certain morphological and functional similarities. It is much the same in principle with typical figures of the unconscious. They are forms existing a priori, or biological norms of psychic activity.' CG Jung *Collected Works* 9,1, p. 281. Jung also compared archetypes to the structure of a crystal, which 'exists' only when manifested in a particular crystal.

This is not to suggest that archetypal patterns are static or predetermined. In Jung's understanding they may be grounded in an eternal and transcendent reality, but the form in which we experience them is strongly influenced by historical and cultural factors.

See J Hillman (1977) *Revisioning Psychology*, p. 138f.

CG Jung *Collected Works* 8, p. 201.

See for example M Wheatley op.cit., M Knowles (1990) *Organizational Behavior*, R Stacey (2000) *Strategic Management and Organizational Dynamics*, A De Geus (1997) *The Living Company*, and F Capra (1996) *The Web of Life.*

See J Lovelock (1979) *Gaia: a New Look at Life on Earth* and (1988) *The Ages of Gaia.*

See M Louis (1985) 'An Investigator's Guide to Workplace Culture', In PJ Frost (ed.) *Organizational Culture.*

See E Marais (1973) *The Soul of the White Ant.*

Support for this proposition comes from the study of synchronization in human behavior. For a discussion of this phenomenon see ET Hall (1976) *Beyond Culture* and (1984) *The Dance of Life.*

WG Bennis, KD Benne, & R Chin (1961) *The Planning of Change*, p. 19.

J Forrester (1969) *Urban Dynamics*, p. 9.

J Goldstein op.cit., p. 90.

See R Stacey (1996) *Complexity and Creativity in Organizations.*

2

ORGANIZATION, CULTURE AND CHANGE

Defining Organizational Culture

A slow revolution has been undermining established notions about organizational structure. Traditional structures have begun to fail under the challenge from what Emery and Trist called 'a more turbulent environment' as long ago as 1965.[1] Since then we have seen various new concepts emerge: matrix structures, quality circles, skunk works, and the like. Of recent times, the quiet but persistent seepage of new thinking in the sciences into the management literature is producing even more fluidity. But as more fluid structures match the greater lability of the environment, organizations have to depend more heavily upon shared meanings to hold themselves together. And that is where culture becomes relevant. This is one of the factors that seem to have stimulated the rise in interest in organizational culture over the last two decades.

One of the difficulties in writing sensibly and clearly about culture comes from the fact that whatever we think or say about culture in general, or about specific cultures in particular, is thought and said from within our own culture and carries that culture's presuppositions and prejudices. This is going to be true whether we are exploring a tribal culture that is very different from our own, or attempting to analyze the culture of an organization to which we belong. We do not pretend here that we are engaged in a totally detached and objective science of culture, but then, neither is anybody else. The best we can do is to be upfront about the particular perspective we are taking and the assumptions that our own experience of organizations has led us into.[2]

Defining an organization is straightforward enough. Following Edgar Schein,[3] we can suggest that any definition of organization will include a number of elements. The first is the notion of a group of people acting together in some sense and coordinating their efforts; a second element is the notion that this is done to achieve some common goal or purpose; thirdly, there will be some sort of division of labor in order to achieve this goal; and finally, there needs to be some structure of authority and responsibility that the members accept in order to attain their common goal.[4]

In accepting this definition we are limiting ourselves to talking about formal organizations, as opposed to social organizations, which arise spontaneously when a group of people cooperate for a common interest (such as enjoying each other's company) without setting up explicit goals or establishing the roles and division of labor that make these explicit goals achievable. There is obviously a continuum here, though the basic distinction is clear enough. The group of friends may decide to make their goal explicit, appoint a secretary, and think strategically about how best to enjoy each other's company, in which case they have become a formal organization. A formal organization may lose sight of any common purpose and yet manage to maintain its formal structures. It may direct all its energy to maintaining its existence, or the power and status of its executive.

A useful way to think about organizations is to distinguish different kinds, or different levels, of organizational reality. The structural level, for instance, is the level of abstract structure, which can be represented diagrammatically without any reference to the particular people who exercise roles and responsibilities. It is possible, in theory at least, to change the personnel entirely without changing the structure. Then there is the social relations level in which actual people communicate with each other and relate to each other within the roles assigned to them by the organization. It is through these constantly ongoing negotiations that the work of the organization is done. This is distinct from the nomological level, the level of individual consciousness, at which the members relate to the organization and to other individual members as unique persons, each with their own particular personality, perspectives, prejudices, and personal style. Fourthly, there is the human encounter level, which includes the whole person, unconscious as well as conscious. Following Jung and Freud, we can argue that conscious behavior has its roots in unconscious processes, and that these are manifested in organizational as well as personal phenomena. Jung talks of individuation, meaning a process of dialogue with the unconscious psyche, in which the ego (or conscious self) negotiates a more harmonious relationship with the unconscious. This level, energized by the unconscious, cannot be ignored if we wish to intervene productively in organizations.[5]

Defining culture is a little more problematic. The extensive literature developing the dichotomy between 'nature' and 'culture' and distinguishing between 'culture' and 'civilization' demonstrates that this is by no means a simple matter. However, all we need here is a working definition of culture as it is used in the context of organizations.

Perhaps the best place to start is with Kluckhohn's cluster of definitions through which he tried to summarize what we mean when we refer to a people's 'culture'. In Mirror for Man (1949) he suggested that we could define culture as:

- the total way of life of a people
- the social legacy the individual acquires from his [sic] group
- a way of thinking, feeling, and believing
- an abstraction from behavior
- a theory on the part of an anthropologist about the way in which a group of people in fact behave
- a storehouse of pooled learnings
- a set of standardized orientations towards recurrent problems
- learned behavior
- a mechanism for the normative regulation of behavior
- a set of techniques for adjusting both to the external environment and to other men [sic]
- a precipitate of history

Putting this more concisely, a group's culture comprises the things that an individual has to know and do in order to be accepted as a member of that group.

This sort of definition is essentially mechanistic and has led some social scientists to believe that it is possible to discover the laws that govern the formation and maintenance of cultures so that we will be able to control and predict this process. This has been particularly marked where the insights and language developed by anthropologists in studying tribal cultures have been applied to formal organizations. Combined with the image of an organization as a machine-like structure, where every element is in a simple cause-effect relationship with the other elements, this approach has led to a fantasy that organizational change can be easily manipulated and controlled, if only we are clever enough.

During the past two decades the complexity of organizational cultures has been increasingly recognized. Writers such as Gagliardi,[6] Schein,[7] Hofstede,[8] Trompenaars[9], and Lundberg[10] have challenged simplistic notions of culture. They suggest that culture resides less in behavior than in the meanings that people attribute to the organizations in which they spend much of their time. This approach has been strongly influenced by Clifford Geertz' work on the interpretation of cultures.

> Believing, with Max Weber, that man [sic] is an animal suspended in webs of significance he himself has spun, I take culture to be those webs, and the analysis of it to be therefore not an experimental science in search of law but an interpretative one in search of meaning.[11]

At its broadest, culture is a coherent system of assumptions and basic values that distinguishes one group or organization from another, and that orients its choices. Geert Hofstede defines organizational culture as 'the collective programming of the mind which distinguishes the members of one organization from another'. He presents an image of culture as 'software of the mind'.[12] To put it a little differently, in the words of Edgar Schein, organizational culture is:

> . . . a pattern of basic assumptions – invented, discovered, or developed by a given group as it learns to cope with its problems of external adaptation and internal integration – that has worked well enough to be considered valid and, therefore, to be taught to new members as the correct way to perceive, think and feel in relation to these problems.[13]

The teaching is often not conscious, but absorbed by the newcomer through observation of how other people behave, and how they react to the newcomer's behavior. The manifestations of an organization's culture are to be found in person-organization interaction and person-person interaction.

While Schein provides a good working definition of organizational culture, it has two problems, from our point of view at least. In the first place, it suggests that culture is more or less static, that it is something that is established and maintained rather than something that is always in process. Of course, our experience of culture in organizations confirms that culture often appears to be fairly constant and even rigid, but this is not a necessary attribute of culture. Indeed, if we imagine culture as ongoing process, constantly emerging from the conversations, conflicts, hopes, and negotiations between members of the organization, we might wonder how we ever manage to see organizational culture as either stable or desirable. In recent years it has become more common to speak of organizations in process terms. Such a perspective leads to an alternative definition of organizational culture, such as that offered by Richard Seel. In such a definition culture is a process that organizations are engaged in, rather than an attribute that an organization 'has'. It is 'the way we do things around here'.

> Organization culture is the emergent result of the continuing negotiations about values, meanings, and proprieties between the members of that organization and with its environment.[14]

Secondly, Schein's definition suggests that culture is unitary. This is a conventional notion of culture that was not challenged until recently. It overlooks the diversity that exists in any group of people, even when they come together in a formal organization. There are certainly plenty of people in executive positions who think that an organization can become strong by suppressing dissent and difference. We would argue that the attempt to do so not only uses up a great deal of energy that could be employed more creatively, but even turns potentially productive members into subversives and saboteurs. We would argue that in the current environment, whether we call it postmodern or not, the ability of an organization to respond to the changing demands being made on it may depend on whether it has supported or even encouraged the existence of different cultures within it.

When Schein refers to a 'pattern of basic assumptions', we should note that this pattern may include assumptions that contradict each other. An organization in which one group of people assumes that the purpose of the organization is pursuing a social good, while another group believes that the organization's purpose is to foster the creativity of its members and still another group can imagine no other purpose than making a lot of money obviously has a culture, but not a unitary one. The managers of the organization may attempt to build a unitary culture by rewarding those who 'fit in' and getting rid of those who do not. The effect of this will be to diminish the organization's ability to respond flexibly to changing conditions. They can try to ignore the situation, but then they risk the fragmentation of the organization. Or they can acknowledge and value the different subcultures and their contrasting positions and thus give the organization access to all the energy and talent of its members. The tension between different subcultures within an organization may be destructive, but it does not have to be. If difference is genuinely valued, this tension and the dialogue that it generates will be the source of a great deal of the organization's energy and inventiveness.

We can argue that the unity or plurality of an organization's culture is really a matter of perspective.[15] One observer may examine a commercial organization from an understanding that culture is more or less unitary. He reads the vision statement, studies the structures and procedures, observes people's behavior, and interviews the people. He finds that managers and workers say much the same things about what the company does and how it does it. What they say matches the company's public statements. He decides that the organization has a strong and cohesive culture.

Another observer looks at the same company and finds that there are two kinds of managers: those who talk about the company's aims in a way which echoes the vision tatement, and those who are rather critical of the way the company is stuck in an outmoded way of operating. She finds that in a particular division of the company, managers and staff have adapted the standard structures and procedures so they can work in a more creative way. When she interviews people she finds that when she asks sufficiently probing questions, she uncovers a significant subculture of people who don't really accept the official company line and are working to change it. She sees this diversity in the culture as a strength, rather than a weakness.

A third observer looks at the same company with no expectation of seeing consistency and consensus. He sees the ways that particular structures are inconsistent with the vision statement. He notices that the things people say don't always match the things they do. He finds that when he questions people for long enough, they often contradict themselves. He finds that in some circumstances there is consensus about values and in other circumstances there is conflict. He sees a great deal of ambiguity in the organization's stated and unstated aims and its ways of achieving them. He finds similar ambiguity in individuals' attitudes to the company and their work. He concludes that there is really no point in trying to paint a picture of a stable and consistent culture. From his perspective, organizational culture by its nature is complex and constantly in process.

If we expect the culture of an organization to be unitary we will judge an organization by the singleness of its vision and the conformity of its members to a particular way of thinking and acting. Peters and Waterman, in their celebrated study of successful American companies, made such a judgment. They assumed that a 'strong' (i.e. cohesive and conformist) culture was necessarily better than a 'weak' culture, and argued that it was possible to describe the kind of culture a company needed to have in order to be successful.[16]

However, this very singleness of vision can prove to be a weakness in a changing environment. Most organizations have both areas of consensus (which give them stability) and areas of ambiguity (which give them flexibility). Insistence on absolute conformity takes away the ability to change without trauma. On the other hand, an organization ceases to be an organization if its members do not share some assumptions about what it is and why it exists.

Stacey provides a useful model for dealing with the complexity of organizational culture.[17] He suggests that we need to distinguish two dimensions in looking at the beliefs and values of members of an organization: agreement and certainty. There are things that everybody in the organization believes and is certain about. There are things that everybody agrees about, but without a great deal of certainty. There are things that people strongly disagree about. There are things about which people have neither agreement nor certainty. We can argue that it is the area of high certainty and high agreement that gives both stability and rigidity to an organization; the area of low agreement and low certainty provides openness to change; the area of high certainty and low agreement contains the threat of fragmentation; and the area of low certainty and high agreement is the site of emerging culture.

Conventionally, discussions of organizational culture deal only (or at least mainly) with what is observable and conscious within the organization. However, there is an entirely different level of analysis possible. We can, for instance, talk about the 'tacit' dimensions of culture, the values and meanings which are expressed in people's actions without ever coming into awareness. Or we can look at organizational culture as the expression of unconscious dynamics in a Freudian or Jungian sense.

Murray Stein refers to the 'intermeshing of the organization's unconscious and the unconscious of the individual'[18] that occurs when an individual joins an organization. One of the effects of this enmeshment is that the organization uses its individuals to act out roles as they become activated in the group's collective unconscious:

> The constellation and enactment of these archetypal roles forms the psychological underpinning for what is called an organization's 'culture'. A group's culture is made up of many such archetypally determined roles and enactments, most of them unconsciously motivated and shaped. Only the rare individual or organization has any insight at all into how this works, or what the most crucial archetypes active in its midst are.[19]

From this perspective organizational culture is the organization's experience of the complex interaction between diverse archetypal energies that are striving for expression.

Describing Organizational Culture

In the anthropological and management literature there are a number of widely accepted ways of describing cultures. When we look at culture, what we see depends on the lens we are looking through. If we assume that power is the most significant dynamic in organizational life, we will see the different ways power is exercised and categorize an organization's culture accordingly. In the meantime, others will be classifying organizational culture according to the way people relate to each other, the way decisions are made, the way organizations are structured, the way particular basic assumptions shape their behavior, and so on.

For example, as early as 1960, researchers at the Tavistock Institute were distinguishing between *mechanistic cultures*, which are appropriate for conditions of high stability, and *organismic cultures* which are suitable to unstable or turbulent environments, and pointing out the difficulty of moving from one to the other as the environment changes.[20]

Writing in the seventies, Charles Handy cited Roger Harrison's classification of *power cultures* (which are dominated by top-down power relationships), *role cultures* (which are characterized by a rational structure where personal power and relationships have limited influence), *task cultures* (which focus on getting the job done and giving people the resources to achieve this), and *personal cultures* (where people's commitment is to their own achievement and satisfaction rather than to the organization). He added his own take on these by associating them with the Greek gods Zeus, Apollo, Athena, and Dionysos.[21]

Edward Hall has distinguished *monochronic cultures* from *polychronic cultures* and *high context cultures* from *low context cultures*.[22] The monochromic/polychronic distinction refers to the way cultures relate to time. *Monochronic cultures* think of time as abstract and linear, believe in time-lines and timetables, value punctuality, and like to do 'one thing at a time'. *Polychronic cultures* think of time as personal and relational and are happy dealing with many things simultaneously and at different paces. *High context cultures* are those in which the ways that people relate to each other are governed by shared knowledge and relationships and unspoken rules that may never have been put into words and that are taken completely for granted. In a *low context culture*, rules and procedures are spelled out in detail because there can be no assumption that people will 'naturally' know how to behave.

Henry Mintzberg has described a number of 'organizational types', distinguishing between them in terms of structure.[23] He lists five distinct types: *simple structure* (as in a small company run by a boss who decides what is to be done and gets people to do it), *machine bureaucracy* (as in a large company characterized by centralized decision making, specialized tasks, and formal operating procedures), *divisionalized bureaucracy* (where a large company is organized as semi-autonomous units), *professionalized bureaucracy* (such as doctors in a shared practice or academics in a university department, where they control their own tasks), and *adhocracy* (characterized by smaller scale, fluid, often temporary structures, responding to needs as they arise).

Geert Hofstede classifies cultures in terms of five polarities.

- *High power distance* cultures are distinguished from *low power distance* cultures by the extent to which the less powerful members of organizations and institutions accept that power is distributed unequally.

- *High uncertainty* avoidance cultures are distinguished from *low uncertainty* avoidance cultures by the extent to which members are threatened by ambiguous situations and find ways (rules, rituals) to feel more secure.

- In *individualist cultures* people feel their main responsibility is to look after themselves, whereas in *collectivist cultures* people's commitment is to the group (family, corporation, or nation).

- *Masculine cultures* care about achievement; *feminine cultures* care about people and the quality of life.

- Cultures with a *long-term orientation* are concerned about the future; those with a *short-term orientation* put all their energy into the present.[24]

Fons Trompenaars and Charles Hampden-Turner likewise distinguish between cultures by proposing a number of polarities based on the value positions held by people in the organizations.[25]

• *Universalism* is distinguished from *particularism* by the tendency of people to base decisions on universal rules rather than judging each case on its merits.

• Some organizations value *achieved status* (being respected comes from productive work) and others value *ascribed status* (e.g. based on age, race, gender, or social class).

• Organizations may value either *individualism* (where personal initiatives are encouraged and successful individuals are rewarded) or *communitarianism* (where no one is singled out because every one is in it together).

• Organizations with a *specific culture* like to show their efficiency by breaking tasks or problems into parts and dealing with them one at a time; those with a *diffuse culture* approach tasks or problems as a whole - including the wider context, past experiences and the social relations between people.

• In *inner-directed* organizations people make their own judgments about the value of their activities; in *outer-directed* organizations they are more sensitive to the way outsiders view them and may also be more aware of their impact on the natural environment.

• Some organizations perceive *time as sequence*; others perceive *time as synchronization*. In the first case they see past, present, and future to be unconnected and accordingly think of achieving tasks in the shortest possible time and getting on with something else; in the second case both past and future are felt to make an impact on current activities and consequently planning is done quite differently.

Organizations value either *equality* or *hierarchy*. Either they think people should all be treated equally or they emphasize the authority and respect accorded to those in charge.

Some organizations have an *affective* or *emotional* culture, and others have a culture that is *neutral* as far as feelings are concerned and disapprove of emotional expression, especially when decisions are being made.

Like Hofstede, Trompenaars, and Hampden-Turner are most interested in the way the value systems of national cultures impact on corporations. However, in applying their framework specifically to corporate cultures they find four distinct cultures dominant, which they label *family* (hierarchical/person-oriented), *Eiffel tower* (hierarchical/task-oriented), *incubator* (egalitarian/ person-oriented), and *guided missile* (egalitarian/ task-oriented).

In a recent classification of national cultures designed to sensitize business people to the hazards of inter-cultural communication and the danger of assuming that a corporation can make a geographical shift without an accompanying cultural shift, Richard Lewis[26] distinguishes between three kinds of culture: *multi-active cultures*, *linear-active cultures*, and *reactive cultures*. People in *multi-active cultures* (Brazil, Sub-Saharan Africa, Saudi Arabia, Italy) are inclined to show their feelings, do several things at once, talk a lot, and have a flexible view of truth. People in *linear-active cultures* (Germany, USA, Australia, Switzerland) like to do things step by step, are job-oriented, depend on the facts, and put truth before diplomacy. People in *reactive cultures* (Vietnam, Japan, China, Indonesia) are inclined to hide their feelings, hate to lose face, are polite and indirect, and avoid confrontation.

Jack Gibb distinguishes nine kinds of 'environmental quality' that characterize organizational behavior. Depending on the relationship of fear to trust, organizational culture can be *punitive*, *autocratic*, *benevolent*, *consultative*, *participative*, *emergent*, *organic*, *holistic*, or *cosmic*.[27] Gibb proposes that, given good will, organizations have a tendency to progress through these stages. Increasing the level of trust in an organization initiates what he calls a TORI process (trusting – *opening* – *realizing* – interdepending – *trusting* –), which spirals the organization through these levels of environmental quality, increasing communication and organizational efficiency, and changing people's values and assumptions as well as the quality of their relationships and their interaction with their environment. Increasing the level of fear sends the organization spiraling in the opposite direction.

One way of classifying culture is to assume an analogy between the personality of an individual and the culture of an organization. Thus we can talk in diagnostic language of a *paranoid culture*, a *manic culture*, a *schizoid culture*, an *obsessive culture*, a *sychopathic culture*, and so on. Alternatively, Jung's personality theory offers us a ich language for talking about organizational culture. We can talk about extraverted r *introverted cultures*, *sensate* or *intuitive cultures*, *thinking* or *feeling cultures*, *erceiving* or *judging cultures*, or combine all these polarities in descriptions of (for xample) *ENFP cultures* or *ISTJ cultures*.[28]

is obvious that there are recurring themes here. Most of these schemes are based n polarities, and they focus mainly on the ways we deal with power and intimacy in ur relations with others and how we experience time, space and environment. The bove attempts to classify cultures are based on a shared assumption that there are a nite number of dimensions to culture and that these are combined in different ways produce the very different cultures that we can observe. Each classification system tempts to find the particular set of dimensions that will cover all cases.

in D'Cruz makes the observation that particular characteristics of culture seem occur together. He argues that cultures can be located on a continuum from ncreteness to abstraction. For instance, a culture located towards the concrete end the continuum will tend to manifest a set of values which includes giving the group iority over the individual, accepting an hierarchical authority; acknowledging the aims of blood relationship; respecting the wisdom of 'the elders', preferring a face--face approach to resolving problems and conflicts and maintaining a relationship of rmony with the natural world.

the language of the writers discussed above, a *concrete culture* can be described as role culture (Handy), organismic (Tavistock), polychronic and high context (Hall), gh power distance, uncertainty avoiding, collectivist and feminine (Hofstede), cribed status, communitarian, diffuse, inner-directed, hierarchical, and emotional rompenaars), or introverted, sensate, and feeling (Jung). By contrast a culture wards the *abstract end* of the continuum will emphasize a very different set of lues: individuality and autonomy, rationality, professionalism, abstract structures, mocratic processes, and personal achievement. It can be described in such words and rases as low power distance, monochronic, low context, masculine, individualistic, alitarian, universalist, and feeling-neutral.[29]

In this book we are looking at organizational culture through a somewhat differer lens, which provides a more complex (or at least more complicated) view of cultur than that used by D'Cruz. Following Jung's writings on archetype, we suggest that ther are a number of specific patterns of human behavior, both individual and collectiv which are grounded in our biological, psychological, and cultural inheritance, an that a language for distinguishing these patterns is to be found in the mythologie of classical civilizations. John G. Corlett and Carol Pearson have taken a simila perspective in distinguishing twelve archetypal narratives which shape the identity an functioning of contemporary organizations: Creator, Caregiver, Ruler, Revolutionar Hero, Magician, Jester, Lover, Everyperson, Sage, Explorer, and Innocent.[30] W have preferred to distinguish between the archetypal patterns we have observed i organizations by giving them the names of Greek gods.

Jung came to the conclusion there is a finite number of archetypal patterns shapin our lives, just as the classical Greeks concluded that there was a finite number of goc shaping theirs. Neither the Greeks nor Jung were prepared to say with any confidenc how many.

Hofstede's classification of cultures was based on the assumption that a culture wi be either collectivist or individualist, either masculine or feminine, and so on. On th other hand, Trompenaars and Hampden-Turner make it clear that they are not talkin about dualities but about polarities. A culture will have both diffuse aspects an specific aspects. Whether we classify it as one or the other will depend on whichev is dominant. Likewise, D'Cruz is explicit that abstractness and concreteness are n dualistic contraries but lie at opposite ends of a continuum.

Whether a culture is abstract or concrete is a matter of how the balance works out a particular time or in a particular environment. In individual psychology, introverte people may become extraverted when intoxicated or under stress. Extraverted peop may become introverted in the same circumstances. The same applies to organization cultures. The egalitarian organization may become authoritarian when under threa the uncertainty-avoiding corporation may suddenly begin to gamble with its assets the excitement of a rising market.

However, in the model we describe in this book we are not concerned with either dualities or polarities. Rather, we are leaning on much older understandings of the world to distinguish things imaginatively. We depict organizational culture as a web of interacting narratives, expecting to find in any organization myths that are dominant, myths that are suppressed or neglected, myths that comfortably co-exist, and myths that are in tension. We distinguish sixteen different images drawn from Greco-Roman mythology, which represent the 'old stories' that still largely shape the culture of Europe and its former colonies.

Accordingly, we write of a *Zeus culture* (which might be described in rational language as being simple structure, hierarchical, autocratic, inner-directed, power-oriented, high context, masculine, Eiffel Tower, high power distance), an *Eros culture* (person-oriented, high context, low power distance, affective, polychronic, feminine, incubator, organic), a *Hermes culture* (short-term oriented, individualistic, polychronic, low uncertainty avoidance, intuitive, adhocratic), and so on through the pantheon. The rational mode of classification is intent on pointing to differences. The imaginative mode recognizes that the energies dominant in any organization and manifested in its culture are constantly in interaction with other energies which are supported, suppressed, or neglected, just as the Olympian gods do not exist in isolation but are constantly interacting and arguing with one another. It is concerned not so much with the simplicity of either-or as with the complexity of both-and.

Layers of Organizational Culture

When describing the culture of an organization, it is tempting to focus on what is readily observable – the organizational structures, the organization's ikons, the things people say or do. However, in every culture there is a pattern of unspoken rules that governs the things that people say and do, and even the things they think. Hall refers to this 'hidden cultural grammar', which defines the way people view the world and establishes the basic rhythm of life, as primary level culture. He distinguishes it from secondary level culture (the screened off, private level of a culture which is generally known only to insiders) and tertiary level culture (the conscious, technical level which is manifested in words and other symbols). The primary level culture is largely unconscious, yet when the rules are violated, people know at once that something is wrong. And it is extremely resistant to change.[31]

Organizational culture is a multi-layered affair. Its expressions range from the behavioral and tangible to the invisible and deeply unconscious. Schein's definition of culture refers to basic assumptions as the source of the particular ways of perceiving, thinking, feeling, and talking that are acceptable in an organization. In discussing this, he distinguishes three distinct layers of organizational culture: artifacts, espoused values, and basic underlying assumptions. Lundberg,[32] who offers a definition of organizational culture very similar to Schein's, likewise distinguishes separate levels of meaning for an organization's culture: artifacts, perspectives, values, and basic assumptions. In this way of thinking we can visualize organizational culture as being structured something like an onion, with a number of layers around an inner core.[33]

Layer 1: Artifacts

In Lundberg's model we find artifacts at the more visible or superficial levels of culture, the outer layer of the onion. Artifacts are tangible things shared by members of an organization or group, including behavioral and physical attributes, language, stories and myths, rituals and symbols, technology, and art. They comprise the surface layer of skills and behaviors, the ways members of the organization behave, the things they have learned to do and say. It includes the organization's visible structures, documents, roles, and material resources.

We can find out what an organization's artifacts are simply by observing them: they are directly accessible to our five senses.

Layer 2: Perspectives

At the next level we find perspectives: the rules and norms the members of a group or organization develop and share socially in any given context. This is a layer o information, ideas and beliefs, the things members of the organization know and think. Perspectives are, if you like, solutions to a common set of problems encountered from time to time. They define situations and prescribe the bounds of acceptable behavior in such situations. They are relatively concrete and members are usually aware of them.

We can find out what an organization's perspectives are by asking its members, or by inferring the shared frameworks within which people operate to solve their problems. They represent the 'espoused theory' of the organization.[34]

Layer 3: Values

Organizational values are the base that members of an organization use for judging the 'rightness' or 'wrongness' of situations, acts, objects, and people. Values reflect the real objectives, standards, and goals in an organization and also define its transgressions, sins, and wrongdoings. Though more abstract than perspectives they can sometimes be articulated by members in such statements as the organizational mission, vision, or philosophy. Some organizations value difference, others value uniformity. In some organizations people value clear, rational, and logical thought processes to reach decisions. In others, intuition and feeling are given priority in decision-making. Some reward creativity, risk-taking, and innovation; others value order, checking, and control. Some value collaboration; others encourage competition. Some give priority to the quality of relationships; others regard this as irrelevant. Some maintain a purely financial 'bottom line'. Others maintain a 'bottom line' of social concern or environmental responsibility.

Values are somewhat harder to get at than artifacts and perspectives, but if people reflect they can usually become aware of what they value, of how their organization judges what is good or bad, right or wrong, nice or nasty, important or unimportant, and how these values affect behavior in the organization. We need to be aware, of course, that people can easily deceive themselves when it comes to articulating their values. What they say they value is not always reflected in the way they behave. The same can be said of their collective behavior in organizations.

Inner Core: Basic Assumptions

At the deepest level we find the tacit beliefs that members hold about themselves and the world, their relationships to one another, and the nature of the organization in which they work. Largely unconscious, these beliefs underpin the first three levels above. If you like, they are implicit and abstract axioms that shape the values, perspectives, and artifacts of an organization's culture.

These basic assumptions are the things people in the organization take completely for granted. Central to this inner core are their basic assumptions about the organization's identity, about what sort of an organization it is (i.e. about 'who we are'). These assumptions are often difficult to get at, simply because they are taken so completely for granted and rarely reflected on. The members of the organization also carry assumptions that may sometimes appear to have little to do with the identity of the organization, but that nevertheless have a profound effect on its culture. These are assumptions about human nature, about humanity's place in the universe, about how people should treat each other, about the nature of reality, about time and space, about what constitutes a good life, about where one's loyalties should lie. Such assumptions are generally pretty firmly embedded in us by our family and cultural group long before we voluntarily join an organization.[35]

Hofstede[36] has shown how these deeper cultural values and assumptions, which are commonly associated with our nationality or religion, persist in people after they have joined an organization that proclaims a contrary set of values. It is common in foreign takeovers of companies that new management runs into trouble by assuming that a corporate culture can simply be transplanted into another environment. The artifacts may be largely accepted and the perspectives may be officially acknowledged, but they may rest on a base of values and assumptions that are very much at odds with them. Such a situation leads to failures of communication, stress, inefficiency, and fragmentation.

Levels of Change

To put Lundberg's understanding a little more concisely, organizational culture is found in the way an organization's employees talk with and act towards clients and each other (artifacts); is expressed in the symbols used on letterhead, on buildings, in advertising (artifacts); is found in the mind-sets members bring to bear on solving problems inside the organization and with clients (perspectives); is found in the attitudes and beliefs members collectively hold about what is good and proper, about what is questionable, about what is unacceptable (values); and occasionally shows us glimpses of its core – the deep and unconscious assumptions an organization's people hold about the world and how it works.

The unconscious is not rationally ordered – either in individuals or in organizations. Those parts of an organization's deep structure that arise from its collective unconscious will not always emerge or unfold in orderly ways. The levels of culture described by Lundberg are not discrete and detached from each other, but constantly interact. Obviously, the organization's basic assumptions will shape the particular values that the organization espouses, which in turn are expressed in perspectives and made concrete in the organization's artifacts. But it is also clear that the influence can run in the opposite direction. A change in the environment in which the organization lives will make its first impact at the level of artifacts, as the organization attempts to adapt to environmental change by substantially changing what it does or by dressing itself up in a different style. If the new artifacts are not consistent with the organization's established ways of thinking about itself (second layer) and the values in which these are grounded (third layer), tensions develop that have the potential to initiate productive change, on the one hand, or fragmentation and collapse, on the other. Which of these occurs is likely to depend on whether the organization's basic assumptions can still be expressed in the new vision, beliefs, and ways of operating. The inner core is very resistant to change, especially if it has never come into the collective awareness, and often the pathway to deep change lies in this domain, in the organization coming to a deeper knowing of its self.

Organizations, like individuals, can change their basic assumptions and their sense of identity. They can even do it quickly and suddenly, through a transformative experience, which may be either positive or traumatic. However, organizations, like individuals, cannot change their values and basic assumptions by simply deciding to change their values and basic assumptions.

An organization's basic assumptions may be rarely articulated, but they are carried in its myths, values, perspectives, and activities. An organization's myths act as long-term memories. The stories, true or imagined, which the members of an organization tell about the organization 'in the old days' are often the repository of the organization's most deeply held values and assumptions. These assumptions can also be found, if we care to look, in the recurring strategies with which the organization tries to manage its internal and external worlds. They are the source of an organization's 'theories in use' – the unstated rules that might be deduced from its behavior.

Organizational culture changes over time. In times of stability it becomes more embedded within the out-of-awareness functioning of an organization. It becomes more and more unconscious. In times of change, aspects that have previously dropped out of awareness may well be lifted once more into consciousness.

Misunderstanding Organizational Culture

Because it is complex, layered, and to some extent unconscious, culture is not totally controllable. The process of working with it always involves unpredictability and risk, and demands creative improvisation. Any technique that is applied 'cookbook style' is likely to be inadequate. Many of these non-mechanistic aspects of culture are now being addressed in the organization literature. For the most part, however, they do not have common currency in the world of management. For example, some of the literature, and much of management thought, seems to ask of 'culture' much more than it can give. Such views tend to ascribe much more predictability to the cultural change process than is warranted, and place more confidence in the ability of 'social engineers' to understand and influence a culture than is wise. Indeed, this type of thinking often rests on five common misunderstandings of culture in organizations. They are listed below as five fallacies: five misleading ideas that may lead senior executives and the student or manager of culture either to look in the wrong direction, or with too narrow a focus, or with inappropriate expectations.

Fallacy 1. Equating a manifestation of culture with culture itself

Culture is often viewed too simply, or is confused with other concepts. In reality it is very hard to capture clearly in words the essential nature of culture. There is often no way of telling if people are using the same terminology in the same way until they begin to tease out its implications. Only then do interpretive differences become apparent. Some people confuse culture with values. Others confuse it with organizational climate. For still another group it seems to be almost akin to management style. Culture is related to all of these things; but is not to be identified with any one of them.

Fallacy 2. Working with, or changing, only the superficial elements of culture

It is common for people to reduce culture to one of its constituents or manifestations. An intervention in this element is then attempted, in a misplaced confidence that the organization will change according to plan. Disappointment follows when unrealistic expectations for change are not met.

Many managers seek cultural change by changing superficial phenomena: the behavior and events and objects that Lundberg calls artifacts. They fail to pay attention to the deeper values and the unconscious assumptions that influence people's attitudes and behavior.

Quite rightly, they see among their employees' behaviors various practices and procedures that are outmoded or inappropriate. They recognize inappropriate ways of approaching problems, non-strategic responses to critical issues, and inattention to the things that matter. These same managers then espouse a new set of behaviors, a new set of norms. They become frustrated when their employees fail to respond to what is obvious, necessary, and common-sense.

Another frequent folly arising from this fallacy finds expression in the upsurge of interest in organizational values, – in particular, the assumption that espousing a different set of values will lead to change in the organization's deeper culture. Argyris and Schon show us how complicated and treacherous it is to sail in these waters.[37]

Culture ranges from the superficial and apparently trivial to the deepest assumptions and feelings that people hold about an organization. The deeper phenomena are harder to define and reach, and surface elements of the culture can change without affecting them at all.

Fallacy 3. Treating culture as key cause and remedy of organizational problems

There are some who engage in simplistic thinking about organizational dilemmas and see culture as both the key cause of, and the key remedy for, quite complex phenomena. Their assumption is that if you change culture, then other changes follow. Some managers see culture as a means of control. If you can establish a culture in which every one is loyal and hard working, you will no longer have to bother about rewarding loyalty and hard work and threatening or punishing those who don't come up to the mark.

This is a fallacy that comes in many guises. For example, some act as if they believe: 'Culture is the cure-all. It'll fix everything.' They seem to operate from a notion that culture is the cause of collective behavior in an organization, where it would be just as logical to see the behavior as the cause and culture as the effect. They seem to assume that inappropriate 'culture' is not necessarily affected by managerial competence, systemic, or structural factors. They think that a program of cultural change will remedy the deficiencies. They believe that a program of cultural change is a straightforward, simple, and sufficient intervention for such deficiencies, and that cultural change can be planned, implemented, and evaluated against the same criteria and within the same frameworks as other more operational aspects of organizational life.

Cultural change cannot take place in a vacuum. We cannot separate it from structure and strategy, nor deal with it as though it were a discrete dimension of organizational life. Strategy, structure, and culture require simultaneous attention.[38]

Fallacy 4. Treating a subculture as if it were the entire culture

This fallacy occurs with the equation of some part of a subculture within an organization with the whole culture of the organization. Or it may involve equating the managerial subculture with the culture of the whole organization, and perceiving those who do not share in it as deviants.

It rests upon the misconception that it is possible to create a unitary culture in a large organization. Unfortunately for the neatness of organizational theory, this simply is not so. We have to acknowledge that if unitary cultures do occur at all, they are rare. It seems that a unitary culture can exist only under certain conditions. In a context where all members of an organization face roughly the same problems, they may well develop the same beliefs and values and form a consensus about what constitutes approved behavior, but even this cannot be taken for granted. There must be some areas of the organization's identity and activity where most people are in agreement, otherwise the organization would cease to be an organization. But there will also be areas where there is no certainty and no consensus.[39]

Louis[40] points out that organizations may be more appropriately thought of as culture-bearing milieus: arenas in which one will find sites of sub-cultures, and through which sub-cultures may develop. Culture involves relationships between interests and groups within an organization; it is about differences in the sets of meanings, values, and beliefs that more or less ambiguously delineate group identity, and also about those social pressures that condition relationships between groups. Unitary cultures in large organizations may not be possible: what may be possible is a unitary set of espoused values, and a more or less common set of espoused perspectives, but these alone do not a culture make.

In our view, this fallacy, combined with the relatively high level of corporate interest in Jungian psychology as represented by the Myers Briggs Type Indicator, has created some fertile fields in which unscrupulous consultants can prey on unsuspecting executives. We now hear of ISTJ, ESTJ, ENFP etc. 'cultures'. Unfortunately such terms are sometimes used to describe government departments or private sector organizations with tens of thousands of people in them. Along with this trend, we also find one-dimensional archetypal labels used as descriptors of the characteristics of very large and complex organizations. It sometimes makes sense to talk of an ISTJ culture, a warrior culture, or a wisdom culture, and we will do so ourselves, but we need to acknowledge that such terms have limited application to large and complex organizations.

The tendency of many executives to worship the quick fix, and the desire of many consultants to provide it, makes this form of simplistic and uni-causal thinking particularly attractive. Unfortunately, the resulting analyses and the strategies derived from them usually fail dismally, and the real power and utility of cultural and archetypal analysis is thereby diminished. The edge of the consultants' understanding is blunted, as is that of their client executives, for they fail to recognize that merely categorizing and labeling the content of a social phenomenon gives you no insight into its internal, dynamic processes, and, consequently, very little real basis on which to plan change.

Fallacy 5. Confusing a concept with reality

This is the inappropriate reification of culture, treating as concrete and tangible what is actually a concept, an image, a fantasy. Culture is not a 'thing'. Psychological and anthropological 'realities' are constructs, ideas in the mind of the observers, and not physical entities. Nevertheless, many psychological constructs have been afforded the status of physical reality by writers and thinkers. In so doing, they have often unwittingly laid traps for themselves. The traps may consist in trying to define a set of technologies for things that are only poorly understood or purely imaginary, or in expecting reality to conform to a favorite theory or model, rather than being willing to deal with the world as it exists. Some managers seem to imagine that corporate culture is an instrument that can be used to increase productivity. This leads them to frustration because, from a different perspective, culture exists only in the subjective experience of all the people in the organization. It is not really a thing to be quantified, categorized, and manipulated. Rather, it is a shared experience.

This final fallacy is a major hazard in the analysis of organizational culture, yet it is possible to draw on this way of thinking to find constructive ways of dealing with the complexity and uncertainty of culture. We often find it easier to talk about mental and social processes as though they are things that can be classified, counted, and set in cause-effect relationship to each other. It enables us to develop neat, elegant, and even useful theories of how organizations work. We will certainly be categorizing and comparing cultures in the following chapters. However, we just need to be careful not to stumble into our own trap, by thinking that we have really got the facts on organizational culture. A theory does not tell us the truth about organizations; it is merely a tool to help us deal with them.

It may be more helpful to think of culture as the evolving process of organizational life. However, most of us lack the skill and the language to consistently talk about culture in this way. We find it easier to talk about culture as a 'thing' that we can observe and, possibly, change. Nevertheless, we will make some effort, in this book, to think and write of culture as a dynamic process in a living system.

Matters of Life and Death

For most of human existence the universe has been imagined as alive, animated, ensouled, peopled by spirits. The earth was our mother and worshipped as a goddess. However, for the last four hundred years or so scientists have understood the universe to be a vast machine, an inanimate physical system operating entirely according to mathematical principles that determine how it will behave. This image of a machine has been extended to plants, animals, human beings, and abstract structures. The same image has dominated social scientists in their understanding of organizations.

Things are changing. There are significant numbers of scientists now who find it more productive from a scientific point of view to think about the planet as a living organism.[41] The notion of soul is returning to psychology. Darwin's theory of evolution, which was hijacked by mechanistic scientists, is being rethought around its central image of organic growth. A significant and influential minority of social scientists are talking about organizations as living organisms rather than as inanimate machines.

Our tendency to imagine our organization as machine or metaphor affects the way we function within it. Richard Knowles suggests that it particularly affects our attitude to change:

> People in more traditional organizations, which usually function according to a machine paradigm, tend to be quite resistant to change. The thinking and behavior of the people in these organizations can be rather incoherent. People in organizations functioning more like living systems, however, proactively and intentionally co-create their future together. The thinking and behavior take on a deeper coherence. Resistance to change almost disappears. With information flowing freely, with strong relationships and trust, with a clear sense of identity and intention, the people in such organizations move into the future together, creating as they go. They embrace the wholeness, variety, and chaos, for with their agreements on how they'll be together, they can trust and have confidence in each other.[42]

Whereas adopting the metaphor of organization as machine involves us in thinking about constructing and fixing and malfunctioning and dismantling, the metaphor of organism has us talking about birth and healing and decay and death. Whichever way we imagine them, beginnings and endings are important. Machines are built, break down, and are thrown away. Living creatures are born and die. For the person or any other organism, birth and death are fundamental boundaries. Similarly, staying with the organic metaphor, every aspect of a group is born and develops, and every development is bound for decline. Paradoxically, decline also carries within it the potential for renewal. No group can remain unchanging forever; the sustained effort to keep it that way will ultimately destroy it. Even in the short term it will render the group ineffective.

It is not only the group or organization as a whole that grows and declines. The same can be said for any of its organic parts: its goal systems, its programs, its structures, its roles, its image, and so on. Everything goes through the same cycle of growth and decline. Death and life are intimately connected. If our cells were not constantly dying to make way for new cells we could not remain alive.

Peter O'Connor[43] suggests that we are engaged in a massive cultural denial, or repression into unconsciousness, of the reality of death. He argues that we can witness in Western society an obsession with Eros, the life force, and that this takes a variety of forms – from hard-core pornography through to the search for spiritual enlightenment.

We want to triumph over death, not accept it as an aspect of life. This is as true in the conduct of organizations as it is in our individual psychology. We want to grow without letting part of ourselves die. Organizations want to renew themselves while fiercely hanging on to everything that makes them what they are.

In an organization, the forced – or even voluntary – letting go of its accustomed identity is often felt by its members as a death. They may have entered into a state of unconscious identification with some aspect of the organization that resonates with their own psychological and social needs, to the extent that they cannot clearly distinguish between themselves and the organization. They may be unconsciously enacting an archetypal role such as savior, scapegoat, mother, or clown, on behalf of an organization that needs these roles to be acted out. Such roles are not easily abandoned. As Murray Stein points out:

> Generally, individuals and groups are not motivated to become conscious of what is going on with such unconscious identifications and archetypal enactments until the shoe starts pinching. Without pain, there is little desire or demand for consciousness. When the pain becomes intense . . . then the demand for consciousness reaches the pitch of life and death.[44]

There is a paradox here in that the sense of dying is associated with becoming conscious, not with losing consciousness. If as individuals we are stuck in a particular myth that tells us who we are and what gives meaning to our lives, we may be unable to imagine any reality outside this myth. We resist any movement towards consciousness of who we really are and what is really going on. This is even more true of groups and organizations, which are, on the whole, much less capable of being objective, rational, and aware than individuals are. Consciousness is resisted because it is only attained through a symbolic death.

Freud suggested that the essence of human existence is the struggle between the life-force (Eros) and the death-force (Thanatos).[45] The problem is that, individually and collectively, we consciously acknowledge one and keep the other in the depths of our unconsciousness.

> Yet the reality is that we live within the dynamic eternal cycle of birth, death and life, a cycle that occurs and re-occurs throughout our lives and of which death, or the separating quality of Thanatos, is a vital component. Thanatos surfaces whenever change occurs – divorce, redundancy, children leaving home, ageing, death of a parent or friend. We prefer to move from life to renewal and avoid the difficulties associated with endings and deaths. Thereby we create a delusion of change, not heeding the French axiom, 'Plus ça change, plus c'est la même chose'.[46]

Nevertheless, if we want to be involved in deep organizational change, death is something that we must confront and consider. John Sherwood is one social scientist who gives us a language for doing so, with his notion of organizational doubt.

Organizational Doubt

John Sherwood[47] developed a model of organizational growth and decline in which he focused on the experience of doubt. In this model, the decline of any organization (or a sub-unit, aspect, function, or the like) can be regarded as a series of steps related to increasing doubt.

Suspended Doubt

At times the general functioning of a group may be highly acceptable to all. This may be indicated by high morale; the people involved are likely to be cohesive; there are common goals and congruent structures, and so on. We can then say that the group exists in a state of suspended doubt. It is not that the group is functionally perfect. Rather, its members have for the time being unconsciously agreed to withhold doubt and skepticism. Everything is fine, or seems to be.

Operational Doubt

The first sign of decline appears when members start to tell each other and their leaders that things are not functioning as well as they might. Some doubt begins to be expressed: 'We've got a problem here'. The first and most typical response to this statement is denial: 'No we haven't. Everything's fine. Let's not fiddle with the system. It's working well.' Nevertheless the evidence that something is wrong begins to affect people. Doubt is expressed about the operations of the organization – plans, decisions, coordinating mechanisms, policies, procedures, budgets, structures. We can call this operational doubt. During times of suspended doubt, people's comments about the group are positive and characterized by enthusiasm and commitment. Operational doubt comes from a position in which the operational norms of the group – the way we do what we do – are questioned or challenged.

If such a challenge continues, it is likely that leaders will ultimately accept the problem to some extent. They then attempt to institute changes designed to address the 'problem'. Their intention is to return the system to a state of suspended doubt. We might typify this response by: 'Yes, we agree. But we've spotted the problem and we're working on it. All we need to do is fix up the system.' Such attempts may involve setting up a committee, doing a needs analysis, undertaking an organizational diagnosis, hiring a management consultant, or the like – all expected to establish accurately the nature of the problem and the most appropriate steps to get things 'back on track'.

Such attempts, in the long term, tend not to resolve the increasing doubt. In such cases, more often than not, the underlying goal is to manage the person asking the question rather than the question itself. The result is often that nothing is really done about the concerns of the members raising the questions. Consequently, their questioning becomes more serious and their doubts deeper.

Ideological Doubt

We now begin to see people questioning the purposes and goals of the group and seeking rational responses rather than the standard 'party line'. Their own convictions or beliefs are in doubt and no longer undergird their practice. Typically, members might say things like: 'All this patching up is worthless; the whole system is bankrupt and we need to renew the whole lot; we no longer know why we are in this business.' Such doubt is termed 'ideological doubt' for it questions the basic purposes and goals of the group. It is typically met by leaders with an ideology-based response through recourse to the group's charter or such attitudes as are exemplified in the comment: 'That's the way we've always done it and we will continue to do it that way.'

The seeds of alienation are now setting in. The leaders tend to adopt increasingly defensive responses to the increasing doubt. This period can be characterized by rational argument and debate, as conventional wisdom is challenged and the assumptions that underlie the organization's activities are critically examined. On the other hand, it may see increasing rigidity disguising the beginnings of panic.

Ethical Doubt

If management remains unresponsive to these concerns, doubt intensifies yet further. Alienation is widespread. The group may be viewed by many of its members as oppressive and uncaring of such things as basic working conditions. Questions about moral or ethical values implicit in the group's goals or practices are now raised openly.

The situation reaches a point exemplified in the statement: 'All this renewal is getting us nowhere; the whole system is losing its meaning for us.' Leaders take up increasingly defensive and entrenched positions in the face of such doubt, and tend to revert to highly arbitrary and autocratic management styles. Commitment and loyalty to the organization vanish. The general systems for communication and coordination break down or become inoperable. This state is called 'ethical doubt'.

People might say: 'Once we were a team pulling together and enjoying our work and each other (suspended doubt). Then we became a club – we had some common interests and generally worked in the same direction but only came together for support and networking (operational doubt). Then for a while we found we really couldn't work together (ideological doubt). Now we are a motel – people coming and going in the night without any real connection to one another (ethical doubt). And if we don't watch out we will soon become a hospice.' This is the last stage before ultimate breakdown or absolute doubt.

An organization can continue to exist when there is widespread ethical doubt, but it will be ineffective and inefficient. Its members get no rewards for their participation and contribution towards common goals. There is widespread breakdown of basic management principles and practices.

Absolute Doubt

Sherwood describes the next stage of absolute doubt as one of widespread cynicism and despair. The system is barely workable. Nobody believes in it any more. It may even cease to function, although this is not always the case. People are saying, 'What's the use? There is nothing at all in this for me.' In times of high unemployment and uncertainty, people in such organizations have fewer options for going to other organizations, so they stay, but without faith in what they are doing. They may suppress such doubt behaviorally yet still experience it emotionally and motivationally.

Transition and Renewal

Sherwood's stages of doubt parallel the levels of organizational culture noted by Schein and Lundberg. When our artifacts are not working for us, we experience operational doubt. Our perspectives and beliefs come under threat and we experience ideological doubt. As our values become shaky we find ourselves in ethical doubt. Finally our assumptions prove to be baseless and we collapse into absolute doubt.

However, absolute doubt may not be an entirely dysfunctional state. It may be a necessary transitional state before renewal can occur. The stages of doubt may be seen as a movement towards consciousness. The organization whose identity is shaky may be in a state of suspended doubt, totally unconscious of its true state. As the crisis intensifies it is forced to confront the reality of its situation at ever deeper levels, becoming increasingly conscious as it sheds its illusions and abandons its myths. Descending into absolute doubt is experienced as death, but death and life are a cyclic process, and organizations can choose not to stay dead.

William Bridges[48] suggests that in order to be reborn and grow, an organization has to answer three basic questions that are a product of doubt.

> Who are we? What is our identity?
> Why are we here? What is our purpose?
> How will we give expression to our response to the 'who?' and the 'what?'?
> What processes will we use to achieve our goals?

A transition implies going from one place or state to another. Bridges speaks of a transition as composed of endings, a neutral zone, and beginnings. The ending phase is characterized by an increasing sense of loss and doubt that creeps into the organization and moves through four phases to despair:

Disengagement
A willing or unwilling separation

Disenchantment
Loss of purpose, direction, and confidence
Experience of confusion and emptiness
Disintegration
Loss of meaningful environment and lack of commitment
'Reality' is not what it really is
Values and traditions fall apart

Disidentification
Loss of meaning and self
Ambivalence and distress

Cynicism and Despair
Disgust with life
Loss of all hope that things might be different

These phases of decline are parallel to Sherwood's stages of increasing doubt, as are the reverse stages according to which an organization or social system seems to rebuild itself:

Dreams
Where am I going?
Rediscovery of new self
Spontaneity, yearnings, and transformations

Beliefs
Why am I here?
Reviewing values, meanings, and attachments
Culture, conscience, passion, wisdom of the heart

Purpose
What do I do?
Identifying new directions and objectives
Grafting old meanings into new sources of meaning

Plans
How do I do it?
Steps, goals, and strategies

Between endings and beginnings lies the neutral zone. Eric March and William Bridges talk of the neutral zone as a time of alienation, of life experienced in a vacuum where there is much chaos. It is also a time filled with a sense of wilderness and being lost, an experience of abandonment and uncertainty in which people no longer have access to the previously established forms of power and authority that had up until now guided their lives and provided certainty for them. March's description of the neutral zone echoes the words used by the anthropologist Victor Turner to describe a liminal condition.[49]

Liminality and Transition

Turner speaks of the importance for cultures of liminal periods, the periods 'in between'. The word 'liminal' suggests a boundary, a place that is not really a place because it is neither 'here' nor 'there', like a doorstep or a crossroad. A liminal period is a period of marginality existing between structures or between situations. It is a transition between an existing order of things and one yet to be born.

Within such a period, one is likely to find 'transitional beings' or 'liminal personae' who seem to be necessary to the transition. The liminal persona is defined by a name and a set of symbols that give an outward and visible form to an inward and conceptual corporate process. The organizational analogue of such persons seems to be the 'innovator' and/or 'early adopter' spoken of in agricultural extension models of organizational change.[50] However, most organizations give little thought or energy to developing symbols around such persons, let alone rituals designed to express new corporate myths.

The liminal period is also likely to be characterized by 'structural invisibility, ambiguity, and neutrality'.[51] In an organization or group there are many different kinds of privileges and obligations, many degrees of superordination and subordination. However, in the period of change such distinctions and gradations tend to be eliminated. In such a period people confront one another integrally and not in a compartmentalized fashion as actors or roles. The person emerges from behind the mask. (In a sense, there is no mask left to hide behind.)

Although it is a period of structural simplicity (or a relative absence of structure), it is nevertheless also one of cultural complexity and turbulence. This phenomenon is most evident as large organizations face severe survival demands and their executives begin to realize they no longer have the strategies and wherewithal to solve the problems the environment is presenting to them.

It seems to make sense to think of Sherwood's state of absolute doubt as constituting the liminal period during which new beginnings are created. It also makes sense to think of it in March's terms, as the phases of disidentification, alienation, and dreaming. As an organization or social system declines through the various stages of doubt, it reaches the liminal phase in which there is a loosening of structures and roles, enabling a transition to a new beginning. Sometimes it goes on to create a new identity and unity, a new set of purposes and directions, and a new set of practices and procedures. Sometimes it decays or dissolves into fragments and its members go off to new beginnings elsewhere. Sometimes it is artificially kept alive long after it is 'clinically dead'.

The notion of a liminal phase provides assurance that the turbulence or ennui of a transition will pass, and that a new, more stable and more consolidated system will emerge. But as the rate and extent of organizational change has increased in recent years this model's limitations have become apparent. It does not satisfactorily deal with the unitary fallacy of organizational cultures, nor does it provide any language with which to discriminate and understand the turbulence of the liminal phase.

Moreover, it now seems to many people that they are forever in liminal phases. The sense that this kind of model no longer matches our experience of stability and change in organizations parallels a rising awareness that Kurt Lewin's model of unfreeze, reframe, and refreeze for personal and organizational change no longer applies, as there no longer seem to be any periods of enough duration in which to refreeze the patterns.[52] Change no longer appears as a shift from one state of equilibrium to another, via a period of relative turbulence. Change now appears to be constant.

Wheatley[53] argues that once we used to see change as something we needed to endure in order to reach the next period of stability, all the while ignoring that the periods of stability were becoming shorter and fewer. She puts succinctly when she says, 'Now, change is all there is.'

Doubt and Transformation

In Sherwood's three-level model of organizational culture the most obvious components of a group's behavior are its normative procedures. These include such things as its programs and actions, its roles and the relationships among them, its policies, its communication patterns, and its treatment of members. In other words, they are its standard operating procedures: what it does and how it does it. These components are collectively referred to as the norm element of the system.

The second element is belief. By this we mean the group's rational statements of what it hopes to achieve. They are embodied in documents and through key people as statements of purpose or mission, broad aims, goals, and objectives.

The third element in the model is myth. Here we are dealing with the unstated values and assumptions that are at the heart of a group. It is from these that its statements of purpose and its goals derive.

By the word *myth*, John Sherwood means an essential 'core of truth' or the basic sense of identity that a group possesses. This third layer he describes as concerned with the fundamental, unchallengeable assumptions we use to order the variety of our experience and give it meaning. It is composed largely of unconscious values and processes. Though pervasive, myth is nevertheless elusive in the rational world; it deals with time yet is outside of it; it is passed down through the organization from one 'generation' to the next. It is essentially non-rational. In using the word myth, Sherwood is indicating that the stories that the organization tells about itself do not have to be true in any objective, factual sense. Nevertheless they represent what the organization holds to be true. Indeed, sometimes the true believers in an organization will cling on to these 'truths' long after it is clear that they do not match the facts anymore.

Setting this model next to the stages of organizational doubt, we can say that an organization that is in a state of operational doubt is confronting the evidence that normative procedures are not working for it, but it is not entertaining any challenges to belief and myth. An organization in a state of ideological doubt is conceding that its beliefs are challengeable, but still hanging on to myth, particularly the assumptions surrounding its identity. Ethical doubt finds the organization desperately defending challenges to its myths, which may collapse at any moment and leave it in a state of absolute doubt.

However, it is only through the experience of doubt or discomfort that transformation becomes attractive. Carl Rogers maintained that for psychotherapy to be effective, the client must be either anxious or 'vulnerable to anxiety'.[54] It is only when we feel discomfort at the dissonance between the way we are and the way we want to be, between the way we imagine our world to be and the way we actually experience it, that we have any capacity to change. Even when our way of being is not 'working' for us, we will continue to resist information that challenges our way of seeing the world, either avoiding it altogether or distorting it so that it ceases to be a challenge. Only when anxiety enters the equation, when we can no longer avoid the evidence that there is something wrong, do we make room for the possibility of change.

This is true for groups just as it is for individuals. As in individuals, it seems that it is the lower levels, or core elements, that control or at least hold together the whole structure. Each layer expresses the layer below it. An organization makes certain unreflected assumptions about what it is and what the world is like; these assumptions are reflected in its value systems, in its tendency to see some things as better and more important than others; these values are expressed in the organization's beliefs, ideas, and opinions, the thoughts the organization has about the world; finally, these beliefs find expression in the organization's normative procedures and artifacts. The surface layers can change to some extent without affecting the deeper layers. Change in the deeper layers generates change all the way through.

Secondly, it seems that while some elements in the surface layers can change readily enough as long as the deeper layers are not affected, change in the deeper levels is strongly resisted. If an organization can add on a new procedure or piece of technology without any change in its values, attitudes, and assumptions, change is pretty straightforward. On the other hand, if taking on this new procedure or technology requires a change in values and attitudes, the organization will resist it. As individuals we hang on very tightly to our values and assumptions, especially to our assumptions about ourselves. As members of groups with shared values and assumptions, this resistance is reinforced. We can argue that when people or organizations change, it is usually in order to remain the same. If we are forced to change the things we do and say, we look for ways of changing that leave our values, our assumptions and our sense of who we are unaffected.

One thing that change agents have to get used to is the way some organizations appear to resist change even when they state that they want it and are prepared to invest considerable resources in bringing it about. They have seen themselves for so long in a particular way that even when they employ consultants to initiate specific changes, they still keep resisting the change, or so it seems. Change may seem desirable when the organization finds its procedures dysfunctional, but it becomes frightening to the organization's members when it threatens to destroy their idea of who they are. They don't yet know any other way to be.

Paradoxically, it is often in coming to know 'who they are' at some very deep level that organizations can manage to let go of the past and embrace a future

Doubt, even absolute doubt, may be a necessary pre-condition for deep organizational change. In this context it is useful to make the distinction between incremental and transformational learning, and apply it to the learning organization.

Incremental learning, whether for an individual or a group, is learning that is simply added on to what is already known. New technology can be embraced, new procedures can be practiced and adopted, new perspectives can be developed, and simply included in the organization's knowledge base without affecting what is already known. On the other hand, transformative learning involves abandoning what is already known in order to know something that contradicts it. What is already known is in systematic relationship to lots of other things that are known by the organization. Consequently the organization's whole structure of knowledge has to collapse and be reconstructed to accommodate the new truth.

A manufacturer geared entirely towards supplying traditional markets finds those markets have suddenly disappeared. A community service organization finds that a change in the law has made its work either redundant or impossible. The organization cannot just add the new facts to its current structure of knowledge. Accommodating

:he new facts of life involves the organization in changing its understanding of what t is. For both individuals and organizations, creation of a new identity involves the leath of one's present identity, and this is usually a painful process.

ȝELF-REALIZATION AND THE FORMATIVE TENDENCY

Carl Rogers introduced the term 'congruence' into our ways of talking about therapy ınd personal growth. It is a term that can readily be applied to organizations. When vriting about the personal context, Rogers described congruence as being a state when my experiencing of this moment is present in my awareness and when what is present in my awareness is present in my communication'.[55] For Rogers, congruence vas the core quality of a psychologically healthy person. It was both the means and nd of therapy. In the first place, a therapist must bring this quality to her relationship vith her client, if the therapy is to be helpful to the client. In the second place, it is an wareness of incongruence – a sense (however vague or fuzzy) that the way I am at the noment does not match the way I can be or the way I want to be – which is the starting oint of therapy. If I can explore this point of discomfort courageously enough (with r without the help of a therapist) I will become more congruent – more aware of who am, what I am experiencing, and more able to communicate this to others. I will be o longer lying to myself, no longer shutting my experience of myself and my world ut of my awareness. And my artifacts, perspectives, values, and core assumptions vill be in tune with each other. It is doubt that provides the stimulus for this process n the individual just as it does in the organization or group. And it is the 'formative ndency' that provides the energy.

ogers rejected the mechanistic psychological theories that were fashionable for most f his career and worked within the 'organic' metaphor. Coming from a farming ackground, he believed that human beings resemble vegetables more than they semble machines! 'Growth' is the central image within his psychology. Growth is ot random. It has direction. The specific seed has a tendency to become a specific ee. It may depend on environmental conditions to germinate and flourish, but its rection and purpose comes from within. All sorts of environmental factors will ncourage, inhibit, or distort its growth, and it may never reach its potential, but the tendency remains the same. Likewise, we all – as individuals – have a tendency to become the whole of the person that we are capable of becoming, '. . . a directional tendency towards wholeness, towards actualization of [our] potentialities'.[56] Rogers was certainly not alone in basing a psychological theory on such a proposition,[57] and the acknowledgement of a 'drive in living matter to perfect itself'[58] is increasingly common in biological and ecological thinking as the industrial age's infatuation with machines weakens in a postmodern world. Rogers' unique contribution was to turn this philosophical position into a particular mode of practice for therapists, educators, and other agents of change.

'Growth' in the psychological or even biological sense cannot be equated with getting bigger. In Rogers' understanding it is a process of 'actualizing' or 'realizing' the self. Rogers uses the word self in much the same way as Jung does – not equating it with the ego, or conscious 'controlling' element of the personality, but referring rather to the whole of the personality: physical and mental, conscious and unconscious, thinking and feeling, acknowledged and denied.

The personal self does not stop at the skin. Any line we draw to separate self from non-self is going to be arbitrary. The self is an open system. When we talk about the self or identity of an organization we likewise find that any boundary we construct around it is entirely arbitrary.[59] An organization is not a closed system, shut in its own capsule. Rather it is open, embedded in a larger system, in a mass of complex relationships with other elements in that larger system. There is evidence from many quarters that it makes at least as much sense to imagine that larger system (with all its human and nonhuman elements) as a living organism, as it does to imagine it as a machine.

The notion of the universe as organism (rather than machine) is intricately tied in with the notion of evolutionary process. If we set aside the metaphor of the planetary system as a machine running according to abstract and eternal mechanical laws, and adopt the image of it as a living organism constantly evolving and renewing itself, we have to include human organizations in this evolutionary organismic process. Not just in some abstract historical way, but in their concrete everyday existence. One characteristic of organisms is their purposiveness. Embryos have a tendency to become adult organisms, and sometimes overcome all sorts of difficulties to do so.

Human beings have a tendency to grow up. Immature organizations have a tendency to become mature organizations. When we stop growing we start to die, and death is intimately connected with the beginnings of new life. The universe is in the process of 'becoming'.

When it came to personal self-realization, Rogers did not conceive of the 'formative tendency' as a purely individualistic thing. The individual's experience is embedded in a much larger context: 'a formative directional tendency in the universe, an evolutionary tendency towards greater order, greater complexity, greater interrelatedness'.[60] The image of the organization as organism belongs within the same context. We believe it makes little sense to talk of organizations as living organisms without acknowledging, as holistic biologists do, that every organism is a living whole that cannot be reduced to, or explained in terms of, its simple elements, and that it has its particular being and discrete identity only through its relationship to the whole organic process of which it is a part. And it makes even less sense to talk about an organization as an organism while making interventions designed to fix it as if it were a machine.

Personal change, in Rogerian theory, is governed by a drive to become the whole of what one 'naturally' is. Organizational change can be framed the same way. But what one is 'naturally', from an ecological perspective, is a healthy cell of a greater organism, and a healthy cell lives 'naturally' in a way that does not destroy the organism of which it is a part. We can say the same of a healthy group or organization. Whatever the espoused purposes and strategies of the organization, it experiences collectively and in its individual members, an unfolding process which, if not inhibited, can bring the organization to live out all of its potential as a manifestation of the cosmic system of which it is a part.

We should think of growth, not as something that people undertake and achieve, but as a universal process in which people exist. We should think of growth as shaping the individual rather than of the individual as determining and controlling the nature of his or her growth. We should likewise think of growth as shaping the organization rather than of the organization as determining and controlling the nature of its growth. In extending this notion to organizations we are suggesting, not only that the members of the organization are individually motivated (unconsciously at least) by this universal evolutionary process towards ever greater degrees of individuation, freedom, and selfhood, but that the process operates also at the collective level.

Put simplistically, this sounds an unrealistically romantic idea. Our experience of organizations does not always provide much evidence of a drive towards wholeness. If anything, organizations are even more 'neurotic' than individuals – more rigid, more deluded, less 'together', less creative, less in touch with their own experiencing, less able to utilize all of their potential, more prone to irrational and impulsive behavior. This in no way falsifies the theory, any more than the evidence of pathological and self-destructive behavior in individuals falsifies the theory that every individual experiences a drive towards self-realization. Theories are merely tools for getting a handle on reality. Good theories are beautiful and useful as well as 'true'. What really interests us here is whether the theory 'works'.

Intervening for Organizational Transformation

Rogers and other client-centered therapists have demonstrated that their theory works at the individual level. If we trust the client's ability to solve his own problems, avoid thinking that we know more about him than he knows about himself, try to see the world the way he sees it, accept that his behavior is the best he can manage in the world as he experiences it, accept and prize him as a human being (even if we find his behavior repugnant), be as congruent and transparent in our interactions as we can manage – in other words, if we can provide an environment in which it is safe for him to explore the dissonance between what his organism experiences and what he habitually tells himself about it – the client's innate tendency to 'become what he naturally is' will provide the energy for change.

Edgar Schein and numerous process-oriented consultants have demonstrated that the theory works at the organizational level also. In this kind of intervention, the change agent abandons the role of 'fixer' and tunes in to the organization's subjective experience of itself. She focuses on the point of incongruence where the organization is 'vulnerable to anxiety', facilitating the organization's exploration of the ways (conscious and unconscious) it experiences the world and trusting the organization's ability to become what it is capable of becoming. She approaches the organization the way a client-centered therapist approaches the client – with empathy, respect, and congruence, understanding that the organization's evolutionary drive to become fully itself will provide the energy for change.[61]

Jung-oriented therapists and organizational theorists practice in a similar way, though the way they think about it may be rather different. For them the starting point is not the subjectivity of the individual but the objectivity of the collective unconscious, and the project of individual consciousness, society, and social relations is the realization of the unconscious. In other words, organizations exist as a means of giving expression to the unconscious. In such a theory, the proper stance for the change agent in an organization is to facilitate dialogue between the shared consciousness of the organization, and the organization's unconscious. The organizational consultant guides a journey through the organization's dreams, fantasies, symbols, stories, rituals, and 'meaningful situations' so that the energy of the unconscious can flow into the organization's awareness and conscious behavior. In this scenario, capacities and potentials that have been suppressed can be discovered and embraced, and artifacts, perspectives, values, and assumptions can be transformed.

The essence of these approaches is the same. Transformation is not something an organization does. It is most certainly not something that a change agent does to an organization. Rather, it is something that happens to an organization, as a seed transforms into a plant, or an egg transforms into an insect or animal when the time and conditions are right. The change agent working in the ways outlined above is not trying to change the organization, but to put the organization in touch with its own transformational energy while helping it become aware of what, at some level, it already 'knows' about itself and its context. Both approaches 'work' when employed with an adequate dose of skill and understanding, but neither approach conforms to the model of 'planned change'. The outcomes may well be creative, energizing, enlivening, enchanting, or just satisfying, but they are not predictable.

It is not our intention to argue that there is no virtue in imagining an organization as a machine and intervening to fix its malfunctioning. Indeed many of the highly technical, known and understood, routine, and predictable patterns of organizational life are maintained with and through the benefits of mechanical metaphors and practices. The machine image has served science and engineering very well for some hundreds of years, and both scientists and change agents have good reasons for sticking with it. The cosmos has machine-like qualities; so have human beings, so have organizations. However, the cosmos as it revealed itself to science in the twentieth century severely stretches the ability of the machine image to accommodate it. And the more we learn about human beings and organizations, the more difficult it is to argue that they are only machines.[62] However, when we discuss organizations within the Dionysian metaphor of the organism that grows or decays, we must remember that this is a way of imagining organizations, not a way of stating a fact about them. Just as we must when we discuss organizations within the Apollonine image of the machine that breaks and is repaired.

It is sometimes useful to study the way an organization operates and calculate that if a particular change is made, in systems or in personnel, the organization will operate much more efficiently and achieve its stated goals. This is generally the fantasy cherished by a concerned management and encouraged by the consultant who wants the gig. The organization-machine is out of balance; it has lost its equilibrium. The consultant undertakes to locate the malfunctioning part or analyze the design fault that is throwing the machine into disequilibrium and recommend adjustment or replacement for the part or suggest how the machine should be redesigned. So the machine returns to equilibrium. This may be exactly what management wants.

There are a couple of problems with this. In the first place, the strategy can only be used at the artifact level of the organization. Structures and procedures can be observed and assessed. If they are not working they can be modified or replaced. Perspectives, values, and assumptions are not so easily changed. Making changes at the artifact level cannot be counted on to make any immediate impact on the deeper levels of the organization's culture.[63] If there is a problem at these deeper levels it will keep finding expression in the organization's artifacts, no matter how much and how often we modify them.

In the second place, the limitations of the return-to-equilibrium approach are becoming very apparent in the postmodern, liminal consciousness that characterizes the current situation. For organizations that are experiencing problems existing in such a context, equilibrium is no longer an appropriate goal. Rather, equilibrium is the problem. For an organization trying to survive and flourish in a world where the ground is constantly shifting, equilibrium represents inflexibility and stuckness. In open systems, equilibrium is equivalent to death.[64] We might add that the sense of equilibrium is often inauthentic. It is a fantasy constructed only by denying and distorting the complexities of the organization's experience of its world.

For half a century organizational development theory has worked from the assumption that equilibrium is the natural state of an organization. This equilibrium may be disturbed from time to time by a period of turbulence, but the organization hopefully returns to equilibrium after this experience. Kurt Lewin's very influential unfreeze-reframe-refreeze model of organizational change is in tune with this 'natural' process. However, this particular truth about organizations is now challenged by another truth. In a machine-like, steady state universe it was appropriate to expect to find machine-like, steady state organizations. In a dynamic, alive, evolving universe, we expect to find dynamic, alive, evolving organizations. Jeffrey Goldstein has set out a number of assumptions that might guide the change process in the kind of universe that science is discovering and non-linear mathematics is attempting to describe:

- Instead of resisting change, organizations and work groups tend towards change and development.
- Instead of hierarchically imposing change, the potential for change is unleashed and activated.
- Instead of 'unfreezing and 'freezing' a spontaneous reorganization emerges representing a more effective way to accomplish the organization's objectives.
- Instead of large changes requiring large efforts, small-scale efforts can facilitate large changes.
- Instead of emphasizing planning, change is an evolving strategy, utilizing chance and random events.

- Instead of only focusing on what is internal to the organization, the self-organization approach includes the paradoxical work of firming up and traversing the boundaries between a work group or organization and its environment.

- Instead of relying only on a rational and cognitive perspective, change needs to incorporate elements of play and what may even appear absurd.

- Instead of consensus-seeking as a means towards participation, nonconsensus-seeking can lead to spontaneous participatory structures.[65]

In such a model, strategies for organizational change depend on the existence of 'far-from-equilibrium' conditions. If we want to find creative solutions to meet new challenges, we should look among those aspects of the organization which do not fit very well into the 'well-oiled machine' image and which, even if they are acknowledged by the shared consciousness of the organization, are usually perceived as aberrations and ignored in planning for change.

Ralph Stacey calls this domain of activity the domain of extraordinary management He goes on to point out that the consciousness that has worked so well for problems around which there is high agreement and high certainty simply does not work in thi domain. A different paradigm is required.[66]

One of the core arguments of this book is that we can find one such alternative paradigm within the fields of deep structure and corporate culture. It is in delving into the unconscious, into the shadow of the organization, in helping the system com to know itself, that we find some different answers to those provided for so long b the machine metaphor. And it is in the 'shadow' or 'dark matter' of the organization that we can most fruitfully search for evidence that the organization is alive, and fo the energy that will allow it to adapt spontaneously and purposefully to a constantl changing world.[67]

It is the universal and largely unconscious acceptance of the mechanistic paradigm tha leads us to assume rest or inertia as the natural state of being in this universe. Havin made this assumption, we then have to explain how movement or change happens. If we abandon this assumption, we can see movement as the natural state of being, and rest or inertia as the aberration that requires explanation. The debate over this goes back to the early Greek philosophers, and is not over yet. We believe it is important to challenge the absolutist pretensions of the mechanistic paradigm in organizational theory as in other sciences, which is what Senge, Stacey, and others have been doing. What archetypal theory offers in addition is a way of developing the notion of multiple realities, not just as a way of being clever and avoiding commitment to any particular position on anything at all, but as a way of acknowledging the true complexity of culture in organizations, and of dealing with it productively.

---

1. F Emery & E Trist (1965) The Causal Texture of Organizational Environments. *Human Relations* 18, pp. 21-23.
2. 'To be able to write about culture presumes the sometimes enabling, yet for many writers, blind prejudice of living the analytic attitude. In short, writing about 'culture' happens only in a certain culture that nurtures a particularly critical attitude. Therefore, no naive claims to transcendental truth are to be found in this paper, except a nod to the paradoxical law of hermeneutics, that all explanations are essentially perspectival, including this acknowledgement itself.' EM Kramer (1992) *Consciousness and Culture*, p. 2.
3. See E Schein (1970) *Organizational Psychology*.
4. ibid., p. 7f. We need to distinguish also between formal and informal organizations. The latter term is often used to refer to the patterns of relationship and interaction, which exist between members of a formal organization, separately from, and sometimes in spite of, the formally acknowledged roles and structures.
5. For a discussion of this model see: OF White & CJ McSwain (1983) 'Transformational Theory and Organizational Analysis', in G Morgan *Beyond Method*.
6. See P Gagliardi (1986) The Creation and Change of Organizational Cultures, *Organization Studies*, 7, 2.
7. See E Schein (1985) *Organizational Culture and Leadership*.
8. See G Hofstede (1980) *Culture's Consequences*.
9. See F Trompenaars & C Hampden-Turner (1998) *Riding the Waves of Culture*.
10. See CC Lundberg 'On the Feasibility of Cultural Interventions in Organizations', in PJ Frost, LF Moore, MR Louis, CC Lundberg, & J Martin (1985) *Organizational Culture*.
11. C Geertz (1973) *The Interpretation of Cultures*, p. 5.
12. G Hofstede (1991) *Cultures and Organizations*, p. 180. Hofstede's focus is on the relationship between organizational culture and national culture. He found in his study of culture in the multinational company IBM that the company culture functioned essentially through common practices, but that there were distinct differences from country to country in terms of employees' values, which they had presumably developed before being inducted into the IBM culture.
13. E Schein op. cit., p. 9.
14. R Seel (2000), Culture and Complexity', *Organizations and People*, 7, 2, May 2000, p. 3.
15. The distinction between the 'integration', 'differentiation', and 'fragmentation' perspectives on organizational culture was developed by Meyerson and Martin. See D Meyerson & J Martin (1987) 'Cultural Change', *Journal of Management Studies*, 24, pp. 623-647.
16. 'Without exception, the dominance and coherence of culture proved to be an essential quality of the excellent companies. Moreover, the stronger the culture, and the more it was directed towards the marketplace, the less need was there for policy manuals, organization charts, or detailed procedures and rules. In these companies, people way down the line know what they are expected to do because the handful of guiding principles is crystal clear.' T Peters & J Waterman (1982) *In Search of Excellence*, p. 75.
17. See R Stacey (1996) *Complexity and Creativity in Organizations*.

18. M Stein (1992), 'Organizational Life as Spiritual Practice' in M Stein & J Hollwitz, *Psyche at Work*, p. 4.
19. ibid., p. 10.
20. See T Burns & G Stalker (1961) *The Management of Innovation.*
21. See C Handy (1976) *Understanding Organizations*, Chapter 7. See also (1979) *The Gods of Management*, passim.
22. See ET Hall (1984) *The Dance of Life.*
23. See H Mintzberg (1983) *Structure in Fives.*
24. See G Hofstede (1991) Cultures and Organizations. Robert House and his colleagues have tested and modified Hofstede's model in their study of leadership in a wide range of cultures. See R House et al (2004) *Culture, Leadership and Organizations.*
25. See F Trompenaars & C Hampden-Turner (1998) op. cit. The seven polarities are based on sociologist Talcott Parson's classification of five 'relational orientations' plus two further dimensions - 'attitude to time' and 'attitude to nature'. See T Parsons (1951) *The Social System..*
26. See R Lewis (2000) *When Cultures Collide.*
27. See J Gibb (1978) *Trust.*
28. Jung's theory of personality type has been operationalized and applied to behavior in organizations by a number of authors. Their focus to date has been on individual rather than collective behavior. Nevertheless, the language of type is readily transferable to a discussion of cultures and subcultures in organizations. See F. Briggs Myers & P Myers (1995) *Gifts Differing*; D Kiersey & M Bates (1998) *Please Understand Me II*; J Singer & M Loomis (1996) *Singer Loomis Type Development Profile*; D Sharp (1987) *Personality Types*; A Brownwood (1999) *It Takes All Types.*
29. See D'Cruz & Steele (2003) *Australia's Ambivalence towards Asia.* D'Cruz is not specifically concerned with organizational culture, but this polarity has considerable utility in application to organizations.
30. See J Corlett & C Pearson (2003) *Mapping the Organizational Psyche.*
31. See ET Hall, op.cit., p. 6f. Hall, like Hofstede, Trompenaars, and Hampden-Turner, is primarily interested in discussing national or ethnic cultures, and the ways in which national cultures affect corporate cultures in transnational corporations. Yet their insights about national cultures can readily be applied in discussing organizational cultures.
32. CC Lundberg, op. cit., p. 171.
33. Hofstede also uses an onion image, indicating four levels at which organizational culture is manifested: *symbols, heroes, rituals, and values.* The three outer layers he refers to as *practices.*
34. The distinction between 'espoused theory' and 'theory in use' has been developed by C Argyris and D Schon (1978) *Organizational Learning.*
35. For a discussion of such assumptions see E Schein (1999) *The Corporate Culture Survival Guide*, p. 48-58.
36. See G Hofstede op. cit.
37. See C Argyris & D Schon, op. cit.
38. The interrelationship of strategy, structure, and culture is discussed by B Cunnington & D Limerick (1986) '*The Fourth Blueprint*'.
39. See R Stacey op. cit.
40. See M Louis (1983) 'Organizations as Culture-bearing Milieux', in L Pondy, P Frost, M Louis, G Morgan, & T Dandridge, *Organizational Symbolism.*
41. See R Sheldrake (1993); J Lovelock (1988) *The Ages of Gaia*; F Capra (1982) *The Turning Point.*
42. R Knowles (2002) *Reaching New Ground*, p. 3.
43. P O'Connor (2001) *Beyond the Mist*, p. 5.
44. M Stein (1992) p. 10. Stein discusses the way that we unconsciously project our pathology onto our organizations and then identify with our projections. To become aware of these projections is both necessary and painful. 'Consciousness is threatening. Becoming conscious of projection sounds appealing in the abstract, but when one actually gets down to particulars, it is extremely upsetting and disturbing. Why is this? To break off participation mystique is to risk loss of meaning and depression. One's unconscious identifications give one a sense of place, of purpose, of attachment, and as long as they do not seem to threaten life itself, one is loath to give them up. Even painful identifications are held on to . . . But the greater Self presses for something else. It wants conscious wholeness.' ibid., p. 11.
45. S Freud (1985/1929) *Civilization and its Discontents.*
46. P O'Connor, op. cit., p. 6.
47. See J Sherwood (1977) *Leadership.*
48. See W Bridges (1991) *Managing Transitions.*
49. V Turner (1970) *The Forest of Symbols*, p. 93-111.

50. See T Dalmau & B Dick (1984) *Promoting and Marketing Internal Consultancy Services.*
51. V Turner, op. cit., p. 99. There are many analogies between anthropological descriptions of liminality and the individual's experience of liminality in midlife. Murray Stein develops the latter notion in *In Midlife* (1983).
52. See K Lewin (1951) *Field Theory in Social Science.*
53. See M Wheatley (1999) *Leadership and the New Science.*
54. See CR Rogers (1961) *On Becoming a Person* for his discussion of the necessary conditions for therapeutic change.
55. CR Rogers (1980), *A Way of Being*, p. 15.
56. ibid., p.120.

57. A similar insight led Roberto Assagioli and Karen Horney to write of 'self-realization', Carl Jung to write of 'individuation,' and Abraham Maslow and others to develop a theory of 'self-actualization'.
58. A Szvent-Gyeorgy (1974), 'The Drive in Living Matter to Perfect Itself', *Synthesis*, Spring, p.17.
59. The boundaries we set to any open system are entirely arbitrary. The organization we call a company may be thought of as consisting only its directors and employees, or we can extend our notion to include its shareholders, its clients, its suppliers, the families of its directors and employees, its past and future employees, the dependents of its clients and suppliers, the clients of its clients, the suppliers of its suppliers, and so on. We can also include the nonhuman and abstract elements of the company: its assets, resources, products, systems, procedures, and history. We could extend its boundaries to include the whole economic, social, and ecological system to which the formal organization is related in complex and evolving ways.
60. CR Rogers, op cit., p.133.
    Current notions of the 'aliveness' of the universe are influenced by the 'process philosophy' of Alfred North Whitehead. Whitehead argued that the universe consists of 'moments of experience' in which the universe 'becomes'. The entire cosmos is constantly renewing itself. According to Whitehead, this ongoing process of becoming new (Whitehead calls it 'concrescence') is directed to the production of beauty. And it is shaped by what Whitehead calls 'eternal objects', that is, possibilities waiting to be made actual. See AN Whitehead (1978) *Process and Reality: Corrected Edition.*
61. See E Schein (1969) *Process Consultation* and (1999b) *Process Consultation Revisited.*
62. It really makes no difference whether we are imagining machines as nineteenth century structures of cogs and pulleys or the sophisticated, self-organizing feedback systems which are now becoming possible. The essential difference is that an organism is alive. It unfolds from within, re-organizing itself to adjust to changes in the environment, not because it is really a machine that has been programmed beforehand by a clever person who has foreseen all possible eventualities, but because it is itself purposive. It differs also from a machine also in that it is an organic whole, which cannot be reduced to simpler systems. And it can regenerate and reproduce. It is not 'caused' by other agencies but 'causes itself'. Holistic or organismic systems theory turns conventional mechanistic theory on its head and treats all nature as alive. In this way of thinking atoms, molecules, and crystals can be thought of as organisms.
63. Certainly, a small change at the artifact level will sometimes produce massive changes throughout an organization, but they are unpredictable and unplannable. This will happen when the change sets up resonances that are amplified disproportionately by feedback. This will only happen in certain conditions. This is often referred to as the 'butterfly effect', on the notion that 'a butterfly stirring the air today in Peking can transform storm systems next month in New York'. See J Gleick (1987), *Chaos*, p. 8 and passim.
64. Margaret Wheatley (1999), op. cit., writes of the need for 'equilibrium busters' to keep the system alive:
    'No longer the caretakers of control, we become the grand disturbers. We stir things up and roil the pot, looking always to provoke, even to disrupt, until finally things become so confusing that the system must reorganize itself into new forms and new behaviors. If we accept this challenge to be equilibrium busters, if we begin to value that it is disequilibrium that keeps us alive, we will find the task quite easy. There is more than enough confusion and ambiguity in our lives to work with. We don't have to worry about creating more, only with how to work more artfully with what we have.' p. 108.
65. J Goldstein, (1994) *The Unshackled Organization*, p. 16.
66. See R Stacey (2000) *Strategic Management and Organizational Dynamics.*
67. The shadow is Jung's term for the repressed or unacknowledged elements of the individual or collective psyche. The ego or conscious element of the psyche exists only in relation to it, and draws its energy from it. Freud and Jung had different notions of the unconscious, but they agreed that human behavior is not explainable without it. Dark matter is the physicist's equivalent to explain the behavior of the universe. If galaxies contained only the matter that can currently be observed by science, their gravitational attraction could not explain the way they behave. The way galaxies cluster together can only be explained by the existence of hidden matter that according to some calculations

3

THE FIVE-MINDED ORGANIZATION

A Note on Psychological Evolution

The Swiss cultural philosopher Jean Gebser, after tracing the emergence of human consciousness, concluded that it has evolved through five stages or 'mutations', each clearly distinguishable from the stage preceding it. He argued that the earlier, simpler structures of consciousness are still functioning in us.[1] Gebser is not alone in suggesting that we can distinguish specific phases in the evolution of consciousness and culture. Merlin Donald writes of the evolution of consciousness going through three transitions: from the episodic cognition of primates to the mimetic cognition of the early hominids, to the mythic cognition of *Homo sapiens sapiens*, and finally to the theoretic cognition of modern culture.[2] MacLean examines the structure of the human brain and finds it to be 'triune', comprising a 'reptilian' brain (the brainstem), a 'mammalian' brain (the limbic system), and a 'neo-mammalian' brain (the cerebral cortex) contributing simultaneously to our experience and behavior.[3] Research on brain hemisphericity has more recently distinguished between 'right-brain' and 'left-brain' in the neo-mammalian brain.[4] Robert Kegan and Kieran Egan build on Piaget's model of cognitive development to distinguish five phases of development that provide a capacity for five kinds of thinking. Kegan labels them simply from first order thinking to fifth order thinking.[5] Egan writes about humans as 'five-minded animals', capable of thinking in five distinct ways which he calls somatic, mythic, romantic, philosophic, and ironic.[6]

In these models, which have been constructed on the basis of very different evidence from very different disciplines, there is the suggestion of an evolution or development (both in the species and in the individual) from a physical experience of the cosmos, with little sense of individual consciousness, to a fully conscious experience in which a sense of oneself as an individual is central. Several of them follow the trajectory of evolution further. Gebser sees the rational culture of the modern age as something of a dead end and claims to observe the emergence in the mid twentieth century of an 'integral structure of consciousness' in which all the earlier, simpler structures are transcended in a new 'integrative' mode of experiencing the universe, a mode that connects mental consciousness with the earlier, simpler structures.[7] Egan points to the emergence of an ironic mode of consciousness that experiences the relationship between individualistic, 'philosophic' consciousness and the simpler modes, while Kegan's fifth order consciousness transcends the other orders to be conscious of its own mode of consciousness. We find in all of these models not only a move from collective, physical identity to individual, mental identity, but a move beyond individual identity towards greater complexity and wholeness. There is also an acknowledgement that while these different structures may represent phases in cultural history or individual cognitive development, we bring them all to our daily experience of the world.

Gebser's model is of particular interest as a framework for looking at organizational culture because his perspective is cultural rather than psychological. He does not focus on the individual, but on the cultural milieu which the individual inhabits.

The earliest state of human consciousness Gebser calls the *archaic* structure of consciousness. For the first million or so years of human existence, human beings lived in an undifferentiated world; they had no sense of themselves as separate from their environment. As far as we can guess, the first humans were governed by instinct and reflex, and their consciousness was exceedingly dim. In this archaic consciousness they had no sense of themselves as individuals, no sense of time and space, and lived in a state of ego-less unity with their environment.

About 750,000 BC[8] we find the first signs of human beings acting in a world of objects, exercising some control over them through the use of simple tools. There was as yet no sense of personal identity, nor any ability to distinguish the part from the whole or internal experience from external. They seem to have experienced no sense of identity apart from the clan, and their world was a world of numinous power that could be dealt with only by magic. They had little language; they communicated through the direct experience of physical sensations or images. Their lives were totally enmeshed in the rhythms of nature. Gebser calls this consciousness magical.

After the last ice age (about 12,000 BC) this primal consciousness seems to have been displaced by a new kind of consciousness, characterized by the development of imaginative thinking and the development of language. This shift, from magical to mythical consciousness took human experience from an instinctual/emotional mode to an imaginative/verbal one. Humans ceased to experience themselves as being totally merged with nature. We see the beginnings of individual consciousness, the separation of internal and external awareness, the expression of human experience of the cosmos in image and story. This period saw the emergence of gods with quasi-human personalities. Through the power of imaginative or 'mythical' thinking the people of the Bronze Age were able to develop the sophisticated civilizations and complex societies of the ancient world, and with them the great narratives that expressed their experience of the universe.

After 1000 BC we find evidence of a fourth structure of consciousness, which Gebser calls mental. Human beings became capable of rational and directed thought, began to identify being with thinking rather than feeling, to be aware of time, space and quantity as we commonly understand them today. The emergence of discursive or abstract thought totally changed the relationship between human beings and their world. They became able to stand outside their world and reflect on it. They even became able to stand outside themselves, finding themselves not merely conscious, but conscious of their own consciousness. They became aware of time as more than duration and natural rhythm. They became fully aware of themselves as individuals, aware of cause and effect, able to act in a directed way on their world, and were no longer submerged in their environment and social group. They became able to build abstract political structures rather than tribal ones, and to develop secular-scientific ways of perceiving and exploring the world.[9]

With the collapse of the Roman Empire, Europe experienced a widespread regression for some centuries to a magical-mythical consciousness.[10] It was only in the twelfth century that the Celtic and Germanic tribes made the same transition as had been made by the Greeks and Hebrews two thousand years earlier, from mythical to mental consciousness. The Renaissance celebrated the discovery of the person. With the emergence of science, the human ego began more and more to assert itself against nature, against faith, against the darkness of myth and magic. By the seventeenth century, consciousness was identified with reason.

In his notion of structures of consciousness, Gebser distinguishes between efficient and deficient structures. Magical consciousness, mythical consciousness, and mental consciousness can all have either efficient (positive) or deficient (negative) manifestations. From Gebser's perspective, the rational structure of consciousness that has dominated European culture for the past three or four hundred years is not a higher form of consciousness that has emerged from the mental structure through an inevitable evolutionary progression, but is actually a deficient form of mental consciousness. Whereas the mental consciousness of classical Athens or renaissance Florence combined conceptual thinking with a rich imaginative life, the rational-scientific age has seen the reduction of the universe from living organism to a collection of objects, the body from the temple of the soul to a piece of matter. It has seen the privileging of the intellect over other human capacities, the identification of intellect with the male, and the relegation of the devalued physical-emotional (magical) and imaginative-intuitive (mythical) to the female. Through their rational or scientific consciousness human beings have achieved a great deal, but it has also given them the means to seriously damage themselves and the planet.

Gebser saw in the collapse of this rational structure in the twentieth century both the danger of slipping back into a deficient magical-mythical structure and the promise of evolution to a new structure. The unwillingness of our rational-scientific civilization to acknowledge the more primitive structures in no way makes them go away. We still think magically and mythically as well as rationally, whether we acknowledge it or not.

The past structures are still present in us. We are inclined to equate consciousness with the sense of self we experience at the mental level. Yet we constantly shift between this mental/rational consciousness and the older and simpler structures that preceded it.

Archaic consciousness can hardly be called consciousness at all. We still slip back into our archaic unity-consciousness in deep sleep, or enter it voluntarily or involuntarily through trance, drugs, or certain kinds of meditation. Certainly, a great deal of our behavior is automatic and unconscious, and we seem to be able to do quite complicated things without any awareness of doing them.

We operate at the magical level when we submerge our identity in that of a group, when we experience events or objects as numinous, when we engage in rituals designed to make things happen or make us feel good, when we come closer to a loved one by kissing a photograph, or when we share in the power and glory of a football team by wearing its colors. A great deal of healing, both physical and psychological, takes place within a magical structure of consciousness. When we sense in our bodies the pain or joy of a loved one, even in their absence, when we know something 'in our bones', when we join in religious ritual, we are acting from our magical consciousness. On the other hand, our superstitions and compulsive behaviors also come from our magical consciousness.

We are engaged in *mythical* thinking when we dream or day-dream, when we get totally immersed in a film or a book, or listen to a story or tell stories about ourselves, because we are receiving or constructing the world in images without any need or attempt to translate them into thoughts. Every metaphor comes from our mythical consciousness. When we give a human name to a car or boat, or talk to an inanimate object as though it can understand us, or get angry with an object because it will not do what we want it to, we are thinking mythically. When economists talk about 'the market' as though it is a person who 'reacts', 'decides', 'dislikes', and so on, they are engaged in mythical thinking. Our mythical thinking enables us to admire and love a work of art, even when we would be hard pressed to explain why we like it. It is our mythical consciousness that induces us to change our behavior after hearing a story that has engaged us, and that binds us to a partner or a group of friends through the stories we tell about ourselves. It is through the mythical structure of consciousness that we remain enmeshed in the 'old stories', the shared narratives by which our family, clan, tribe, or nation defines its identity and its understanding of the world. Such narratives seem to be more potent shapers of behavior than abstract reasoning.

Since Galileo and Descartes we have been content to define our humanity within the *mental/rational* structure. Through this structure we perceive ourselves essentially as individuals. We have a sense of history as a sequence of events starting at a beginning and moving towards an end. We quantify both space and time. We find ourselves standing apart from an objectified world and acting upon it. We dichotomize our experience of the world in all sorts of ways: good/bad, matter/spirit, male/female, progressing/regressing, true/false, self/other, subject/object. Our way of perceiving the world is shaped by an awareness of three-dimensional space, through the metaphors of hierarchy, perspective, quantity, scale, and progress.

Gebser's investigation of the evolution of human consciousness came from his sense, in the thirties, that European consciousness was undergoing some sort of change, that something new was emerging. As a refugee in Paris in the late thirties, he sought in art, literature, music, science, architecture, psychology, the evidence of a new sort of consciousness – against the background of a disintegrating mental/rational world and a regression to magical consciousness. He saw the assumptions of narrow rationality being seriously tested by science. He saw a new willingness to take myth and imagination seriously, and conventional rational notions of time and space and ego being destabilized. He found in the arts attempts to perceive the world in ways that challenged the assumption that our perceptions are anchored in a particular time and place. He gave the label *integral* consciousness to this new aperspectival consciousness that he saw emerging.

In Gebser's model, our contemporary consciousness is multi-structured or, to change the metaphor slightly, multi-layered. We may thank Freud and Jung for pointing out to us that even when we are acting 'rationally', our magical and mythical consciousnesses are hard at work. The complexity of human behavior comes out of the interplay of these several 'layers' or 'levels' of consciousness in whatever we do.[11] Gebser suggests that the acknowledgment and appreciation of these discrete structures is a step towards their integration with the rational structure in a more 'integral' way of experiencing the world. From the point of view of the rational-scientific culture that has been dominant for a few hundred years, magical and mythical thinking are primitive and inferior forms of thinking that have limited value in the contemporary world. However, we can argue that it is our capacity for mythical, and even magical, thinking that enables us to find meaning in our lives and gives us a grounding in the concrete world that rational thinking seems bent on destroying. It makes more sense to say that magical and mythical consciousnesses are neither better nor worse than mental/rational consciousness. They are simply older and different.

The Archaic Organization

There are a number of elements in Gebser's theory that are particularly relevant when we look at the culture of organizations. We are inclined to see groups or organizations as collections of separate individuals. Yet there were groups long before there were individuals. The notion that we are separate individuals living inside the boundaries of our own skins and communicating by passing messages to other individuals walking around in similar capsules is a very recent one, relatively speaking. We are inclined to think of consciousness as a personal, self-reflective phenomenon. If we think of group consciousness at all we are likely to think of it as the sum, or maybe the consensus, of the consciousnesses of all the members of the group. Gebser's theory is based on the evidence from archaeology that, in evolutionary terms, it goes the other way around. Group consciousness comes first. It is more basic than individual consciousness, which has emerged from it only recently. We may have a considerable investment in the notion that we are free, choosing, initiating individuals, but we have to admit that sometimes a group – or a mob – of so-called individuals acts as though it were a single organism.

When we examine the behavior of a termite or ant colony, or study schools of fish, flocks of birds, or herds of animals, we find evidence that groups of creatures sometimes behave as though they are single organisms. The simpler or more primitive the forms of life, the more sense it makes to describe them in this way. If we could view the human species from a great enough distance we might have an impression of it as a single organism. Gebser argues that individuals in archaic humanity could only behave as elements of a single organism. As individual consciousness evolved humans came to act independently, so that, in the past three or four centuries, they have thought that human beings are essentially discrete and separate beings. When we look at the way human groups behave, we can see that, in spite of our individuality and separateness, we have retained some sort of connection with other people that causes groups to act as one. It sometimes makes sense to talk about a tribe, a nation, or an organization as though we are talking about a single person. Jung, with whom Gebser was associated for some years, developed his own way of talking about this. He became convinced that individual consciousness has grown out of what he called the 'collective unconscious' or the 'objective psyche' – a collective, impersonal, unconscious mind that is older than individual consciousness and that goes on functioning as the ground of individual consciousness. If we follow Gebser and Jung here, we will be acknowledging that, while we are usually conscious of ourselves as separate individuals, there is another level of our experiencing in which we are not separate at all. Research on flocking behavior in various animal species, such as birds and fish, seems to indicate that the behavior of the flock can best be understood if we suppose that there are particular forms of connection between the animals in the flock that give the flock its collective behavior.

Bion's observations of the ways groups function suggested to him that individuals in groups are constantly seeking to regain within the group their infantile relationship with mother. This explains the irrational behavior of what he calls the 'basic assumptions group'. Gebser and Neumann suggest rather that in seeking to explain this behavior, we should look beyond the individual's attachment and separation from uterus and breast to the experience of the species losing its primal 'participation mystique' in the life of Mother Earth herself.[12] The collective consciousness of the group is much more primitive than the individual consciousness of those who comprise it. According to this argument, we have a residual awareness of oneness with the earth, an awareness that some of us may rarely acknowledge, but which is the ultimate basis of the sense of 'belonging' that we seek in group membership; it may well be the source of our capacity to feel empathy with others.

Neumann, in discussing the original 'uroboric' state of primal human beings, argues that unconsciousness is our 'natural state'.

> One has no need to desire to remain unconscious; on the contrary, one is primarily unconscious and can at most conquer the original situation in which man [sic] drowses in the world, drowses in the unconscious, contained in the infinite like fish in the environing sea.[13]

In mass behavior or mob behavior we see groups of human beings acting out of collective instinct and impulse to preserve or propagate the collective identity. Neumann argues that, since contemporary urban human beings have lost their connection both to the earth and to a clan to which they might be consciously and unconsciously bound, there is a schism between conscious and unconscious experience. There is still a largely unconscious mass component in modern human beings, but it is irrational, emotional, anti-individual, and destructive; the primal group consciousness, on the other hand, was constructive, synthetic, and creative. We do not have to either romanticize primal cultures or take an entirely negative view of mass phenomena in the twentieth century to acknowledge that his argument has some grounding in experience. Neumann's contrast between primal group consciousness and contemporary mass consciousness echoes Gebser's distinction between the 'efficient' and 'deficient' structures of consciousness. In Gebser's language, the archaic, instinctual consciousness of primal humans was 'efficient' in that it represented a valid and creative way of experiencing the world. By contrast, mob behavior, as we might witness it today, represents a takeover of rational consciousness by a repressed archaic structure, and accordingly is likely to be negative in its manifestations. In Jung's language, it signals the emergence of the collective *shadow*.

Merlin Donald has a different take on the phenomena that Neumann associates with primeval consciousness. In *The Origins of the Modern Mind*,[14] he traces the evolution of human cultures through three stages: the mimetic, the mythic, and the theoretic. These correspond fairly closely with Gebser's descriptions of archaic-magic, mythic, and mental-rational structures of consciousness. Like Gebser, he imagines the culture of the primeval hominids to be not so much unconscious as pre-linguistic. He suggests that *mimesis* forms the core of human culture in its beginnings and that, no matter how intellectually and linguistically sophisticated we manage to be:

> The use of patterns of mimetic representation in modern society has remained distinct from the uses of our later cognitive acquisitions (like language and literacy). In effect, there is still a vestigial mimetic culture embedded within our modern culture, and a mimetic mind embedded within the overall architecture of the modern human mind.[15]

If we reflect on the way mimesis functions in a contemporary organization, we might imagine organizational culture as the effect of 'everybody copying everybody copying everybody'. Margaret Wheatley, in commenting on the 'fractal'[16] nature of organizations, draws attention to this phenomenon.

> I can't think of any organization that isn't deeply patterned with self-similar behaviors evident everywhere. I am often struck by eerily similar behaviors exhibited by people in an organization, whether I'm meeting a factory floor employee or a senior executive. I might detect a recurring penchant for secrecy, or for openness, or for name-calling, or for thoughtfulness. These recurring patterns of behavior are what many call the culture of the organization. I believe we all experience this fractal nature of organizations in any of our encounters with them. As customers, we can learn how employees are treated by their bosses by noticing how employees treat us. As a consultant, I was taught that I would be able to spot the dominant issues of the client system by noticing how the client interacted with me.[17]

We are not talking here about conscious imitation, where an employee copies an executive's behavior out of admiration, fear, or sycophancy. This may indeed occur, but mimesis[18] is grounded in a pre-reflective, pre-linguistic consciousness; it is an expression of the connectedness of human beings. As adults we may indeed learn to behave in certain ways by observing and copying others, but as infants we learned to be not only human but members of a particular tribal and family group by absorption rather than observation. This capacity survives as an underlay in our adult collective behavior. We are drawn into collective habits (fashions, ideologies, cultural movements) because we are organically connected to others. It is only when we start consciously observing and reflecting that we are able to choose to resist this drift and assert our individuality.

A great deal of our behavior is robotic. It requires no reflection and is performed while we are thinking of something else – if, indeed, we are thinking at all.[19] If this is observable of individual experience, it is even more apparent in collective behavior, in corporations and elsewhere. Kieran Egan writes of *somatic understanding*, sharing Gebser's view that before ever we 'think' about our experience, we prehend it through our physical, organic sense of the world.[20] Collectively, we feel the rhythms of nature 'in our bones' and respond to them without reflection. We tune in to the rhythms of the groups we belong to in the same way.

Edward Hall called attention to the evidence of synchrony in cohesive groups. It seems that people quite unconsciously act 'in sync' with others in their group – in gesture, speech rhythms, biological cycles, and so on, so that the group as a whole may be performing a dance of which the individuals are unaware. The capacity for synchrony is rooted in the biology of our archaic consciousness. When it is frustrated, as it is by corporate routines or assembly lines that are 'out of sync' with the human rhythms of the group, both satisfaction and productivity are impaired.[21]

Where we see the archaic structure functioning in contemporary organizations, it may well be in deficient manifestations, but not necessarily. The archaic structure of consciousness is the basis of our 'togetherness' in groups and organizations. Our very capacity to understand each other, feel for each other, and identify with each other is grounded in archaic consciousness, which knows nothing of authority structures, goals, roles, reason, ethics, personal boundaries, or even verbal language. However, if the culture of an organization is such that the need for belonging goes unacknowledged, it becomes vulnerable to a takeover by a regressive, pathological, archaic consciousness, where the organization collectively behaves in infantile, pre-rational ways, driven by fear, greed, or vengeance, and the individuals find themselves caught up in an energy that they cannot control.

The archaic structure of consciousness is profoundly passive. The world of archaic consciousness is a world where 'things happen' without any understanding or control by human beings. Where an organization is stuck in the inertia of collective habit and fixed ideas, we can detect the drag of the primordial archaic consciousness. We find it in the urge to satisfy our natural need to belong by dissolving our ego boundaries.

We find it in the power that the group's collective habits and rituals have over the individual's ability to think, in the way the organization's unquestioned assumptions can suck in the individual, in the group member's loss of the ability to discriminate between right and wrong, sane and silly, and in the stress experienced by those members who begin to doubt.

In our experience of groups, the archaic structure of consciousness is overlaid by the magical, mythical, and mental structures. The essence of the kind of group we generally call an 'organization' is the attempt to establish a level of abstract structure that transcends the instinctual collectivity of the clan. We don't see 'pure' archaic consciousness in contemporary organizations. Yet, following Gebser, we might argue that the natural basis of organizational life is our 'oneness', not only with each other, but with the earth itself.

The Magical Organization

Gebser argues that, in spite of our illusion that we are rational individuals, the older structures of consciousness still continue to function in us, and that part of our brain knows nothing about either individual identity or rationality and inhabits a magical-mythical world. If we accept this argument we will expect to find evidence for it in contemporary organizations.

Magical consciousness as Gebser describes it has no sense of personal self at all. The individual has no existence except as a member of a clan. Not *I doubt, therefore I am*, or even *I think, therefore I am*, but *I belong, therefore I am*. The clan exists in a world where everything is connected to everything else, where there is no notion of logical cause and effect. The clan participates in the life of this world and deals with its dangers through magic and ritual. In our contemporary clans we are still doing this, though we generally cover it up with all sorts of rationalizations, because we believe ourselves to be rational people. Underneath the contemporary organization's rationally stated policies and strategies and decisions, there is a 'group think' that tends to respond to the world in the same way our stone age ancestors did – through magic.

In primitive magical consciousness, human beings did not experience themselves as psychically separate from the tribe. They felt an identity with the community and an emotional bonding to it. This was constantly reinforced by the 'closedness' of the clan and the repetition of its rituals. We find a similar phenomenon manifest in organizations in times of crisis. There is often a marked increase in the frequency of allusions to 'the way we do things around here' or 'the company style'. At such times there seems to be a huge propensity for the sentiment surrounding and imbuing the organizational entity to seep very deeply into the emotional experience of individual members.

In a culture where primary groups have largely disappeared (except for the family, which is itself under the threat of disintegration) people still seek group membership, and largely find it in organizations that have been designed for other purposes than for simply giving people a group to belong to. In organizations, no matter how 'rationally' structured, we find people responding to a need to be bound emotionally to a group and participate in its rituals. The 'closedness' of an organization, the development of clear distinctions between those who belong and those who do not, the distrust of or antagonism towards strangers, the strong notions of correct behavior, the taboos, the punishments meted out to those who offend against usage and custom, are as manifest here as in the stone age clan or the mediaeval village.

In magical consciousness, if two objects are similar in some way they are taken to be identical. Likewise a part of an object is taken to be the whole. So it is that I can harm my enemy by sticking pins in a doll that looks like him or contains some of his hair. I can turn myself into a buffalo by wearing the buffalo mask, or into a woman by wearing woman's clothing. When it is time for the rains to come we dance the rain dance, and it rains. We always do the dance at this season and it always rains. If it does not rain this time, it is because we are not doing the dance correctly. We will have to keep doing it until we get it right. In our experience many organizational practices have these characteristics, particularly and especially in the area of organizational advancement – a more recent coinage for what used to be called organization development. They are amply described in an article by Robert Schaffer and Harvey Thomson, who speak of activity-centered interventions: they speak of such rain dances as the ardent pursuit of activities that sound good, look good, and allow managers to feel good, but in fact contribute little or nothing to fundamental corporate performance.[22]

We do not have to look very far to see this magical consciousness at work in some curious and often poignant ways. The chairman of the board gets frightfully agitated when some lesser mortal sits in his chair, as though power will leak out of the chair into the interloper. The bureaucrat gets a larger desk and a more imposing office and immediately feels (and becomes) more powerful. The department spends a million dollars on the latest in information technology and expects this ritual act to shift it from the nineteenth to the twenty-first century. Last time the firm was in crisis we sacked our chief executive (or we did a major re-structure, or we called in the consultants, or we got a new logo, or we renovated head office) and the crisis ended. The firm is once again in crisis, so we repeat the ritual. If it doesn't work we know we've got it wrong somehow, so we repeat the ritual once more, hoping to get it right this time. In some ancient cultures the king had to be sacrificed at the end of winter to make land fertile again. It worked! It is fortunate for chief executives (or other available scapegoats) that human sacrifice is no longer fashionable as a ritual of renewal.

Of course, being intellectually sophisticated people, we can have perfectly good and logical explanations for taking our course of action, no matter how irrational or superstitious it may actually be.

In our magical consciousness we are not initiators of our behavior, but controlled by external forces that we must use magic to keep in check. If something terrible happens in a magical community, it is because someone has broken a taboo, and it is of no significance whether the infringement was conscious or deliberate. Magic tends to be used to keep things the way they have always been, rather than to change things. Many of the artifacts that are taken for granted in an organization are maintained simply because 'This is the way we've always done it'. Sometimes the situation that the procedure was designed to deal with has long ago changed, but the procedure is still followed because it provides the security of magical ritual. The organization is unconsciously engaged in magical thinking: 'We've done it this way for thirty years and we've always been OK; if we stop doing it, something terrible will happen!'

Geert Hofstede argues that rituals are employed in organizations to avoid uncertainty, and that the response to uncertainty is one of the key dimensions that distinguishes organizational cultures from each other.[23] The more anxious we are about the uncertainties of our situation, the more we depend on rituals to give us a sense of security. These rituals may be dressed up as rational exercises, such as establishing more appropriate rules and regulations, but they are often not rational at all. Among the uncertainty-avoiding rituals to be observed in organizations in times of stress he counts meetings, memos, and reports, aspects of the accounting, planning, and control systems, and the employment of consultants. These rituals do not actually make the future more predictable or less dangerous, but they relieve stress by giving people a sense of certainty in which they can keep functioning as a group.

In times of external threat and crisis, those that lead and manage organizations are particularly susceptible to the seduction of the magical consciousness. At first glance they do not appear caught in the trap of conservatism and oft-repeated ritualistic behavior. Their language, decisions, and behavior speak of change, development, and transformation. However, this may not so much represent their purpose to achieve a change through action, as serve as an incantation to make it happen by magic. Often such leaders will have by their side a magician to weave the magic for them. The magician will be a consultant – or group of consultants – in whom the senior management have invested their own hope for the future as a way of resolving a much deeper and unconscious impotence, doubt, or anxiety. The consultants can come in many forms and guises: they can range over the full gamut, from rational, systematic, advice-givers to skills providers, systems analysts and strategic problem-solvers, to those with a more facilitative, value-based, and relational focus, and, finally, to those who call on large group awareness for their magic. The cloak, potions, and spells of the magician are less important than the fact that, at some level, the leader has cast the consultant in the mould of a magician. CEOs newly appointed to organizations in crisis or under threat are especially vulnerable to this seduction, often presented to them by their assistants and trusted lieutenants.

We have an advantage over early humans in that we do have the ability to reflect on our own behavior, to detach ourselves from the group and the world and look at what is going on, so that our magical behavior can be recognized and modified, if it serves no useful purpose. But it is always easier to do such reflecting from outside an organization rather than from within it. It is easier for an outsider to see the ritualized hatred, self-destruction, or scapegoating within a nation, a corporation, or a club, and declare that on any rational ground it ought to stop. Those who are enmeshed in the situation are likely to be caught up in the 'group-think', taken over by something 'bigger than themselves', and unable to see clearly or act rationally. The magical structure acts out of impulse and emotion. Reasons and justifications are constructed later by the mental/rational structure.

Jung has a great deal to say about unconscious processes, but he makes very little direct contribution to a discussion of group behavior. His observation of group behavior, especially his observation of the rise of Nazism, convinced him that group behavior is generally stupid, and often immensely dangerous. He declared that the larger a group becomes, the less intelligence it has. In referring to the same mass movement, Theodor Abt talks about 'the headless regression into archaic *participation mystique*' where 'one has handed oneself over to the world of drives', and contrasts it with the magical-mythical consciousness of the 'real folk person' of the traditional Swiss village.

> . . . the real folk person is anything but a creature of drives lacking a head. Having a precise knowledge of the dangers of humanity's chaotic drive nature, the primordial folk person is continually alert to living correctly in harmony with the whole.[24]

The folk community controls instinct and impulse by developing rituals and taboos, for this is essential to keeping 'harmony with the whole'.

It is a frequent source of wonder that people who are capable of sane and intelligent behavior as individuals can become completely irrational as members of a group. Each time they emerge from the group and reflect on their behavior they may express amazement that they could have behaved so strangely. Then they re-enter the group and behave exactly as before. The group identity and emotionality have swallowed them. As individuals, we think of emotion as something we have. It may be difficult to control at times, but it is ours. However, at the level of our magical consciousness it is the emotion that 'has' us. Our rage, or lust, or depression, or exhilaration are not initiated by us or owned by us. Rather, they are energies that take possession of us, dominate us for a while, and leave us if and when it suits them. For our pre-scientific ancestors it was natural to think of them as gods.

Being immersed in group emotionality is not necessarily a negative experience. As individuals we often regress to infantile (magical) or childish (mythical) behavior. Sometimes it is just a matter of being playful. Sometimes it 'happens' to us in reaction to a shock or a crisis. We sometimes deliberately join a group in order to regress in this sort of way. We may go to a football match and allow ourselves to become emotional and irrational participants in a quasi-religious ritual. Or we may let ourselves get totally caught up in dancing or drinking, gladly abandoning our self-conscious, reasonable, and respectable selves for the time being. We can participate in a political demonstration, a religious celebration, or a rock festival and experience a powerful sense of being one in heart and mind with our companions. There is a certain intoxication in the dissolving of boundaries between ourselves and others. After the event we return to our rational consciousness, either refreshed or embarrassed by the experience.

Likewise, we don't have to be totally negative about the impact of magical behavior in organizations. Magical behavior was a quite adequate way of dealing with the world in well-functioning tribal communities, and there are still aspects of our experience that we deal with through our magical consciousness. Our ability to heal ourselves by means of placebos, and the power of group religious ritual to heal and transform, attest to magical consciousness being a valid response to the world. And because we can bring our rational consciousness to bear on our magical ways of behaving, we can have some control over them. We can create rituals to express the organization's commitment to a common enterprise or to shared values, and this ritualizing can create or transmute energy for a specific end. We can invest particular icons with the power to express our identity and the meaning of our group activity. This process can be malicious and destructive (as in the Nazi use of the Nuremburg rallies to transform German consciousness). But it can also be transformative in a positive sense (as in the ritual singing of the incantation *We Shall Overcome* in the American Civil Rights movement). On the other hand, sometimes the attempt to create a ritual is embarrassingly ineffective.

While Jung did not have much to say to us about working with groups, what he says about individual psychology is relevant here because, in the magical structure, groups behave very much like persons.

For instance, Jung says a good deal about the associated phenomena of *projection* and *transference*. By *projection*, Jung meant our tendency to attribute to others aspects of ourselves that we are unable to acknowledge. Robert cannot acknowledge his hostility to women, but constantly perceives women as hostile to him. Robyn fails to recognize her own wisdom but has an obsessive admiration for a teacher or guru who puts words to Robyn's half-articulated thoughts. By *transference* he means the projection on to another person of that part of our personality which is still embedded in relationship with some one else, particularly with one of our parents. Charles is always transformed into a submissive and dependent child (or a defiant adolescent) the moment he enters the boss's office. In such cases, the recipient of our projection or transference has presented us with a 'hook', something in their appearance, behavior, or role that immediately stimulates the projection or transference. If we were purely rational we could say, 'This person has some similarity to so and so. I should be careful not to confuse them.' In practice, our magical consciousness usually gets in first, so that we unconsciously mistake the part for the whole, or the similar for the identical, and react to this person as though they were really someone else. In magical consciousness there are no impermeable ego-boundaries, no clear distinction between what is *me* and what is *you*.

Organizations are very prone to project their pathology on to other organizations. Organizations that close their collective eyes to their own lack of ethical principles can be loud in their criticisms of the low ethical standards of other organizations. Corporations that perceive themselves as providing a humane working environment while actually oppressing their employees will stridently condemn other firms for their poor treatment of their workers. Of course, this may be conscious and manipulative, but it can happen without any awareness at all. In his study of International Telephone and Telegraph, Sampson describes how the company's self-image and rhetoric of enabling and supporting democracy (and the slogan *Freedom Dying Everywhere*) proved to be quite compatible with its collusion with the CIA in undermining the democratically elected government of Chile. He suggests that the reality of a brutal and coercive management style, combined with the rhetoric of a moral crusade against totalitarianism, had the predictable effect of projecting on to Allende all the anti-democratic prejudices of ITT and its chief executive.[25]

Sampson uses the Jungian term *shadow* to refer to the unacknowledged totalitarianism of the company in this instance. At the personal level, the Jungian shadow contains all the aspects of our personality that do not fit in with our self-image. Jung means this to include the positive aspects (such as creativity and altruism) that we are not able to acknowledge in ourselves, as well as the negative aspects, but in popular usage the shadow is often identified with the negative. The shadow is experienced collectively as well as personally. In pre-scientific societies, the shadow is dealt with magically. Rituals are performed for allowing the shadow expression and, in some cultures, for exorcising it. Sometimes, an individual is delegated to ritually perform actions that violate the standards of the group. Sometimes an individual is made to carry the clan's pathology and is really or symbolically killed or driven out of the clan. Sometimes an animal (scapegoat) stands in for a clan member in this role.

Organizations still use such methods to deal with the shadow. The phenomenon of scapegoating is too common to require much comment. The delegation of particular individuals or sub-groups to act out the shadow-dynamic of the organization is likewise readily recognized. An organization that cultivates a self-image of order, rationality, and propriety may tolerate within its ranks an individual or a group of individuals who behave in disordered, irrational, and disordered ways. Or it may ritualize a regular celebration of the shadow, for example an annual 'retreat' or an 'office party', which allows the shadow suitable expression and then shoves it back into the organizational unconscious for a year. The more the shadow energy is repressed in the conventional activities of the organization, the more outlandish this officially sanctioned 'carnival' behavior is likely to be.

Power relations in organizations are deeply embedded in magical consciousness. Often this is by way of transference, as we invest a leader with the qualities of the omnipotent parent who dominated our infantile consciousness. Investing another person with power over our emotional life, finding divinity in our guru, or satanic evil in a hated superior, is not a rational act. The notion and experience of authority belongs to our rational consciousness; our experience of power belongs to the magical. It is something that happens to us, rather than something we choose and do reflectively.

Another sign of magical consciousness at work is the unreflective identification of an organization with its leader or, even more bizarrely, with an external consultant or proponent of a particular ideology. This is most striking in religious cults, but the phenomenon can be widely observed in all sorts of organizations. The tendency of groups to identify sympathetically with individuals or representative groups is well attested as the fortunes of nations or cities rise and fall with the success or failure of a national or local football team.

Even in organizations structured in rational ways, morale can be dependent on the fortunes of a powerful leader. When the organization is organically structured around the personality of a charismatic leader, the leader's failure can have a catastrophic effect on the group. In a magical culture, the most effective way to defeat the tribe is to kill the chief. If the projection is centered on an external consultant, the urge to find ways to kill the magician and replace him or her with another can be both more extreme and more immediate than when it is centered on the leader.

The Mythical Organization

Magical consciousness functions through shared emotionality and ritual behaviors. The mythical structure functions through image and story. Though it is more 'evolved' than magical consciousness it still has no clear sense of individual selfhood. To be in mythical consciousness is to be enmeshed in story, and the stories we are enmeshed in are the collective stories, the 'big' stories, of our tribe. From the standpoint of our rational consciousness we are inclined to see story and images as things we have, things that are in us. In our mythical consciousness it is we who are in the story.[26]

Our late Stone Age and Bronze Age ancestors lived in a world that was alive with gods, and whatever happened in this world was a manifestation of these gods and their interaction with each other and with humanity. The stories they told were simply stories of how the world is, not of how it once was or how it ought to be. Mythical consciousness, as Gebser describes it, has no sense of measured, sequential time. Time is rhythmical, always returning to its beginning. Everything has already happened in the time of the gods. It was only with the development of mental consciousness that history was invented.

As far as our mythical consciousness is concerned, the old stories are still true, and we are still in them. From the perspective of archetypal psychology we are always in one archetypal fantasy or another. In this way of thinking, even the notion that we are reasonable beings able to observe the world objectively, reflect on it rationally, and deal with it scientifically is simply one story among many. It is a way of imagining the world, a story, a myth. It has been a dominant story in European culture for some time, and it is certainly a powerfully dominant story in corporate culture but, as stories go, it is relatively new. It is less than three thousand years old. It started to really take hold of Western thought with the advent of Rene Descartes and Isaac Newton and the subsequent age of rational enlightenment, a mere three hundred or so years ago.

We can thank Freud and Jung for calling our attention to the stories we act out in our lives. Freud documented a couple of stories in particular that he claimed we are scripted to re-enact. Jung, when he looked at the common patterns in human lives, claimed that there are a number of different stories that we find ourselves enmeshed in. Jung and Freud were most interested in the way we live out the myths without any awareness that we are doing so. We live out the old stories both personally (the *Oedipus* story, the *Hero* story, the *Cinderella* story) and collectively (the *Oppressed Minority* story, the *Master Race* story, the *God's Special People* story, the *Daddy Will Look After Us* story).

Even our personal stories are variations on the collective ones. Our stories still belong to the tribe. When Jung listened to the stories his patients told him about themselves, and the images they reported from their dreams, he was impressed by the way the same images and patterns kept turning up. It was his attempt to find an explanation for the way his patients' intensely private experiences were expressed in specific, apparently universal, images and narratives that led him to the notion of archetypes. He saw myths as the ancient narrative expression of these patterns or energies.

There has been increasing recognition of the narrative level of human experience in recent years, even among people who have little time for Freud or Jung. It is increasingly fashionable to talk about culture and personality in terms of dominant narratives and discourse rather than in terms of dominant ideas or values. The tendency of human beings not only to tell and listen to stories but also to live out collectively held 'scripts' is being acknowledged and studied.

Myths are powerful in shaping individual behavior. We can argue that they are even more powerful in shaping group behavior. Gebser argued that it was in the very nature of pre-rational mythical consciousness to be a group consciousness. We can now see readily enough that it is a shared story that shapes behavior in areas of inter-cultural or inter-ethnic conflict: in Northern Ireland, in Kosovo, in Rwanda, in Palestine, in Kashmir, in Iraq. We can see how a shared story gives identity and meaning to a group of people, and how the conflict between two stories resists rational analysis and rational solutions. We can see former imperial nations, whose story of cultural and racial superiority no longer 'works' for them, clinging to the story that once gave them identity, or trying to write themselves a new one. Likewise we can see corporations clinging to a story of who they are and what they exist for, long after changed social and economic conditions have created a world different to the world of their story.

To return to Sampson's account of ITT's operations in Chile, it is apparent that the promulgation and acceptance of a myth of moral and political superiority allowed the company to behave in utterly immoral ways without any sense of dissonance. The facts were overwhelmed by the power of the shared narrative.

There is an attempt in many organizations to articulate the organizational myths in a 'mission statement' of some kind. When this statement actually articulates the shared narrative in which members of the organization declare where they have come from, what they are about and where they are going, it can be an effective device for building cohesion and a sense of purpose. Where it is thrust upon the organization from outside or represents the fantasy of a non-representative managerial subculture, it is not likely to have much impact.

One of Jung's most useful ideas was the notion of inflation. He used the word to refer to the state of an individual who is 'taken over' by a specific archetypal energy and image, so that it entirely shapes their thinking, valuing, feeling, and behavior. We sometimes describe a person as having a 'power complex', meaning that the drive to power dominates their way of being in the world. All other values have become insignificant. Their view of life is narrowed to a single dimension. In their obsession with power we see them acting irrationally and obsessively, and they don't seem to have any control over this. Such an inflation may suddenly come and suddenly go. It is something that happens to us, rather than something we do. Sane and rational people fall obsessively in love, become overwhelmingly doting parents, become paralyzed by stress or depression, or become consumed by a thirst for vengeance or a conviction that they must save the world, and they forget everything else in their lives. Their sanity and rationality seem to be set aside until this condition decides to let them alone.

Jung pointed out how such a 'complex' seems to behave like an autonomous agent. It was natural for pre-scientific cultures to see in it the work of a god. Jung and later archetypal theorists have found it useful to follow this lead and use the language of polytheistic religion to label such phenomena, so we can talk of a Zeus (patriarchal power) inflation, a Demeter (mothering) inflation, an Ares (rage) inflation, and Eros (love) inflation.

In Gebser's way of thinking, we would say that an 'inflated' person has regressed to a simpler (magical-mythical) structure of consciousness, and has lost their individual identity in a collective image and narrative (mythical) or in the impersonality of fixed ideas and compulsive behaviors (magical). They have also lost their capacity to detach themselves from their experience and reflect on it. Magical-mythical consciousness does not have such a capacity, which belongs to rational consciousness.

Inflation and regression occur in organizations just as they do in individuals. For Jung, being taken over by a single archetypal energy was pathological, whether at the individual or group level, and the most obvious example of a group inflation was the experience of Nazi Germany, which he saw as an inflation by the Wotan archetype. The German nation let itself be caught up in the energy and imagery of the myth of Wotan. At one level there were opportunistic choices made by individuals, and a conscious manipulation of images and ideology, but this rational activity was soon swept up in the irruption of a collective emotion and a collective myth.

In a similar vein, organizations can become inflated with a dominant archetypal energy represented in a dominant organizational narrative. This collective obsession blinds the people within the organization to a more detached and multi-perspectival assessment of their experience. In the first place they are caught in a collective emotion sustained by ritual ways of behaving; in the second place, they are caught up in a particular story that gives meaning to their behavior. They may consider that they are acting reasonably, according to a theory of good organizational practice, but it is theory swallowed whole without opportunity, or even desire, for critical reflection. For example, we saw a rise through the sixties, seventies, and eighties of training and organization development activities premised on the belief that more effective and healthier relationships among people in the workplace would lead to more effective organizational performance and a better quality of work life for employees. It was associated in some fields with a rise in emphasis on values as key drivers in relational activities. This became a quite seductive and powerful movement, which is still strongly represented in some places.

During this period many organizations invested heavily in human relations training of one form or another. The movement provided a deeply entrancing alternative to the linear, mechanistic, male, dominating, power-oriented environment that it was set against in such sharp relief. We might say it represented the Eros narrative. Those in its grip became blinded both to its negative aspects and to the existence of other, and equally legitimate, value systems. They were blind to any evidence that a strong relational orientation does not necessarily translate to corporate performance and environmental relevance. At the core of this narrative as it is lived out in organizations are images of total inclusion and mutuality; separation and contained roles are frowned upon. The Eros myth is very seductive, especially when seen against a background of barren and life-inhibiting corporate environments. But the myth can blind people to the hard decisions they have to make in the marketplace and to the realities of how people actually behave, rather than how we would like them to behave. We need more than love to make the world go round.

In the same period, we saw the rise of a 'human potential' orientation, enacting the myth of Dionysos, the god of new life and growth. It took a number of different forms, and derived from a number of sources (among them humanistic psychology, Scientology, and the EST movement of Werner Erhard). It is currently offered in many different guises and from a wide range of consulting and training providers who offer personal and corporate transformation. The focus is on the psychology and philosophy of a person's experience – past, present, and future; individuals are asked to bring into existence new realities both individually and collectively as they become part of a shared narrative of emergence. Like any myth, it has the power to blind those gripped by it to other ways of thinking and feeling about the world.

The eighties saw the rise on a global scale of another narrative, that of economic rationalism. Once again we found a story about the world presented as a universal truth. The self-evident truth this time was the centrality of the unregulated marketplace as the final arbiter of values. We saw an economic theory being turned into an unchallengeable truth that was applicable in every field - human relationships, health, education, and welfare. Where organizations embraced this view of the world, or had it forced on them, we saw market value taking the place of all other ways of valuing, not only in the organization's relation to its products and processes, but also in its relation to its people. Market value in a particular marketplace gave many CEOs salaries out of all proportion to their contribution to the company, and led to the sacking of many employees whose actual contribution to the company was not matched by their monetary value in the same marketplace. Where this narrative was so powerfully dominant that it overwhelmed all other voices and drowned out all critical reflection, we can call it an inflation, this time associated with Hermes, god of the marketplace.

Through these decades we saw the Eros, Dionysos, and Hermes myths being accepted in various organizations as 'the way things are', in clear contrast to Zeus archetype that preceded them. More recently we have seen a more conservative element assume the high political ground. The moral majority took control of the argument in the USA after the 1994 election, and it was no longer seen as fashionable or ideologically legitimate to engage in deep psychological inquiry or to abandon traditional values. About the same time we saw the return of a reductionist and rationalist approach to human influence in organizations. No more vivid expression of this trend can be found than in the fields of competency modeling and performance management. This shift is described by Michael Grinder as a movement from a psychological model to a professional model.[27] It is probably better described as a trend away from interventions that focused on changing the interior experience of individuals to those that focus more on their external reality. Grinder describes this latter form as change from the 'outside in' rather than 'inside out'. Underlying this shift is the rise of (or perhaps more properly, a return to) different myths: Apollo (the universe is rational and systematic and we will understand all about it if we think hard enough) and Prometheus (if we become more systematic and technically skilled we can create a new and better world).

It is ironic that the image of the universe as machine hangs on in myth, while the idea of the universe as machine has been long ago been challenged by science, through such developments as Einstein's relativity theory, quantum theory, and nonlinear dynamics, and the replacement of the idea and image of the universe as machine with a different idea and image, that of the universe as a self-organizing system.[28]

Over the past few years the image has come to be applied in organization and management literature also, and much of what we say in this book is shaped by it.[29] However, we must be careful not to confuse image with fact. If this way of thinking represents our own taken-for-granted, uncontestable assumptions about organizations, so that we are simply unable to examine the theory critically and look at evidence that challenges it, we are ourselves being constrained by the images of a specific myth – this time the myth of Gaia, the ancient mother-goddess whom the Greeks identified with the earth.

Those who promote a particular way of imagining organizations and organizational change do not generally perceive themselves to be promoting a myth. They believe that they are constructing a theory and applying it in practice. Yet if the theory does not critically reflect on its own assumptions, if it will brook no contradiction, it is likely to be the rationalization of a myth. People stuck in a particular narrative don't cease to think rationally; it is just that their rational thinking takes place within a framework of taken-for-granted assumptions that determine what the truth is in their tribe or organization. Myth doesn't allow for contingency. It asserts that 'the way things are' is inevitable and natural. Organizations stuck in a particular myth have no desire to change and no understanding of why they might need to do so. Their members are engaged in what developmental psychologist Robert Kegan calls 'third order' thinking, where 'truth' is something given to the individual by the consensus of their cultural group, rather than something arrived at through their own observations and reflections.[30]

Being stuck in a single story, being able to imagine the world in one way only, prevents us from responding flexibly and appropriately to the world as it is. Fortunately most of us in our personal lives experience the archetypes (or gods) as interacting energies and interacting fantasies without giving ourselves over entirely to one of them alone. The same thing happens in a psychologically healthy organization. Many organizations have a dominant narrative, a dominant fantasy, but it is balanced by other complementary narratives. In earlier, simpler societies individuals and organizations could conduct their lives within a single narrative. That option no longer seems to be available. When leaders or their magicians try to impose a single story and image on an organization, they are more likely to generate confusion and demoralization than constructive energy.

The Mental/Rational Organization

When writing about the evolution of consciousness, Gebser distinguishes between the mental structure of consciousness that characterized the high culture of the classical world and the Renaissance and the rational structure that has been dominant more recently. Mental consciousness develops out of mythical consciousness and retains an awareness and appreciation of non-rational (e.g. religious and poetic) ways of understanding the world. Rational consciousness (in Gebser's use of the word) cuts itself off from its non-rational roots, and attempts to deal with the world only within its own terms, that is, in terms of science. It denies that any other ways of experiencing the world are valid. In Gebser's language, it is the 'deficient' form of the mental structure.

In the emergence of the mental structure in classical Greece and Asia about 800 BCE and its flowering in enlightenment Europe, we find the notion of the self-conscious, decision-making individual given political application in a movement towards participative democracy. However, genuine participative democracy, grounded in the mental structure of consciousness, proved to be fairly elusive. In most places it was overwhelmed by myth and magic, as the narratives and rituals of monarchy or 'the mob' proved more powerful and enduring.

We also find the mental structure manifested in the development of science in the classical and renaissance worlds. European scientific culture between the sixteenth and twentieth century believed that it was at last possible to look at the world 'objectively' and assumed that we could get rid of magic, myth, and gods. Human beings, it was believed, only needed to exercise their powers of reason and they would be able to understand exactly how the world works. They would eventually know everything there was to know. They would be able to control the chaos of nature and, if they cared to, fashion a world in which everyone would be happy and prosperous. Light would replace darkness; objective, scientific truth would replace myth and superstition. Nobody doubted that man was the center of the universe, a notion that was reinforced by conventional religion as well as by science.

With the development of technology, the earth itself came to be seen as a vast machine operating on precise laws of cause and effect in quantifiable time and space. Human beings themselves came to be viewed as machines. Just as man should, could, and would control the 'forces of Nature', so the ego, the individual's rational self, should, could, and would control instinct, imagination, and emotion.

The development of organizations during this time has been based in the same assumptions. It came to be accepted without argument that the ideal organization is one based on scientific principles, that is, an organization that is rational, objective, and impersonal. The success of technology in the nineteenth century made it inevitable that organizations would be viewed as machines, designed to deliver designated products. Richard Denhardt[31] points to the way both science and organization took on greater and greater significance. They became important for their own sake, not simply as instruments to accomplish something. The rational organization came to be an end in itself, and a model of how society ought to function.

The mental/rational organization is built on the premise that its members are essentially individuals who join, by choice or necessity, in a common task. Commitment to the organization is only understood as an expression of self-interest. Whereas the members of the magical organization are connected in a common emotionality expressed in ritual, and the members of the mythical organization are linked in a common narrative, connections in the rational organization are abstract and bureaucratic. Because the rational organization is a collection of individuals, the roles and functions of these individuals are differentiated. Moreover, the roles and functions are not confused with the individuals who perform them, but are reified abstractions, independent of changes in personnel.

It is significant that the thinking behind both modern science and modern organization is blatantly elitist. Both the scientist and the manager of the rational organization distinguish themselves from the objects of science and the objects of management. The scientist/manager does the thinking and controlling; the objects, human or otherwise, are thought about and controlled. The rational organization operates out of the rationality of the chief executive and the elite leadership team who look at the facts, develop strategies and systems, and put them into operation. Individuals at other levels of the organization may be invited to contribute information and ideas from time to time, but the 'thinking' is done at the top.

This is not surprising. Organizations cannot 'think' at all. By 'thinking' we detach ourselves from the group consciousness and assert our separateness. As a member of a group we express the group identity by sharing the established ideas and values of the group, but as soon as we 'think', in the sense of applying our logic, our capacity for critical analysis and our ability to construct new ideas, we are acting as individuals. Our individuality and our capacity to manipulate ideas are inextricably tied together in our mental/rational structure of consciousness. The mental structure of consciousness enables us to reflect critically on the myths in which our organization is enmeshed, the taken-for-granted assumptions out of which the organization's dominant narrative is constructed. It enables us to test an organization's propaganda against the available evidence. In mental consciousness we look at the past through the lens of history, not myth. History is a tool we have invented to allow us to make sense of changing conditions, and to accept the information about changing conditions for what it is, instead of distorting it to make it compatible with our particular narrative.

The mental/rational organization self-consciously distinguishes itself from organizations that are trapped in a deficient magical or mythical structure. Murray Stein suggests that 'one of the essential functions of a good organization is to contain the spirit of the organization's unconscious and to keep it from devouring its members'.[32] The latent archaic structure pre-disposes the individual to lapse into an instinctual and unreflective oneness with the organization. The magical structure pre-disposes them to be caught up in collective impulse and emotionality. The mythical structure tends to keep them uncritically embedded in a narrative. The mental/rational structure makes them individuals and sets them free from the 'diminished responsibility' attendant on the other structures. In so far as the mental/rational structure can carry over into the collective behavior of the organization, it can inhibit a takeover by collective instinct, emotion and image.

However, there is a twin paradox here. The mental/rational structure of consciousness gives individuals the capacity and inclination for reflection. It is a capacity that has been cherished by the science-dominated culture of the modern European era. However, this capacity is acknowledged only in the context of a single reality that is ultimately discoverable by science. Not only modern science, but modern organizations – religious, political, and cultural – have been built upon the assumption that there is 'one truth' which is discoverable by intelligent, thinking people. The nature of this 'one truth' varies enormously, but the assumption is constant. Modern, rational organizations are, in Gebser's words, perspectival, that is, they see the world from one direction only.

The deficient rational, perspectival consciousness of the modern era leads us to assume that the maintenance of order depends on the acknowledgment of a single reality. This assumption has been used to justify political and intellectual oppression for centuries. The assumption still lurks behind the rational organization's fantasy of a unitary organizational culture. In such an organization, difference is feared as a threat to order. If people 'think right' they will accept the truth as given to them and enjoy the order that depends on it; the alternative is chaos and disintegration.

The other side of this paradox is that unthinking acceptance of the organization's narrative of what is true and what is worthwhile is a function of the mythical structure; our unthinking participation in its rituals and our immersion in its emotionality belong to the magical structure. And in both of these structures the group consciousness is more powerful than the individual. Reflection, in the fantasy of rational organization, as in the fantasy of scientific culture, is reserved for the elite.

A peculiar irony in this is that the group consciousness of the 'rational' organization is itself always a mythical one. The organization's consensus reality is the experience of a shared, ongoing story.

When James Hillman declares that we are always in one archetypal fantasy or another he is making the point that we cannot get away from our mythical consciousness. Even when we are self-consciously being modern, rational, logical, objective human beings, exercising our extraordinary capacity for abstraction and our ability to find the truth by looking objectively and critically at the evidence, we are in the midst of a fantasy that this is the way the world is. We are telling ourselves a story. This happens to be a story that has dominated European consciousness for some time, but it has no absolute grip on the truth. It represents a partial truth, like the story that *it is love that makes the world go round*, the story that *the earth is our mother and we her children*, the story that *might is right*, the story that *beauty is truth and truth beauty*, the story that *you can't stop progress* or the *story that globalization made me do it.*[33]

In the 'rational' organization there is an official story promulgated, reinforced by rituals of status and procedure, and individuals 'belong' to the organization to the degree that they accept this story. The problem with this particular story is that those who tell it and live it are inclined to assume that it is the only story. They will cling to this story even when they see their organization behaving irrationally, as when it spends a great deal of energy and expense on getting objective data to assist decision-making and then actually makes its decisions according to prejudice or whim.

What passes for a 'rational' organization, then, is not necessarily rational at all. It may be a mythical organization enacting its particular myth of rationality. The more genuinely rational an organization is, the more it will allow for individual reflection, for critical analysis of its own processes, for truly objective appraisal of its situation, for genuine democratic processes.

However, even in our individual lives we are not able to act out of pure rationality without being affected by of the irrational elements in our nature. In our group membership this is even more so. Ironically, a genuinely rational-scientific view of organizations will acknowledge and assess all the aspects of human behavior, unconscious as well as conscious, magical and mythical as well as rational.

This brings us back to Gebser's argument that the rational structure of consciousness that has characterized the modern, industrial world is a deficient mental structure. Rational consciousness has so narrowly defined reality that it cannot see what is there. The only way rational consciousness can be an effective instrument for dealing with the world is by re-admitting aspects of reality that it has defined out of existence, aspects that were admitted in an efficient mental structure.

An organization functioning within the efficient mental structure of consciousness is able to utilize the rational thinking of its members without denying the magical and mythical dimensions of group life. The reflection and dialogue of the organization's members enable the organization to function in the way most appropriate to its situation. Recognition of the organization's collective myths enables meaningful and purposive common action. Group ritual is acknowledged and honored for its effectiveness in developing a common identity. The mental organization cherishes soul as well as mind.

However, such organizations are hard to find. Many are stuck in a deficient and exhausted rational structure of consciousness.

The Integral Organization

While Gebser proposed that the rational consciousness that has characterized European scientific-industrial culture for the past few centuries was something of a dead end, he pointed to evidence that there was a significant change in consciousness taking place in the twentieth century. Gebser noted some dimensions of this change when he examined the arts and sciences in the middle of the century, and he tried to determine the kind of change that was taking place. His conclusions are compatible with more recent observations of the change in intellectual sensibility associated with late capitalism.[34]

Gebser suggests, logically enough, that just as archaic humanity could not feel what the experience of magical consciousness might be, and just as mythical humanity could not imagine what mental consciousness might be like, rational humanity cannot conceptualize the experience of the structure of consciousness that is at present emerging. Gebser himself claims only to have observed the past and present trajectory of consciousness and on this basis to have guessed at its future direction. The nature of his guess is implied in the label he gave this structure: integral consciousness.

When Gebser was developing his theory in Europe in the thirties and forties he was confronted with some evidence that humanity was regressing to an older and more collective form of consciousness. As he studied the evidence, he became somewhat less pessimistic. Alongside the regression, there seemed to be a movement to a more complex, rather than a less complex form of consciousness. His interest was originally sparked by his observation that European poets were using language in quite new ways, but he soon turned his attention to the other arts and to economics and science.

His conclusion was that not only were the magical and mythical modes of perceiving the world being once again taken seriously, but that the magical and mythical structures of consciousness were being integrated with rational consciousness to produce a totally new way of perceiving and thinking.

Certain elements stand out in Gebser's analysis of what he calls the *integral* structure of consciousness: freedom from the constraints of linear time and space, and freedom from the constraints of ego.

There is rather more to Gebser's speculations about the nature of the emerging structure of consciousness than this, but this is sufficient basis for some speculation on the emerging nature of organizations. However, there is no sense in here trying to describe fully integral organizations. We have neither the experience nor the language that would enable us to do so. What we can now observe is the confusion of organizations inhabiting a world where there is a growing sense that the political, environmental, social, economic, and health problems that the late modern-industrial age was so confident of solving are not only too complex to solve but too complex even to think about. It is in this state of confusion and instability that Gebser sought for signs that a new way of experiencing and dealing with the world might be emerging.

The world as we generally perceive it follows certain rules regarding time and space, yet when we get beyond the range of our naked senses and look at the macro-world of outer space or the micro-world of the sub-atomic realm, the rules don't seem to hold any more. Time goes backwards as well as forwards. Space is curved. Matter becomes so dense it disappears. Particle can act on particle instantaneously at a distance. We can no longer think of time and space as quantifiable, for their dimensions are constantly changing. Like everything else in a postmodern world, science has lost the steady ground it used to stand on. The reality we can observe with our senses is a very partial reality indeed. The universe, as Schrodinger observed, is not only stranger than we think, but stranger than we *can* think. The high technology of our civilization is based on sciences and mathematics that have long ago left behind the assumptions of the machine age, yet the ways most of us think about technology and use it are still the ways of a hundred years ago. Moreover, many of the organizations by which we try to manage this high-tech world are extremely low-tech in their structures and ways of operating.

However, there are signs that we are learning to think in new ways. In the first place, we are prepared to challenge some of the assumptions on which the 'old science' of the past four hundred years has been based. We are prepared to acknowledge that the rules of rational thinking that have been so useful for us in the past may not be universally applicable. Gebser warns us against assuming that the only alternative to rational thinking is irrationality. Integral consciousness is not irrational but arational.[35]

What might this mean for organizations and those who belong to them? One of the features of integral consciousness, as Gebser imagines it, is the transcendence of the dualism that is at the core of rational thinking. In all sorts of fields we find that we no longer absolutely have to think in terms of either/or. Either spirit or matter. Either true or false. Either male or female. Either human or divine. Either wave or particle. Either living or non-living. Thinkers in various fields have given us ways of thinking outside these limitations. In organization theory there is still a great deal of dualistic thinking going on, but it is under challenge. The emerging integral organization does not assume that there must be a choice between concern for product and concern for people, between tradition and progress, between authority and chaos, between self-interest and altruism, between technology and humanity, between company business and personal business.

Another feature of integral consciousness is the transcendence of a single perspective. The emerging integral organization is, to use one of Gebser's key expressions, aperspectival. It does not locate itself (physically or metaphorically) on a particular spot and see the world from there. It attempts to see the world from no spot in particular and from all possible spots at once. The integral organization is able to hold different perspectives and different value systems. The deficient rational, perspectival consciousness is unable to do this. The rational organization prefers the security of one truth to the freedom and limitless possibility of many. The assumption of a single reality still lurks behind the fantasy of a unitary organizational culture. Both contemporary science and postmodern social analysis have challenged the feasibility of assuming any longer that there is a single reality. Gebser and contemporary constructive postmodernists challenge the assumption that order depends on believing in it.

In the integral organization, difference is valued. There is no fantasy about 'objective truth' to determine what the organization believes about itself. The world is as it is experienced and interpreted by the members of the organization, each from their own perspective. Reality is conceived to be not one of these things but all of these things.

The emerging integral organization is also *time-free*. It is not locked into a particular spot in history, a particular mark on a time line. In the integral organization the past and the future are simultaneously experienced with the present. Time can now be stretched or compressed, and it has become possible to talk of the *quality* and *intensity* of time as well as its extent. The organization is not locked into its history or its traditional ways of categorizing people and events, which are a product of both mythical consciousness (through shared narratives) and rational consciousness (through history). Among the products of myth and history are essentialist views of race, gender, class, and cultural difference, including an essentialist view of its own identity.

The integral organization is no longer trapped in historically-based assumptions about people – assumptions that particular groups of people have particular traits and accordingly are suitable only to fill particular roles. It does not have to limit its members' activities on the basis that they are essentially such and such because of race or gender or geography and cannot change. It does not have to limit its collective activity because of an essentialist view of what it is and what it does. It does not have to protect itself from incorporating people who will not 'fit in' because of cultural difference. It is difference that gives the organization the capacity to 'go with the flow' through ongoing self-organization. Where the mythical organization seeks conformity through immersion in a shared narrative, and the rational organization seeks stability and planned change, the integral organization values the multiplicity, creativity, and spontaneity that come with *time-freedom*.[36]

Jung made an intense study of magical and mythical phenomena, and gave us a psychological language for talking about them. He also perceived, like Gebser, that rational thought alone could not deal with the kind of universe that his studies were revealing. He did not accept that dualistic thinking could have the last word about the world. While Einstein was proposing that the physical universe is four-dimensional, Jung was saying the same of the psychic universe.[37] With his notion of archetype he challenged conventional psychology by positing a psychological structure that is 'eternally present', that is *time-free*.

The emerging integral organization is also 'ego-free'. It does not have a narrowly defined sense of self analogous to the ego in the individual psyche. It does not separate out a particular person or group of persons as the decision-making, controlling center of the organism (or machine). Jung argued that the development in the individual of a strong ego is only a stage in psychological growth (a particular task of adolescence and young adulthood) rather than the goal of it. A strong ego enables us to have a strong sense of who we are and what we value, but this is at the cost of one-sidedness. It ignores or suppresses a great deal of who we are and what we are capable of. To live to our full potential we have to admit into our consciousness all the suppressed and underdeveloped parts of our personality. Archetypal psychologists emphasize that we have many selves, actual and potential. To concentrate on a single identity and self image is a denial of most of what we can be. The integral, or individuated, organization likewise owns up to all of its potential, giving all of its selves expression.

There is another aspect to this transcendence of ego. Not only do we seem to be abandoning the notion that the ego is the center of the personality, but there is also doubt about whether human beings are the center of the universe. The spread of Buddhism in the West has clearly been dependent on the psychological readiness to abandon the fantasy that we are essentially separate encapsulated egos, and to imagine us rather as distinct manifestations of a greater reality. Jungian psychology suggests that the personal ego is merely a secondary phenomenon, that our personal consciousness is just a momentary expression at a point in space and time of what Jung calls the *objective psyche*. It is becoming increasingly difficult to place human beings at the center of the universe, or even to maintain that they are at the center of the planet. The anthropocentric fantasy is under attack from Gaia consciousness in one direction and from 'selfish genes'[38] in the other. It is becoming incumbent on us to relativize ourselves, to imagine ourselves not only as choosing and acting individuals in our own right, but also both as an environment for smaller organisms and as cells of a larger organism. We are part of something bigger than ourselves, and the boundaries of our selves are not as fixed and impermeable as they used to be.

This kind of thinking about our place in the universe, even when it does not reach conscious expression, affects the way we think about organizations. It demands that organizations see themselves and structure themselves in ways that are consistent with a sense of themselves as open systems in a web of relationships that blur the boundaries between *inside* and *outside*. The boundary between the postmodern integral organization and its human and nonhuman environment is exceedingly permeable.

Gebser developed his notions of what integral consciousness might be like without being witness to the developments in communications and information technology that are peculiar to the present time. Yet these are highly significant for the intellectual sensibility of a postmodern world and the functioning of postmodern organizations.

The shift in our modes of thought that Gebser was documenting in the forties has been reinforced by an information technology that operates outside our conventional notions of space and time. The idea of exploring 'cyberspace' and of handling complex transactions in this place that is not a place, may be difficult for conventionally rational minds to handle, but increasing numbers of people are doing it. It is possible now for an entire organization to exist outside the conventions of time and place that we have taken for granted for nearly three thousand years. It seems to be becoming possible to transcend not only time and space but ego, as communication scientists pursue the fantasy of enabling a hundred minds (or ten thousand) in instantaneous communication to function as a single great mind. This transcendence of the limitations of the individual's mental powers is a very different thing from the submergence of the individual in the group that characterizes magical-mythical consciousness. It has enormous implications for the ways organizations operate. Organizations may at last be able to 'think'.

The integral organization's potential for thinking is different from that of magic, mythical or mental-rational organization. Magical thinking in the organization is dominated by emotion and fixed ideas. Magic and ritual are used in a constant attempt to keep the organization safe in a world where unexplainable things happen. Mythical thinking in the organization operates within a narrative, one – it is assumed – that everyone accepts and that cannot be questioned. Rational thinking in the organization looks at the evidence in an objective way and comes to conclusions about what is true and not true. It can even critically examine the organization's myths to judge whether they correspond to reality. Integral thinking, as Gebser understands it, is more than the aggregation of these simpler ways of thinking. It is a new kind of thinking in which the emotion (magic), imagination (myth) and objectivity (mental) of the other structures are integrated in an understanding of the world that is complex, fluid, and paradoxical. The capacity of information and communication technology to flood us not only with information, but with information about the information, and even information about the information about the information, only reinforces the need for organizations to develop a fluid and ironic appreciation of the world in which they operate.

We increasingly find organizations that, through the application of information technology and the abandonment of the mechanistic model of organization, appear able to transcend the limitations of ego, sequential time, and linear space. However, we find ourselves in the same messy paradox as we were when discussing the rational organization. The structures of consciousness are in constant interaction, and the integral corporation cannot escape from myth any more than the rational corporation can. The rational corporation says, 'This is the way the world is and the way it has to be' and goes on to relate Apollo's myth of abstract rational structure, role definition, and the importance of hierarchy, Athena's myth of shared expertise and participative decision-making or Prometheus' myth of salvation through technology. When the flexible, pluralistic, de-centered, post-rational organization takes its experience and turns it into a statement of 'This is the way the world is', it demonstrates that it is also caught in a myth – Hermes' myth of multi-perspectivism, fluidity, relativism, and transformation.

LIFE AT THE CROSSROADS

Gebser was adamant that his model was not developed within a fantasy of progress. He was not proposing that our species has moved through successive mutations of consciousness in some determined way that represents an improvement in the conditions of human life. On the contrary, he argued that all of the structures persist in us in our every day grasp of reality. Magical and mythical consciousness have not been discarded because we have evolved to a higher state called 'reason' or even 'integrality'. They are an essential part of our experience as individuals or as members of groups and organizations. We may want to distinguish between archaic, magic, mythical, mental, and integral organizations, but we are likely to find them all occupying the same space and populated by the same people.

In the condition of liminality and doubt in which we find ourselves, we have a tendency to reach for old certainties, old solutions. Fundamentalists of all kinds proclaim that they possess the only truth. Managers cling to old ways of managing, based on the rational-mechanistic principles that enabled the achievements of the industrial age. Unfortunately, it is the old certainties and old solutions that have got us into the position we are in. We have to accept that we are living on an edge, that liminality and doubt is where we have to be right now, to accept that perhaps our experience of the world in the times that are coming will be an experience of ambiguity and paradox.

Many individuals and organizations have arrived at their present state by following a particular narrative path that took them from a known past to a predictable future. Now we find ourselves at a crossroads where we are conscious of other paths crossing the one we have been following. Nationally we have become increasingly aware that the dominant national narrative is only one narrative among many, that our nation has a 'herstory' as well as a history, and that there are indigenous and ethnic stories that have been left out of the conventional account of our past. In our personal lives we are conscious that we are entangled in more than one story and that our actions have more than one meaning. Our organizations are in the same situation, as they are challenged to abandon the illusion that they have a simple definable identity and a simple definable script to follow. They can't even look around the crossroads, choose a clear path, and confidently move on. At the present time, the crossroads is where we are and where we have to be. This need not stop us traveling, but choosing a path no longer sets us on the way to a predictable future. We take the crossroads with us.

Some people view the changes in consciousness signaled by Gebser and by postmodern philosophers like Lyotard with alarm or despair. Others view them with excitement. Gebser warns us not to view integral consciousness as either innately positive or innately negative. It has, or will have, deficient as well as efficient forms. We might plausibly argue that we can find such deficiency in the groundlessness, radical relativism, fragmentation, cynicism, and nihilism commonly associated with postmodernity. Gebser also warns us that we will survive only if we achieve the new integral structure without forfeiting the efficient forms of the previous structures. Archaic, magical, mythical, and mental structures of consciousness all experience the world in different ways, but they are all legitimate ways of experiencing it, and we need to experience it in all of these ways. Our present cultural and ecological dilemmas may be a consequence of too long a neglect of them.

We can, if we like, take Gebser's evidence to support a romantic notion that everything will be all right in the long run, or even that things will get better and better, but that was certainly not his intention. He was certainly interested in the possibilities of integral consciousness, but he was not making a statement about how things ought to be or how things have to be. He was just looking hard at the complexity of contemporary culture and announcing that he had found a pattern in it.

When we approach a 'big' theory like Gebser's, we may find ourselves engaging in a debate with ourselves or others about whether it is objectively 'true' or not. We need to remind ourselves with James Hillman that 'we are always in one archetypal fantasy or another'. We might just as legitimately argue about whether it is beautiful, whether it is ethical, whether it is socially responsible, whether it is ecologically or culturally sensitive, whether it is politically correct. All of these different perspectives are grounded in different narratives, different myths, different 'archetypal fantasies'. For the present we choose the perspective that a theory like Gebser's is a tool for examining the world of organizations, and our concern is not whether it is true or beautiful but whether it is useful. Obviously, we think it is, and the following chapters are based on this premise.

Gebser and Jung knew each other, and their ideas intersect at a number of points, not the least of which is the sharing of a pluralistic notion of truth. To those (even their own disciples) who want to proclaim the truth about human beings and their relation to the universe, they might reply that truth is not so simple that it can be proclaimed unambiguously. For Gebser, such proclamations come from unreflecting acceptance of a particular myth, or from rational thinking which believes that it has found objective truth when it has really only found a perspective. For Jung or Hillman such proclamations are expressions a particular archetypal pattern, while truth resides not only in all the archetypes together but also in the tensions and contradictions between them. This is very different from the nihilism of much postmodern writing, which claims that because we cannot claim objective truth for any particular statement we might make, then truth does not exist.

Gebser's model provides a framework for thinking about Jung's notion of archetype. Jung starts from Plato's idea that archetypes are pure forms that can only be known through their manifestations. When we consider the ways in which archetypes may be manifested, we can follow Jung in finding them manifested in our instincts (the archaic structure), our rituals and emotions (the magic structure), our dreams and myths (the mythical structure), our ideas and theories (the mental structure) and our spiritual experience (the integral structure). It is the manifestation in myth that we want to focus on in the following chapters by taking a 'polytheistic' approach to organizational processes and change.

---

1. Gebser's key work, *The Ever Present Origin* (1985), was first published as *Ursprung und Gegenwart* in 1949. It should be noted that though the evidence Gebser uses to support his theory comes almost entirely from Indo-European sources, he universalizes his conclusions. For commentary and critique of Gebser's model see EM Kramer (1992) 'Gebser and Culture', in EM Kramer (ed.) *Consciousness and Culture*; G Feuerstein (1987) *Structures of.Consciousness*; A Combs (1995) *Radiance of Being*. Ken Wilber's model of consciousness evolution had a key source in Gebser's ideas. See particularly *The Atman Project* (1980) and *Up From Eden* (1981).
2. M Donald (1991) *The Origins of the Modern Mind.*
3. See P MacLean (1990) *The Triune Brain in Evolution.* According to MacLean, in the course of evolution the brain was not transformed into a single integrated new unit. Rather, we function with three interrelated but distinct brain systems, each with its own unique patterns and needs. He compares the brain to a car with three drivers who are all seated up the front and have different ideas about where they are going. Accordingly, our reptilian need for safety and routine is sometimes in conflict with our mammalian need for emotional contact and our neo-mammalian need to be reasonable. Reptilian instincts preserve a perfect memory for what their ancestors learned over millions of years, but the reptilian brain is poorly equipped for learning to cope with new situations.

4. See J Hellwige (1993) *Hemispheric Asymmetry.*
5. Kegan defines the stages of cognitive development in terms of increasingly complex subject-object differentiations: between sensations and environment (first order), between experiencing self and sensations (second order), between thinking self and experiences (third order), between critical self and the contents of mind (fourth order), between transcendent self and mode of thinking (fifth order). In first order consciousness we identify with our sensations, in second order with our experiencing, in third order with the contents of our minds, in fourth order with our capacity for critical reflection. In fifth order thinking this very capacity becomes the object of our knowing. Our way of thinking, our way of determining the truth, is relativized as only one out of many ways of constructing reality. We cease to see either ourselves or our truths as complete. See Kegan (1994) *In Over Our Heads: The Mental Demands of Modern Life.*
6. 'We have, you might say, a fivefold mind, or, more dramatically, we are a five-minded animal, in whom different kinds of understanding jostle together and fold on one another, to some degree remaining 'somewhat distinct". K Egan (1997) *The Educated Mind*, p. 80.
   Other contributors to the model of 'multiple minds' are Marshall McLuhan, who proposed that the evolution of consciousness should be viewed in terms of five successive quantum leaps in our capacity to communicate, and numerous writers who have focused on the shift from magical/mythical consciousness to mental/theoretic consciousness. See M McLuhan (1965) *Understanding media: the extensions of man*; J Jaynes (1976) *The Origin of Consciousness in the Breakdown of the Bicameral Brain*; M Eliade (1991[1954]) *The Myth of the Eternal Return: or Cosmos and History*; K Jaspers (1953) *The Origin and Goal of History.*
7. It should be noted that Gebser's model is not based on an assumption of progress from an inadequate to an adequate understanding of the universe. On the one hand the earlier, simpler structures provide just as valid a way of experiencing 'the ever-present origin' as the later, more complex structures. Secondly, the experience of time as linear and sequential (and consequently the very notion of evolution) belongs to a specific structure of consciousness – the mental/rational structure – and is in no way an essential attribute of time.
8. Gebser was reluctant to attach a chronology to the mutations of consciousness. I have followed Feuerstein's chronology here. See Feuerstein, op. cit. Gebser was more interested in exploring twentieth century culture than developing a chronology of the evolution of consciousness.
9. Karl Jaspers (1953) argued that there was a distinct shift in the nature of thinking in the centuries following 900 BCE, and that this occurred simultaneously in Greece, Western Asia, China, and India. He referred to this period as the *axial age.*
10. The mental structure of consciousness endured for some centuries outside continental Europe, e.g. in the Byzantine, Iranian, and Arab world. Gebser restricted himself to analyzing the structures of consciousness for which he found evidence in Western Europe. This is not surprising, considering the difficulties of pursuing his research as a refugee in war-time and post-war Europe.
11. Gebser himself avoided referring to 'layers' or 'levels' of consciousness, on the grounds that the terms were embedded in a spatial, hierarchical metaphor. More recently emerging structures should not be valued as 'superior' to earlier ones. Nor should they be regarded as determined by the earlier ones.
12. The archaic, undifferentiated union of human and environment was first called 'participation mystique' by Levy-Bruhl in *La Mentalite Primitive* (1922). In the face of adverse criticism he later modified his theory, but the phrase has been adopted by many later theorists, to refer to the consciousness both of primal human beings and of newborn infants.
13. E Neumann (1973) *The Origins and History of Consciousness*, p. 16. Gebser does not talk about the unconscious, but rather refers to different degrees of consciousness.
14. See M Donald, op. cit.
15. ibid., p. 163.
16. Fractals are geometric objects that demonstrate self-similarity across several size scales. For discussion of the applicability of fractal geometry to human events and processes see R Robertson & A Combs (1995) *Chaos Theory in Psychology and the Life Sciences.*
17. M Wheatley (1999) *Leadership and the New Science*, p. 128.
18. Donald is careful to distinguish between mimesis on the one hand and mimicry and imitation on the other. Mimesis is not mere duplication of another's behavior as externally observed. It involves intentional representation. When an infant waves her hand or shakes her head she is expressing meaning and feeling, not merely copying an action she has seen. And she performs this action before she ever has the words (or thoughts) to be aware that she is integrating action, meaning, and feeling in this way. See Donald, op.cit., p. 169.

19. See Jaynes, op. cit. We are also aware of such phenomena as 'driving trance', where we can drive long distances and perform quite complex operations without any awareness. Our 'robot' is not dependent on awareness to operate efficiently in many circumstances.
20. See K Egan (1997) *The Educated Mind.*
21. ET Hall (1976) *Beyond Culture*, p.72ff. See also Hall (1984) *The Dance of Life.*
In Complex Responsive Processes in Organizations, Ralph Stacey (2001) develops a similar theme in discussing the ways human beings communicate with each other. Our relationships are essentially the responses of bodies to each other. He writes of 'protoconversation' as 'the unconscious communication of feelings as bodily resonance, expressing the need to be met and understood at a deep existential level, in the realm of sensuous lived experience, which is ultimately what gives meaning to life 'It seems to me that it is in the rhythmic, protoconversational exchange between us that a felt sense of reality, of existing, continually emerges. Protoconversations take a theme-and-variation format, with patterns of beat, rhythm, duration, and intensity. Through them, we directly express in our looking, vocalizing and touching, the rhythms and intensities of our bodily experience, our own temporal feeling dynamic, thereby evoking responses in terms of feeling rhythms from others.' p. 104.
22. See R Schaffer & H Thomson (1992) 'Successful Change Programs Begin with Results', *Harvard Business Review*
23. G Hofstede (1980) *Culture's Consequences* p. 114 ff.
24. T Abt (1989) *Progress Without Loss of Soul*, p. 264.
25. See IS Sampson (1973) *The Sovereign State.*
26. Magic is conventionally distinguished from religion on the basis that whereas magic attempts to change the world directly by the performance of ritual actions, religion appeals to higher beings through prayer and ritual to change the world on our behalf. Religion in this sense is the product of mythical consciousness.
27. Presentation at Group Dynamics workshop, Clear Mountain, Brisbane, Australia, in Sept 1997.
28. AN Whitehead in *Modes of Thought* (1938) attests to the power of myth to resist the evidence. Referring to the 'commonsense' picture of the universe as composed of 'bits of matter', enduring in space which is otherwise empty, an image which has been accepted since about 1500, he argues that '... the development of natural science has gradually discarded every single feature of the original common-sense notion. Nothing whatever remains of it, considered as expressing the primary features in terms of which the universe is to be interpreted. The obvious common-sense notion has been entirely destroyed, so far as concerns its function as the basis for all interpretation ... [Yet] this common-sense notion still reigns supreme in the workaday life of mankind. It dominates the marketplace, the playgrounds, the law courts, and in fact the whole sociological intercourse of mankind. It is supreme in literature and is assumed in all the humanistic sciences.
'... The state of [recent] modern thought is that every single item in this general doctrine is denied, but that the general conclusions from the doctrine as a whole are tenaciously retained. The result is a complete muddle in scientific thought, in philosophic cosmology, and in epistemology.' p. 130f.
29. While there are differences in the way such writers as Stacey, Goldstein, Senge, and Wheatley understand complexity and apply the theory to organizational development, they are clearly working with the same organic image. There are different ways of theorizing chaos, non-linearity, and complexity, and these provide quite different ways of explaining in rational language the phenomena which present themselves as 'organic'.
30. See R Kegan (1994) .
31. DT Denhardt (1981), p. 38ff.
32. M Stein (1992) 'Organizational Life as Spiritual Practice' in M Stein & J Hollwitz, *Psyche at Work*, p. 4.
33. 'There are no whole truths; all truths are half-truths. It is trying to treat them as whole truths that plays the devil.' AN Whitehead in L Price (2001) *The Dialogues of Alfred North Whitehead*, Prologue.
34. Gebser's analysis of the emerging integral structure in the 1940s is in many respects parallel to the more recent analyses of postmodernity by such commentators as Lyotard and Baudrillard. Like them, he focuses on diversity, multiperspectivism, relativism, and process, and the apparent abandonment of dualism, rationalism, hierarchical structures, and all the 'grand narratives'. However, where postmodernist thinking leads to fragmentation through the 'deconstruction' of what has so far passed for reality, Gebser's interest was in integration - in gaining a new, intuitive grasp of the whole.
35. 'It is of fundamental importance that we clearly distinguish between 'irrational' and 'arational', for this distinction lies at the very heart of our deliberations. ... There is a fundamental distinction between the attempt to go beyond the merely measurable, knowing and respecting it while striving to be free from it, and rejecting and disregarding the measurable by regressing to the immoderate and unfathomable chaos of the ambivalent and even fragmented polyvalence of psychic and natural interrelation.' Gebser, *Origin*, p. 147.

36. For a discussion of the implications of time freedom for our experience of difference see J Murphy & M Jung (1992) 'Jean Gebser, The Commonweal and the Politics of Difference'.
37. Dimensionality is one characteristic by which Gebser distinguishes the structures. The archaic consciousness is zero-dimensional, magical consciousness is one-dimensional, mythical consciousness is two-dimensional, mental/rational consciousness is three-dimensional, and integral consciousness is four-dimensional. Jung also, in a number of different ways, insists that the psyche is four-dimensional: e.g. in his discussion of the trinity-quaternity and his discussion of the superior and inferior functions of the psyche.
38. See R Dawkins (1990) *The Selfish Gene.*

4

GODS, MYTHS AND ARCHETYPES

Images and Myths in Organizations

Archetypal psychology's preferred approach to understanding the unconscious patterns at work in an organization is through an exploration of the organization's myths. Wendy Doniger O'Flaherty defines myth as follows:

> A myth is a story that is sacred to and shared by a group of people who find their most important meanings in it; it is a story believed to have been composed in the past about an event in the past, or, more rarely, in the future, an event that continues to have meaning in the present because it is remembered; it is a story that is part of a larger group of stories.[1]

When we talk about myths we may fall into the trap of assuming that our listeners are giving the word the same meaning as we are. If our understanding of ancient myths is that they represent the deep truth about the universe as it was experienced by human beings before they learned the laws of logic, and that they still richly represent human experience, there can be some confusion when we are addressing people for whom it is axiomatic that myths are false. If we use the word in the popular sense of a story or belief that isn't true, we may not communicate with those with more romantic notions of myth.

Myths are both true and false. If we define truth in terms of 'objective facts', such truth may be irrelevant to myth. The truth of myth is not the truth of fact or logic. It is the truth of image. People carried images of what the world is like before they ever learned to have thoughts about it, or even to think of themselves as separate from it. The great myths carry these ancient images, expanded and refined over thousands of years, but maintaining their essential form. They have survived simply because they have never ceased to be true to people's experience of the world. We may pride ourselves on nearly three thousand years of rationality, but we have not outgrown our need to mythologize. We still comprehend the world through our myths. Even the most rational of us still act out the same patterns as our ancestors; we are still moved by the same images as moved them; and we still tell ourselves the same stories as our ancestors, and worship the same gods, no matter how thoroughly we may disguise them.

The great myths were not invented. They were not thought up by logical minds seeking an explanation for some phenomenon or other. The myths were originally experienced, not told and recorded. Pre-rational humans lived in a world of energies that they did not understand and did not control, energies that were larger and more powerful than they, energies that they felt to be alive. Primal human lives were lived in the interplay of these energies that were acted out in ritual long before people learned to tell stories. When they did come to tell stories, the stories they told reflected their experience of those energies as living beings.

There is little to be gained by trying to establish an authentic 'original' version of the great myths. Human beings experienced the gods long before they had a verbal language in which to express this experience. The earliest imagining of the divine seems to have come from primitive humans' experience of the Earth as the Mother who gives us birth, feeds us and eventually devours us, so that eventually new life came to be personified as a child, and the eternal cycle of birth, growth, death, and decay came to be imagined through the ritual and narrative of the Great Mother and her Divine Child. It was only very recently, in the last few thousand years, that changing environmental, political, and social conditions brought the Father and his Hero-Son into the story.

It is important to recognize that myths have two kinds of origin. In the first place, myths represent humanity's primal experience of the world. In the second place, with the development of psychological, social, and political life, myths could be consciously modified or constructed to represent the new ways that life was experienced. The myths of the great classical civilizations come to us as literary representations of 'the way the world is' in particular sophisticated and complex civilizations. Or rather, of 'the ways the world is', for the polytheism of classical civilizations represents an ability to hold more than one perspective on life.

It used to be commonplace to talk about mythical thinking as something peculiarly characteristic of primitive human beings, who did not have the capacity to think about the world in an abstract, rational way as we do. Primitive humans, it was understood, thought in pictures and experienced the natural world as the interplay of gods, whom they imagined vividly, and about whom they told the stories we know as myths. But as they evolved the ability to think rationally, they ceased to need these myths as explanations of the way the world is. Mythical thinking came to be seen as an inferior form of thinking that modern 'civilized' human beings had outgrown.

In the past few decades it has become conventional to speak more respectfully of mythical and magical thinking. This is largely through the influence of Freud (who demonstrated that we all engage in a great deal of magical and mythical thinking, whether we acknowledge it or not) and Jung (who argued that mythical thinking is as necessary and as valid a way of approaching the world as rational thinking). Similarly, Gebser argued that the mythical structure of consciousness was not simply a primitive structure that we have outgrown, or that is latent in us but irrelevant; within its limitations, it provides as valid a way of experiencing the world as the rational structure. More recently we have seen brain research differentiate between 'left-brain' and 'right-brain' functions, and this has led to a revaluation of the 'right-brain' functions associated with mythologizing.

At any rate, when we talk about myths nowadays, we accept that myths do not belong only to people in pre-scientific cultures. We can examine the mythology of contemporary, sophisticated organizations, just as we can examine the myths of ancient, tribal cultures. When we do this we are likely to find, strangely enough, that the myths of contemporary organizations and those of ancient cultures have a great deal in common. We find in organizational mythologies both the traces of primal myths, pointing past themselves to mysteries of universal import, and the conscious or unconscious generation of 'local' myths that explain what needs to be explained or emphasize what needs to be emphasized in the organization's meaning system. What is fascinating for a student of myths is the ways in which even these culturally generated myths reproduce variations on the 'old stories'.

In the context of contemporary organizations, we can say that a myth is the narrative constructed by the people of an organization to embody a theory that explains their experience of themselves and their world. Every organization develops such narratives in order that people can understand, share and use them to define themselves. Implicitly, the members acknowledge that the narrative, the story, has meaning for all of them and that it provides a moral system through which they can make decisions and go about their work together. The story does not have to be 'true' in any factual sense, but is believed and communicated because it carries the organization's meaning and identity.

Organizational myths emerge out the experience of a group of people and they provide a medium of expression for the underlying strata of the group's awareness. Myths are not time-dependent. They talk about the past and present (and sometimes the future) simultaneously. They allow a group to discern the essential meaning they give to their collective existence. They become vehicles for deeper insight into the day-to-day experience of people in groups, organizations and, communities.

Joseph Campbell distinguishes four different functions of a living mythology. The first he calls the *metaphysical-mystical* function:

> . . . to awaken and maintain in the individual a sense of awe, humility, and respect, in recognition of that ultimate mystery, transcending names and forms, 'from which' as we read in the Upanishads, 'words turn back'.[2]

Campbell's statement assumes that human beings have some sort of natural religious sense, a tendency to find 'numinosity' in the universe. There is enough evidence of this in human experience for organizations to go to great lengths to provide their members with objects of religious devotion. We find this phenomenon even in avowedly atheistic political systems, as in the elevation of Lenin and Mao to objects of worship and their tombs to shrines. We find it no less in commercial organizations and football clubs, where 'ancestor worship' is promoted as a way of focusing people's natural religiosity in the interests of group cohesion or 'club spirit'.

Campbell calls the second function of a mythology *cosmological*. Myths explain where things come from, how they work, why they are the way they are.

> The second function of a mythology is to render a cosmology, an image of the universe, and for this we all turn today, of course, not to archaic religious texts but to science.[3]

Of course, the mythologies of some organizations promote explanations that have little to do with the respect for hard evidence and logical thought by which science likes to identify itself. However, Campbell is making the point that, on the one hand, such mythologies function as explanatory systems for pre-scientific humans the way science is supposed to function for us now, and that on the other hand, science itself functions for us as a mythology, doing for us what stories of the gods did for pre-scientific peoples.

The third function is a *social* or *moral* one. Myths support and validate the current social order within an organization.

> . . . the enforcement of a moral order, the shaping of the individual to the requirements of his [sic] geographically and historically conditioned social group.[4]

We see myths functioning in this way in many contemporary organizations. Stories of the feats of former heroic leaders, dedicated workers, or brilliant sales people, and stories of the punishment exacted on the slack or unworthy, constantly assert what sort of behavior is valued in the organization. Or alternatively, in an oppressive organization the most repeated stories may be stories of successful attempts to beat the bosses and the system.

Campbell's fourth function is a psychological one. Myth functions to foster '*the centering* and unfolding of the individual in integrity'.[5] Each of us has our own responsibility to achieve integrity through the creation of our own unique and authentic story in tension with the established mythology of our culture.

> Creative mythology . . . springs not, like theology, from the dicta of authority, but from the insights, sentiments, thoughts, and vision of an adequate individual, loyal to his [sic] own experience of value. Thus it corrects the authority holding to the shells of forms produced and left behind by lives once lived. Renewing the act of experience itself, it restores to existence the quality of adventure, at once shattering and reintegrating the fixed, already known, in the sacrificial creative fire of the becoming thing that is not thing at all but life, not as it *will* be or as it *should be*, as it *was* or as it *never will be*, but as it is, in depth, in process, *here and now*, inside and out.[6]

This tension between the metaphysics, cosmology, and morality expressed in the collective mythology of nation, tribe, or organization, and the individual's need to create a meaning system that is true to his or her unique experience of the world, is particularly powerful in the present age. The spread of education and increasing access to knowledge about other organizations and to critiques of our own has ensured that acceptance of a nation's or organization's mythology by its members is no longer automatic. Doubt and change are becoming constant conditions rather than occasional aberrations. In many organizations the living mythology is a mythology in constant process of creation out of the members' experience. Meanwhile, the mythology promulgated by the executive and the public relations manager is dead or dying. Where management has employed consultants to initiate a cultural change involving a re-writing of the organization's myths, the mythology is usually *born* dead.

The same is true of ritual. We are reminded of a scientific organization with which we are familiar. The new CEO had taken over and arranged for the amalgamation of former separate but similar organizations into the larger one. He had also become recently aware of the power of both ritual and mythology, and went to great pains to create a new story for the new organization, and especially for those who were being annexed from the other place into this new creation. Stories honoring its past were told. Stories for its future were created. New rituals were enacted. But in the time since then, all the members of the annexed organization remember not these events, but the funeral soon thereafter of one of their former colleagues. It was at his funeral and wake that they told for themselves the stories of their past that mattered to them. It is widely felt in the organization that it was only with the passing of this colleague and the telling of the old stories that they were finally able to let go of the past and allow themselves to become part of the new CEO's grand dream for the future.

Myth is generally more powerful than history. Myth resists or distorts 'the facts' with great tenacity. Mircea Eliade points out the tendency of people's memories of actual events to shift towards some version of an 'old story' rather than stick to the historical facts.[7] We have plenty of evidence of the ability of political and religious groups to hang on to a story that outside observers can see to be a distortion of history, or even of current events. The continuing struggle between competing stories of civilization and dispossession in many parts of the globe shows the resilience of myths and their capacity to distort or deny any new information that purports to present the 'real facts' of history.

Organizational myths are vehicles for understanding the images that drive and grip organizations. One client group we have worked with is a unit within a large federal government department. Over the time we spent time with them, we heard many stories. Like many other organizations, these were stories of the past. Only the past went back to 45 years ago and finished about 20 years ago. (Not one of the current employees had worked in this unit for more than 11 years!) The stories told of how they were the original department, how they once had nearly four times the number of staff than currently, how they achieved great things, how they had pioneered many innovative practices in their time. These stories of a 'golden age' evoked images of past potency, of past power, of past creativity. They implied present impotency, present powerlessness, present flatness.

The scope and applicability of organizational myths can range from sub-cultures within organizations, through to the organization as a whole, and even beyond the organization into the wider environment. The archetypal psychologist seeks understanding through discerning, exploring, and playing with the images latent in the myths. She seeks to understand the least conscious and deepest depths of a group in order to appreciate better the more surface elements. The power of a myth is as much visual and kinesthetic as it is verbal. Wendy Doniger O'Flaherty highlights this when she states:

> The myth combines the functions of philosophy (the plot of the myth: what happens, and why) with the symbolism of ritual and cosmology (the actors in the myth: gods, animals, elemental powers). Myths are both events and images, verbs and nouns. To analyze a myth in terms of either element alone is to reduce and distort it.[8]

Myths are imaginal manifestations of archetypal patterns, but they are not the only manifestations. Following Gebser's model of the structures of consciousness, we can see the regularities we call archetypal patterns[9] being manifested in different ways in each of the structures. In archaic consciousness they are manifested in sensation and instinctual behavior. In magical consciousness they are manifested in emotion, ritual, taboo, and compulsive behavior. In mythical consciousness they are expressed in image and myth, and in the values and meanings these carry. In mental-rational consciousness they find expression in ideas, perspectives, ideologies and belief systems.

It is myth that we wish to deal with in particular, but myth and ritual are intricately connected, as are myth and belief, so both rational and magical structures are necessarily included in this discussion.

One of our tasks in studying an organization is to discover the myths that are idiosyncratic to the organization and to compare them with more universal images. Studying specific organizational myths is but the first step on an archetypal journey. A richer and deeper insight into these specific organizational myths can then be derived by comparing them with the 'old stories'. The 'old stories' can be found in Roman,

Egyptian, Phoenician, Celtic, Teutonic, Persian, Indian, Chinese, Japanese, Oceanic, Amerindian, African, or Greek mythologies; indeed, in any of the 'grand' mythologies. The particular source for our comparisons in this book will be Greek mythology, because our observations specifically concern organizations that have been constructed within European or post-colonial cultures, and such cultures have been largely shaped by the myths of Greco-Roman civilization. [10]

Working with archetypal images arising from organizational myths becomes a way for celebration and affirmation, for wonder, order, and insight. When a person senses that there is a mythic dimension to something that he is undertaking, the knowledge that arises from this awareness touches him deeply and creatively. The same is true of organizations as a whole. Myths evoke feeling and imagination and touch on themes that are part of our collective inheritance. They take us beyond personal experience to tribal and even species experience.

Habits of Imagination

It is tempting and easy to take a simplistic view of myths. One such view is that they represent fixed and stable ancient patterns in which we are still embedded and which determine the ways we experience, imagine, think, and behave. Another is that they are stories that we collectively make up to explain the ways we experience, imagine, think, and behave. Or again, that they are stories that the powerful members of society make up to ensure that those whom they control experience, imagine, think, and behave in ways that maintain the status quo and the power of their masters. One way of dealing with this complexity is to suggest that the word myth has quite different meanings; 'pretend' myths are untrue and changeable, while 'real' myths are ancient and immutable. We suggest that this is a nonsense. We suggest that myths are all of these things: archetypal image, creative imagination, and social engineering are forever in tension in our mythology.[11]

A lot of 'Jungian' writers reduce myth to the first of the above definitions, but this is not true to Jung's own position. Archetypal images, in Jung's way of thinking, are both 'given' and 'created'. On the one hand, they reflect the enormous influence of the past on our behavior; our tendency to imagine the world in certain ways is inherited, grounded in instincts that are themselves grounded in our biology. On the other hand, we are constantly creating new ways of symbolizing our experience, putting it into words and images that will contain it and enable it to be communicated to others. As human experience changes, the old images may become less able to symbolize our experience and we create new ones. Certainly, in classical Jungian thought, archetypes exist as transcendent forms, but they cannot be known in themselves. The archetypes themselves have no content; they only get content when they enter time and space. We do not experience them in 'pure' form, but only in images and behaviors that are inevitably conditioned by their social, historical, and political context.

There appears to be no question that myths are sometimes constructed and spread by those in power in order to maintain their power. We can find myths to justify practices of social control that we might find morally repugnant or aesthetically disgusting; genital mutilation, infanticide, slavery, wife-beating, and ethnic cleansing all find mythological justification. Such myths may be grounded in deliberate lies or distortions of history. Nationalism, fascism, and racism depend on them. In an organization we may find official propaganda in the shape of stories to illustrate the heroism of the firm's founder, the loyalty of the guru's disciples in previous times of crisis, the wisdom of the current management. The increasing trend to use multi-media in quite sophisticated ways inside organizations to create myths around a newly arrived CEO is a pattern we find very familiar. The stories may be originally based in deliberate lies, in some group's belief about what might be the most appropriate image to create, or simply in some one's psychological need to believe; they become myths when they become part of the collective imaginal life of the clan, nation, or organization. We also find myths created and adopted by the oppressed to underline their difference from, and even their moral superiority to, their oppressors. The archetypal psychologist will be inclined to see both the oppressors' myths and the myths of the oppressed as versions of 'old stories'. There do seem to be 'regularities' in the ways in which what Gebser calls 'the mythical structure of consciousness' deals with experience.

There is a tendency among romantic 'new age' Jungians to believe that archetypes exist as stable and unchanging entities outside of time and space waiting to find concrete expression. Yet we find that myths and other archetypal expressions are enmeshed in both physiology and culture. There is a tendency also to regard the archetypes, or the myths that are their imaginal expression, as repositories of ancient wisdom. Yet we see that, while societies may use myths to make a metaphysical or moral point, they can also use them to justify oppression or other evils.

What sort of truth can lies have? We can reiterate Joseph Campbell's assertion that myths do not describe the world the way used to be, or the way it ought to be, but the way it is '. . . in depth, in process, here and now, inside and out'.[12] Moreover they represent regularities in the way we experience the world. The violent or oppressive social system is one aspect of how the world is and the myth that represents it is 'true'. (It certainly does not contain ancient wisdom about how the world ought to be.) The violent or oppressive social system is certainly a pattern that recurs regularly in human collective experience. It is also a pattern that recurs *inside* – in individual internal experience – when one part of the personality oppresses the rest. Some essentialist and simplistic explanations of archetype would lead to the conclusion that this pattern is inevitable because there is an ultimately real 'archetype' that determines it. We acknowledge rather more complexity than this. Such explanations make sense within a static, clockwork universe, but it is over a hundred years since science last found a static clockwork universe. We prefer to see myth within the image of an evolving universe. Besides, we prefer to take an agnostic position as regards ultimate reality and content ourselves with understanding myth, not as representing a transcendent reality, but as representing human experience.

It makes some sense to think of our mythology as the outcome of a natural selection process. Literature is full of stories of heroes who establish their independence, go on some necessary journey, perform difficult tasks, and slay the dragon or the bad guys. The story is common also in the mythologies of organizations. This story obviously has survival value. In romantic novels we still find the story of the young girl who is swept off her feet (or raped) by an older (and fabulously wealthy) man and carried off to his dark world where she becomes queen. And we find the same story re-enacted in some business takeovers. Some stories (like those of Herakles and Persephone) successfully represent psychological experience and survive. Others are rejected and forgotten. This explanation is all right as far as it goes, but it does not account for the felt power of myth.

The power of myth to influence our perception and behavior and the 'numinous' quality that we sometimes experience when caught up in one of the 'old stories', comes in part from its grounding in instinct, in the primitive patterns that precede human awareness. Rupert Sheldrake[13] uses the language of field theory to explain instincts, calling them 'habits of nature' which set up 'morphogenetic fields' which in turn make the same events more likely to happen again. According to his hypothesis of morphic causation, the more times a particular event is repeated, the more likely it is that a present member of the species will repeat this event.

> New bodily forms can arise suddenly, for example as a result of genetic mutations or unusual environmental conditions, and so can new patterns of behavior. These are then subject to natural selection, and the selected, oft-repeated patterns become increasingly habitual. According to the hypothesis of formative causation, this happens not only because of genetic inheritance, but also because of morphic resonance from previous similar organisms.[14]

This has a great deal in common with a Jungian understanding of archetypes, which, as Jung says, 'can only be explained by assuming them to be deposits of the constantly repeated experiences of humanity.'[15] For Sheldrake, as for Jung, our instincts, our inclination to behave in specific ways and our individual and collective memory are all aspects of the same phenomenon – they are our past (our species past, our tribal/ cultural past, and our individual past) still living in us in the present moment.[16]

Myth-finding and Myth-making

The executive, consultant, or other change-agent who takes myth seriously has the twin tasks of myth-finding and myth-making.[17] Myth-finding involves 'seeing through' the organization's artifacts, beliefs, symbols, and local narratives to the old stories and the gods who people them, on the understanding that 'something archetypal is going on' in even the most trivial behaviors and events.

Having done that, what next? - other than announce that an 'archetypal' pattern has been detected, that this organization has an obsession with its golden age, or has a hero-inflation, or is populated by Father-worshippers, or is infatuated with progress? A label is just a label, but does not have much explanatory value. Even when we go further and point to the god behind the organization's particular energy – Kronos, Herakles, Zeus, or Prometheus – we may not have added anything besides confusion. Pointing to an archetypal pattern in an organization does not necessarily reveal anything. It simply imposes a particular template on a complex phenomenon. The problem with templates is that they give us an illusion of clarity by hiding most of the information.

There are certain kinds of rewards in being the expert archetypal analyst and interpreter who studies the organization and announces that it 'is a Zeus organization' or 'has an Eros culture' or 'is suffering a Hermes inflation', but these rewards have little to do with enduring transformation in organizations. The expert diagnose-and-fix-it approach, besides entrapping us in the narcissism of the consultant, takes us back to the clockwork universe of the eighteenth century. Organizational transformation demands more than that.

Archetypal work with organizations involves the change agent in helping the organization to become conscious of dimensions of its experience of which it is normally only dimly aware. More than that, it involves helping the organization to acknowledge and own these dimensions of experience. This is not something that can be achieved by studying an organization within an archetypal framework and then presenting a report.

Personal transformation involves an ongoing dialogue between the conscious and unconscious dimensions of an individual's personality, so that both one's understanding of oneself and the freedom of one's action are enhanced and expanded. We suggest that the same is true in organizational transformation. The consultant's most useful contribution is to facilitate a similar dialogue between the conscious and unconscious dimensions of the organization's identity, so that the organization gains access to all that it is and all that it has the potential to be. It involves the consultant being in a collaborative I-thou relationship with the organization. Within such a relationship myth-finding can be transformative of and by itself.

Archetypal investigation of an organization looks for the present in the past and the past in the present. And it looks for the future in both. The organization's collective memory is trawled for stories and practices of the 'old days', with an eye to the endurance of the same patterns in the present; the organization's current stories and practices are examined with an eye to the organization's imaginal history. Through both processes we become aware of organizational habits of imagining the organization and its relation to the world outside it. Present experience loses its uniqueness and becomes something that is shared by others over time. But it is not presented as something static. Against the background of real and imagined history, present experience can be presented as process, a point in a trajectory from past to future.

This collaborative myth-finding can unearth both authentic and inauthentic myths. Authentic myths are lived by the organization and contain the values and meanings that are shared by the organization's members. Inauthentic myths may have been inherited from the organization's past history, and still adhered to, at least notionally, even though they no longer represent the organization's experience. Or they may have been thrust upon the organization by management in an attempt to manipulate the organizational culture, but have never been owned and lived by the members. Inauthentic myths may indeed be versions of the 'old stories', but they are not true to the organization's current experience.

This kind of inauthenticity is common in organizations of all kinds. We have seen a sustained propaganda exercise in Anglo-Saxon countries over the past two decades to persuade their populations that an unregulated global market is the key to universal prosperity and happiness. The lack of solid evidence that this is true has not greatly inhibited the spread of the myth, to the degree that people now commonly talk the language of economic rationalism and fast capitalism as though they were referring to universal truths rather than to a fantasy promulgated by those who stand to profit by it.

There are academic departments in universities whose self-image and consciously espoused values are conveyed in a myth of intellectual rigor and commitment to the advancement of understanding, yet whose behavior can be seen as an increasingly flexible response to market forces. There are community organizations whose self-image and values are carried in a history of liberating the oppressed and distressed, but whose current activities and constraints now make them agents of social control on behalf of the State. There are churches that talk the talk of spirituality, morality, and service to God's children, while the energies of their leaders are devoted to the less heavenly concerns of property and power.

In the myth-finding process, the emergence of such contradictions can be disturbing. But disturbance is essential to change.

The myth-making process starts from here. It is simplistic to say: 'The organization's mythology represents the real organization. Its current behavior is inauthentic. We must change our behavior to fit the traditional mythology'. It is equally simplistic to say: 'The organization's current behavior represents the real organization; the traditional or official mythology represents an organization that no longer exists or never existed. We must create a new mythology to fit our changed circumstances and identity'. Behavior is not always a good indicator of who we 'really' are. It can be copied inappropriately from others, or adopted to satisfy some higher authority, or forced upon us by the need to survive in a hostile environment. The inauthentic behavior and the going along with an inauthentic mythology are elements of the complexity that makes up the organizational identity. We are not dealing here with a shift from one steady state to another steady state. What the consultant must do in myth-finding is to recognize that the organization is in process, and help it to become aware of that process. It is an axiom of this approach that the organization is purposive, that it has an organic life that is more than the sum of the lives of its members, and that the direction of this life is not only to survive but to enhance the quality of its life.

When, in this process, the organization finds itself to be living in 'false consciousness' through its acceptance of an inauthentic mythology, it is really finding something it already knows. When experience and its symbolization do not match, the incongruence is felt and expressed, if not in words then in physical or psychological symptoms – stress, absenteeism, workplace accidents, interpersonal conflict, scapegoating. Organizations entrapped in this kind of inauthenticity are in a state of ethical or ideological doubt, where people's expression of the dissonance and discomfort they feel is still constrained by a degree of hope. If the organization has already reached the state of absolute doubt, they are not even pretending to accept the organization's inauthentic mythology.

In the exploration of organizational myths, attention must be paid to the 'alternative narratives' – the 'deviant' or 'marginal' stories that do not figure in the official organizational mythology. Myths are repetitive; we tell the same story over and over. Adherence to a single dominant myth in an organization gives stability, but inhibits both change and creativity – which are dependent on the experience of discomfort or contradiction. If stability is what the organization wants, if it exists within a stable environment and has no desire or need to change, living within a single myth may be feasible and safe. Yet we cannot depend on stable environments any more.

We do not expect the culture of a healthy contemporary organization to be unitary. Where there is an attempt to impose a unitary culture, alternative value systems and the stories that embody them are being suppressed. If we are to unlock the energy of the organization to allow transformation, the alternative myths have to be allowed to emerge, not for the purpose of imposing a different unitary culture, but to discover the organization's unique 'personality' through the plurality of its cultures and the relationships and tensions between them. For an organization wishing to flourish in a postmodern, relativistic environment, identity and cohesion can no longer be founded on the unitary fantasy. The fantasy of belief in and commitment to a single dominant narrative is certainly still attractive to many people, but we suggest it is no longer a viable option. For better or worse, late twentieth-century consciousness in advanced democracies turned from the assumption that truth is one to the assumption that truth is many. An authentic organizational mythology will be pluralistic.

In undertaking mythmaking to stimulate organizational transformation, the change agent within or outside the organization is engaged in the task of helping the organization to express its experience and identity symbolically. It is not enough to understand conceptually where the organization has been, how it responds to current circumstances and where it may go in the future. Human beings are imagining, symbolizing entities, and their collectives – families, tribes, nations, or organizations – are imagining, symbolizing entities. Individuals and organizations, we suggest, function more basically in terms of symbolic images than they do in terms of literal concepts and are moved more fundamentally by images than by concepts. We would argue further that, while the organization is indeed a collection of individual members who may be stimulated and motivated by concepts, the organization as an organic whole functions through the more fundamental archaic, magical, and mythical structures.[1] Though the organization may claim to be guided by shared ideas and principles, these ideas and principles are likely to be embedded in an ideology whose self-evident truth is taken for granted rather than subjected to any testing critique. An ideology may be dressed up as a set of concepts, but it usually a way of telling the organization's story about itself. In other word, it belongs to the mythical structure of consciousness rather than the mental.

Gods and Archetypes

Myths become constellated into mythologies, and mythologies are particularly fertile fields for the person seeking an understanding of the unconscious in organizations. They contain within them god-symbols – manifestations of archetypal motifs. Of all the possible archetypal motifs, the god-symbols have the greatest energy associated with them. And, like the myths, the god-symbols are rooted in the deep past.

The use of the Greco-Roman gods as metaphors for different perspectives on life, different patterns of behavior, different constellations of values, needs, instincts, and habits, has been conventional in most of European history. When Jung developed his own archetypal theory, he continued in this poetic tradition, finding the manifestations of the gods in personal and collective behavior and convinced that the archetypal images are most powerfully and resonantly manifested in the great myths. Contemporary archetypal psychologists continue to use the same language and share the same conviction. They concentrate their attention on the patterns they find in our ways of apprehending the universe and of acting in it. They are fascinated by the recurring patterns in our ways of imagining the world, in our cultural movements, in our architecture, in our scientific paradigms, in our dreams, in our diseases, in our obsessions, in our relationships, in our organizations. They find that mythical or metaphorical thinking offers a fruitful way of exploring them. Each of the god-images personifies a different way of apprehending and comprehending the world.

For thousands of years, human beings imagined the energies of the universe as gods. God-archetypes still achieve the greatest momentum in the individual and corporate psyche and they are the most autonomous, i.e. the least able to be controlled. Jung found god-archetypes to be expressions of the life energy within individuals and groups. Because they are largely autonomous it is possible for individuals and groups to become over-identified with a particular archetypal god-images, to become possessed by them and engage in exaggerated one-sidedness. The unconscious within the corporate organism can become unbalanced.

It has become unconventional to use the word 'god' outside a very narrow sense, but there are plenty of people who might plausibly be accused of worshipping wealth or pleasure or technology, of committing their lives to this worship, of sacrificing all else to it, of treating wealth, pleasure, or technology as transcendent values worthy of their entire devotion. There are plenty of people who are taken over by an obsession with wealth, pleasure, or technology (or lust, work, gambling, or alcohol) so that they appear to be no longer in control of their actions. The ancient Greeks and other polytheistic peoples would see here the presence and action of a god who has a name, a personality, and a story. We may pride ourselves on our rationality, on our detachment from such superstitions, but there are levels of our consciousness at which we still respond to the world and its events in the magical-mythical ways of our biological and cultural ancestors.

The gods and myths of the classical Greeks are the gods and myths of an urban, sophisticated, self-reflective people, with a complex social and political system, and a highly developed cultural life. They wove a web of myths from many sources to represent the complexity of life, a web of overlapping and interpenetrating personalities and stories that provided a rich source of meaning for the philosophers and poets of the European Renaissance and that now serves the same function for contemporary archetypal psychologists. The patterns we find in European culture in the late twentieth century are not entirely new patterns. The stories through which we construct and express the meaning of our lives are rarely new stories. The conflicts between competing meanings and competing values are not new. The same squabbling gods whom Homer described are still present in our personalities and in our institutions.

The Greeks did not believe that the number of gods was infinite, but they did find them too many to count. Jung, on the other hand, seems to have entertained the notion that there are a limited number of archetypes and that he would eventually have names for them all. For Jung, ego and self, persona and shadow, animus and anima were all suitable labels for archetypal structures and he was careful to distinguish them from one another. Later archetypal psychologists are somewhat less fussy about essential distinctions between this archetype and that. They can see that if we chose to work with the Hindu or Celtic pantheon rather than the Greek, we would be dealing with the same energies and issues, but they would be distributed and packaged rather differently. Most contemporary archetypal psychologists are not much interested in archetypal structures as entities anyway. They do not focus on what reality is, but on how we now imagine it.

Each god-image has associated with it positive and affirmative functions. However, if an organization becomes gripped by those functions to the exclusion of all other god-images (or fails to recognize the darker and more shadowy aspect of each god-image), then they become dysfunctional, pathological. To use John Sherwood's language, there is a breakdown in the purposes and directions the organization pursues (belief level) and ultimately a disintegration of its practices and procedures (norm level).

The Gods of Ancient Greece

The people we call Greeks (and who called themselves Hellenes) entered the Balkan Peninsula in successive migratory waves between about 2000 and 900 BC. They were an Indo-European people (like the Latins, Celts, Persians, and Germans) who seem to have originated somewhere north of the Black Sea. They were a nomadic, cattle-driving, horse-riding people who worshipped a family of sky-gods. The society of the gods, like their own tribal society, was dominated by the most powerful male – Dan or Zdan, the Thunder-god. When they entered Greece they found the land inhabited by a peaceful, agricultural people who worshipped the Great Goddess, in her various manifestations. In particular they worshipped her as the Earth-mother, who gave birth to them, fed them, and took them back to herself. With her they worshipped her divine boy-child, who died each Winter and was born again each Spring. Their social and political system, like their religion, was matricentric. The role of men seems to have been minor. These people were no match, in either aggression or military technology, for the invaders, and the society that emerged from the conquest was a strongly patriarchal one. However, the Greeks did not suppress the indigenous religion, but incorporated the old nature-gods into the family of their sky-gods. The different local forms of the Great Goddess became the wives, lovers, and daughters of the Thunder-god, and the divine boy-child under his different names became his sons. Besides this, there were other influences. All of the principal Greek gods are of mixed origin – Indo-European, Pelasgian, Cretan, or Asian – and there are residues of primitive animal-worship.

When the Greeks began to get a sense of themselves as a single people, after about 800 BC, they collected the tales of their various local gods and heroes into a body of songs and stories that spoke to them all. Homer's epics were not composed to be sung for a single local warlord and his court, but were meant to be heard and appreciated all over the Balkan Peninsula. By the sixth century BC the city-states each had an official pantheon of gods. It was agreed that there were twelve major gods who were most entitled to public honor and worship. Besides these, there were countless other gods and spirits who received special worship in particular places or on particular occasions. And there were countless nature gods, spirits of trees, caves, springs, and mountains, who were felt to be everywhere present.

Whatever the process by which the Greeks of the fifth century BC arrived at their official pantheon of twelve major gods, they gave European civilization a set of images that have been enormously powerful. The stone-age clan could find in the worship of the Earth-mother or the Thunder-god an adequate expression of their relationship to the universe. The universe in a sophisticated urban culture is a bit more complicated than this. One of these complications is in people's ability to reflect on their experience, so that the gods for the classical Greeks are images of psychological patterns as well as cosmic ones. They have remained so for us.

The Greeks knew they ought to have twelve key gods, like their Egyptian and Asian neighbors, but they could not quite agree on which twelve they should be. The identity of the twelve differed slightly from place to place. In the following chapters we have settled on sixteen gods of organization, omitting Poseidon (who is usually one of the twelve) and including Hades, Herakles, Prometheus and Eros (who are not). Both Dionysos and Hestia, who seem to share twelfth place, are included. There is no logical place to end a list like this and, having gone past the magic number of twelve, the next magic number of sixteen was as good a place to stop as any. Unfortunately, this means omitting not only Poseidon, but also Kronos, Hekate, Pan, and Persephone, not to mention the nymphs and satyrs and fates and furies, all of whom may be found to influence the culture of particular organizations.

Greek God-Images in Organizations

Each of the god-images within the Greek pantheon represents a powerful inner pattern at the level of deep unconscious assumptions within a group. The Greek myths or god-images remain current and personally relevant for they each resonate with a particular understanding of our shared human experience. When we seek to re-tell these myths in the context of the particular organization we are studying, we open ourselves up to the possibility of much intuitive understanding and insight.

So what then are the organizational god-images? They are all complex and multi-dimensional, and resist summary statement. Nevertheless, some such statement seems warranted here. How would we describe an organization that is given over to a particular god-energy, carried along by the myth of a particular god? The following summary is based in the first place on the personalities of the gods as represented in classical Greek mythology, and secondly on our experience of imposing this particular template on the organizations with which we have worked.

Aphrodite: An organization that focuses on beauty and pleasure, that seeks to be admired and desired.

Apollo: A rationally structured organization that seeks clarity, understanding, and meaning in all its activities.

Ares: An organization in which people challenge and are challenged, in which energy is expressed through activity.

Artemis: An organization that focuses on achieving harmony with nature, an environment in which the affirmation and protection of 'feminine' values is privileged.

Athena:	An organization characterized by cooperation, the sharing of power, the manifestation of balanced and practical wisdom.
Demeter:	An organization that mothers and nourishes its members.
Dionysos:	An organization that values growth, emotional excitement, spiritual experience, and rewards creativity and spontaneity.
Eros:	An organization that focuses on intimacy and community, in which people can express their need to love and be loved.
Hades:	An organization characterized by extreme indifference and apathy; an organization from which life has departed.
Hephaistos:	An organization devoted to the values of work, skill, and craft excellence.
Hera:	An organization that demands great commitment from its members, in which the members give organizational loyalty precedence over their individual needs.
Herakles:	An organization that sees itself involved in an heroic struggle.
Hermes:	An organization focused on communication, process, and transition, and which abhors all regulation.
Hestia:	An organization characterized by quiet, focused, centered, and receptive activity in the service of others.
Prometheus:	An organization with a mission to save humanity through the application of technology.
Zeus:	An organization based on centralized power.

In the following pages we will look at each of these gods more closely, pointing to the ways their presence and activity is discernible in organizations. Our examples will be taken from academic studies of organizations, from fiction, from history and from our own experience as consultants. Though we will treat the gods separately, we acknowledge that they never act alone. Even in an organization dominated by a particular god, the other gods are making their presence felt. Hera is harassing Dionysos and Herakles. Hermes is stealing Apollo's cattle or competing with him for the favor of Aphrodite. Demeter is making every one suffer out of her rage at Zeus. Athena, Hera, and Aphrodite are engaged in a beauty contest. Hephaistos is making Ares look ridiculous. Prometheus is undermining Zeus' power. The dynamics of organizational life echo the constant squabbling of the gods.

---

1. WD O'Flaherty (1984) *Dreams, Illusions and Other Realities*, p. 33.
2. J Campbell (1968) *The Masks of God*, p. 609.
3. ibid., p. 611.
4. ibid., p. 4.
5. ibid., p. 6.
6. ibid., p. 6. Emphases in original.
7. M Eliade (1991) *The Myth of the Eternal Return*, p. 43.
8. WD O'Flaherty, op, cit., p. 33. There used to be arguments among anthropologists as to whether myths were invented to explain magic rituals and dances, or whether the rituals and dances were invented to enact the myths. In Gebser's model, magical consciousness, in which ritual and dance are grounded, is prior to mythical consciousness. However myth does not depend on the pre-existence of ritual. Myth and ritual are different but connected expressions of a particular apprehension of the cosmos.
9. 'When we talk about myths as expressions of archetypal patterns, we are not talking about stereotypical patterns of behavior, which are sometimes confused with archetypes. We are talking rather of: 'invisible, unformed sources of light and radiance; a veritable 'Heraklitian fire' which has nothing cozy, secure, or comfortable about it. It is only the social engineering and manipulation of archetypes that produces stereotypes, those entirely predictable and usually conservative constructs of psychosocial reality.' D Tacey (1997) *Remaking Men*, p. 20.
10. This is not to suggest that these organizations are unaffected by other mythologies, including indigenous ones.
11. Gebser distinguishes between an 'efficient' and 'deficient' mythical structure of consciousness. The efficient mythical structure is found in the primal myths that directly represent human beings' experience of the cosmos. Literary myths and myths constructed for political purposes, emerge late in the 'mythical' era when the mythical structure has become exhausted and the mutation to mental consciousness is taking place. Such myths will be more or less 'deficient'.
12. Campbell, op. cit.., p.6. There is a tendency among some commentators on Jung's theory of archetypes to equate what is with what ought to be. Demaris Wehr makes this criticism of Jungian explanations of archetypes of the feminine and the anima. If archetypes are given status as eternal, unchanging entities, 'Jungian theory can function as a quasi-religious or scientific legitimation of the status quo in society, reinforcing social roles, constricting growth, and limiting options for women.' In E Lauter and CS Rupprecht (eds.) (1985) *Feminist Archetypal Theory*, p. 37. We acknowledge that the Greek pantheon as we know it, and which we use as a framework in this book, is largely a literary construction of the patriarchal society of classical Greece. However, we suggest that one reason why the Greek pantheon provides a useful framework for looking at the mythologies of contemporary organizations is that it reflects a society like our own, in which there is tension between essentially patriarchal power structures and a suppressed feminine energy.
13. Sheldrake's theory is developed in detail in *A New Science of Life: The Hypothesis of Formative Causation* (1981) and *The Presence of the Past: Morphic Resonance and the Habits of Nature* (1988).

14. R Sheldrake (1990) *The Rebirth of Nature*, p.109.
15. CW Jung, Collected Works 7: 109.
16. Sheldrake acknowledges the similarity between his biological theory and Jung's psychological one on this point: 'Individual memory and capacities for learning take place against the background of a collective memory inherited by morphic resonance from previous members of the species. In the human realm such a concept already exists in Jung's theory of the collective unconscious as an inherited collective memory. The hypothesis of morphic resonance enables the collective unconscious to be seen not just as a human phenomenon, but as an aspect of a far more general process by which habits are inherited throughout nature.' (1990) op. cit. p.94.
17. 'The process of understanding myths has often been called a science. I think it is an art. In any case, like both of these enterprises it proceeds through alternating phases of finding and making.' WD O'Flaherty op. cit., p. 297.
18. This is consistent with Gebser's conclusion that in the archaic and magical structure human beings have no sense of individual identity, and in the mythical structure have only a dim sense of it. Myth and the various forms of magic are by their very nature collective phenomena.

5

THE BOARD OF DIRECTORS

Zeus, Father of All

I shall sing of Zeus, the best and greatest of gods,
far-seeing, mighty, fulfiller of designs who confides
his tight-knit schemes to Themis as she sits leaning on him.
Have mercy, far-seeing Kronides, most glorious and great.[1]

Zeus is father of the divine family. He was originally the Thunderer, the Cloud-gatherer, the ancient and powerful weather-god who ruled the sky and dominated the consciousness of the Indo-European nomads. He was the personification of power. More exactly, he was the personification of male power, and he ruled the heavens the way the Indo-European warlord ruled his clan. Over the centuries he gradually became more benevolent until, partly through Jewish influence, he became the loving father 'in whom we live and move and have our being'. In the myths, however, which date from the Bronze Age and the Dark Age that followed it, he seems to have little interest in human beings, except for the occasional mortal woman whom he rapes or seduces.

Behind his benevolence, he is arrogant and capricious. He does exactly what he wants, beyond the rule of law. If he wants something, he takes it.

Zeus represents patriarchy. He is the last of the line of old gods who ruled by brute force. His grandfather, Uranus, was the ruthless ruler of the first age of all, the Golden Age, until he was mutilated and overthrown by his son, Kronos. Kronos, in his turn, was overthrown by his youngest son, Zeus. Zeus faced the same fate himself, until he learned from the cunning Titan, Prometheus, how he could avoid having the son who would usurp his throne, and how the best way to maintain his power unchallenged was to share a little of it with the other gods.

Zeus does not have to answer to anyone. He makes all the decisions, sometimes after a show of consultation with the other gods in Council. He punishes those who offend him but rewards with great generosity those who please him. But his rewards are as unpredictable as his punishments. He has favorites who can get away with behavior that would not be tolerated in others. He acts according to whim rather than according to reason. He is just, but he is the one who makes the laws anyway. Like the eagle, with which he was once identified, he hovers way above the common world and sees everything that goes on. And he swoops like lightning on those who offend him.

Zeus got his power over the universe by fighting for it, first against an older race of gods, the Titans, and then against the Giants who threatened his rule. The establishment of his rule, which meant the end of chaos and the beginning of order, was welcomed because order, even Zeus' autocratic order, was obviously better than the primitive savagery that came before it. As long as his rule is not challenged he can be benevolent and generous, but when he is challenged, for instance, by Prometheus (who helps men free themselves from Zeus' absolute power) he is ruthless in his retribution.

Some of the gods are friendly to mortals (e.g. Prometheus and Hermes) and prepared to descend to their level occasionally, but not Zeus. He always acts from a position of power, and when a human demands to see his face as his lover Semele does, the sight of it incinerates her. He spends a lot of his time keeping order, for human beings are on the whole a very inferior species, nasty and stupid and brutish. Zeus saves his worst punishments for those who forget their limits as human beings and try to behave like gods. He is very touchy about mere mortals who try to get above themselves. He uses his thunderbolt on Asclepius, the healer, for raising someone from the dead. He punishes Tantalus for giving away his secrets and Sisyphus for being too clever. (The former spends eternity surrounded by food and drink that he cannot quite reach. The latter forever rolls a rock up a hill and watches it roll down again.)

Zeus is productive, for all his many lovers bear him children. As a rule, however, he shows little interest in his offspring until they have made a name for themselves. His grandfather, Uranus, buried his children and his father, Kronos, ate his. Zeus belongs to this tradition of paranoia. He swallows one of his wives (Metis) because he fears her child will overthrow him. Only after he finds out how to preserve his power forever can he afford to become less savage.

Examining the Zeus archetype in organizations seems to come down to the examination of the personality of the chief executive and how he (almost invariably he) operates. This is the nature of the Zeus organization, where the boss is everywhere present and his power is effectively absolute. He is not anybody's agent, is beholden to nobody, makes the laws, and sees that they are carried out. He surrounds himself with executives whose status comes from their closeness to him. All power comes from above, as do truth, justice, self-esteem, and condemnation. It is difficult to escape the presence of the all-knowing, all-seeing, all-powerful one who hands out his bounty with one hand and hurls his thunderbolt with the other. Rewards are as unpredictable and arbitrary as punishments, for no one must think of deserving them

Sometimes the Zeus figure has long retired or died, yet his personality lives on the traditions of the organization. In such a case we might more accurately refer to the 'Senex' organization, for Senex is the 'grandfather' god.

In his study of the Garrett Corporation, a highly successful aircraft accessory company, Stephen Stern was interested to find that the influence of the company's founder, Clifford Garrett was still strong twenty-two years after his death.[2] Managers consciously modeled their behavior on the behavior of Garrett as it was remembered, or as it had been re-created in myth and story, and engaged in exactly the same rituals as Garrett had initiated. When he interviewed over one hundred current and past employees without hearing one negative comment about the company and became aware of the loyalty and devotion to Garrett's memory, he came to the conclusion that

Garrett had founded a 'symbolic organization' in which the personality of Garrett, a benevolent father-figure, was enshrined in shared stories about him, and had come to symbolize the collective identity of the employees. He argues that the Garrett name, which figured on the company's logo, served as a totem – a sacred image that generates group identification in the 'clan', promotes respect and admiration for the group, and provides meaning for the group's activities. Organizational logos do not generally have this much power (except in religious organizations) but in this particular organization the personality of the founder served as an image of power that management was still using, fifty years after Garrett started the company, to 'Garretize' employees, that is, to infuse them with the company culture.

The Zeus boss may have great contempt for lesser species. He is outraged when politicians and bureaucrats block his schemes. The myths of the Zeus organization may be stories about the good old days (the Golden Age), about the battles the god-boss had to fight to get supremacy, about his unassailable arrogance and superiority in his dealings with lesser beings, about the rape or seduction of other organizations that took his fancy, about his ruthless destruction of those who stood in his way, about his spectacular generosity to those who have found favor with him.[3]

There are lots of benefits in being part of a Zeus organization, as long as you know how to carry out instructions and avoid the boss's wrath. Generally speaking, you know what is what. You know what counts for right and wrong. You know which way to turn. If you like being part of a culture that has a sense of history and a sense of moral superiority, if you like having a strong leader, if you like decisive action, if you are impatient with ethical subtleties, if you like to be respected for the power you share in, you may work very well in a Zeus organization. Zeus organizations can be very efficient in producing goods and services, and at handling crisis situations. The Zeus culture may be the best culture for dealing with a major emergency. There is good reason why dictatorships generally emerge out of chaos. People are generally willing to exchange freedom for a guarantee of order and security.

The Greeks saw no clear division between good and evil. They did not have good gods and bad gods: all the gods have nasty aspects as well as nice ones. Furthermore, it is not even possible to talk about the good side of a god and the bad side. Good and bad are totally mingled together. The Greeks saw pathology to be an essential part of the way things are, in the gods as well as in humans.

Zeus, the benevolent despot, protects his followers from chaos and provides the security of clear expectations and unambiguous rules of conduct. Yet he has his pathological side, and the Zeus organization is likely to manifest this pathology. One aspect of this is the conflict between the organization's view of itself as an ordered, hierarchical structure and the reality of being ruled by the whims (sometimes very productive whims) of the great man. The organization may have a self-image based on a continuing tradition of inherited power and status, but its chief executive's behavior may be quite unpredictable. You can see the thunder-clouds gathering, but you can never be sure where the lightening will strike. Zeus' omniscience can also be a problem to his subordinates. Because he knows everything, he does not readily take advice. What is more, he is inclined to become impatient with executives who cannot anticipate his directives. His arrogance is a powerful weapon in his dealings with lesser mortals, but it blinds him to the possibility that he may not always get his own way, and that others may not accord his wishes the same respect as his worshippers do. Just as Kronos eats his children for fear they will supplant him, the Zeus organization may be afraid of really creative individuals and inclined to get rid of them. This may leave the organization stuck in the past. The Zeus organization may not get the best out of its people: a smiling paternalism can be as great an obstacle to individual talent as a ruthless dictatorship. The inability of the organization to take women seriously (except Athena women, who must fight for acknowledgment) is another serious limitation. Zeus may expend a deal of energy chasing women, but he either oppresses or patronizes them.

One of the biggest downside effects of a Zeus organization is the manner in which information is handled, or not handled. The omnipotence and capriciousness of Zeus combine to make it very unsafe for subordinates to provide Zeus with bad news, especially and particularly if it is bad news about something for which he has a very positive disposition. It is downright dangerous to provide such information if it is about one of Zeus' whims. For example, we are aware of a large multi-national company dominated at most levels by the Zeus archetype which invested and, some would say, wasted more than $2.5 billion of shareholder funds in a new technology.

This represented a cost over-run of $1 billion. But the company's commitment to this technology could have been reviewed, harnessed, and redirected much earlier in the project's life cycle if the CEO had been told of the potential cost implications and over-runs.

But this was not to be. For no one near him was prepared to lay out to him in simple, blunt, and clear terms the progress on cost estimates. The project was seen as one of Zeus' personal favorites. This was despite the fact that one of the senior financial officers is quoted as saying that the financial fraternity within the company knew a good six months before the 'shit hit the fan' about the scale and scope of the cost blowout. No one was prepared to risk Zeus' unpredictable temper and scorn, something for which he was famous throughout the organization.

It is very difficult for clean, authentic performance information to flow freely upwards in Zeus organizations. The end result is what Chris Argyris and Donald Schon[4] call a Model I system or organization. In such systems, the hidden ground rules are:

- to maximize winning and minimize losing
- to minimize expressing negative feelings
- to be rational
- to decrease the opportunity for confrontation
- to define the task unilaterally and have the others agree to it
- to maximize cooperation and collaboration
- to maximize free and informed choice

Not only is bad news censored as it travels up such a system, so also is non-rational information such as that arising from intuition and feelings. Zeus organizations thus find it difficult to make judgments and decisions in response to rapid environmental changes because the 'data base' on which strategy rests is inauthentic and limited. Invariably, there will be one or more very noticeable miscalculations by the system, e.g. huge cost blowouts, massive environmental embarrassment, human loss of life, etc . . . and eventually the embodiment of Zeus (the CEO) will be asked to move on.

But because the CEO is the embodiment of the culture and not the cause, his removal will not address the deeper pattern. Invariably, a new CEO is found. Liberation from the yoke of dependence, improved performance, new worlds and tomorrows are promised. The workforce invests its hope in these and optimism replaces depression, confusion and disempowerment . . . for a while.

Unfortunately the Zeus archetype is a strong, pervasive 'something' that grips the members. As with all archetypal inflations it is not the people who have the archetype, rather it is the archetype that has the people, and in so doing finds many and subtle ways to express itself. So the new CEO is often taken over by the archetypal pattern in the system just as his predecessor was. We are familiar with an organization in which one CEO was replaced by another. The successor spoke of focus and commitment, equality and contribution, involvement and results. Yet within a very short period he took his most senior and close people away to draft and proclaim a new vision and set of values for the institution. This act was portrayed by the spin-doctors as being for the good of the company and its people. Such an act is typically Zeus-like, so much so that those caught in it do not see the blinding contradictions between what they espoused and what they did. The Zeus-energy had survived the previous CEO and was now well and truly alive in his successor.

The deep and pervasive influence of the Zeus pathology also finds common expression in the way information is often handled around senior executive and middle management selection procedures in large corporations.

It is not unusual to find senior operational managers of large departments, units, or projects totally uninvolved in the creation, selection, and appointment of their next 'level up', i.e. boss. Zeus sits a layer or two above this operational manager and in his benevolent wisdom decides that the unit or project could benefit from some additional leadership and capability and that a senior executive should be appointed to oversee the operational manager. This is not the mistake. The mistake comes in excluding the operational manager from all information in regard to the decision until after it has been made and the executive appointed. Because Zeus sits in a position of hierarchical superiority and power, he fails to see how much of the information on which he bases his decisions is severely compromised and filtered. This applies as much to his selection processes as to any other aspect of his behavior. The very people who have the most valid and useful perspectives on who should be appointed to lead them and what is required of such a person, i.e. the operational manager and his colleagues, are not put in the loop at all. Moreover the unidirectional nature of the processes induces passive aggressive responses in them both towards Zeus and towards his appointed executive. Little wonder then that we see so much wasted effort and energy spent in managing unresolved feelings, resentments and confusions in such situations.

Joseph Heller paints a vivid picture of Zeus pathology (and Apollo's attempt to contain it) in his description of General Dreedle in *Catch 22*:

> 'What was that?' roared General Dreedle incredulously, and whirled around in a murderous rage upon Major Danby, who staggered back in terrified confusion and began to quail and perspire. 'Who is this man?'
>
> 'Major Danby, sir,' Colonel Cathgart stammered. 'My group operations officer.'
>
> 'Take him out and shoot him,' ordered General Dreedle.
>
> 'S-sir?'
>
> 'I said take him out and shoot him. Can't you hear?'
>
> 'Yes, sir!' Colonel Cathgart responded smartly, swallowing hard, and turned in a brisk manner to his chauffeur and his meteorologist. 'Take Major Danby out and shoot him.'
>
> 'S-sir?' his chauffeur and his meteorologist stammered.
>
> 'I said take Major Danby out and shoot him,' Colonel Cathgart snapped. 'Can't you hear?'
>
> The two young lieutenants nodded lumpishly and gaped at each other in stunned and flaccid reluctance, each waiting for the other to initiate the procedure of taking Major Danby outside and shooting him. Neither had ever taken Major Danby outside and shot him before . . .
>
> . . . As soon as Major Danby began to cry, Colonel Moodus, who had been vacillating wretchedly on the sidelines, could restrain himself no longer and stepped out diffidently towards General Dreedle with a sickly air of self-sacrifice.

> 'I think you'd better wait a minute, Dad,' he suggested hesitantly. 'I don't think you can shoot him.'
>
> General Dreedle was infuriated by this intervention. 'Who the hell says I can't?' he thundered pugnaciously in a voice loud enough to rattle the whole building. Colonel Moodus, his face flushed with embarrassment, bent closer to whisper into his ear. 'Why the hell can't I?' General Dreedle bellowed. Colonel Moodus whispered some more. 'You mean I can't shoot anyone I want to?' General Dreedle demanded with uncompromising indignation. He pricked up his ears with interest as Colonel Moodus continued whispering. 'Is that a fact?' he inquired, his rage tamed by curiosity.[5]

It is not only the chief executive of an organization who manifests the Zeus archetype. At each level of the hierarchy the organization's particular manifestation of Zeus may be re-iterated. This is particularly obvious in the ways middle management responds to first line supervisors in large manufacturing and other industrial settings. Managers often complain of the supervisors' lack of leadership skills, their rather brutish behavior towards those for whom they are responsible, their arbitrary autocratic style in resolving conflicts, and their simmering alienation from the goals and dreams of the company. As outside consultants to such organizations, we often sit down and talk with the senior executives and find them describing middle management in identical terms. We are also accustomed to witnessing the managers behaving in exactly the ways they find objectionable in the supervisors. The language may be more genteel, the actions more elegant, yet the patterns are deeply similar.

In the organization dominated by the Zeus myth, it is not only the chief executive who regards power as all-important. The organizations members may individually have much or little power, but they share the assumptions that might prevails over right, that the powerful are entitled to privileges, that powerful people should look impressive, that inequalities between people are to be both expected and desired, that powerful people should be able to demand respect. All these assumptions are characteristic of what Hofstede calls the *large power distance culture*.[6]

The gods are complex. We can find in each of the gods traits that appear to be contradictory. In his Indo-European origins Zeus is a transcendent sky-god. In his Cretan origins he is a youthful vegetation god, child-lover of the Great Goddess. In his Asian origins he is the child of earth and sky who wins dominion over the universe.

As imagined by the Greeks of classical times, he is both order and unpredictability, oppression and beneficence, the all-knowing father and the bully, the old god who wants things to be always the same and the new god who wants to act for himself.

The genius of the Greek mythographers was in their recognition that in human personality and in human culture generally, there is a pattern in which these things belong together.

Deborah Layton, in describing her experience as a disciple of Jim Jones at Jonestown, portrays a culture, where a pathological Zeus is supported by both Ares and Dionysos.

> We were being trained to survive under desperate conditions, with few comforts and little sleep.
>
> We were taught to put our faith in Jim Jones, our leader, and never question him. We were to let go of such petty desires as living in a nuclear family. Father had a vision greater than any we could have. None of us was evolved enough to understand or question him.
>
> Whenever my inner voice began to caution me, Jim would intuit my doubt and quickly dispel my 'capitalist' anxiety. On one occasion when he told us to close our eyes and pray while he turned the water into wine, I peeked. Suddenly he bellowed,
>
> 'For those unbelievers, still too caught up in the material world, who cannot trust, who think they can secretly learn something and in the process only prove how small their minds are . . . Ha! . . . Shame on you! . . . I have turned the water into white wine!'
>
> I was terribly embarrassed that he had seen me doubting. I promised myself that I would no longer try to outsmart God . . . Father was teaching us that doubting him was a sign of conceit and selfishness, vestiges of the material world that I was trying to shed. He always knew how to address my hesitations and dilute my apprehensions.[7]

The gods do not usually act in isolation. Zeus in organizations is usually accompanied by other gods. The power that comes from superior strength (Zeus) is often supported by the power that comes from charisma (Dionysos). Hera, Zeus' queen and the goddess of social obligations, represents one pattern that modifies the Zeus organization.

Hera domesticates Zeus somewhat and gives him an interest in social respectability. Apollo, god of order and rationality, is another god who may work closely with Zeus, providing rational power structures to moderate the chief executive's impulsiveness and unpredictability. However, there is often a conflict between Zeus energy and Apollo energy, especially in large organizations. The Zeus-inflated executive is most comfortable in a simple structure where he or she gives the orders and they pass quickly down the hierarchy to be executed promptly and efficiently. As an organization becomes larger and more complex, this is no longer feasible, and bureaucratic procedures frustrate the boss's desire to turn his or her ideas into immediate action. The Zeus organization may be young and energetic (through the presence of Ares and Herakles, Zeus' sons) or may lose touch with the world and lose its capacity for action (evidence of the presence of Hades, Zeus' elder brother).

There are organizations where we can recognize the Zeus pattern very clearly. Military-type organizations, for instance, have traditionally been strongly Zeus in their culture, although there is now evidence in some Western forces of the limitations of this culture for battle effectiveness. Indeed the Zeus culture seems to be more a characteristic of military forces in peace time, rather than in battle. In the heat of battle, Zeus may give way to alternative gods – the mateship of Eros, the loyalty of Hera, the heroic individualism of Herakles, and the spontaneity and initiative of Dionysos.

Zeus culture appears to dominate in the media and publishing empires that have sprung up in the past hundred years or so, for Zeus wants power over truth and morality as well as power over people. The symbols of such organizations – their buildings, their logos, their choice of cars, the dress-code of their executives – point to power as their supreme value. One consequence of this identification with power is that when the Zeus-figures who control such organizations take sick or hint that they are contemplating retirement, the share market immediately responds by lowering the value of the corporation.

The consultant who looks at an organization from a Zeus perspective will focus on the way the directives of the chief executive get to be put into action. The model organization will be one in which the chief executive is able to make decisions on the best available knowledge basis (through a wise choice of advisers), and in which these decisions become actions with the minimum of delay, inhibition, or distortion.

Glorious Hera

Of golden-throned Hera I will sing, born of Rhea,
queen of the gods, unexcelled in beauty,
sister and glorious wife of the loud-thundering Zeus.
All the gods on lofty Olympos reverence her
and honour her together with Zeus who delights in thunder.[8]

Telling a woman that she has eyes like a cow may not be particularly complimentary in our culture. However, 'cow-eyed' is a common epithet for Hera in the myths. It links her with the ancient goddess-worship where the goddess, in her aspect of provider and nourisher was linked with, and even identified with, the cow.

Hera is queen of the gods, and reigns with her husband Zeus on Mt. Olympus. The assimilation of the Greek culture with the indigenous culture was symbolized in the marriage of Zeus and Hera, for Hera is 'the Lady', who ruled the land before the Greeks arrived and who now accepts the reality of the patriarchy and attempts to domesticate it.

In the Greek imagination, Hera represents social stability, without which the city-state cannot survive. She is the goddess of marriage, and a very jealous goddess at that, who savagely harasses Zeus' many lovers and their offspring. She is goddess of family, of social obligations, of the bonds of blood and the bonds of commitment, loyalty, and fidelity that unite people. Hera persecutes Zeus' sons, Herakles and Dionysos, not only because they are children of her rivals, but also because the individual heroism of Herakles and the impulse and ecstasy of Dionysos are subversive of a well-ordered society.

'Lady' is a fitting title for her. On the one hand it denotes her dignity and the honor due to her as queen of the gods. On the other, it has an old-fashioned feel to it, with connotations of old-fashioned values, 'proper' behavior, and keeping up appearances. She is a great and glorious goddess who is capable of extraordinary pettiness and spite. She sometimes appears as an old woman, for she represents the wisdom of the old ways. She stands for tradition and conservative values. She is more often represented as a mature and fulfilled woman, who can occasionally bend even Zeus to her will. She is also a girl, for she bathes every year in a spring to renew her virginity, a symbol of the independence of the woman who is not possessed by or beholden to any man.[9]

Greek myths often carry a moral message. Hera offers a very different morality from Zeus. Zeus commands us to 'Do it because I say so!' Hera reminds us of social obligations. When the hero Jason first sets out on his journey to find out who he really is, he comes to a river. He is about to step in and wade across when a bad-tempered old woman asks him to carry her. At first he refuses because, like most heroes, he is in a hurry and he does not think old women are very important. However, he eventually relents and lifts her on to his shoulders and steps into the river. As he wades through the water she keeps scolding him for her discomfort, and she gets heavier and heavier, so that he barely makes it to the other side. When, at last, he lies exhausted on the bank, she reveals herself as the great and glorious queen of the gods, blesses him, and becomes his protector.

Many Greek myths carry the message that we meet the gods constantly in our daily lives, in the weak and infirm as well as in the strong, in the stranger as well as in the lover. In this story Hera is manifest in our obligation of honor to carry the aged and powerless, an obligation that we need reminding of as much as Jason does.

The typical Hera organization is the family company, where the image of the family shapes the way the organization thinks and talks about itself. New members of the organization, if they are not already members of the family, are adopted into it, and if they 'fit in' are likely to stay with the organization for many years. There is an expectation that members socialize with each other. The company organizes family picnics and other outings. What makes the company special are the bonds between people. Loyalty to the organization is highly valued. Disloyalty to the organization is the worst of crimes. The company reciprocates the loyalty of its employees. Loyalty to employees may actually be more important than profit, and inefficient and unproductive (but loyal) employees may be retained by the company because to sack them would be immoral. In some Hera organizations, especially in family-oriented cultures, it would be regarded as immoral to hire a competent stranger rather than an incompetent family member.

The British royal family is an organization that upholds Hera values. Family comes first. Members have status and identity only as members of the family, and if they betray the family's values they will be expelled from it. Honor is all-important. Appearance must be kept up at all costs, and part of the appearance is conservative moral values. The disasters that have befallen this organization in recent years have come in part from having introduced into the family a couple of individuals who were 'women' rather than 'ladies'. There is no place in Hera's world for the individual giving priority to personal fulfillment. Every member must put commitment and loyalty to the organization ahead of personal whims and satisfactions.

In *Men of Honour: the Truth about the Mafia*,[10] Giovanni Falcone describes the ultimate Hera organization, the Sicilian Mafia. Entry to the Mafia begins with a sort of religious initiation. Not everyone can join. Knowing how to kill is not enough.

> The candidate is taken to a room in a secluded house and learns the Cosa Nostra code: not to desire the woman of another man of honour; not to profit from prostitution; not to kill other men of honour except in cases of absolute necessity; not to talk to the police; not to seek conflict with other men of honour; to behave responsibly and correctly; to keep absolutely silent about Cosa Nostra to all who are not part of it; never to introduce oneself to another man of honour; and to execute the decisions of the commission or cupola – the governing body of Cosa Nostra – at all costs.[11]

The Mafia is not run by a high profile figure, but by the godfathers, the elders of the family. The chief executive is elected by secret ballot of the godfathers and his identity is kept secret. The basic unit of Cosa Nostra is the family, with all its traditional values: respect for parents and relatives, friendship, honor, putting the family before oneself. Conservative Christian values are displayed, sometimes ostentatiously.

> A man who has had more than one wife or who has had very public affairs is judged incapable of self-control on a sexual and emotional level and is not to be trusted on a professional level either. The only truly important woman for the Mafioso is the mother of his children; the others are all whores. If he marries the wrong woman, too bad: marriage isn't such a vital part of life. He'll have to

> stick with her and abide by the traditional family values, ensuring that mother and children are respected and adequately maintained. A much quoted proverb in the world of Cosa Nostra goes: *Meglio commandare che fottere* – Better to command than to fuck.[12]

Hera's sentiments exactly! If the Mafioso is unfaithful to his wife he must ensure that she is not humiliated in her social circle. As long as gossip is avoided there is no problem for him or her. Appearances must be kept up. On the other hand, if a public affair humiliates the wife, retribution will be immediate and violent.

In the Hera organization, there is a lot of attention given to honor and morality. But honor and morality may have different meaning inside the organization to the meanings commonly held outside it. Lying, stealing, and cheating within the family will not be tolerated, but there may be no objection to such behavior in one's dealings with outsiders.

When Gareth Morgan describes Japanese corporate culture, he does so largely in Hera terms:

> Coupled with an amazing capacity to borrow ideas from elsewhere, first from China, now from the West, the cultures of the rice field and of the Samurai blend to create a hierarchical form of social organization within a modern industrial context. The managerial echelons are elitist and highly meritocratic, as they have been for centuries. Workers readily contribute to the material goals of their industrial masters and defer to their authority, because that has always been the traditional relationship between worker and samurai. No surprise, therefore, that so many people are prepared to sing the company song and commit a lifetime to the corporate family.
>
> The system of organization is feudal rather than modern, and from outside the culture seems distinctly oppressive, particularly since mobility between ranks is highly restricted, being determined for each individual from a very early age. However, it is important to realize that the kind of submissiveness and deference to authority found in Japan is not necessarily experienced as demeaning. Hierarchy in a Japanese corporation is as much a system of mutual service as one of top-down control.
>
> . . . In many Western countries individualistic culture leads us to seek and gain self-respect by competing with others, or against the wider system, thus emphasizing

> our uniqueness and separateness. In Japan, on the other hand, cultural conditions allow workers to achieve self-respect through service *within* the system, even though there may be aspects of the system which they find distasteful.[13]

There are great satisfactions in being part of a Hera organization. You know where you fit in, because 'fitting in' is an essential aspect of the Hera culture. You can count on people to act in the best interests of the organization rather than out of personal ambition. You can serve something bigger than your personal whims, and share this service with others. You will happily work long hours for little or no remuneration rather than let the organization down. The sense of relationship may be horizontal, between family members with different roles and responsibilities, rather than vertical, between you and the boss or bosses. (Of course, senior members of the family will be treated with great respect.) You and your colleagues do not criticize the organization to outsiders. Rather, you are zealous in showing its positive side. These satisfactions may be balanced by some frustration at the excessive stability of the organization. There is likely to be a strong sense of the established and 'proper' way of doing things. You may be made to feel that you are disloyal if you insist on your right to leave work at the official closing time or take your full entitlement of annual leave. Even if your work in the organization is voluntary, a lack of commitment will be considered shameful. Leaving the organization to work for another (especially if money is involved) may be looked on as outright betrayal.

We often find Hera as a dominant archetype in trade union settings. In work with union members and officials it is common to hear them speak of their shared experience in terms of family. Indeed it is a very strong motif throughout all their dealings, particularly in times of external threat. As with other Hera organizations, loyalty within the family is prized over values that the external world would perhaps see as more important. For example, unapproved practices are sometimes tolerated by supervisory staff or union officials. One hears stories from supervisors (union members) of their unwillingness to complete injury reports for management. The supervisors may know that the individual concerned has suffered the injury at home rather than in the workplace, and they turn a blind eye when the injured party seeks medical treatment, time off or some other company-sourced response. They say they are caught between their loyalty to 'their family member' and their own personal integrity that would be compromised by completing a false document: Their solution is non-compliance with management's requirements, thereby honoring both drives. One of the settings where the Hera archetype is dominant is the coal mining industry. Similar dynamics are played out throughout this industry on a regular basis, and union members regularly speak of working for the family (i.e. the industry union) rather than a particular company.

In his study of Disneyland, John Van Maanen shows a very different culture dominated by the same Hera values of social conformity, stability, and clear role definition.

> [Ride operators] are also a well-screened bunch. There is – among insiders and outsiders alike – a rather fixed view about the social attributes carried by the standard-make Disneyland ride operator. Single, white males and females in their early twenties, without facial blemish, of above average height and below average weight, with straight teeth, conservative grooming standards, and a chin-up, shoulder-back posture radiating the sort of good health suggestive of a recent history in sports are typical of their social identifiers. There are representative minorities on the payroll but, because ethnic displays are firmly discouraged by the management, minority employees are rather close copies of the standard model Disneylander albeit in different colors.[14]

Van Maanen describes how appearance and conduct are strictly regulated. There is a clearly defined status hierarchy among employees. In their training at the 'University of Disneyland' employees learn the norms, myths, and assumptions of the Disney culture.

- First, we practice the Disney smile.
- Second, we use only friendly and courteous phrases.
- Third, we are not stuffy – the only Misters in Disneyland are Mr. Toad and Mr. Smee.
- Language is also a central feature of university life and new employees are schooled in its proper use. Customers at Disneyland are, for instance, never referred to as such; they are 'guests'. There are no rides at Disneyland, only 'attractions'.

- Disneyland itself is a 'Park', not an amusement center, and it is divided into 'back-stage', 'on-stage', and 'regions'. Law enforcement personnel hired by the park are not police but 'security hosts'. Employees do not wear uniforms but check out fresh 'costumes' each day from the 'wardrobe'. And, of course, there are no accidents at Disneyland, only 'incidents'.[15]

Employees who fail to conform are dismissed. Nevertheless, according to Van Maanen, there is a flourishing underground Dionysian subculture among employees as they find ways to express their individuality and resist the pressure to wear a perpetual smile and be nice to their 'guests'.

The lessons taught at the 'University of Disneyland' are based on the kind of assumptions that Hofstede sees as characteristic of a *strong uncertainty avoidance*[16] culture: that what is different is dangerous; that there should be tight rules regarding what is dirty or taboo; that people are naturally more comfortable in structured situations; that rules should be respected; that *our way is best*. People in Hera-dominated organizations also make assumptions characteristic of *collectivist*[17] or *communitarian*[18] cultures: group interests should prevail over individual interests; the more deeply you belong to the organization (family) the more privileges you should have; the organization gives you your identity; employer-employee relationships have a moral dimension; you shouldn't try to stand out in the group; you shouldn't compete with each other. Status in the Hera organization is likely to be *ascribed* rather than *achieved*.[19] In a family company, for example, family membership gives a status that a non family member cannot achieve through hard work. Ethnicity or social class may also be significant in ascribing status.

Hera obviously has a strong connection with Zeus. Her maintaining the societal status quo is her contribution to maintaining the patriarchal political status quo. Falcone points out that the Mafia through its organizational skills and its involvement in legitimate business activity actually contributes to the stability of Sicilian society. The Hera culture seems to be particularly strong in organizations dedicated to maintaining the political and social system, such as police departments and service organizations.

Other gods who have a close relationship with Hera are her sons Ares, the god of war, and Hephaistos, the god of crafting. She is not often found in the company of

Aphrodite or Dionysos. She is a determined enemy of Herakles. The personal growth of the individual, like the individual's heroic struggle, is a threat to the good order and stability of the organization. Hermes has an interesting relationship with her. Though originally hostile to him for good reason, for he is subversive of conservative values, she is seduced by him when he disguises himself as the infant Ares and sucks at her breast. It is apparent that in past two decades Hermes, who is the god of marketing, has been busy seducing and subverting Hera organizations.

The consultant who looks at organizations from a Hera perspective will focus on those aspects of an organization that contribute to its stability: the functional relationships and roles, the loyalty of its members, the shared values. These are seen as strengths to be maintained and enhanced, while heroic individualism will be seen as destructive.

Shining Apollo

I shall remember not to neglect Apollon who shoots afar.
The gods of the house of Zeus tremble at his coming,
and indeed all spring up from their seats
as he approaches, stringing his splendid bow.[20]

Apollo is the eldest son of Zeus, the symbol of what the classical Greeks understood by being Greek and civilized. He represents perfection in art, science, music, athletic prowess, law. He is a god of healing and prophecy. He is reason and moderation personified. The Greeks were inclined to identify Apollo with the sun. They imagined him as showing clearly what is what, as illuminating the world, bringing light to the darkness, enabling us to make sense of our experience.

Apollo establishes order and the rule of law. Not autocratic do-it-because-I-say-so law (which is the law of Zeus), but rational law, based on a reasoned estimation of what constitutes good and bad behavior. Carved in the lintel of Apollo's temple at Delphi were the following maxims:

Abstain from inauspicious words.
Fear authority.
Do not glory in strength.
Make obeisance to the divine.
Hate hubris.
Govern your spirit.
Observe the limit.
Nothing in excess.
Know yourself.
Rule women.[21]

These maxims give a sense of where Apollo stands in the scheme of things. For one thing, he affirms the authority of Zeus; for another, he firmly puts women in their place.

Apollo was originally a version of the divine child, the vegetation god who was everywhere worshipped alongside the mother-goddess. He appears to have had an Asian origin, and the myth of Apollo makes him the son of Leto, an ancient earth-goddess who was certainly Asian.

Leto wandered all over the world looking for somewhere to give birth to her twin children. She eventually found a place, the island of Delos, which was prepared to give her shelter, and gave birth first to Artemis. The newborn goddess then helped in the birthing of her brother Apollo. The story to this point could well be a version of the myth of the young vegetation god who is both child and lover to the goddess, a myth in which fatherhood plays no part. However, as soon as this child was born he announced to his mother and the assembled goddesses that he had come to do the work of his father Zeus. Then he went off to establish his own shrine at Delphi. Before he could do so he had to do battle with a great she-dragon. He slew her and left her corpse to rot. Then he established the shrine and oracle of Delphi, the place where people came from all over the world to learn the will of the gods. They would ask Apollo and he would tell them. If they were clever enough they would understand the answer.

Apollo's slaying of the she-dragon (most monsters in Greek mythology happen to be female) and the evidence we have from other sources that Delphi was originally the shrine of Gaia, the earth-goddess, and that it was she who originally spoke through the oracle, point to a shift in culture and consciousness. The old religion has been put down by the new. Heroic male consciousness has been triumphant. Order has conquered chaos. In cult and politics, power has passed to men, and it is Apollo who represents their fantasy of themselves.

Apollonine consciousness has generally been hostile to women, whom it marginalizes as trivial, intuitive, emotional, sensual, and irrational. In mythology, Apollo appears to be unable to have any sort of satisfactory relationship with a female – goddess, nymph, or mortal – except with his mother and sister. One of the best-known stories is his pursuit of Daphne.

Eros, god of love, has two kinds of arrows, which he fires off irresponsibly at gods and mortals alike. The arrows with golden points cause the wounded to fall hopelessly in love with whoever happens to be passing. The ones with leaden points cause them to be filled with revulsion. After a quarrel with Apollo, Eros got even with this most rational of gods by shooting him with one of his gold-tipped arrows. He fell in love with the nymph, Daphne, whom Eros immediately wounded with one of his leaden arrows. She rejected Apollo's advances and fled from him. After a long pursuit he was on the point of seizing her when she prayed in terror to Gaia, the earth-goddess, who turned her into a laurel tree. All Apollo got for his pursuit was a branch of laurel, which he broke off and wore in his hair as his special emblem. Accordingly, it was the special emblem of poets and musicians, who were thought to be inspired by Apollo.

Apollo also fell in love with Cassandra, a Trojan princess. In order to impress and seduce her he gave her the gift of prophecy. When she still refused to make love with him, Apollo punished her by making sure that no one ever believed her prophecies. In classical Greece, Apollo was the god of prophecy, healing, law, poetry, and music, as well as science and philosophy. He was the god who gives mortals the capacity to think clearly, to understand how the world works, to find meaning and beauty, to organize their lives in an ordered way. He demands that we seek moderation in all things and look at the world in a detached and reasonable way, without being carried away by emotion. He insists that clear thinking will enable us to solve all our problems.

The organization whose culture is dominated by Apollo will place a high value on a rational approach to its operations. Individual whims and impulsive decision-making are strongly discouraged and emotional outbursts are looked on with distaste. It is assumed that all problems can be solved and all crises dealt with through the application of cool intelligence. The power of the executive is subject to checks and balances, designed to moderate any excesses. Considerable emphasis is placed on developing and maintaining structures that are truly rational – not based on mere tradition, superstition, or personal taste. People are expected to behave rationally and there is some surprise when they do not. There is an assumption that if matters are clearly explained to people, they will understand and act on that understanding. There is a great deal of faith in universal abstract principles.

Obviously there are some settings where such characteristics are to be greatly valued: in the planning and conduct of highly specialized and technical operations such as space missions, for example. But as with all the gods, problems arise when the organization becomes inflated with one archetype. At such times the excesses are present in both their healthy and pathological forms. It surprises us little that public service organizations (bastions of worship to Apollo), whilst honoring Athena in their quest for gender equity, have also been among the institutions defending most strongly against women taking their equal role and influence alongside men. Formal policy has not always matched informal practice, and the Delphic temple's Apollonine injunction to 'rule women' still seems to dominate the senior ranks of these systems.

Max Weber, in considering the dominance of bureaucratic structures, points to their capacity to be both efficient and dehumanizing.

> The decisive reason for the advance of bureaucratic organization has always been its purely technical superiority over any other form of organization. The fully developed bureaucratic mechanism compares with other organizations, as does the machine with the non-mechanical modes of production.
>
> Precision, speed, unambiguity, knowledge of the files, continuity, discretion, unity, strict subordination, reduction of friction and of material and personal costs – these are raised to the optimum point in the strictly bureaucratic administration ... Its specific nature develops the more perfectly the more bureaucracy is

> 'dehumanized', the more completely it succeeds in eliminating from official business, love, hatred, and purely personal, irrational and emotional elements which escape calculation.[22]

The Apollo organization is unselfconsciously elitist, for it is only right that power should belong to those who are best able to use it wisely. As in the Athena organization, there is a conscious pursuit of excellence, but the Apollo organization does not have Athena's interest in power sharing. As the eldest son of Zeus, Apollo believes that in the natural order of things power comes from above. What he provides is a hierarchical structure to ensure that this power is exercised in a rational and orderly way.

The Apollonine fantasy of 'scientific management' was voiced most strongly and most influentially by Frederick Taylor. Writing in 1912, he had no doubt that applying his radical 'scientific' principles to management would make industry more efficient than it had ever been before.

> The first great advantage which scientific management has . . . is that under scientific management the initiative of the workmen – that is, their hard work, their good will, their ingenuity – is obtained practically with absolute regularity, while under even the best of the older type of management this initiative is only obtained spasmodically and somewhat irregularly. This obtaining, however, of the initiative of the workmen is the lesser of the two great causes which make scientific management better for both sides than the older type of management. By far the greater gain under scientific management comes from the new, the very great and the extraordinary burdens and duties which are voluntarily assumed by those on the management's side.[23]
>
> Taylor went on to list the four principles of scientific management:
>
> - the development of a scientific knowledge to replace the old rule of thumb knowledge of the worker;
> - the scientific selection and training of the workers;
> - the bringing together of the scientific knowledge and the trained workers;
> - the equal division of the work between the workers, on the one hand, and the managers, on the other.

For Taylor it was obvious that a good organization is one where roles and tasks are defined with absolute precision, where ambiguity is eliminated, where rules, laws, and formulae can be applied to every aspect of the organization's operations. He was convinced that conflict and inefficiency could be abolished simply by explaining clearly to people what is expected of them and why it is in their best interests to behave in the way that has been 'scientifically' demonstrated to be the best. For Taylor it was perfectly clear that the most rational way to run an organization was for the workers to do the working and the managers to do the thinking. There is no acknowledgment in Taylor's Apollonine vision that human behavior has irrational as well as rational sources, or that there might be more to being human than is satisfied by being part of a perfectly efficient machine.

Aldous Huxley satirizes 'scientific management' in *Brave New World*:

> It was a small factory of lighting sets for helicopters, a branch of the Electrical Equipment Corporation. They were met on the roof itself (for that circular letter of recommendation from the Comptroller was magical in its effects) by the Chief Technician and the Human Element Manager. They walked downstairs into the factory.
>
> 'Each process', explained the Human Element Manager, 'is carried out, as far as possible, by a single Bokanovsky Group.'
>
> And, in effect, eighty-three almost noseless black, brachycephalic Deltas were cold-pressing. One hundred and seven heat-conditioned Epsilon Senegalese were working in the foundry. Thirty-three Delta females, long-headed, sandy, with narrow pelvises, and all within 20 millimeters of 1 meter 69 centimeters tall, were cutting screws. In the assembling room, the dynamos were being put together by two sets of Gamma-Plus dwarfs. The low work-tables faced one another; between them crawled the conveyor with its load of separate parts; forty seven blond heads were confronted by forty-seven brown ones; forty-seven receding by forty-seven prognathous chins. The completed mechanisms were inspected by eighteen identical curly auburn girls in Gamma green, packed in crates by thirty-four short-legged, left-handed male Delta-Minuses, and loaded into the waiting trucks by sixty-three blue-eyed, flaxen and freckled Epsilon Semi-Morons.
>
> 'O brave new world . . .' By some malice of his memory the savage found himself repeating Miranda's words. 'O brave new world that has such people in it.'
>
> 'And I assure you', the Human Element Manager concluded, as they left the factory, 'we hardly ever have any trouble with our workers.'[24]

The pathology of Apollo is present in the elitism and dehumanization of what has come to be called Taylorist management. It emerges also in a tendency to dogmatism and rigidity. Once the Apollonine executive sees the way things are, he or she has little tolerance for those who cannot. He wants things to be obvious, and has little patience with ambiguity and illusion. He is inclined to insist that people accept his assessment of a situation, because its reasonableness is perfectly clear to him and those who can't see this must be stupid or bloody-minded. She is blind to the critical influence of emotions, relationships, and unconscious drives on people's behavior, and he sometimes makes bad decisions because his perspective prevents him from taking in certain kinds of information. She can be quite unaware of her own irrational prejudices and the ways in which her own precious clear-sightedness is governed by impulse.

This is most evident in the upper ranks of public sector organizations. Well portrayed with humor in the British television series 'Yes, Minister' and 'Yes, Prime Minister', it can have a more sinister and destructive side as well. It is not uncommon for senior bureaucrats to use public sector regulations and processes to remove difficult people, block unwanted initiatives or individuals, or maintain their own power base. The sheer vindictiveness and individual human suffering occasionally associated with these behavior patterns and their irrational basis are invisible to one inflated with Apollo.

In the Daphne myth it is Apollo's confidence in his own rationality and emotional detachment that makes him such an easy prey for Eros. It is possible for a management structure, founded on thoroughly reasonable Apollonine principles, to become completely ineffective because of the narrowness of its vision. When you know you are right it is difficult to be flexible. The Apollo organization may pride itself on the excellence of its theory, but it may not be particularly productive and may treat its people very badly.

We are familiar with a large organization that restructured itself into an elaborate set of matrix structures and functions, designed to bring maximum rational benefit to the system through formal networking and other processes. Its elegance as a design was outstanding, yet its designers (the CEO and his few close advisors) were blind to its irrelevance and unworkability in the eyes of those entrusted to work within it. Consequently, as a design, it had no deep permission in the company and was unable to help the organization adjust to the turbulent environment. For all their great ideas, the CEO and his advisors were soon moved on by the march of circumstance.

An organization dominated by Apollo values may treat its women members particularly badly and be rather contemptuous of 'feminine' values and behavior. The Apollo organization may be so interested in the elegant efficiency of its structures that it may pay little or no attention to its products. It may even become so intent on maintaining its structures and the power and status relationships between people that it forgets what larger purpose these structures are supposed to serve. Like the Hera organization it has little tolerance for uncertainty and, consequently, little openness to change from within. It may also not be very good at protecting itself against the forces that threaten it. Change, when it comes, is likely to be traumatic.

Apollo culture is likely to be dominant in scientific organizations. Science is a manifestation of Apollo, and organizations made up of scientists and pursuing scientific goals are inclined to bring both the good and the bad qualities of Apollo into the way they organize themselves. The god of scientific healing is particularly powerful in the culture of medical organizations.

Apollo is closely associated with Zeus, and Apollo may often be found moderating, or attempting to moderate, the Zeus culture of an organization. Sometimes Zeus and Apollo cultures are in conflict within the same organization; the organization may officially function through formal, hierarchical structures, but key executives actually by-pass these structures and go straight to the chief executive for a decision. Apollo may have to struggle against Zeus' tendency to favoritism, arbitrary authority, and discrimination. Apollo organizations have a great deal in common with organizations dedicated to another scientist-god, Prometheus. However, Apollo lacks Prometheus' sense of mission and his focus on the applications of his science. Bureaucratic organizations may also experience tension between Apollo's need to uphold abstract organizational principles, Hera's need to maintain cohesion and a sense of common identity, and Prometheus' need to get the job done.

The consultant approaching an organization from the Apollo perspective will examine the organization in as detached and objective way as possible. This will enable an accurate diagnosis of its ills and the application of abstract principles of good management to its treatment. There will be a tendency to simplify complex situations, to reduce them to basic principles, which are held up as obviously true. The report and recommendations will show enormous faith in the ability of people to follow a rational course of behavior as soon as it is pointed out to them.

This Apollonine approach to consulting is particularly prevalent in the large professional service firms, such as the former 'big six' accounting practices. Here we see an unusual alliance of Hermes and Apollo. In their desire to sell their services and grow their markets (Hermes) and in the face of the relentless forces of globalization, we see a trend towards designing consulting and accounting support services in some center of excellence (almost always pre-ordained as the USA simply because of its sheer market size and the dominance of the US economy). These 'programs' are then distributed world wide with the expectation of implementation largely unchanged for local conditions. This particular form of the Apollonine fantasy is elaborated in the belief that standardization of product and service will lead to greater efficiencies (e.g. profit per partner) but fails to recognize or account for the local settings and dynamics. The confidence in rationality leads to abstract, universalist solutions. *Once we have found the correct solution we can apply it everywhere.* It overlooks the evidence that there are significant differences among regional and ethnic cultures and among regional and ethnic 'truths', and the evidence that when it comes to organizational problems and their solutions one size doesn't fit all.

---

1. A Athanassakis (trans. and ed.) *The Homeric Hymns* (1976), p. 64. The Homeric hymns are a collection of devotional songs once ascribed to Homer but apparently the work of various poets between the eighth and fifth century BCE.
2. S Stern (1988) 'Symbolic Representation of Organizational Identity', in M Jones, M Moore, and R Snyder, *Inside Organization*, p. 283.
3. In Trompenaars' terms the Zeus organization is 'inner-directed' considering itself sole judge of the rightness of its activities. F Trompennars & C Hampden-Turner (1998) *Riding the Waves of Culture*.
4. See C Argyris, & D Schon (1974) *Organizational Learning*.
5. J Heller (1962) Catch 22, p. 218f.
6. See G Hofstede (1991) *Cultures and Organizations*, Chapter 2.
7. D Layton (1999) *Seductive Poison*, p. 47.
8. A Athanassakis, op. cit, p. 59. Rhea is an ancient earth-goddess. In the Olympian myth she is wife to Kronos and mother of Hestia, Demeter, Hera, Poseidon, Hades, and Zeus.
9. The primal earth-mother was a virgin because she obviously produced life without the intervention of any male. The mythic virginity of Hera, Athena, Artemis, and Hestia represents this link with the original Great Goddess. We see the symbolism carried through centuries later to the Virgin Mary.

10. G Falcone (1992) *Men of Honour*. Judge Falcone, who was conducting an investigation into the Sicilian Mafia, was blown up with his wife and bodyguards before this book was published.
11. ibid., p. 85.
12. ibid., p. 62.
13. G Morgan (1986) *Images of Organization*, p. 116.
14. J Van Maanen (1991) 'The Smile Factory: Work at Disneyland', in PJ Frost, LF Moore, MR Louis, CC Lundberg, & J Martin (eds.), *Reframing Organizational Culture*, p. 59.
15. ibid., p. 65f.
16. See G Hofstede op. cit. , Chapter 5.
17. ibid., Chapter 3.
18. See F Trompenaars & C Hampden-Turner op. cit., Chapter 5.
19. ibid., Chapter 8.
20. A Athanassakis, op. cit., p. 15.
21. Cited in R Eisner (1987) *The Road to Daulis*, p. 142. This is a selection from a much longer list of maxims. The actual inscription no longer exists, but there are several lists of the maxims surviving from classical times. *Hubris*, which involves being inflated, having a higher opinion of oneself than humans are entitled to have, was regarded as very offensive to the gods.
22. M Weber (1947) *The Theory of Social and Economic Organization*, p.194.
23. F Taylor (1947) *Scientific Management*, p. 39.
24. A Huxley (1932) *Brave New World*, p. 128.

6

GODS OF LIFE AND DEATH

Golden-Haired Aphrodite

Sing to me, O Muse, of the works of golden Aphrodite,
the Cyprian, who stirs sweet longing in gods
and subdues the races of mortal men as well as
the birds that swoop from the sky and all the beasts
that are nurtured in their multitudes on both land and sea.[1]

Among the Greek gods, Aphrodite was pretty clearly a foreigner. Her origins can be traced to an Asian fertility goddess and an Egyptian fish goddess. She does not seem to have had any Greek origin at all. Yet, as far as the Greeks were concerned, she was one of the most popular gods.

Aphrodite, for the Greeks of classical times and for European culture ever since is the goddess of beauty and sensuality. She is overtly and unselfconsciously sexual, the only goddess who appears naked to mortals. She believes in fun, in immediate gratification, in the ultimate power of beauty. She gives great attention to her appearance, seeking before all else to be infinitely desirable. She has none of Hera's concern for respectability and social obligations.

Some of the stories of Aphrodite point to her origins as a sea-goddess. She was said to have emerged from the foam of Uranus' genitals when Kronos cut them off and cast them over the ocean. The sea is a powerful image of her beauty, her fluidity, and her unpredictability. She is irresponsible and self-indulgent, careless of the consequences of her actions.

Other stories of Aphrodite show her as a fertility goddess, the personification of Nature. One such is the story, Asian in origin, of Aphrodite's romance with Adonis.

When the princess Smyrna is turned into a myrrh tree, after an incestuous relationship with her father (a relationship engineered by Aphrodite), her child Adonis is born from a gash in the tree. When Aphrodite finds the infant, she immediately falls in love with him. Since he is not of an age to satisfy her desires she locks him in a box, which she gives to Persephone, the goddess of death, for safe-keeping. In spite of strict instructions to the contrary, Persephone looks in the box and also falls hopelessly in love with the child. Of course she refuses to give him back. The quarrel between the two goddesses is arbitrated by Zeus, who decides that they should share him. So he spends part of each year in the underworld with Persephone and returns to the living world and Aphrodite each Spring. Aphrodite dotes on him, and as he grows into manhood reluctantly gives him permission to go hunting. He is killed by a wild boar, allegedly put in his way by Ares, Aphrodite's jealous adult lover, and Aphrodite is, of course, heart-broken.

This version of the ancient vegetation myth of the great goddess and her child lover was very popular among the women of Athens, who celebrated the worship of Adonis each year by growing 'Adonis gardens' in shallow pots each Spring. The grass sprang up quickly and withered just as quickly, and the women mourned the brevity of youth and beauty.

When the Greeks were busy incorporating the various manifestations of the great Goddess into the Olympian family, they made Aphrodite the daughter of Zeus. As daughter of Zeus, she was given in marriage to the ugly blacksmith-god, Hephaistos.

They were obviously incompatible, and Homer tells the story of Aphrodite's affair with the divine macho-man, the war-god Ares. Hephaistos suspected something was up, and made a net of the finest metal mesh, so fine that not even a god could see it. He set it up over the marital bed and announced to his wife that he was going to his favorite Greek island for a holiday. Ares saw him leave, made his move, and took Aphrodite most willingly to bed. The trap was sprung and Hephaistos brought the gods in to witness the lovers so tightly bound together that they could not move. Hephaistos expressed his rage, the gods enjoyed the spectacle, Ares departed shame-faced, and Aphrodite was not put out at all.

The divine beauty-contest between Aphrodite, Hera, and Athena was won by Aphrodite when she bribed the judge (the Trojan prince, Paris) with an offer of the most beautiful woman in the world to be his bride. The fact that the woman in question, Helen, was already married to king Menelaus of Sparta did not bother her at all. Nor did the fact that the seduction of Helen would precipitate the Trojan War. Most stories of Aphrodite are about her love affairs, including her one night stand with the mortal Anchises. She had a casual affair with Hermes, the trickster-god, who gained her favors in exchange for a stolen sandal. The offspring of this union was Hermaphrodite, who was both male and female. She even helped Hera (who didn't generally approve of her) when the latter wanted to seduce her husband, Zeus, and get him to change his mind.

Aphrodite is a goddess of life, of delight in experience, of unembarrassed enchantment by beauty.

Beauty is a powerful force in human affairs of all kinds. In the organization given over to an Aphrodite culture, it is the key value around which all else revolves. Some organizations are essentially Aphrodite-dominated. The fashion industry, especially cosmetics distributors and modeling agencies, is involved in the worship of Aphrodite by its very nature. Advertising and marketing organizations, which are engaged in various kinds of seduction, are likely to have something of Aphrodite in their culture. Organizations whose focus is on creating or displaying beautiful products, such as orchestras, art galleries, and ballet companies, are likely to live out the myth of Aphrodite, as are health and fitness clubs.

Predictably, Aphrodite has a strong presence in the culture of organizations involved in the marketing of beauty products. Anita Roddick describes how Aphrodite values are promoted in *The Body Shop*.

> But I also try to bring beauty, style, and excitement into the office. I like the concept of a workplace that is as visually stimulating as you can make it. We hang art not just in the boardroom, but everywhere. All over *The Body Shop* the walls are hung with photographs, blow-up quotes, charts, and illustrations. We have eight life-size men flying about near the ceiling and 12-foot-long bottles and bananas in our warehouse. We have a full-scale fiberglass replica of Manet's Dejeuner sur l'herbe outside the office in Littlehampton. It's funny and it's charming. There is a whimsical dummy of a cleaning lady with a mop and bucket in our entrance lobby. We have Oscar Wilde quotes painted in two-foot high letters on walls and exhibitions about human rights issues in our hallways. And it's the same in the Child Development Centre as it is in the office; creative activities are an essential part of play.
>
> The language of design is very important to *The Body Shop*. Our messages tend to be visual rather than verbal and they are very rarely word-dense. As a franchise operation, it is very important that we create a style that becomes a culture. It may be designed, but whatever we do, we have to preserve that sense of being different and of doing something that hasn't been done before.[2]

People living in an Aphrodite culture may pay a lot of attention to personal appearance; they may be obsessed with the need to be attractive; they may be more interested in the elegance of what they do than with its usefulness or efficiency; they may not have much interest in doing anything at all if it is not fun. They may pursue the fantasy of perpetual youth and perfect beauty (and be always disappointed). The Aphrodite organization will give attention to the environment in which people work, ensuring that it is not only the chief executive who experiences beauty in his or her surroundings. The Aphrodite organization not only values beauty for its own sake but recognizes the need of every member of the organization to find beauty close at hand.

There may be a relatively small number of organizations that are driven entirely by the pursuit of beauty, but it is a drive experienced by individuals in every organization. In writing a report, developing a product or a strategy, attacking a problem, conducting a meeting, they may, consciously or not, be seeking the most elegant and beautiful solution rather than the most efficient, useful, or economical one. In most organizations they may have to keep this eccentricity secret; in the Aphrodite organization they may be actually encouraged in such behavior.

In organizations dominated by Zeus and Apollo, sub-groups inflated with Aphrodite tend to be publicly ignored, treated as if they do not exist. Such groups may pay particular attention to their appearance, find opportunities for indulgent celebration, and strive to make the physical environment in which they work as pleasant and beautiful as possible. Invariably they will be found in the staff and service functions of the organization rather than line management functions. We are reminded of an intelligence organization (populated by many ex-military personnel) devoted to Zeus, in which there existed a pocket of human resource personnel led by a worshipper of Aphrodite. This area came to be one of the most beautiful workplaces we have seen. The people dressed immaculately, and did not let a day go by without capturing opportunities for fun and celebration. Eleven of the fifteen or so people in the group went together to the same gym to workout three times each week. This subculture could be labeled ESFP (Jung): organismic (Burns), personal (Handy), short-term oriented and feminine (Hofstede), diffuse, particularist, equalitarian and emotional (Trompenaars), high context and polychronic (Hall). It contrasted with the dominant Apollonine culture of the larger organization, which was INTJ (Jung), mechanistic (Burns), role-based (Handy), long-term oriented and masculine (Hofstede), specific, universalist, hierarchical, and neutral (Trompenaars), low context and monochronic (Hall).

It was curious to see line managers deal with this phenomenon in their midst. Their forays into the HR area were few; they preferred to deal only with the two HR people who 'look like us' and progressively limited their use of the function to basic personnel administration and training. Any attempt by the senior HR executive to engage these executives in more strategic HR development was politely and awkwardly ignored.

As this group became more marginalized from the power centers within the organization, Aphrodite's pathology began to appear. Whilst maintaining their celebratory rituals they also began to argue and fight among themselves in some of the most 'bitchy' ways (except of course when an outsider was present, on which occasions they became gushing and effete in their behavior with one another). The group began to disintegrate, and the more this social fragmentation grew, the more elegant and sophisticated became their HR systems, until finally Zeus had had enough and summarily sacked ten of them.

An Aphrodite organization operating within the commercial sector may need to frame Aphrodite values in terms of work. Even having fun can become a serious matter. Mats Alvesson, in a study of advertising agencies, found advertising people balancing the hedonistic values of an Aphrodite culture against the need to be part of an efficient commercial operation.

> When the advertising people at AD AG are asked to describe themselves, their workplace, and advertising work the following themes are salient and, based on observations and impressions, they seem to be part of the way-of-talking and interacting in everyday life. Friendship and 'personal chemistry' seem to be vital. It is important that people are having fun and can laugh; that advertising workers are emotionally involved in their tasks; that they are free, independent, and even a bit lawless. One has to know better than the customer what is good for him or her and one has to be, in comparison with the other advertising agencies, 'serious' . . .
>
> According to themselves it is very important that advertising persons should have 'fun' and be able to laugh. An interviewee stated that those at AD AG 'should have more fun'. This remark indicates the high level of expectation (or the inclination to talk about fun) and the significant measures that were taken to achieve 'fun' situations. A conference trip turned out to include much more entertainment than conferencing ... It seems that playfulness, a sense of humor, and being relaxed are part of the arsenal of values and norms that are necessary in order to be the 'right material' to become a good advertising person. Serious (in the wrong sense of the word) and boring people seldom fit into advertising agencies, according to AD AG staff. At the same time, it is also important that the fun does not take over. Then it becomes foolery, which is seen to be 'unserious'.[3]

Some cultures have a much more comfortable relationship with Aphrodite than others. James Hillman points to this as a distinguishing feature of Japanese industrial culture as compared with that of the United States:

> We believe that we have lost out to [the Japanese] because they have better management techniques; because they plan farther ahead; they coordinate better among the bankers, researchers, industrialists, and government; because they work like slaves. These economic reasons don't cut it. There is also an aesthetic reason for their guaranteed quality, which our puritan mind cannot even imagine. The Japanese are trained aesthetically early on and live in a culture devoted as much to the chrysanthemum (beauty) as to the sword (efficiency) - to use their symbols.
>
> Japanese people, ordinary people – have hobbies of calligraphy, flower arrangement, dance gesture, paper twisting and cutting. They live in a world of very small detail, which we call quality control. Their eye is trained to notice, their hand to tastefully touch. Watch the sushi chef. Even their language takes immense care. It's aesthetic training that gives them the economic edge, even if they get as drunk as we do and as tired.[4]

The Aphrodite organization provides a stimulating and satisfying environment for all sorts of activities, but it may have to cope with the pathology of the most beautiful of the gods: bitchiness, vindictiveness, superficiality in relationships, self-obsession, and self-indulgence, lack of awareness of social obligations of any kind, inability to tolerate the grittiness of reality, distaste for work, carelessness of consequences.

Aphrodite is often found in the company of Ares, her lover, or Eros, her son. In her contempt for the restraints of conventional society and her delight in immediate experience she has a lot in common with Dionysos and Hermes. She is also forced to spend some of her time with her husband, Hephaistos, the smith and craftsman.

The consultant who looks at organizations from an Aphrodite perspective will look at the quality of experience of those who work in the organization. Are they enlivened rather than deadened by their participation? From this perspective the strength of the organization is to be found in the delight people find in their work and the elegance of their process and product.

Mother Demeter

Of Demeter, the lovely-haired and august goddess,
and of her daughter, the fair Persephone, I begin to sing.
Hail, O goddess! Keep this city safe, and guide my song.[5]

Demeter was originally an Indo-European sky-god, the consort of the Thunder-god. She was very easily assimilated to the Earth-goddess, mother of all, who was worshipped by the indigenous tribes. Her mother, Rhea, and her grandmother, Gaia, were other personifications of the earth. Demeter is distinguished from them in being a more domesticated form of the Earth-mother. She is the harvest, the cultivated and nurturing earth, rather than wild nature or chthonic depths. When the urban Greeks first made a list of the twelve great gods, they left Demeter off the list, just as they left off Dionysos. Presumably it was because she was mainly worshipped by peasants, descendants of the conquered races. Eventually, however, as aristocracy gave way to democracy, her popularity among the common people made it impossible to ignore her. She presided over the crops, especially over grain, for the ripe corn was her golden hair.

The myth of Demeter tells of her reaction to the disappearance of her daughter, Persephone. For nine days and nights she wandered the earth, trying to find some one who had witnessed the disappearance. On the tenth day she came across the goddess Hekate, who told her that her daughter had been abducted, but could not say by whom. The two goddesses hurried off to enquire of the sun-god, Helios, who sees everything. Helios was able to tell them that Hades had driven up out of the earth in his chariot and abducted her. Helios pointed out that Zeus had given his approval for the marriage, and that Persephone was lucky to have such a highly esteemed and powerful husband. Demeter was not the least comforted by this. Furious at Zeus, Hades, and everyone else, she wandered the earth, overwhelmed by grief, bringing famine over the land. The vegetation died, people began starving to death, and the gods became alarmed. Demeter refused to listen to their entreaties to let the crops grow again, so Zeus sent Hermes down to the Underworld to negotiate with Hades for Persephone's release. Hades made no objections to her return, and kindly gave her a pomegranate seed to eat. Demeter welcomed her daughter with great joy, but was aghast at the knowledge that Persephone had eaten the food of Hades. This meant that she would have to return to the Underworld.

So Persephone spends a third of each year with Hades, and Demeter grieves in her absence. However, on her return each year Demeter lets the grain grow again, and the world rejoices.

There is clearly a pattern in human affairs that we call mothering, and Demeter personifies it. She is represented in Christian art in the images of the Madonna and the Pieta. She gives birth, she suckles, she provides, she is anxious for her child, she grieves. This is a psychological pattern as well as a biological one, and men as well as women share in it. Many people in the ancient world, both men and women, used to travel to Eleusis, a small town near Athens, to participate in the secret rituals of Demeter. They believed that it was only by initiation into her mysteries that they could become fully human.

The organization with a strong Demeter culture takes mothering seriously. Central to its image of itself is its task of providing a safe and supportive environment for its members. It must look after them, as a mother does. It undertakes responsibility for the care of its members and sees this as essential to its nature. The executive exercises the power of the carer and nourisher, rather than the power of the bully or manager. Mother Demeter says, 'Trust me. I know what is best for you.' For their part, the members or employees are content to be looked after; they even take it for granted, seeing it as the organization's duty. Efficiency and productivity are not usually central concerns of the Demeter organization. The Demeter organization will continue to look after its children even when they are not financially viable!

The Demeter organization provides what Jack Gibb calls the 'benevolent' environment (Do this because I love you!), which he contrasts both with the 'punitive' environment (Do this or I will punish you!) and the 'autocratic' environment (Do this because I say so!). Demeter-power is still power, though it generates dependency rather than fear. For Gibb, benevolent power relations are a stage in the evolution of organizations from structures dominated by fear to structures in which everyone is empowered and free to realize their personal and collective potential. If Demeter really loves her children she will let them grow up.[6]

In Deborah Bosco's[7] description of a community mental health center, she shows how Demeter-consciousness is expressed not only in its values, goals and organizational structures, but even in its architecture:

> The building itself is actually a hexadecagon, but from the outside it looks round. It has a protruding skylight in the very center of its shingled roof. And it is with this breast-shaped dwelling that we encounter the most primordial aspect of the Eternal Feminine, in the symbol of the breast or container.[8] The shape of the building was deliberately and successfully designed to provide a non-threatening space for the people who enter. Indeed it evokes the experience of 'participation mystique between mother and child . . . the original situation of container and contained'[9] As vessel, it evokes 'the whole scope of basic feminine functions - the giving of life, nourishment, warmth, and protection.'[10] When these aspects of the Great Mother are constellated and projected onto the center, one experiences it as safe, protective, and nurturing. The building further evokes the attributes of the primordial Great Mother by its location at the top of a gently sloping rise or hill. Its architecture does not reflect the work of a psyche intent on transcending its earthly fetters by spiraling towards the heavens, but rather a psyche which reflects the sedentary, stable, grounded aspect of the primordial Great Mother who 'belongs like a hill or mountain to the earth of which she is a part and which she embodies.'[11] This vessel, as symbolized womb or breast, also evokes the transformative aspect of the Great Mother. The womb gives birth to new life. The breast not only sustains life, but enables it to grow. For the client, whether child or adult, this environment not only engenders change and growth, but the gradual withdrawal of these projections and their concomitant integration into self-soothing, self-sustaining, and self-directing capabilities, could be viewed as a process whereby the client gains the ability to 'mother' him or herself. In fact, '25% of the clients return to be trained as facilitators'[12] bringing to life the center's logo: 'People helping people to help themselves'.

The Demeter organization may make strong demands on the trust of its members. At one stage in her travels, Demeter disguised herself and worked as a nurse for a local chieftain and his wife who gave her shelter. Each night she took the woman's infant and placed him in the fire, to burn away his mortality. One night, the child's mother investigated, saw the nurse putting her infant in the fire,and screamed. Demeter was outraged at her lack of trust, threw the infant on the floor, and revealed herself as the goddess, declaring that the woman had destroyed her child's chance to be immortal.

Demeter is not interested in consultation or participative decision-making, nor in rational management structures. If you accept the notion that mother is always right, if you love mother as mother loves you, she will take care of your every need. If you are not a good child, if you bite the breast that feeds you, she will withdraw it. There is plenty of room for the pathology of dependence in the Demeter organization. The members may be unwilling to grow into adults, and the organization may be unwilling to let them. Mother may care or abandon, nourish, or deny, give birth or devour.

Geert Hofstede found a clear distinction in national cultures between those he labeled 'feminine' and those he labeled 'masculine'. In his definition, the former value caring for others, warm relationships, modesty, emotional expression, intuition, beauty. The latter value material success, progress, assertiveness, emotional control, intelligence, size, and speed.[13] When an organization's culture is feminine, but it has to survive in a masculine cultural environment, there will obviously be problems. Often these are resolved through fabrication. The organization meets the demands of the masculine culture for evidence that it has an adequate focus on competition, performance, and accountability, yet people within the organization knows that this is really a pretence. Within the organization members get satisfaction out of celebrating their difference from the mainstream culture.

The traditional Japanese company is often perceived as a Demeter culture. The company holds all its employees in an enormous embrace, and they remain fondly her children, spend their lives in her embrace, and gladly make whatever sacrifices she demands. Many government departments in other countries have traditionally been dominated by Demeter, with employees happy to give up personal ambition and the thrills of freedom in order to feel safe with mother. The situation is changing, however, with such departments now being taken over by more fashionable gods. Community organizations are also likely to have a dash of Demeter in their make-up.

Bernard McCnaimhan gives us a portrait of a Demeter-dominated community organization in *The Centre*:

> Bruce decided that he was more than a little nauseous. He knew there was no escape; something he had done in a previous incarnation had destined him to

be locked in this room with Sylvia for the evening. He set his attentive smile on automatic, and scanned his brain for tried procedures for bearing unbearable situations.

He tried calculating how nauseous he was, on a scale of one to ten, but that only made his condition worse. He tried competing with the others in telling Sylvia how much they had all missed her, but he choked on his first attempt. He tried guessing what each of the other committee members was about to say, and caused some distraction when he mouthed (in perfect sync) Glenda's declaration of 'how much nicer the meetings are when Sylvia's here.' He smothered his laugh with a cough, but a glance at Sylvia was enough to show that she was wise to him. He decided to settle for inertia, frustration, and silence. Who was he to be the serpent in Paradise, any way? Sylvia was what they wanted and Sylvia was what they got. He even kept his smile throughout Sylvia's report on her trip to the UK where, it was apparent, there was enormous admiration for the work of the Centre. There was a lovely little warm glow all round when Sylvia reported that she had made it clear that the Centre's achievements would not have been possible without the specially wonderful and dedicated people of the management group. The very, very special smile she beamed at Bruce at this point was nearly enough to break him, but he managed to hold on.

It was the final item on the agenda which beat him. What had appeared to Bruce's cursory reading as a motion to revise the method of electing the Director, somehow turned into a proposal to renew Sylvia's appointment for another five years. By the time it had passed with acclamation Bruce was trembling uncontrollably. Sylvia turned to him with motherly concern. 'You don't look very well, Bruce. Is there something we can do?'

Sylvia paused for a few seconds. Even in his extremity, Bruce had to admire her timing. Then she confided her diagnosis to the world around her.

'I think somebody needs a cuddle,' she said.[14]

Organizations inflated with Demeter become very safe places for those who value safety and predictability. Uncertainty is generally avoided. However, there is a significant price to be paid. One large corporation with whom we work a great deal is often described in the following terms: 'We may resent the company, but you have to admit it does look after us'. This company offers its employees an extremely generous health plan, more than ample relocation expenses, strong family support systems for expatriates on assignment. It also has a history of negotiating quite satisfactory deals with unions in claims cases. These things do not go unnoticed by the employees, and it is true that, when questioned, they will (far more often than not) speak of being cared for by the organization. But the pathology of Demeter is a smothering dependency, and this in turn breeds passive aggressive responses – even outright irrational rage. Demeter feels the utmost dismay and bewilderment when things get to this stage, and cannot understand how her children whom she has nurtured and protected can be so irrationally ungrateful. In this organization, it is not unusual for senior executives to experience this dismay and bewilderment as they 'cop' the resentment and anger from their workforce that they have genuinely sought to nurture and protect.

The Great Mother, of whom Demeter is one personification, has a double aspect. On the one hand, she nourishes, cares and contains. On the other she smothers, devours, and destroys our individuality. Murray Stein points out the risks of projecting this archetype onto an organization.

> A well-run, consciously-managed organization – if there be such a thing – would attempt to ameliorate the negative side of this archetype by setting limits on involvement, which would protect its members from being overinvested and devoured. Because members of these organizations project the Great Mother upon them and then become so dependent and so look to them for the very basis of material life and comfort and sustenance, the power held is enormous. This is especially true in a materialistic, non- or anti-spiritual culture such as ours is. Beyond rational considerations, it is felt that the organization controls life and death. To be banished from one of them is to starve and collapse into an abandonment depression. The base of support for the ego's existence in the world is threatened. So tied into organizational life can the individual become that the self seems at stake, the core of the personality at risk. Promotion comes to mean self-esteem and life; demotion, abandonment, and death.[15]

Demeter and Dionysos, the Great Mother and the Divine Child, are likely to be found together. She is quite distinct from Hera, as mother is distinct from wife. She is also often associated with Zeus, who is both her brother and her husband. Eros and Hermes (other images of the Divine Child) share her interest in intimacy and transformation.

The consultant who approaches an organization from the perspective of Demeter will be most impressed by the way an organization looks after the interests of its members. He will assume that any business that genuinely cares about its employees will be a business whose employees will repay this concern through their reliability and their willingness to make sacrifices.

Dionysos the Loosener

> *Hail, child of Semele with the fair face! There is no way one can forget you and still compose sweet songs.*[16]

Zeus, in the appearance of a man, seduced the mortal girl, Semele. Hera, jealous as usual, disguised herself as Semele's old nurse and suggested that the girl ask her lover to prove he was Zeus by showing her his true face. Semele asked Zeus to prove his love by swearing to grant whatever she asked. Then she made her request. He had no choice but to appear as he really was. This was too much for her; she was immediately incinerated by the sight of the god. Zeus rescued the child from her womb and sewed him in his own thigh. After a couple of months he opened up his stitches and Dionysos was born. The divine child was, in Greek as well as Christian mythology, the son of the father.

In another story, Zeus lay with Persephone in the form of a snake, and she conceived a child. Hera persuaded the Titans to tear the child to bits and eat him. Athena managed to save his heart and took it to Zeus. Zeus swallowed it and fathered the child again. Dionysos was often called the 'twice-born'. He is a fertility god, a symbol of the rhythmic renewal of nature.

Because of Hera's persecution, so the story goes, Hermes took the baby god off to Asia and changed him into a goat until he was old enough to look after himself. In another story he escaped Hera's anger for some time by being brought up as a girl. The Homeric Hymn to Dionysos tells of the boy-god being kidnapped by pirates. Their plans to rape and sell him came to an end when the ship suddenly stood still. Grape-vines and ivy grew from the masts; the oars turned into snakes; panthers, bears, and lions appeared on the deck. The pirates in terror leapt into the sea, where they were turned into dolphins. Only the helmsman, who had attempted to protect the boy, was saved.

Dionysos was not counted among the Olympian gods until classical times. However, he had been god for the natives of the Balkan Peninsula long before the Greeks arrived. He was the son and lover of the Earth-mother long before the Greeks introduced Zeus into the story. As a god of the indigenous people, a god who did not fit comfortably into the Indo-European sky-family, his worship was neglected and even suppressed by the Greek rulers. Aristocratic governments tried to stamp out the orgiastic rites associated with his worship, but were unable to do so. When eventually his popularity among the common people forced his admittance into the pantheon, he was presented as a foreigner, an Asian god whose worship had at last reached Greece. However, there is evidence that he had been in Greece all the time.

From his beginnings as a vegetation god Dionysos came to personify impulse and ecstasy. His presence is felt in drunkenness as well as in religious experience. He is the god of the flow of life, the god of the sprouting seed, the god of feeling, of joy, of tragedy, of spontaneity, of newness, of creativity, of growth. He is the god of becoming fully oneself. He is also the god of fragmentation, of uncontrollable emotions, of tearing apart and devouring. Hera persecutes him for good reason (in her value system, at least) because he is dangerous to social stability. The Athenians knew the dangers of ignoring him, and attempted to civilize him by dedicating their theatre to his honor. Their playwright Euripides, in The Bacchai, showed the disastrous consequences of failing to acknowledge him. He was depicted wandering from place to place with his band of wild women, establishing his worship, and grievously punishing those who rejected him.

Some organizations are largely devoted to the worship of Dionysos. From Apollo or Athena's point of view, they might not be rightly called organizations at all, for they lack the kind of structures that those gods recognize. Yet they have their own kind of structure, based on feeling rather than rationality, on satisfying the individual's need to do their own thing rather than on serving group needs or causes. Patriarchal (Zeus/Apollo/Hera) organizations rightly regard Dionysos as subverting their values, and are inclined to see the wearing of a floral tie as the first step to full frontal nudity. In the Dionysian organization, people are encouraged to be spontaneous, to be totally engaged, to immerse themselves in the flow of life, to put more value on personal growth than on role or status. Eccentric or bizarre behavior is tolerated. The ability to improvise is highly valued. The criteria of effectiveness in a Dionysian culture are criteria of personal satisfaction, not of service or productivity. Leadership in a Dionysian culture comes from the power of a charismatic personality, rather than from hierarchical or democratic structures. Dionysian organizations are friendly to the feminine. (Dionysos was mainly worshipped by women, and was the only god whose myth makes him eternally faithful to his wife, Ariadne.)

The stories of the creation and early development of Apple Computer have a distinctly Dionysian air to them, as do the stories of many start-up companies in Silicon Valley and elsewhere in the IT industry. Dress codes, formal structures, and standard procedures were eschewed in favor of providing individuals with an environment in which they could flourish and where their creativity could be harnessed to business innovation and growth. Not for them the regulation suit and tie of IBM. These were places to wear jeans, T-shirts, and sweaters so the people would not be constrained by the organization in pursuing their ideals and making their unique contribution.

In the Dionysian organization, each individual has the opportunity to set his or her goals, to make his or her own choices, to create his or her own environment. Life in such an organization is a continuing, flowing process, where experience constantly enriches the individual. It is an organismic, high context, low uncertainty-avoidance, individualistic, and particularistic organization, where people resist any notion of regulating behavior or delineating roles and responsibilities the way an Apollo organization does. When a large organization dominated by Apollo-values takes over a small Dionysos organization (a common enough scenario) there is immediate and enduring friction. The new administration conducts its business by a proliferation of 'low context' procedures, such as memos, reports, meetings, regulations, job specifications, time-lines, and performance audits. This is intolerable for those who have been immersed in the high context, polychronic, open score[17] Dionysian culture. They believe they know what to do without wasting time on such nonsense, and will as likely as not find their satisfaction in subverting or sabotaging it.

In the Dionysian culture the individual's energy and sense of growth comes largely from the group. Being a member of such a group is like dancing - 'where leading and following merge.' As Hillman puts it:

> The phrase in our language that most simply captures the Dionysian spirit is: 'Go with the flow'. Not merely adrift, floating, without compass or port - but flowing with the motions of the psyche. It is like dancing - the Dionysians are depicted usually dancing - where leading and following merge; it is the fusion of one's private consciousness with the field, where borders become imprecise. One develops a special sensitivity to underground reverberations, so that one's will is embraced by the group and represents the group. (Dionysos appears nearly always surrounded by his group, his thiasos.) One embodies the consciousness of the group and is ruler (Lord) of its soul by feeling into all that goes on throughout the organization. [18]

In Mia Nijsmans' description of a London therapy and training institute, whose modes of organization she labels 'Dionysian', the image of 'flow' is central:

> As with the psychodynamic counseling approach, where destination sounds like a contradiction in terms, both structurally and purely processually, 'destination' was a mythical predicament. As in clinical practice, the process is the destination. Growing, individuating, evolving is the pursuit of personal counseling and therapy. That is how the staff was trained. Hence, there was an implicit attitude of 'not forcing things' but letting the experience 'flow'.
>
> This internalized professional culture was reflected in daily morality. Endless hours of talk about apparently unrelated topics, in ever expanding committees or ad hoc working parties, were a case in point. The color of the paint in a reconverted room might become as controversial as the requirements for assessment or the annual budget. I am not suggesting that the people in the organization did not have a value or priority system, neither that everything was equally important or trivial. Instead, I am trying to emphasize the more 'irrational' aspect of organizational life as a real and nearly taken-for-granted component, not only in the clinical but in the organizational setting as well. People's feelings, doubts, hunches were considered equally meaningful along with their logical and rational performances. The wandering, the exploring, the circular, was thus a virtually institutionalized feature which seemed to satisfy most members' needs and may therefore be called 'effective'. There was certainly an element of 'pleasure in the process' that kept people in the organization. The need to belong, the need to share with one's colleagues, the need to participate in organizational activities, were recurring reasons staff members mentioned for staying in the organization. Such benefits compensated even for lower salaries than the ones they earned in their private practices. The generative social and organizational processes seemed to satisfy people's 'higher order needs'. They liked to be in groups, to participate in meetings, to wander. That's where the pleasure principle was prevalent.[19]

Ray Bradbury, writing of 'management from within' sets up the Dionysian organization as an ideal:

> If your meeting room, your board room, or your office (take your pick) isn't a nursery of ideas, a rumpus room where seals frolic, forget it. Burn the table, lock the room, fire the clerks. You will rarely come up with any solutions worth entertaining. The dull room with the heavy people trudging in with long faces to solve problems by beating them to death is very death itself. Serious confrontations rarely arrive at serious ends. Unless the people you meet with are fun-loving kids out for a romp, tossing ideas like confetti, and letting the damn bits fall where they may, no spirit will ever rouse, no notion will ever birth, no love will be mentioned, no climax reached. You must swim at your meetings, you must jump for baskets, you must take hefty swings for great or missed drives, you must run and dive, you must fall and roll, and when the fun stops get the hell out. The whole idea of brainstorming, unless it is a storm of hilarity and ideas clamoring to be born, is silly and non-productive. God deliver me from such.[20]

The pathology of the Dionysian culture is often found in the relationship of membership to leadership. Dionysian cultures are not given to reflection, and they do not have much capacity for self-criticism. In spite of their devotion to personal expression and personal growth, they sometimes give an inordinate amount of power to a 'charismatic' leader, whom they then follow blindly. Dionysian cultures have a tendency to collapse into self-indulgence and chaos, especially when the organization is enmeshed in a wider socio-economic or financial ecosystem. The environment and the Dionysian system exchange energy. Inevitably there are discontinuities and the more open the organization, the more these discontinuities insert themselves into the freedom and creativity characteristic of a Dionysian culture. Descriptions of the collapse of Apple Computers, the exit of Steve Jobs and his replacement by John Sculley, illustrate the way this discontinuity is sometimes played out. Dionysos' morality is the morality of self-fulfillment, and takes no account of formal obligations towards others. If Dionysos is the only god worshipped in an organization, there will be an absence of those qualities, whether of Hera, Eros, Athena, or Apollo, that bind a group together and enable it to act according to conventional notions of effectiveness.

In her novel Babel Tower, A.S. Byatt describes the establishment of a Dionysian community by a group of refugees who have fled from oppression in another land.

Culvert, their charismatic leader, makes a speech outlining the principles on which the community is to be founded:

> The community must strive towards complete freedom for each and every member to live and express himself – or himself – at the utmost.
>
> To this end all false distinctions of the corrupt world from which they had fled must be abolished. There must be no masters or servants, no payment or debt, but a common consent about the work to be done, the delights to be enjoyed, the just sharing of these, and the proper remuneration of all from the common fund of goods and talents. Professions must be abolished, along with privileges, all must turn their hands to all that was possible, as their desires led them, for the work desired to be done is work well done, and slave labor is always ill done.
>
> It will be found, Culvert said, I believe, upon just reflection, that many of the evil distinctions and oppressions in our world come from institutions we have not dared to question. Most of us have already questioned and rejected the religions of our forefathers and compatriots, but we have not sufficiently studied how those unnatural institutions – marriage, the family, the patriarchy, the pedagogic authoritarian relation between teacher and pupil – have also harmed our natural impulses and inclinations.[21]

Culvert goes on to set out various ways in the community's 'natural impulses and inclinations' may be freed from the constraints imposed by traditional society. Needless to say the narrative eventually takes a nasty turn, as Dionysian freedom and charismatic leadership metamorphose into Dionysian humiliation and torture.

Organizations devoted to the arts and performance, especially small ones, are often dominated by a Dionysian culture. It is much more difficult for a Dionysian culture to survive as the dominant culture in a large organization. On the other hand, the Dionysian culture is commonly strong in particular sub-groups within a large, hierarchical organization. Religious organizations are sometimes Dionysian, as are rock bands, self-help and support groups, and fringe political organizations.

Zeus and Dionysos, though they may be seen as polar opposites, are often found together. Dionysos is Zeus in his youth, and Zeus is Dionysos grown old. A Dionysian individual or group can sometimes be found flourishing in an autocratic organization where the CEO gives them free rein to be creative and irresponsible. On the other hand, Hera and Dionysos are hostile towards each other, and they cannot be worshipped together without conflict and tension. Dionysos is often found in organizations in the company of Aphrodite, Eros, and Hermes. He flourishes in the presence of Demeter.

The consultant who approaches an organization from the Dionysos perspective will be looking for the free flow of energy and ideas, the utilization of the full potential of its members, the engagement of all concerned in the creation of something new. In the criteria that are supposed make organizations effective, efficiency will rank much lower than creativity. Abstract structures will be seen as inhibiting rather than facilitating the work of the organization.

Dread Hades

> *How did you dare to come below to Hades' realm,*
> *where the dead live on without their wits as disembodied ghosts?*[22]

Homer says that when the gods had won their battle with the Giants and Titans for control of the universe, Zeus and his two older brothers divided up the world between them by casting lots. Zeus won and got the sky for his kingdom; Poseidon got the sea; and Hades won the Underworld. They decided that the earth could be shared between the three of them. So Hades ruled in the realm of the dead, and stayed there except for one brief excursion to the living world.

The occasion was the abduction of his niece, Persephone, daughter of his sister, Demeter. Eros, eager to demonstrate his power even over the Lord of the Underworld, wounded Hades with an arrow, causing him to fall in love with the young goddess. Hades made the necessary enquiries and learned her identity. With Zeus her father's permission he drove up from the darkness in his chariot and carried her off to be his queen. When the enraged Demeter brought famine on the earth, Zeus ordered his brother to release Persephone. Before she returned to earth, Hades tricked her into eating some pomegranate seeds so that, having eaten the food of Hades, she was obliged to return to the kingdom of the dead for four months each year.

Persephone here symbolizes fresh, new life. Hades is the image of death. Hades rules his kingdom with absolute power. He is grim and inexorable, but not malicious. He is certainly not a manifestation of pure evil, like the Devil. He has no favorites; he applies the rules without discrimination. He keeps his kingdom locked, and has a three-headed watch dog, Cerberus, to prevent any one from leaving. A handful of the inhabitants, mostly defeated Giants and Titans, are subject to eternal torture for crimes against the gods, but most wander as phantoms, mere shadows of their former selves, without their bodies and forgetful of their former lives. They exist without passion. Their forgetfulness is a result of drinking from the river Lethe, a merciful requirement, for memories of the pleasures of life would otherwise cause them intolerable pain. On rare occasions, a hero manages to enter the kingdom of Hades on special terms and leave again[23] but most of the shades must wander forever, without joy or pain or sensation of any kind, over plains of asphodel.

When Odysseus came to the underworld to interview the ghost of the prophet Tiresias, he met Achilles, greatest of the Greek heroes. The latter declared that he would rather be a slave in the house of a landless man on earth than a king among the dead. Hades may not be evil, but it is difficult to say anything nice about him, other than that he is simply doing his job! Apparently, the Greeks did not bother worshipping Hades. They understood that, because he was responsible for ruling the dead, he would have no interest in the living.

Hades, which is the name of the place as well as the name of the god, is a fit image for some organizations. They are inhabited by lost souls, who lead a flavorless existence in a place without life or light. They are systems in a state of absolute doubt. They make no attempt to escape for they do not have the energy, and escape appears impossible in any case. They have no power over their situation, nor is there any point in seeking it. They go through the motions, but without hope, purpose, or feeling. Power in the organization is held by some one remote, cold, detached, and invisible. Life in a Hades organization is dreary and mechanical, without the prick of ambition or the joy of social intercourse. And it goes on forever.

Open systems in high exchange with turbulent environments ruled by Zeus and Apollo often tend to have within them large groups controlled by Hades. As the corporation tries to cope with change (e.g. lost markets, falling prices, lower volumes etc) Zeus and Apollo seek to reorganize, demand more, use power very explicitly, and seek higher levels of compliance, all the while making one strategic change after another. It is not long before Hades inserts himself into this milieu and the workforce becomes desensitized to the promises, the changes, the requests for that extra effort. They have seen it all before, they are all 'changed out'. They outwardly comply, but inwardly have lost all sense of future and shared purpose.

Hades is apparently the assimilation of two quite different gods. In his Indo-European origins he is probably the same god as Zeus. In his Mediterranean origins, he is an earth-god, a god of fertility and plenty. In the old fertility cult the same divine earth-force devoured life and created it. The personality of Hades carries two contradictory images; the image of the permanence of death, and the image of the rhythmical cycle of birth, death, and rebirth. Hades was also called Plouton (Pluto), which makes him the god of wealth. On the one hand, this was a euphemism, for the Greeks preferred not to use his real name. But it also represents a relic of Hades' origin as a fertility god, child of the Great Mother. Wealth, both vegetable and mineral, comes from under the ground. When we die we return to earth and even, in some societies, are planted in it. The domination of Hades culture in an organization may signal the total cessation of life. Paradoxically, acceptance of this situation may be the only way to a new birth.

This understanding is graphically illustrated by Mike Boon, in his description of events that happened on the troop ship 'The Mendi' during World War I:

> On February 21, 1917, the troop ship Mendi was transporting a section of the South African native labor contingent from England to France, when it was involved in a collision with another vessel. The night was particularly dark, with visibility further obscured by thick fog. The Mendi began to sink immediately. In the chaos caused by the darkness and the sloping deck, it rapidly became clear that there would not be time to clear all the lifeboats from the deck. This meant that many men would not have a place on the lifeboats that had been launched. The water was freezing and many of those who jumped into it died of extreme cold. As the ship began to slide under the waves, a lone voice called loudly to

> those who knew, without a doubt, that they were about to die. It was the voice of the Reverend Dyobha, who had been recruited as a clerk and an interpreter.
>
> 'Be quiet and calm, my countrymen, for what is taking place is exactly what you came to do. You are going to die . . . but that is what you came to do ... Brothers, we are drilling the death drill. I, a Xhosa, say you are my brothers. Swazis, Pondos, Basutos, we die like brothers. We are the sons of Africa. Raise your war cries, brothers, for though they made us leave our assegais in the kraal, our voices are left in our bodies.'
>
> And they took off their boots and stamped the death dance on the deck of the sinking ship.[24]

Sometimes the only chance of revival for an organization is to go through a period of absolute doubt. In the organizational decay, in the compost, the seeds may sprout if the environmental conditions are right. This phenomenon of organizational rebirth from the ashes of death is well described by William Bridges.[25] Bridges makes a clear distinction between change and transition. Change can be forced on an organization but, unless the members of the organization undergo a psychological process of transition, the attempted change is likely to be destructive. Where the leaders have joined their staff in a journey into doubt, their attempts to sow the seeds of a new life through a new identity, new purposes, and new processes may be welcomed by the organization at large. Where the bulk of the organization's people are still in a state of suspended doubt, and see no need for substantial change, the leader's efforts will bring demoralization and despair. For a change to be effective, people must own it. Change efforts that disregard the process of transition have little hope of success. Sometimes there has to be a death to allow new life to emerge, but the death has to be acknowledged and honored if this sort of energy is to be generated from it. Bridges warns us that, though change can be implemented very quickly, transition can take a long time. He suggests, however, that leaders with an understanding of the process and appropriate strategies can accelerate it significantly. Unfortunately, the usual story of the Hades culture is not one that involves change. In Greek mythology, only a handful of heroes ever come back from Hades.

In Kriegler's description of work in the Whyalla shipyards in the 1970s, we see how a brutal-paternalistic culture has come to be dominated not by Zeus but by his brother Hades.

> We are treated like children at work. For example, when we are supposed to clock off at the end of the day, the foreman comes along at three minutes to four with our cards and instead of giving them to us in an ordinary rational way, he starts walking towards the clocks which are about fifty yards away and shouts out the person's name. It is usually a nickname which he has made up for each of us. One chap, for reasons known only to the foreman, is called 'shitlegs'. And if you don't dash to his side to accept the card, he shouts 'Too late!' and puts it in the bottom of the pack. Once he has handed out the cards, we are to stop walking and if you walk any further he shouts, 'That's far enough', and you have to stay there. This happens every single evening. The men don't despise him for this because this is just one of the thousands of unpleasant things about the place. It happens so much that the men are not concerned about it any more, they are not even conscious of it any more.[26]

An organization that is dead or dying is likely to be dominated by a Hades culture. There may be a few Giants and Titans who suffer significant tortures, who rage against the dying of the light, but most of the inhabitants accept their fate without much protest. The loss of morale, the loss of the will to fight, is one of the first symptoms of the condition. Occasionally a hero may arrive, create a stir and leave, without changing the condition of the shadowy beings who continue to go about their mechanical tasks without hope of change.

In *The Informed Heart* Bruno Bettelheim describes the adjustment of prisoners to the Hades culture of the concentration camps.

> The chief concerns of new prisoners were to remain physically intact and return to the outer world the same person who left it. Therefore all efforts were directed towards these goals, and they tried to combat as much as possible any weakening of their maturity or self-sufficiency. Old prisoners seemed mainly concerned with the problem of how to live as well as possible inside the camp. Therefore they tried to reorganize their personalities as well as they could to become more acceptable to the SS. Once they had embraced this attitude, everything that happened to them, even the worst atrocity, was 'real'. No longer was there a split between a figure to whom things happened and the prisoner who observed in detachment. The split in personality had disappeared, but at the price of the prisoner's personality no longer being integrated. It dropped to a different, lower level; one of resignation, dependency, submission, and passivity.
>
> Old prisoners could accept this because they could scarcely believe they would

> ever return to the outer world which had grown strange to them. But once they had changed, there was every indication that they were afraid of returning. They did not admit it directly, but from their talk it was clear that in their own minds, only a cataclysmic event – a world war or world revolution – could free them. They seemed aware of what had happened to them as they aged in the camp. They realized they had adapted to camp life and that this process had brought a basic change in their personalities.[27]

Hades does not associate much with the other gods. He is close to his brother Zeus, and shares some of his qualities. Hermes visits him from time to time, as might be expected of the god of transformation. Dionysos, the god of new life, visits him to rescue his mother, Semele, and take her to Mt. Olympus. In a mythical consciousness, life and death are not mutually exclusive; they are opposing aspects of a single reality; there is no new life without death. Hades is death, but in the Orphic rituals he was identified with Dionysos. Persephone is new life, but she is also Queen of the Underworld. The tension between Death and Life, between Hades-Thanatos and Hades-Dionysos is picked up by Robert Linhart in his description of work on the assembly line at the Citroen works near Paris. He describes a culture in which the Apollo/Prometheus fantasy of machine-like efficiency has been pushed to the point of pathology, and Hades has taken over:

> Through the gaps in this gray, gliding line I can glimpse a war of attrition, death versus life and life versus death. Death: being caught up in the line, the imperturbable gliding of the cars, the repetition of identical gestures, the work that's never finished. If one car's done, the next one isn't, and it's already there, unsoldered at the precise spot that's just been done, rough at the precise spot that's just been polished. Has the soldering been done? No, it's waiting. Has it been done once and for all this time? No, it's got to be done again, it's always waiting to be done, it's never done – as though there were no movement, no result from the movement, no change, only a ridiculous illusion of work which would be undone as soon as it is finished under the influence of some curse. And suppose you said to yourself that nothing matters, that you need only to get used to making the same movements in the same way in the same period of time, aspiring to no more than the placid perfection of the machine? A temptation to death. But life kicks against it and resists. The organism resists. The muscles resist. The nerves resist. Something in the body and head braces itself against repetition and nothingness. Life shows itself in a more rapid movement, an arm lowered at the

> wrong time, a slower step, a second's irregularity, an awkward gesture, getting ahead, slipping back, tactics at the station; everything, in the wretched square of resistance against the empty eternity of the work station, indicates that there are still human incidents, even if they are minute; there's still time, even if it is dragged out to abnormal lengths . . . Life is still hanging on.[28]

What of the consultant who approaches an organization from the Hades perspective? If he has been given the task of recommending how to close an organization down, he knows the Hades routine and follows it. It involves taking away light and power and hope. Decisions are best made by people who are remote and, most desirably, invisible. Those who wish to challenge them will find no one to whom they can put their case. Compassion is not only unnecessary but impossible. New life may come, or not come. Hades' key maxim is, 'This is the way it is, and there's nothing to be done about it'.

---

1. A Athanassakis (trans. and ed.) The Homeric Hymns (1976), p. 47.
2. A Roddick (2000) Business as Unusual, p. 84.
3. M Alvesson (1994) '*Talking in Organizations: Managing Identity and Impressions in an Advertising Agency*', Organization Studies, 15, p. 549.
4. J Hillman (1992) *We've Had a Hundred Years of Psychotherapy and the World's Getting Worse*, p. 133.
5. A Athanassakis op. cit., p. 60.
6. See J Gibb (1978) Trust.
7. D Bosco (1994) '*The Great Mother's Work is Never Done*', p. 11.
8. E Neumann (1955) The Origins and History of Consciousness, p. 39.
9. ibid., p. 29.
10. ibid., p. 43.
11. ibid., p. 98.
12. EH Faulk, J Glickman, & M Middleton (1988) '*Low-cost Group Therapy: An Alternative to the Traditional Mental Health Delivery System*', Bulletin of the Meninger Clinic, 52 (4) p. 328.
13. The Anglo countries in Hofstede's study (including Australia, USA, and UK) are all moderately masculine. The most masculine countries are Japan, Austria, Venezuela, Italy, Switzerland, and Mexico. The most feminine are Sweden, Norway, Netherlands, Denmark, Costa Rica, and (the former) Yugoslavia. The latter was the only Eastern European country included in the sample, which was drawn from employees of IBM in fifty countries. While we might argue that IBM has a particular culture (men in dark suits) that is in no way representative of the general population, Hofstede found that there were distinct and significant differences in the values of IBM employees from country to country. See G Hofstede (1991) *Cultures and Organizations*, Chapter 4.
14. B McCnaimhan (1982) *The Centre.*
15. M Stein (1992) Organizational Life as Spiritual Practice' in M Stein & J Hollwitz, *Psyche at Work*, p. 4.
16. A Athanassakis op. cit., p. 58.
17. The distinction between 'open score' and 'closed score' procedures as aspects of culture has been made by Hall. The analogy is taken from music. In closed score music (e.g. classical music) the musician follows the given notes and dynamics and her achievement is judged on how successfully she does so. In open score music (e.g. jazz) achievement consists in producing something new. A computer program is closed score. It follows a determined sequence to a

determined end. An open score procedure is the opposite; if you achieve what you set out to achieve in exactly the way you planned, you have failed! See ET Hall (1976) *Beyond Culture*, p. 112f.

18. J Hillman (1995) *Kinds of Power*, p. 114.
19. M Nijsmans (1992) 'A Dionysian Way to Organizational Effectiveness', in M Stein and J Hollwitz, *Psyche at Work*, p. 148.
20. R Bradbury (1984) 'Management from Within', *New Management*, 1 (4), p. 15.
21. AS Byatt (1966) *Babel Tower*, p. 63.
22. Homer, *The Odyssey*, 11: 444.
23. Herakles descended to the Underworld to capture the watch dog, Cerberus. Orpheus came to rescue his wife, Euridice. Aeneas came to speak to the shade of his father, Anchises. Theseus and Pirithous came to carry off Persephone, but were imprisoned by Hades in the chains of forgetfulness.
24. M Boon (1996) *The African Way*, p. 83.
25. See W Bridges (1991) *Managing Transitions*.
26. RJ Kriegler (1982) *Working for the Company*, p. 123.
27. B Bettelheim (1986) *The Informed Heart*, p. 161.
28. R Linhart (1981) *The Assembly Line*, p. 20.

7

HEROES AND SAVIORS

Fierce Ares

Mighty Ares, golden-helmeted rider of chariots,
stout-hearted, shield-carrying and bronze-geared savior of cities,
strong-handed and unwearying lord of the spear, bulwark of Olympos
father of fair Victory, and succorer of Themis,
. . . from above shine a gentle light on my life
and my martial prowess, that I may be able
to ward off bitter cowardice from my head.[1]

Ares is the son of Zeus and Hera. He was not a particularly popular god in Greece, but he was worshipped with some enthusiasm in Thrace, a wild region in the North, where he seems to have originated. He is the god of war. Though he belongs to the Olympian family, the other gods seem to have little respect for him.

The two Greek war-gods provide a strong contrast, and it is easy to see why the Greeks generally preferred the clear-sighted, cool-headed Athena. Athena fights to protect civilization and her citizens; Ares fights in rage, or for wild excitement and blood-lust. He loves fighting for fighting's sake. However, he does not seem to be a particularly good fighter, and he is not even very brave. Homer in the Iliad, tells how the Hero Diomede, urged on by Athena, seriously wounded Ares. The god, yelling with pain, rushed off to Mt. Olympus to complain to Zeus. Zeus gave him no comfort, simply pointing out how much the other gods detested him. On another occasion he dared fight Athena herself, but the goddess flattened him with a huge rock. When his lover, Aphrodite, came to his assistance, Athena laid her out as well.

The affair between Ares and Aphrodite is supposed to have resulted in four offspring: Eros (Love), Harmonia (Peace), Deimos (Fear), and Phobos (Panic). He also had affairs with other goddesses and women. When his daughter Alcippe was raped, Ares killed the rapist, and was the first person, divine or human, to be tried for murder. He was acquitted by the gods, establishing a precedent for the legitimate use of violence.

Ares is a much simpler god than most of the others. He does not have any of the complexity of Athena, Apollo, or Artemis. The stories about him indicate that he is not very smart. However, we would be wrong to over-simplify him by identifying him with the pathology of warfare. The positive side of Ares must not be overlooked. Ares is the god of energy, of vehemence, of conflict, of activism, of challenge, of fire in the belly and fire in the eyes. He may be emotionally immature and inclined to act without thinking. When he gets too carried away he can be enormously destructive. Yet we cannot live a human life without him. We must honor him as we do the other gods. Without him we have no passion.

Some organizations are completely dominated by Ares. They operate within a macho ideology in which conflict is relished for its own sake, any sign of subtlety or sensitivity is viewed with suspicion or contempt and relationships are entirely competitive. People enjoy kicking each other around the office. The 'manly' virtues of toughness and courage are extolled; any sort of softness is despised. The organization's heroes are those who crash through obstacles rather than negotiate their way around them.

During the eighties aggressiveness came to be seen as a positive and constructive dimension of corporate life.[2] In The Predators' Ball Connie Bruck describes the Ares energy driving Michael Milken and Drexel in the mid eighties:

> On April 2, 1985, the conference room on the eighth floor of the no-frills National Can headquarters in southwest Chicago was packed with the usual armies of deal advisors – M&A lawyers from Skadden, Arps, Slate, Meagher, and Flom as well as from Paul, Weiss, Rifkind, Wharton, and Garrison, and investment bankers from Salomon Brothers. There were some new investment banking faces too, troops who were still a little green but who had launched a juggernaut that was now commanding the attention, and fear, of corporate chieftains across the country, as well as the one in this room.
>
> Drexel – in the spirit of the GI Joe poster hanging behind the desk of one of Drexel's senior executives, a poster which had been designed as a mock ad for the firm and featured the hero leading his platoon, their guns spitting fire – had arrived.[3]

Many people cannot tolerate the Ares culture, but the Ares energy has much to recommend it. The Ares organization is full of challenge and excitement. Conflict is not suppressed or avoided but is welcomed and even enjoyed. Arguments are valued. Management and staff revel in each other's energy. The organization acknowledges people's need to resist, to assert their right not to be pushed around, and if they want something they know that they can fight for it. They know also that they don't have to concern themselves about offending sensitive personalities, because people who can't take the heat don't stay around. Intellectual subtleties may be neglected, and the delight in fighting for fighting's sake may lead to some unfortunate decisions, but there is real engagement in what is going on. Ares is often mistaken, but never boring. He does not care too much what is done, as long as it is done energetically.

Ares has little interest in the future and little ability to plan for it. Like Aphrodite, he is focused on immediate experience. He may get so engaged in the fight that he forgets what the fight is about. The Ares organization may experience a lot of excitement and expend a lot of energy yet produce very little. At his best, Ares is a mover and energizer who makes things happen. At his worst, he is a bully and blusterer for whom the obvious solution to any problem is the random application of violence. The Ares organization may manifest the best and worst of him together.

The Greek city-state of Sparta was organized on military lines, and it was one of the few places in Greece where the citizens gave much attention to the worship of Ares. Plutarch's description of the Spartan education system shows an Ares culture at work:

> As soon as the boys reached the age of seven, Lycurgus took charge of them all himself and distributed them into Troops: here he accustomed them to live together and be brought up together, playing and learning as a group. The captaincy of the Troop was conferred on the boy who showed the soundest judgment and the best fighting spirit. The others kept their eyes on him, responded to his instructions, and endured their punishments from him, so that altogether this training served as a practice in learning ready obedience. Moreover as they exercised boys were constantly watched by their elders, who were always spurring them on to fight and contend with one another; in this their chief object was to get to know each boy's character, in particular how bold he was, and how far he was likely to stand his ground in combat.
>
> The boys learned to read and write no more than was necessary. Otherwise their whole education was aimed at developing smart obedience, perseverance under stress, and victory in battle. So as they grew older they intensified their military training, and got into the habit of cropping their hair, going barefoot, and exercising naked. From the age of twelve they never wore a tunic, and were given only one cloak a year. Their bodies were rough, and knew nothing of baths or oiling: only on a few days in the year did they experience such delights. They slept together by the Squadron and Troop on mattresses which they made for themselves from the tips of reeds growing along the river Eurotas, broken off by hand without the help of any iron blade.[4]

Another aspect of the Ares culture is brought out in Mike Royko's description of council meetings presided over by Mayor Daley, of Chicago:

> The meetings are seldom peaceful and orderly. The slightest criticism touches off shrill rebuttal, leading to louder criticism, and finally an embarrassingly wild and vicious free-for-all. It can't be true, because Daley is a man who speaks highly of law and order, but sometimes it appears that he enjoys the chaos, and seldom moves to end it until it has raged out of control.

> Every word of criticism must be answered, every complaint must be disproved, every insult must be returned in kind. He doesn't take anything from anybody.[5]

The Ares organization often has the atmosphere of the men's locker room, and indeed the culture of sports clubs is often dominated by Ares. Military organizations will have an Ares culture, as will any organization dedicated to activism – political, environmental, or social. Sales and marketing are areas where Ares energy may be prominent, for this god reveals himself in the ethos of competition. Women are not necessarily excluded from Ares organizations and many women enjoy working in an Ares culture. Like the Demeter culture, Ares culture is affective. There is no shame in expressing emotions, but the emotions expressed are very different from those of Demeter or Eros. It is also diffuse; there is not much concern to distinguish task from task, role from role, work from play, thinking from feeling, or public space from private space. All seem to be blended in passionate action. The Ares energy in an organization is oriented towards immediate experience. If the organization does have a long-term orientation, it gets it from one of the other gods, probably Zeus or Prometheus.[6]

The leader in the Ares organization is expected to be a model of heroism and discipline. Getting the best out of subordinates involves both encouraging and controlling their urge to compete with each other for the spoils and glory of war. Wess Roberts, in The *Leadership Secrets of Attila the Hun*, stresses this aspect of the leader's role in the Ares-dominated corporation when he has Attila advise his chieftains on the distribution of booty.

> Never reward a Hun for doing less than is expected of him. Otherwise, he will doubt your sincerity in rewarding appropriate acts and, even worse, expect reward for performing deeds for which you hold no approval.
>
> Never reward a Hun for every act completed correctly. Otherwise, he will not act in the absence of your presence or without the certainty of recognition.
>
> Grant small rewards for light tasks. Reserve heaps of booty for dangerous, gallant, substantial effort and worthy accomplishment.
>
> Praise those who are simply good Huns. Their need for gratification tends to parallel their level of ambition. Security is utmost for those who risk not. Give them, therefore, assurance – not great booty – lest they learn large value is given to those who just get by.
>
> Sincere concern for and purposeful mingling with your Huns will raise their spirits and encourage greater valor.

> Teach your Huns that the booty of battle is nothing more than wages for their service. Heaps of booty, promotion through the ranks and recognition as being a mighty warrior are reserved for those who go beyond the normal call of duty.
>
> Grant your Huns the benefit of your interest in the welfare of their families and the condition of their stores; share your riches with those who are loyal and stand in need. They will be certain to willingly follow you into the mouth of hell, should the occasion arise.
>
> Care more for the rewarding of your Huns than for rewarding yourself. Your own rewards will then far exceed even your greatest hopes and dreams.
>
> Never give a Hun a reward that holds no value for yourself.
>
> Never underestimate the ability of the empire or other foes to gain the support and loyalty of Huns you fail to heed and rightfully reward.
>
> Be generous with small tokens of appreciation – they will multiply in returned loyalty and service.[7]

Ares has a strong connection with Aphrodite, and the two patterns – pleasure and energy – are simultaneously present in the passionate organization. Ares is often found with Zeus or Hera, who use him to confirm their power and who moderate his tendency towards indiscriminate destruction. He is also closely associated with Herakles. On the other hand, he is usually at odds with Athena, and has nothing in common with Hestia.

The consultant who approaches an organization from the Ares perspective will see competition as an end in itself. She believes that the best way to make the organization competitive with other organizations is to force its members to compete with each other. Athena's notions of participative decision-making and Artemis' notion of intuitive collectivity have no place in the competitive organization. People must meet to do battle, not to reach consensus. Only through conflict and confrontation will the organization function effectively.

Bold Herakles

I have a splendid theme: Herakles
Is the son of Zeus;

And has surpassed the glory of his birth
With the labors of his noble life;
By destroying beasts by which men lived in terror
He won for us the tranquility we enjoy.[8]

The Greek myths are full of heroes, men who lived a long time ago and dealt with the gods directly – often, it appears, on equal terms. The most popular of the hero stories were the stories of Herakles the hero who was not only a man but a god.

King Amphitryon married his niece, Alcmene, the wisest and most beautiful of women. She refused to sleep with him until he had gone to war and avenged the murder of her brothers. One evening Zeus disguised himself as the battle-weary Amphitryon. He arrived at the palace and announced that vengeance had been exacted. Then he spent the night with Alcmene. She was somewhat surprised when the real Amphitryon arrived home next morning. The outcome of these events was the birth of Herakles, the greatest of the heroes.

There are many tales of Herakles. The picture we get is of a man of great energy and drive, plenty of good will towards people, and a tendency to take the most direct path to any goal. He is good-humored, generous, and courageous. On the other hand, compared to other heroes like Odysseus, Perseus, and Jason, he is not very clever, and not particularly charming. His lack of subtlety is symbolized in his choice of the club as his preferred weapon. He has a violent temper and an enormous appetite. He is macho man.

Most of the stories about Herakles are concerned with the tasks he had to perform to expiate his crime of killing his own wife and children. (*It was Hera who was actually responsible for this. In her unrelenting persecution of Zeus' illegitimate children she had driven Herakles mad, so that he believed he was hunting wild animals.*) In expiation of his blood-guilt he had to serve as a slave to King Eurystheus, a coward and liar. On Eurystheus' orders he had to clear the sea of pirates. He had to capture or kill assorted monsters and wild animals (including Cerberus, the three-headed hound that guards the gates of Hades, and Hydra, a monster whose many heads grew again as fast as the hero cut them off). He had to go to the land of the Amazons and bring back the girdle of Hippolyta, their queen. He had to find the garden of the Hesperides, at the very edge of the world, and bring back the golden apples that grew there. In the course of these journeys he had many adventures. For instance it was Herakles who shot the eagle that was devouring the liver of Prometheus and set the Titan free. He also had many sexual adventures. He made love to the fifty daughters of King Thespius in a single night. Wanting to make the most of the presence of so great a hero in his house, the king got Herakles drunk so that he thought he was with the same girl all night. Of course, each of the daughters bore him a son.

When Herakles won the hand of the lovely Deianeira, he had to cross a flooded river with her. The centaur Nessus offered to carry Deianeira across the river, and then tried to rape her in mid-stream. Herakles shot the centaur with an arrow. As he was dying Nessus gave the girl a mixture of his blood and semen, telling her that she should use it as a love potion to ensure that Herakles would love her forever. Years later, when Herakles was returning home to her after his adventures, she heard that he was bringing another woman home with him. This seemed a good time to use the love potion, so she dyed a shirt in it and sent it to her husband. When he put it on, the centaur's poisonous blood (poisonous because Herakles' arrow tips had been dipped in the poisonous blood of the Hydra) began to eat into his skin, and when he tried to take it off his flesh came away with it. In agony he begged his son to build a funeral pyre for him and begged a passing traveler to set it alight. There was a flash of lightning and Herakles was at last taken to be with the gods, having earned divinity through his many trials.

Contemporary European images of the hero continue to follow the classical Greek masculine model, personified in Herakles. Heroes are fighters. They overcome obstacles, escape from captivity, transcend suffering, kill monsters, tame the wilderness, save people, are pathologically competitive, and leave a trail of wreckage behind them. It is a perspective that has been the source of a great deal of the achievement of Western society. It is also the source of much of the damage that we continue to do to the planet and each other. It can be argued that Western culture has suffered from a hero-pathology for some time. In collective as well as personal life we have been too much inclined to think of the goals of life in terms of 'mastery' and 'achievement' and to ignore the random destruction that goes with this perspective. This is not to suggest that we should abandon the hero-image. We should, however, avoid being stuck, personally or collectively, in what is essentially an adolescent way of being.

In his reported interview with the Australian entrepreneur Alan Bond, at a time when Bond's businesses were failing and he had been largely discredited, Gerard Henderson shows us a man intent on depicting himself as a hero:

> When I spoke to Alan Bond early in 1989 he was still in buying mode and had his eyes firmly on John Fairfax Limited (*the publishers of the advertising-rich newspapers The Sydney Morning Herald, The Age, and The Australian Financial Review*). An offer was apparently made in January 1989 but there was no acceptance. Within a few months it was apparent that Bond Corporation was in even more trouble than John Fairfax Group Limited.
>
> GH Currently you are the proprietor of the highly profitable newspaper The West Australian. Do you have any plans for a long-term move into the print media?
>
> AB Well if we are doing something in newspapers, it won't be by half measures. They said we couldn't build an aluminum plant in Western Australia. All the big guys were against it but I built an aluminum plant there and made a huge success of it.
>
> GH They said you couldn't win the Americas Cup.
>
> AB They said we couldn't build an automated brick factory in Western Australia. We built an automated brick factory there. They said we would never build an offshore oil platform in Western Australia, that you just couldn't do it. But we did it.
>
> GH It's a bit like the beer advertisement, isn't it?.
>
> AB Yes, I do believe that people can take the assumption that it's all too hard and never do anything. We do things. We are a builder - a builder of businesses.[9]

Bond's self promotion depicted him in the role of 'businessman as hero', the 'little Aussie battler' fighting for a place in the world against the stupidity of the bureaucracies, the mediocrity of the general populace, the lack of vision of the politicians, and the malice of the 'big guys'. It is a myth that bore little relation to the reality of Bond's business dealings – which were dominated rather more by the pathology of Hermes, the thief and liar. Nevertheless, Bond was successful for a decade in identifying himself as a hero, and the companies that he controlled mirrored Bond's personality in their culture.[10]

The organization that has a strong Herakles culture sees itself cast as a hero. It has a quest to fulfill, a mission to perform. There are giants to wrestle, dragons to slay, maidens to rescue, tyrants to overthrow, rivers to divert, mountains to flatten, forests to clear. There is a sense of having to do all this single-handed. Leadership in such an organization is given to a powerful individual, whom the members do their best to emulate. Organizational structures are minimal. The chief executive leads by example rather than by giving orders or by consultation. Subtleties, ethical, intellectual, or operational, are not greatly respected. The organization is dominated by an individualistic macho ethos, which values the ability to crash through, by sheer strength, to endure pain, to resist higher authority, to aim at the impossible. There is little sense of social obligation or responsibility. However, the hero can be extraordinarily generous. The hero (whether an individual or an organization) does what he does because he chooses to, not because of the directives or expectations of others.

In The Right Stuff Tom Wolfe describes the Herakles culture of young fighter pilots, for whom:

> [T]he idea here (in the all-enclosing fraternity) seemed to be that a man should have the ability to go up in a hurtling piece of machinery and put his hide on the line and then have the moxie, the reflexes, the experience, the coolness, to pull it back in the last yawning moment – and then go up again the next day, and the next day, and every next day, even if the series should prove infinite – and, ultimately, in its best expression, to do so in a cause that means something to thousands, to a people, a nation, to humanity, to God. Nor was there a test to show whether or not a pilot had this righteous quality. There was, instead, a seemingly infinite series of tests. A career in flying was like climbing one of those ancient Babylonian pyramids made up of a dizzy progression of steps and ledges, a ziggurat, a pyramid extraordinarily high and steep, and the idea was to prove at every foot of the way up that pyramid that you were one of the elected and anointed ones who had the right stuff and could move higher and higher and even – ultimately, God willing, one day – that you might be able to join that special few at the very top, that elite who had the capacity to bring tears to men's eyes, the very Brotherhood of the Right Stuff itself.
>
> None of this was to be mentioned, and yet it was acted out in a way a young man could not fail to understand. When a new flight (i.e. a class) of trainees arrived at Pensacola, they were brought into an auditorium for a little lecture.

> An officer would tell them: 'Take a look at the man on either side of you.' Quite a few actually swiveled their heads this way and that, in the interest of appearing diligent. Then the officer would say: 'One of the three of you is not going to make it!' – meaning, not get his wings. That was the opening theme, the motif of primary training. We already know that one of you does not have the right stuff – it only remains to find out who.
>
> Furthermore, that was the way it turned out. At every level in one's progress up that staggeringly high pyramid, the world was once more divided into those men who had the right stuff to continue the climb and those who had to be left behind in the most obvious way.[11]

The Herakles organization is beholden to nobody. Within such an organization, individuals who resist orders are likely to be admired rather than chastised. (Tom Wolfe's young pilots are forbidden to transgress a strict safety code, but they know that they are expected to demonstrate their manhood by taking risks, even though it means the occasional loss of millions of dollars worth of hardware.)

The organization has the same resistance to being pushed around. Since it recognizes no one's right to tell it what to do and since it has little capacity for reflecting on the consequences of its actions, it can be randomly and unintentionally destructive. The life of Herakles is characterized by the inadvertent slaying of innocent people. It is also characterized by a constant battle against the various manifestations of the Earth-mother.[12] In the contemporary corporation the pathological Herakles culture may be revealed in a reckless destruction of the natural environment.

The development and construction industries provide many examples of Herakles cultures. Corporations engaged in mining are also likely to have a strong Herakles aspect to their culture. Small businesses often live within a myth of Herakles as they battle for survival against the giants. Herakles cultures can also be found in activist organizations of all kinds, including environmental organizations.

Herakles is the favorite of Zeus. Herakles has a lot in common with his father, and the Herakles organization may be a youthful stage in the development of a Zeus organization. Herakles also has a lot in common with Ares, though he readily got into a fight with both this god and Apollo. He is hostile to Hera, and she to him.

The consultant who comes to an organization from a Herakles perspective will talk a lot about 'mission statements' and 'organizational goals', but rather less about organizational structures. Relationships are of little interest to him. Neither is operational efficiency. What matters is that the organization drives towards its goals with no concern for the bruises it may endure on the way.

Cunning Prometheus

You did not tremble
At the name of Zeus. Your mind
Was yours, not his, and at its bidding
You regarded mortal men
Too high, Prometheus.[13]

Prometheus was not one of the Olympian gods. He belonged to an earlier race of gods, the Titans, whom Zeus and his family had to battle to gain control of the universe. Prometheus, whose name means Forethought, realized that the gods were going to win this war, and accordingly changed sides. When the gods had established their domination he expected to be rewarded, but Zeus denied him. Accordingly, he set out to make life as difficult for the gods as he could by creating men. He fashioned them out of clay and, when they remained nothing but dead clay, he asked Athena to breathe soul into them.

Zeus did not think much of these creatures and tried several times to wipe them out. Each time, Prometheus came to their rescue. When Zeus demanded that men sacrifice to the gods all the animals they hunted, Prometheus tricked him into accepting the fat and bones in sacrifice and letting men have the meat. When Zeus turned out all the lights so that men would starve to death in the cold and dark, Prometheus went up to Mt. Olympus and stole the fire from Hephaistos' forge. He brought men this fire, which not only lighted up their world and kept them warm, but also gave them technology, for Prometheus taught them the crafts (including the craft of writing) by which they could civilize themselves and get control of the earth. When Zeus tried to destroy the human race in a great flood, Prometheus taught them how to build a boat and escape. For the Greeks, Prometheus was the savior of mankind and a god of science and technology.

Prometheus was the savior of mankind quite specifically, for he did not much approve of womankind. According to the Prometheus myth, the first woman, Pandora, was created by Zeus to make things difficult for Prometheus and the men he supported and defended. When Prometheus refused to take her as wife, she was given to his stupid brother Epimetheus. She accidentally let loose all the diseases and other disasters that plague the human race, and her daughters have consistently inhibited men in their mission to control the earth (and their associated tendency to destroy it).

Eventually Zeus lost patience with Prometheus completely and, with the help of Hephaistos, nailed him to a rock on the outer reaches of the universe. He sent his eagle each day to feast off the Titan's liver. After thirty thousand years Herakles shot the eagle and Zeus set Prometheus free in exchange for some useful advice on how to be powerful forever.

The Prometheus myth is a fantasy of setting people free from the power of the gods, of inevitable progress towards a better world, of gaining control over natural forces. It is a fantasy that has had enormous power in the history of Western civilization, especially in the past three hundred years. Indeed, civilization has come to be defined in terms of the gifts that Prometheus can bring: science, the machine and the better world that only they can deliver. This is a peculiarly masculine fantasy, for science and technology have been peculiarly male domains.

A key image of the Promethean culture is technology. It sees the universe as a machine, the political and economic system as a machine, the organization as a machine. The managers of such organizations are disposed to see themselves as free, decision-making individuals in control of this machine.

There are plenty of Promethean organizations around. They are designed like machines and are driven by technocrats. The well-oiled machine of the Promethean organization does not perceive any reason to take account of human needs and human diversity, because the system will function more efficiently if such differences are transcended. It wants its executives to be highly functioning individuals, with the specific competencies demanded by the particular task, and it wants them to fit into the structures provided. Structures are all important, for the efficiency of the organization depends on them. Promethean organizations like to build complex organizational structures, and accordingly are likely to be stable and enduring. Promethean organizations have a long-term orientation, looking to the future rather than focusing on immediate experience. Prometheus was a craftsman, and an important aspect of the Promethean culture is its mission to make things, to build, to control the chaos of the natural world. The great industrial corporations which emerged in the nineteenth century and survived well into the twentieth were characterized by a strongly Promethean culture. By the beginning of the twenty-first century many of them have been taken over by one of the 'short-term' gods, Ares or Hermes.

In his study of The Action Company, Edgar Schein describes an organization dominated by the Promethean personality of its founder: In the organization as he describes it, the management culture is embedded in the Promethean narrative of progress, control, and the triumph of rationality.

> Murphy believed completely in a proactive model of human nature and in people's capacity to master nature, a set of assumptions that appeared to be closely correlated to his engineering background. Hence, he always expected people to be on top of their jobs and was very critical of them, both in public and in private, if he felt they were not completely in control. Recognizing that circumstances might change the outcome of even the best laid plans, Murphy expected his managers to renegotiate plans as soon as they observed a deviation. Thus, for example, if an annual budget had been set at a certain level and the responsible manager noticed after six months that he would overrun it or else miss the schedule, he was expected to get the situation back under control, according to the original assumptions, or come back to Murphy and senior management to renegotiate. It was absolutely unacceptable either not to know what was happening or to let it happen without informing senior management and renegotiating.
>
> Murphy believed completely in open communications and the ability of people to reach reasonable decisions and make appropriate compromises if they openly confronted the problems and issues, figured out what they wanted to do, and were willing to argue for their solution and honor any commitments they made. He assumed that people have 'constructive intent', a rational loyalty to organizational goals and shared commitments. Withholding information, playing power games,

> competitively trying to win over another members of the organization on a personal level, blaming others for one's failures, undermining or sabotaging decisions one had agreed to, and going off on one's own without getting others' agreement were all defined as sins and brought public censure. But thinking for oneself and doing the smart thing were so highly valued that subordinates were expected to argue with their bosses if they thought what was being asked was 'stupid' or, if the boss still insisted, were licensed to be insubordinate. Because the bosses lived in the same culture, they were, of course, less likely to issue peremptory orders and more likely to listen when their subordinates raised questions.[14]

Nineteenth century industrialists were infatuated with their machines, and one of the fruits of this infatuation was a tendency to see their workers as machines. It was only natural that a theory of industrial management would emerge in which workers were reduced to being extensions of the machines with which they worked. It is not much of a step from there to seeing the organization itself as the machine, and its members as its wheels and cogs and levers. The industrial age may be in its final spasms, and the image of the machine may have become more sophisticated, yet this vision of management persists in many organizations, especially those dominated by engineers.

> Engineers make machines which control themselves and each other. These machines 'appreciate the situation', measure the divergence of what is from what ought to be and adapt their behavior accordingly. In doing so, they apply 'rules' which they have previously learned; and some, in the absence of an appropriate rule, will find one and remember it next time. In all this they behave very much like men, who they excel in accuracy though not in variety of response.
>
> Such machines do not need to be continually 'directed', like a chisel or a lathe or a bus. They do not even have to be continually supervised. They will do these things largely for themselves. The job of the engineer is to maintain them in optimum condition and to define from time to time what they are expected to do.
>
> Now this is precisely the goal of all managers of men. How simple life would be if all management, having defined the common purpose, could confine itself to the care of health, welfare, and working conditions, leaving the organization to run itself! This is also the goal of all the managed. Who would ask more than to be given the general objective and allowed to get on with the job, self-directed and self-controlled, in working conditions as favorable as single-minded attention could make them? The automatic factory is a model to the 'directed' factory not merely in efficiency but also in what for want of a better word we might call 'ideology'.

> It used to be a reproach to a manager that he treated men like machines. We may be in sight of the day when it is a reproach to the manager that he has to treat machines like men.[15]

The scientific mindset and the image of the machine are to be found in both Apollonine and Promethean organizations. They differ in that Apollo represents 'pure' science and Prometheus represents 'applied' science. For Apollo, the organization-as-machine is the most rational mode of organization, the most elegantly scientific way of managing people. Prometheus' focus is on the task. The organization-as-machine can get the job done and make an impact on the world. Where the organization dominated by Apollo is likely to be hierarchical, the Promethean organization may be equalitarian. Where the Apollo culture is universalist, the Prometheus culture is particularist.[16] The best form of organization for the Promethean manager is the one that works best in practice, not the one that conforms to some abstract principles of good management.

Prometheus was unable to give men souls. He totally rejected the feminine. He saw himself as a hero defying the tyrannical patriarchy, yet he finally colluded with it. He found that his every attempt to save men through his cleverness left them in still deeper trouble. Promethean organizations are a bit like that. And because, like Prometheus, they have an arrogant and unshakeable conviction of their own rightness and righteousness, they find it very hard to change - in spite of their inventiveness.

The Promethean culture is often found in the manufacturing industry. Engineers have a special affinity for it. State bureaucracies are often designed along Promethean lines but, unless they have a strong sense of mission to accomplish some Promethean task, the machine quickly gets rusty.

The excessive worship of Prometheus, the divine champion of humankind, paradoxically leads to dehumanization. On the other hand, every organization needs something of the Promethean spirit if it is to become a learning community.

> Among the many managers and consultants I have encountered, the most effective ones take a scientific-engineering approach to managerial issues. The organization learns. It makes a series of provisional tries at solutions to problems as they occur, building up a store of wisdom as to what works for this organization. The more members of the organization are involved in each informal experiment, the more effective is the provisional trying process. If the whole organizational unit is involved in all of the processes, it provokes an organizational climate of empiricism and excitement: in making preliminary guesses, in planning on data collection, in discussing alternative problem solutions, in collecting data, and in generalizing about the findings. This conception of management makes managing a highly professional process that is more than a job for technicians, rule-makers, fire-fighters, or prescription-followers.[17]

Prometheus obviously has a lot in common with the other craftsman, Hephaistos, with the other scientist, Apollo, and with the other champion of individual empowerment, Athena. However, where Hephaistos focuses on the skillfully fashioned product and the dignity of crafting, Prometheus sees the products as means to a greater end - gaining control over the chaos of nature and building a technical civilization. Where Apollo's interest in cause and effect leads inevitably to an image of the machine as representing the ideal organizational model, Prometheus pursues the fantasy of emancipating humankind through technology. Where Athena seeks balance and consensus through the application of common sense, Prometheus uses reason as a tool to gain mastery of his environment. Prometheus has a close, conflict-ridden relationship with Zeus. In a strongly Promethean culture, there is not likely to be an obvious presence of Eros or Dionysos, or of the nature-goddess, Artemis.

The consultant bringing the Promethean perspective to bear on an organization will be guided by the image of the smoothly functioning machine designed to fulfill a particular mission. He will look to whether the organizations structures and procedures are appropriate to achieve its goals. He will look for faults in the operation of the machine and will deal with them. He will have the greatest confidence in his ability to find the correct technical fix for every problem, and a tendency to recommend bringing in sophisticated machines wherever feasible to replace human personnel.

1. A. Athanassakis (trans. and ed.) *The Homeric Hymns* (1976), p. 58.
2. We find the legitimization of Ares in the image of management and corporate culture presented by such writers as R Buskirk (1989) *The Frontal Attack*; M Kennedy (1985) *Office Warfare*; W Roberts (1989) *Leadership Secrets of Attila the Hun.*
3. C Bruck (1988) *The Predators' Ball*, p. 105.
4. Plutarch (c.100 A.D.) in R Talbot (ed. and trans.) (1988) *Plutarch on Sparta*, p. 28. According to Plutarch, girls were similarly educated to toughness and competitiveness, being made to 'run and wrestle and throw the discus and javelin'. ibid., p. 24.
5. M Royko (1971) *Boss: Richard J. Daley of Chicago*, p. 97.
6. For the affective/ neutral distinction and the diffuse/specific distinction see F Trompenaars & C Hampden-Turner (1998) *Riding the Waves of Culture* Chapters 6 and 7 respectively. For discussion of the short-term/long-term orientation see ibid., Chapter 9 and G Hofstede (1991) *Cultures and Organizations*, Chapter 7.
7. W Roberts op. cit., p. 179.
8. *Euripides*, Herakles (trans P Vellacott) (1982), lines 691 - 696 p. 174.
9. G Henderson (1990) *Australian Answers*, p. 67.
10. Greg Bailey explores the myth of 'businessman as hero' in *Mythologies of Change and Certainty in Late 20thCentury Australia* (2000). For his discussion of Bond, see p. 158 - 166.
11. T. Wolfe (1979) *The Right Stuff*, p. 88.
12. The many and monstrous serpents that Herakles has to battle are images of the old mother-cult. Psychologically, Herakles is the adolescent male who has to break free from the power of his mother.
13. Aischylos. Prometheus bound, in D Grene & R Lattimore (1960), p. 84.
14. E Schein (1991) 'The Role of the Founder', in PJ Frost et al. *Reframing Organizational Culture*, p. 21.
15. G Vickers (1967) *Towards a Sociology of Management*, p. 15.
16. For the hierarchical/equalitarian distinction see G Hofstede (1991) *Cultures and Organizations*, Chapter 2; for the universalist/particularist distinction see F Trompenaars & C Hampden-Turner (1998) *Riding the Waves of Culture*, Chapter 4.
17. J Gibb *Trust* (1978), p. 179.

8

THE VIRGIN GODDESSES

Gentle Hestia

> *Hestia, you who tend the sacred dwelling*
> *of the far-shooting lord, Apollon, at holy Pytho,*
> *from your tresses flowing oil ever drips down.*
> *Come to this house! Come in gentle spirit*
> *with resourceful Zeus and grant grace to my song.*[1]

When the ancestors of the Greeks were driving their cattle across the northern plains, there was a woman in each clan who had the task of carrying the fire. At each stopping place she would use her carefully preserved heap of hot coals to light a fire that the clan could gather round in the darkness, for cooking and for security. Because of the single-mindedness necessary for such a task, she was an unmarried woman or a widow, who received the status appropriate to this responsibility. Since the gods were assumed to have the same social organization as mortals, the Indo-Europeans worshiped a fire-goddess who performed the same function for the Thunder-god and his family. When the Greeks eventually decided on the constitution of the Olympian pantheon, this goddess emerged as Hestia, elder sister of Zeus and goddess of home-making and the hearth.

Hestia is one goddess about whom there are very few stories, and she is rarely depicted in Greek art. She is hardly personified at all. Indeed, she seems to be more of a place than a person. She dwells in the heap of glowing coals in the hearth, the center of the home, around which the family gathers to keep warm. She dwells also in the community fire, around which the larger community gathers for warmth, light, and ritual. The Latin word for hearth is focus, and Hestia is the focus of the city, the clan, and the family. She is not a flamboyant goddess, but she is crucially important nonetheless. She was highly honored by the Greeks, who offered her the first and last sacrifice at their festivals. She had few temples, for the hearth in every home was her shrine.

One day the gods were sitting around the great table in their board room in the palace of Mt. Olympus, when there was a knock on the door. There was a young god standing there, dressed in womanish clothing, with vine leaves in his hair. He declared, in an Asian accent, that he was Dionysos, son of great Zeus, returned from his travels abroad and claiming his seat at the table. The gods looked around uneasily, for there were only twelve seats and they were all filled. After a moment's pause Aunt Hestia stood up, gave him her seat, and presumably retired to the kitchen to make every one a cup of ambrosia.

As the maiden aunt of the gods, Hestia has no interest in being the center of attention. She is the humble goddess. Yet what she represents is the center of things. She is the center of the individual, the center of the family, the center of the city, the center of the world. She represents the place of stillness that we circle around, the focus towards which everyone faces. She does not enter into the squabbles of the gods, but sits quietly and works at her weaving. She is quiet and self-effacing, but demands considerable honor from humans. A virgin goddess, like Athena and Artemis, she insists on being her own person, and calmly resists marriage overtures from Apollo and Poseidon. She is so upset to find them fighting over her that she ends the conflict by vowing perpetual virginity.

There are societies where 'just sitting' is regarded as a legitimate activity. Obviously, our mainstream society is not one of them. There is not much value placed on looking inward, on stopping to rest in what is essential. Things have been falling apart for so long that there is little sense of a focal point around which everyone is happy to gather from time to time. Yet Hestia, like the other gods, represents both an individual and a collective need that demands satisfaction.

Hestia provides a center for an organization, and without such a center organizations can easily find themselves fragmented or lost. Paradoxically, perhaps, organizations with a strong Hestia-energy, rather than being inward-looking, are likely to be devoted to the service of a wider community, in the image of the self-effacing divine maiden aunt who can be relied on to be there when things are going wrong. Not only will she be there for you, but you know that she will not judge you.

James Hillman, in discussing the notion of service as a dimension of corporate activity, notes that most ideas of service have been imported from ideas of production, as if good service can be defined by the criteria of productivity. He argues to the contrary, that service and production need to be kept clearly distinct because they grow out of fundamentally different psychological attitudes.

> Production masters material; service submits to it. In the language of myth, our ideas of productive employment indicate the influence of Prometheus, the Greek Titan, upon the do-it-yourself ego, or of Hephaistos, the Olympian craftsman and arms-maker, because production constructs; whereas service employment, because it protects, conserves, and furthers, more likely indicates Hestia, the Goddess of the hearth. She is almost invisible in her service, although instrumental in maintaining the daily round.[2]

Hestia gives an organization a strong sense of place. Phil Slattery describes the Nunawading North Neighbourhood Centre:

> The first question people coming to the Centre ask is not usually, 'I'm feeling terrible, what will I do?' It is more likely to be, 'Do you have any dressmaking classes?' We are prepared to discuss that. Yes. Discuss. Not just answer, 'Yes,

> we do, on a Monday morning' – because through discussion the feeling terrible comes out coupled with more questions about the availability of the crèche and cost of classes, and other classes. Eventually, a visible look of relief spreads over the face of the questioner. The person has taken the initial step and has been given the choices the Neighbourhood Centre has to offer.
>
> The House provides a place for people who feel frightened, who feel life is dangerous; it provides a place for people who tremble, for people who are terrified. It is a place where understanding can be understood, where terror is calmed. It is a place where the neighbourhood can build its own community, where each person can be the centre of the neighbourhood and not be afraid, where restlessness can find peace, where we can all be still and humble, and laugh and know people will laugh with us. The Neighbourhood Centre also begins to identify the struggle of people for a voice and choice in their education, a struggle for a better qualification, a struggle for access to public moneys and government policies.[3]

The security provided by a Hestia-place gives people the courage to go out and meet the world.

In the organization dominated by a Hestia culture there is no great anxiety to do things, no frantic activity. Too much excitement is frowned on. People like to take things quietly, concentrating on what is essential and avoiding anything that might distract them from it. The Hestia organization is 'home' for its members. The culture is both introverted and collectivist. In such a culture people look inward rather than outward for the justification of their existence, for the organization contains its meaning within itself, and does not have to seek it in the outside world. The focused community is more important than the individual members of it. There is not much value placed on personal growth or individual potential. In the Hestia organization people are not expected to seek power, and when they do have leadership roles thrust upon them, they take them on as a service to the community. Often the most influential people in the organization are not those who have formal authority but those who most represent the focus of the organization. There is not much interest in management structures, or in the complications of participative decision-making. The ideal leader or executive group is so closely in touch with what is of the essence of the organization's meaning and purpose that the correct decisions present themselves simply and unambiguously, without the need for consultation. In Hall's terms, it is a *high context* culture.[4] There is no need to constantly spell out the organizations values and processes, as these are taken for granted, and communicated more through imitation, rhythm, and narrative than through memos.

Thomas Merton, in discussing the relevance of the contemplative monk in the contemporary world, writes from the perspective of a Hestia culture:

> A monk seeks silence and solitude because there his mind and heart can relax and expand and attain to a new perspective: there too he can hear the word of God and meditate on it more quietly, without strain, without forcing himself, without being carried away in useless abstract speculations. The monk is by definition a man who lives in seclusion, in solitude, in silence outside of the noise and the confusion of a busy worldly existence. He does this because seclusion provides certain necessary conditions for his life: an interior freedom, silence, liberation from trivial concerns that arise from the overstimulation of the appetites and the imagination . . . An apt saying of the Moslem Sufis comes to mind here: 'The hen does not lay eggs in the market place.'[5]

Hestia has her own pathology, which is often manifested in inertia. The inwardness of the Hestia organization may leave it unaware of the environment around it, and unable to take steps to protect itself when that environment becomes threatening. There may be a complete lack of acknowledgment of members' need to grow as individuals, and harsh treatment of those who betray the organization by seeking personal growth and satisfaction outside it. One way in which the Hestia organization protects its members against a dangerous outside world is to strictly regulate their behavior. When the Vestal virgins (priestesses of Vesta, the Roman equivalent of Hestia) were found guilty of unchastity they were buried alive.

The Hestia culture may be found in monastic communities. It may also be found in other religious organizations. In Australia we are seeing a rise in the number of 'retreat houses' provided by religious organizations and, increasingly, people simply committed to a deep spiritual existence, without the trappings of formal religion. Whereas in the past such facilities were not readily available outside formal religious institutional life, these houses increasingly provide a haven for contemplation and regeneration for members of the public who seek the quiet they offer. Many community organizations have strong Hestia elements to balance the activist elements that come from Ares, Artemis, or Herakles. It has become increasingly common for organizations to acknowledge Hestia by dedicating a particular place to her – a 'quiet room' or 'meditation room', or perhaps a country retreat – where people can get out of the rush of activity and distraction in order to focus again on what is essential, for themselves and for the organization. Hestia is present also in the events (festivals) through which an organization celebrates itself as a community.

Hestia has a great deal in common with her sisters, Hera and Demeter. As wife, mother, and virgin they were originally aspects of the same goddess. As elder sister of Zeus, Hestia combines a sense of the honor due to her with a great respect for authority. It is not uncommon for organizations that perceive themselves in Hestia terms to be actually governed by Zeus. Hestia is in most respects opposite to Dionysos, as she is to Ares and Herakles. She has no interest in excitement or heroism, and she hates conflict.

The consultant who brings a Hestia perspective to her work with an organization will be looking for a sense of centeredness in the organization. Do people feel 'at home' there? Can they deal with the essential purposes of the organization in an efficient, unhurried fashion, without conflict or hysteria? Does the organization have an uncomplicated sense of what it is about, and does it go about its work without fuss, and without being distracted by the expectations and pressures of outsiders? An effective organization needs focus and communal identification.

Grey-Eyed Athena

I sing of Pallas Athena, the glorious goddess,
grey-eyed, resourceful, of implacable heart.
This bashful maiden is a mighty defender of cities,
the Tritogeneia, whom Zeus the counselor himself
bore from his august head, clad with golden and resplendent
warlike armor, as awe lay hold of all the immortal
onlookers.[6]

The best way to get a sense of how the Greeks imagined Athena is to read the *Odyssey* of Homer. Athena is the patron and protector of Odysseus on his long journey home. She is shrewd and sensible. She comes to his assistance in emergencies and negotiates on his behalf with Zeus.

Athena is the virgin goddess of arts, crafts, and war. Her origins are mixed. We can trace her, on the one hand, to an Indo-European war-goddess, daughter of the sky-father, and on the other to a Cretan palace-goddess, responsible for the crafts of urban life. She eventually emerges in classical times as a goddess of civilization, of household arts and crafts, especially weaving, and of the defense of civilization against those who would destroy it. More than any other god, she represents a point of balance between the male-dominated and autocratic culture of the Greek invaders and the concrete, matricentric culture of the people they conquered and assimilated. She represents normality, consensus, balance. In political terms she is democracy.

Athena, so the story goes, is the daughter of Zeus by his first wife, Metis, whose name means wisdom or cunning. When Metis was pregnant with Athena, Zeus learned that if she bore a son after this daughter, he would supplant his father. Accordingly Zeus swallowed Metis alive. Some months later, he suffered a severe headache, which was only relieved when Hephaistos (or Prometheus) took an axe, and split his head open. Athena sprang out, fully grown and fully armed, to the consternation of the assembled gods.

As a god of warfare Athena presents a contrast to the other war-god, Ares, whom she hates. Where Ares is mindless violence, Athena is clear-sighted strategic warfare. She is very much an urban goddess, in contrast to the agricultural goddess, Demeter, and the goddess of wild nature, Artemis. She is patron of all who seek excellence in crafting. Her particular domain is the domestic crafts, while Hephaistos is more concerned with industrial crafts. Nevertheless, it was Athena who showed the Argonauts how to build the boat in which they sought the Golden Fleece, and it was she who helped construct the wooden horse by means of which the Greeks took Troy. She is so jealous of her skill as a weaver that, when the girl Arachne demonstrated that she could weave as well as the goddess, Athena turned her into a spider.

The story of Orestes' trial shows her role as the mediator between the old culture and the new. Orestes was pursued by the Erinyes (avenging earth-spirits whom the Romans called the Furies) for killing his mother Clytemnestra. He was impelled to do this by Apollo (who always supports patriarchy) because Clytemnestra had, with some justification, murdered her husband Agamemnon, Orestes' father. The two principles, father-right and mother-right, appeared irreconcilable. Athena intervened and put the case to the vote of the Athenian court. When the vote was tied, Athena's casting vote forced the Erinyes to stop persecuting Orestes. She is represented as the voice of moderation and normality, but she can be very fierce when crossed.

The beautiful Medusa offended her by boasting of her beauty and by making love with her god-lover, Poseidon, in Athena's shrine. (This was particularly offensive to a virgin goddess.) The goddess transformed Medusa into a Gorgon, turning her hair into serpents and making her face so hideous that men were turned to stone by looking at it. She then helped the hero Perseus in his mission to kill Medusa, after which she celebrated her triumph by wearing the Gorgon's severed head upon her breast.

Whatever her historical origins, Athena is certainly a daughter of the patriarchy. She represents the female principle, accepting and accommodating the rule of the father, and making the best of it. In contemporary terms she represents liberal feminism, acknowledging the realities of living in 'a man's world', demanding an equal share of power and competing for it on the same terms as men. In this she is in complete contrast to Artemis, who wants nothing to do with the world of men.

Athena is a goddess who has many attributes that we stereotypically call masculine. She is, like her half-brother Ares, a war-god. Not crude, brutal warfare, waged for the thrill and glory of it, but cool, intelligent, calculating, strategic warfare, waged to defend one's city and citizens. However, she is also a god of peace, and of the civilized living that comes with peace. She is not easily fussed. She is the goddess of practical wisdom, of common sense. (In later Christian times she became Sophia, the personification of transcendent wisdom.) Like Artemis and Hestia she has the containment and self-reliance symbolized by virginity. She has little interest in relationships, except in so far as they have strategic value. As the god of citizenship and the democratic process she was worshipped most intensely in Athens, where our democratic institutions had their source.

The city-state of Athens can be taken as an illustration of an Athena organization at work. At the peak of its political and cultural domination in the fifth century B.C., Athens was the site of a radical democracy combined with an intense focus on artistic and technical accomplishment.[7] Excellence was highly valued. Artist-craftsmen were highly respected. Citizens felt great pride not only in their obvious contributions to civilization – in the visual and tactile arts, in the theater, in science and philosophy, in literature, in scientific warfare, and so on – but they had equal pride in the civilized manner in which they went about their business. All male Athenian citizens, through a complicated system of elections and balloting, had an equal opportunity to be nominal head of state for a day. The chief executive was elected by vote of all the citizens, and could as readily be dismissed and exiled by the same means. The citizens spent a great deal of their time in political activity, or in serving on juries in legal disputes. Decisions could only be made after debate in the appropriate committees. The Athenian statesman, Perikles, described the culture of his city in his celebrated funeral oration (431 B.C.), recorded by the historian Thucydides:

> Our love for what is beautiful does not lead us to extravagance; our love of the things of the mind does not make us soft. We regard wealth as something to be properly used, rather than as something to boast about. As for poverty, no one need be ashamed to admit it; the real shame is in not taking practical measures to escape from it. Here each individual is interested not only in his own affairs but in the affairs of the state as well: even those who are mostly occupied with their own business are extremely well-informed on general politics – this is a peculiarity of ours; we do not say that a man who takes no interest in politics is a man who minds his own business; we say he has no business here at all. We Athenians, in our own persons, take our decisions on policy or submit them to proper discussion: for we do not think there is an incompatibility between words and deeds; the worst thing is to rush into action before the consequences have been properly debated. And this is another point where we differ from other people. We are capable at the same time of taking risks and of estimating them beforehand. Others are brave out of ignorance; and, when they stop to think, they begin to fear. But the man who can most truly be accounted brave is he who best knows the meaning of what is sweet in life and of what is terrible, and then goes out undeterred to meet what is to come.[8]

Ancient Athens also showed the pathology to which an Athena organization is vulnerable. For all the rhetoric of equality and participation, it was an organization that limited participative decision-making to those thought capable of it – actually a minority of the population. Women, resident aliens and slaves had no part in it. Pride in their civilization gave the Athenians a justification for imperialist expansion. The conviction that they possessed an advanced culture and advanced political structures provided them with a high-minded rationale for subjugating others less fortunate and enabling them to share in the benefits. In addition, the decision-making processes of the radical democracy proved too cumbersome to operate effectively in emergencies and left the way open for a takeover by shrewd politicians who knew how to manipulate the system while outwardly respecting its forms, or by demagogues who gained power and popularity by appealing to the people's baser instincts.

Organizations that are committed to the values of Athena give a great deal of attention to the sharing of power. Horizontal structures are preferred to vertical ones. Decisions regarding policy and practice are perceived as decisions of the organization as a whole rather than of the chief executive or ruling clique. People are respected for their technical and professional skills. The preferred way of developing strategies or dealing with problems is a collaborative approach, which recognizes and utilizes people's different kinds of expertise. The preference for group-based decision-making comes from a sense that this is the best way of making decisions, not from any desire for intimacy. People in such organizations believe that decisions should be made coolly and sensibly, after full debate, with full attention to practical implications. And they should be properly documented. (The Athena culture is *low context* rather than *high context*). Too much emotionality is frowned on. Women may be prominent and valued members of such organizations, but only in so far as the feminine perspective that they bring is compatible with the ethos of the organization. Women who wish to challenge the essentially masculist assumptions of the organization by approaching it from the perspective of Artemis or Demeter may not be welcome at all. Athena may represent the independent, resourceful, clear-sighted feminine, but she accepts the ground-rules laid down by Zeus. She does men's work in a men's world. And she probably power-dresses.

Organizations dominated by the equalitarian Athena culture may experience a peculiar pathology when it comes to decision-making. There may be so much insistence on complete debate, so many committees to consult, so many people whose voices need to be heard, that it is impossible to make any decision at all. We have seen this of late in a number of organizational settings where significant energy has been devoted to social skills development and leadership development using a relational focus. The end result is often that the work done in such environments becomes vague, ambiguous, and diffuse, and the end game sees the bankers coming in to take over. Alternatively, the chief executive may be forced to take on a Zeus role and make a decision that over-rides legitimate objections and leaves many people resentful. Sometimes an organization may have an espoused ideology of power-sharing but actually restrict the joys of power to an elite group who are considered worthy of them.

Where the Athena culture has arisen within or alongside a strong Zeus culture, it is common in times of stress to find Zeus' resuming of his rightful place in the scheme of things and being welcomed by a strong and silent sub-group who had no legitimate voice under Athena's reign. Organizationally, this is manifest in statements such as: 'It's about time we got some order and authority back in here'; 'At last the boss is exercising the authority he should have all along'; or 'Thank goodness some one other than a committee is starting to make some decisions around here'.

Athena is often found in organizations alongside the patriarchal gods, Zeus and Apollo. She shares with Apollo and Hephaistos a concern for excellence. Like Hephaistos she approaches life as craft. She may be present in the same organization as Ares, but there is likely to be conflict between them.

Ricardo Semler's description of Semco, the Brazilian company he shaped, shows an Athena culture with strong Hermes and Dionysos aspects. In *Maverick* he relates how he and his colleagues dismantled the corporate hierarchy to establish a 'circular' management structure, handed over decision-making to the workers, including decisions on important matters such as plant relocations, appointment of managers, salaries, and profit-sharing arrangements. The power-sharing, the pride in crafting, and the concern for balance that belong to Athena are joined with an emphasis on communication and flexibility (Hermes) and a respect for 'natural' structures and the autonomy of the individual worker (Dionysos).

> At Semco we did away with structures that dictate the 'hows' and created fertile soil for differences. We gave people an opportunity to test, question and disagree. We let them determine their own training and their own futures. We let them come and go as they wanted, work at home if they wished, set their own salaries, choose their own bosses. We let them change their minds and ours, prove us wrong when we are wrong, make us humbler. Such a system relishes change, which is the only antidote to the corporate brainwashing that has consigned giant businesses with brilliant pasts into uncertain futures.
>
> People often assume that at Semco we have strict selection procedures to ensure that those who come to work for us are philosophically attuned with our system. In fact, it's the other way round. We look for competence, and ignore all else. Many of our employees regularly question our concepts. There are even pockets at Semco that are autocratic, and people who like to work in that kind of environment have slowly migrated there. But how can we lock out people who don't think the same way we do without becoming people who say things like, 'This is not the way we do things around here'.
>
> Semco is more than novel programs or procedures. What is important is our open-mindedness, our trust in our employees and distrust of dogma. We are neither socialist nor purely capitalist, but we take the best of these failed systems and others to re-organize work so that collective thinking does not overpower individualistic flights of grandeur; that leadership does not get lost in endless search for consensus; that people are free to work as they like, when they like; that bosses don't have to be parents and workers don't act like children. At the heart of our bold experiment is a truth so simple it would be silly if it wasn't so rarely recognized: *A company should trust its destiny to its employees.*[9]

A consultant bringing an Athena perspective to the study of an organization will be interested above all in the way power is shared, the way the members at all levels have a sense of owning the organization and its works. A good organization, from this perspective, will be one that is highly professional in all its undertakings, which values its human resources and counts on them to deal with crises with cool grace and precision.

ARTEMIS THE HUNTRESS

I sing of Artemis of the golden shafts, the modest maiden
who loves the din of the hunt and shoots volleys of arrows at stags.
She is the twin sister of Apollon of the golden sword,
and through shady mountains and windy peaks
she delights in the chase as she stretches her golden bow
to shoot the bitter arrows.[10]

Artemis was originally an Asian goddess of wild animals, who was worshipped on mountain tops. When the Greeks made her part of their Olympian family she became the virgin daughter of Zeus and twin sister of Apollo. In the mythology of the classical period she is depicted as an adolescent girl, but there remain traces of her older and fiercer manifestation as 'Mistress of the Beasts'.

According to the story as the Greeks told it, she was born before her brother and assisted her mother Leto at his birth. She is, accordingly, a goddess of childbirth, and is associated with the protection of fragile life, both in human infants and in the young of animals. The goddess of animals, she is also the goddess of hunting, for hunters must pray to her to persuade her animals to give themselves up to the spear or arrow. As a young girl she begged Zeus to let her remain a virgin, avoiding the male-dominated world and going off to live in the wilderness with her girlfriends. Zeus assented, and Artemis tries to protect the virgin forest and her virgin followers from male exploitation and oppression.

Virginity is an important symbol in Greek mythology. Artemis, Athena, and Hestia are quite specifically virgin goddesses, and their virginity symbolizes their independence and self-reliance. Artemis is always surrounded by a band of nymphs and girls with whom she enjoys her freedom from any relationship or obligation to men. She has neither the need nor the desire to give either power or pleasure to men. She imposes on her followers her own strict standards of behavior in this matter and ruthlessly punishes those who betray her ideals. She uses all necessary violence to protect her own virginity when it is threatened.

Artemis is a goddess of sisterhood, of female separatism. In Athens, she was the goddess responsible for girls' initiation into womanhood. However, she is by no means a gentle goddess. When Callisto, one of her followers, was raped by Zeus (who disguised himself as Artemis for the purpose), the unfortunate nymph was unable to hide the ensuing pregnancy. When she noticed Callisto's condition, Artemis was enraged. She asked no questions but turned her into a bear and drove her out of the sisterhood. Poor Callisto wandered through the wilderness for years, and only avoided being shot by her own son, Arcas (whom Hermes had rescued and given to his mother to raise), when Zeus took pity on mother and son and set them in the sky as the Big Bear and the Little Bear.

Artemis is the female warrior. She was associated in the Greek imagination with the Amazons, those warrior women (real or imagined) who threatened to overturn the Zeus-given order of things by taking power to themselves. The Greek gods defy our stereotypes of 'feminine' and 'masculine'. Artemis and Athena have attributes that our culture is inclined to categorize as 'masculine', while Eros and Dionysos are very 'feminine' gods.

When Actaeon, a young hunter (and, accordingly, a worshipper of Artemis), accidentally came upon her bathing with her companions, he was so overwhelmed by her beauty that he stood transfixed. Artemis, assuming that he had come to mock her, threw water in his face, thus changing him into a stag. His own dogs then turned on him and tore him to pieces. When she became too friendly with the giant hunter, Orion, Artemis was tricked by her brother Apollo into shooting and killing him. Artemis and Apollo share the tendency to put principle before relationship.

The picture of Artemis and her companions living in the forest tells us something about the culture of the Artemis organization. It is based on a fantasy of companionship rather than hierarchy, natural rhythms rather than abstract order. It values its difference, sees itself not only as special, but as constantly under threat from an outside world that would destroy it. It places great stress on ideological purity, and gives its members status on the basis of their adherence to the official ideology. It also ruthlessly expels those who are not sufficiently pure. The bonds between people, which are very important in such an organization, are based on the sharing of an ideology rather than on intimacy. People in such an organization are expected to be passionate about its mission, which is generally concerned with the protection of the fragile, the natural, or the oppressed. Whereas in the *low context* culture of the Athena organization decisions are made consciously on the basis of informed discussion and probably recorded in the minutes, the *high context* culture of the Artemis organization sees decisions being made through casual conversation and telepathy. People who truly belong to the organization may be expected to know intuitively the correct response to make to any eventuality. If they habitually make the wrong decisions they obviously don't belong.

The Artemis organization tries to live in harmony with the natural order rather than exploit it. There is often an attempt to do away with formal management structures in order to engage in more 'organic' decision-making. Intuition is highly valued, and there is some distrust of conventional structures. Even the power-sharing structures of Athena's participative democracy may be regarded as oppressive. People are expected to know what to do (and know what other people are talking about) without having it spelled out. Artemis, Mistress of the Beasts, is manifest in organizations whose structures imitate the organic and symbiotic relationships of the natural world rather than the abstract relationships of the controlled or manufactured world. She is found also in the current interest in self-organizing or living systems theory as it is applied to organizations. The voice of Artemis can be heard, for instance, in the work of Margaret Wheatley[11] and Fritjof Capra.[12]

Richard Raspa describes an espoused Artemis culture in his study of Ocean World:

> At Ocean World symbiosis may be observed while individuals are working. In the performance event there are moments when human beings, even different mammals, come together so beautifully, so intimately that two appear as one. Ultimately, symbiosis is a metaphor for the entire Ocean World organization where unlike phenomena – nature and culture, land and sea, people and animals, work and leisure, manager and managed, self and other – are brought together in an expression of planetary wholeness and connectedness. Ocean World is an ecological drama of the late twentieth century. It plays out the symbiotic possibilities of human beings cooperating to achieve organizational goals.

> Ocean World is a drama about organizational life and the ways in which people relate to each other, to other species, and to the organization . . . Although everyone has specific tasks to perform, as defined in a catalog of job descriptions, the symbolic job at Ocean World is to facilitate people's experience of their connection to other people and forms of life. It involves every employee, even those whose job seems marginal, such as parking lot attendant, taking on a role in the ecological drama and hosting the encounter between humans and mammals.[13]

Artemis is a goddess who is very easily offended, and responds to offence with a degree of violence that sometimes seems out of proportion to the transgression. Artemis organizations sometimes manifest this pathology. They are also sometimes paranoid, assuming hostility without or betrayal within where these do not exist. A self-image built around notions of comradeship or sisterhood can be associated with a great deal of manipulation and destructiveness in personal relationships. The equalitarian and collectivist culture of the Artemis organization is vulnerable to a takeover by Zeus. Artemis organizations are sometimes poor judges of human nature, and ready to give power and status to people who can mouth the ideology without really embodying it. The distrust of formal structures may leave the organization open to domination by an individual or group who claim to represent the 'correct line'. Zeus disguised himself as Artemis in order to rape Callisto, and he can do so again in such organizations, raping the sisters while talking about sisterhood.

Radical feminist organizations naturally provide examples of Artemis culture: in the value they place on sisterhood, their need to protect their difference, and their preference for collective decision-making. However, Artemis can also be present in organizations populated by men. Organizations with ecological concerns may be characterized by an Artemis culture, as are political organizations, especially those on the political left. Community organizations provide other examples. When the organization is devoted to a specific Artemis concern, such as the protection of children, its culture is likely to be intensely Artemisian.

A very different Artemis culture was found in the traditional Moroccan harem, where the supportive feminine culture of the single woman is depicted by Fatima Mernissi as a refuge from the Zeus and Hera cultures of the outside world.

> But the grownups never noticed anything, especially on the courtyard level, where life was very proper and strict. Only upstairs were things less rigid. There, divorced and widowed aunts, relatives, and their children, occupied a maze of small rooms. The number of relatives living with us at any one time varied according to the amount of conflict in their lives. Distant female relatives would sometimes come to seek refuge on our top floors for a few weeks when they got into fights with their husbands. Some would come to stay, with their children, for a short time only, just to show their husbands that they had another place to stay, that they could survive on their own and were not desperately dependent. . . . But other relatives came to stay for good, after a divorce or some other serious problem, and this was one of the traditions Father always worried about whenever someone attacked the institutions of harem life. 'Where will the troubled women go?' he would say.
>
> . . . Life upstairs was so much easier, especially since everything was also accompanied by hanan, a Moroccan emotional quality that I rarely have encountered elsewhere. *Hanan* is hard to define exactly, but basically it is a free-flowing, easy-going, unconditionally available tenderness. People who give *hanan*, like Aunt Habiba, never threaten to withdraw their love when you commit some unintentional minor or even major infraction. *Hanan* was hard to come by downstairs, especially among the mothers, who were too busy teaching you to respect the frontier to bother with tenderness.[14]

Artemis is sometimes found alongside her brother, Apollo, for both have a keen interest in the truth. She has some concerns in common with Hera and Demeter, but she rejects the former's support for the patriarchy and the latter's interest in mothering. Hermes sometimes insinuates himself into an Artemis culture, and she has a great deal in common with Athena. There is even a rumor that Eros was the product of an affair between Artemis and Hermes. Like Prometheus she is *outer-directed*, being very sensitive to her environment, but where the Promethean organization imagines itself to be outside Nature, and seeks to control and exploit Nature for the benefit of human beings, the Artemisian organization imagines itself as part of Nature and seeks to live in harmony with the natural world.[15]

Valuing the feminine and valuing Nature may appear to be distinct, but they both manifestations of Artemis-energy. It is no coincidence that women are more likely than men to be concerned about the planetary crisis and prepared to be active in the environmental movement.

Hawken, Lovins, and Lovins bring an Artemis perspective to their discussion of *Natural Capitalism*, which they define as 'capitalism as if living systems mattered'. They outline the fundamental assumptions underlying their perspective, which aims to integrate the values of Artemis with those of Athena and Hermes.

- The environment is not a minor factor of production but rather is 'an envelope containing, provisioning, and sustaining the whole economy.
- The limiting factor to future economic development is the availability and functionality of *natural capital*, in particular, life-supporting services that have no substitutes and currently have no market value.
- Misconceived or badly designed business systems, population growth, and wasteful patterns of consumption are the primary causes of the lack of natural capital, and all three must be addressed to achieve a sustainable economy.
- Future economic progress can best take place in democratic, market-based systems of production and distribution in which *all* forms of capital are fully valued, including human, manufactured, financial, and natural capital.
- One of the keys to the beneficial employment of people, money, and the environment is radical increases in resources productivity.
- Human welfare is best served by promoting the quality and flow of desired services delivered, rather than by merely increasing the total dollar flow.
- Economic and environmental sustainability depends on addressing global inequities of income and material well-being.
- The best long-term environment for commerce is provided by true democratic systems of governance that are based on the needs of people rather than business. [16]

In her story of *The Body Shop*, Anita Roddick describes a company whose culture is defined by the sometimes uneasy relationship between Artemis and Aphrodite. While the product belongs to Aphrodite, the core values reflected in the company mission statement come from Artemis. The mission statement calls for *The Body Shop* to:

- dedicate our business to the pursuit of social and environmental change
- creatively balance the financial and human needs of our stakeholders: employees, customers, franchisees, suppliers, and shareholders

- courageously ensure that our business is ecologically sustainable: meeting the needs of the present without compromising the future
- meaningfully contribute to local, national, and international communities in which we trade, by adopting a code of conduct which ensures care, honesty, fairness, and respect
- passionately campaign for the protection of the environment, human and civil rights, and against animal testing within the cosmetics and toiletries industry
- tirelessly work to narrow the gap between principle and practice, while making fun, passion, and social care part of our daily lives.[17]

The virgin goddess of Nature may appear to the corporate observer to be something of a lightweight among the gods – spending her time playing with her girlfriends and smelling the flowers, rather than confronting the harsh realities of the marketplace. However, her basic toughness is becoming apparent as corporations increasingly face the need to create sustainable products and procedures. Dexter Dunphy and his colleagues have documented the ways in which many corporations over the past couple of decades have been persuaded or forced to abandon their cultures of environmental neglect or exploitation and create cultures of ecological sustainability, if only to remain profitable. In the 'sustaining corporation':

> The organization becomes an active promoter of ecological sustainability values and seeks to influence key participants in the industry and society in general. Environmental best practice is espoused and enacted because it is the responsible thing to do. The organization tries to assist society to be ecologically sustainable and uses its entire range of products and services to this end. The organization is prepared to use its influence to promote positive policies on the part of governments, the restructuring of markets and the development of community values to facilitate the emergence of a sustainable society. Nature is valued for its own sake.[18]

A consultant approaching an organization from the Artemis perspective will be predisposed to see the organization's sense of identity, its assertion of the feminine, and its commitment to environmental responsibility as its greatest assets. It will seem reasonable to minimize the importance of formal management structures in order to take full advantage of the ability of the membership to generate policy intuitively within their ideological framework, and to engage in collective action.

---

1. A Athanassakis (trans. and ed.) *The Homeric Hymns* (1976), p. 64.
2. J Hillman (1995) *Kinds of Power*, p. 69.
3. P Slattery (1983) *Nunawading North Neighbourhood Centre*, p. 78.
4. For the high/context/low context distinction see ET Hall (1984) *The Dance of Life*, Chapter 6.
5. T Merton (1968) *Contemplation in a World of Action*, p. 64.
6. A Athanassakis, ibid., p. 66. The name Tritogeneia is of pre-Greek origin. Its meaning is uncertain.
7. It is interesting to note that the Greeks did not distinguish between artistic and technical accomplishment, and used the same word, *techne*, for both.
8. Thucydides, *The Peloponnesian War*, (trans.) R Warner (1975), p. 147.
9. R Semler (1995) *Maverick*, p. 146.
10. A Athanassakis, ibid., p. 65.
11. See M Wheatley (1992) *Leadership and the New Science*; M Wheatley & M Kellner-Rogers (1996) *A Simpler Way*.
12. See F Capra (1996) *The Turning Point.*
13. R Raspa (1991) 'The Ocean World Paradox: Managing Nature as Carnival', p. 4.
14. F Mernissi (1995) *The Harem Within*, p. 16.
15. For a discussion of attitude to the environment as a distinguishing characteristic of specific cultures, see F Trompenaars and C Hampden-Turner (1998) Chapter 10.
16. P Hawken et al. (1999) *Natural Capitalism*, p. 9.
17. A Roddick (2000) *Business as Unusual*, p. 246.
18. D Dunphy et al. (2003) *Organizational Change for Corporate Sustainability*, p. 84.

9

SONS AND LOVERS

Winged Eros

Eros, the fairest of the deathless gods
. . . unstrings the limbs and subdues both mind
and sensible thought in the breasts of all gods and all men.[1]

In the beginning, the huge black bird, Nyx (Night) hovered over the void. As she hovered, she was impregnated by the cosmic wind, and laid a silver egg, which lay for aeons in the lap of darkness. In the fullness of time, the silver egg broke open and Eros emerged.

According to one tradition, Eros was the most ancient of the gods. It was Eros who brought Sky (Uranus) and Earth (Gaia) together to generate the gods, who presided over the unions of gods and mortals, and who is ultimately the source of life.[2] This personification of cosmic harmony was present at the birth of the gods and mortals and present also in their love-making, for love and the generation of life are obviously manifestations of the same god, the god of union, harmony, and creativity. Eros was present, then, to join in the rejoicing at the birth of the goddess of beauty and love, Aphrodite.

When the Greeks of later times imagined this god, it was as an adolescent boy, for their experience of love included more than the simple drive to union. Eros, as they imagined him, was unpredictable and irresponsible and destructive as well as delightful and creative. In imagining him in this way, they did not diminish his power, for Eros, when he chooses to, can control even Zeus. In the Olympic pantheon, he is pictured as the son of Aphrodite. He is not one of the twelve Olympians, but is still part of the family.

The power of Eros is felt by humans and gods alike, in their propensity to fall obsessively in love. It is felt in the delight and anguish of intimacy. Eros is singularly the god of relationship, and of the creativity which is generated by relationship. There are many Eros myths. One of the most popular in classical times was the story of Eros and Psyche, which is the story of the engagement of Eros with the human soul.

Psyche (Soul) was a princess who had the misfortune to be exceedingly beautiful, more beautiful perhaps than Aphrodite herself. This aroused the mean streak in Aphrodite, and she decided to destroy the girl. Her plan was for Psyche to fall in love with some utterly revolting monster who would carry her off and get her permanently out of the way. Eros was sent to arrange this. Of course he fell in love with the girl himself and carried her off to his palace. Here he came to her only at night and would not reveal his identity. Psyche was happy with this relationship until her sisters, who were visiting her, persuaded her to check the identity of her lover. She hid a lamp, and shone it on Eros while he slept. He woke and fled, leaving her grieving.

Psyche went in search of her husband, begging Aphrodite to help her. The goddess agreed, but made the girl her slave and forced her to perform various impossible tasks if she was to find Eros again. Eventually she sent Psyche to the Underworld to fetch the beauty-cream of Persephone, the Queen of Death. Psyche fetched the cosmetics but, contrary to instructions, looked in the container. She immediately fell down dead. Eros found her at last and revived her by pricking her with one of his arrows. The marriage of Psyche and Eros was celebrated by all the gods, as was the birth of their daughter Voluptas (Pleasure).[3]

In the organization dominated by Eros, the highest value is intimacy. The ideal emotional climate is positive, supportive, free of risk. In its purest form the Eros organization has a structure which is entirely horizontal. Notions of hierarchy, or even of authority, have no place in its ideology. Nor have notions of role. What holds the organization together is the intensity of the relationships between its members. The organization may have a sense of common purpose, may be productive in many ways, may have established ways of going about its work, but these are secondary to the satisfactions of relationship. People think more in terms of their relationships with people, rather than their responsibility to the organization. Community is an end in itself.

In the Eros organization, good communication between members is seen to be the key to effectiveness, and good communication is obviously the product of good relationships. It is love which makes the organization go round.

In the *Acts of the Apostles* we find an assertion of the primacy of love in the primitive Christian community of Jerusalem:

> All who believed were together and had all things in common; they would sell their possessions and goods and distribute the proceeds to all, as any had need. Day by day, as they spent much time together in the temple, they broke bread together at home and ate their food with glad and generous hearts, praising god and having the goodwill of all the people.[4]

This theme is ubiquitous in early Christian writing. In the first letter of John we find love asserted again as the guiding motif of the early Christian community:

> God is love, and those who abide in love abide in God, and God abides in them. Love has been perfected among us in this: that we may have boldness on the Day of Judgment, because as he is, so are we in this world. There is no fear in love, but perfect love casts out fear; for fear has to do with punishment, and whoever fears has not reached perfection in love. We love because he first loved us. Those

> who say 'I love God,' and hate their brothers or sisters, are liars; for those who do not love a brother or sister whom they have seen, cannot love God whom they have not seen. The commandment we have from God is this: those who love God must love their brothers and sister also.[5]

The tendency of Eros organizations to assume that if we love each other, everything else will look after itself, often leads to problems, even problems in loving. We have evidence in early Christian writing that 'espoused theory' and 'theory in use' were sometimes in conflict in the communities. Paul's celebration of love in his letter to the Corinthians is obviously inspired by his observation that the Corinthian Christians were attempting to maintain a myth in which they figured as a loving community, in spite of behaving in ways which did not meet espoused Christian standards of love at all.

> If I speak in the tongues of mortals and angels, but do not have love, I am a noisy gong or a clanging cymbal . . . Love is patient; love is kind; love is not envious or boastful or arrogant or rude. It does not insist on its own way; it is not irritable or resentful . . . And now faith, hope and love abide, these three; and the greatest of these is love.[6]

An Eros organization will have a 'flat' structure. In fact there is often very little in the way of formal structure at all. Mechanisms of control are absent and freedom is paramount, for as John told the early Christians: 'Perfect love casts out fear.'

Jack Gibb describes a workshop environment that is assumed to facilitate this sort of development:

> A circular, octagonal, or nearly square space creates a centering flow, and high-interaction seems to be a critical factor in successful community development. This flow is enhanced when there is no furniture to interfere with free and spontaneous physical movement; when members are visible to each other at most times; when there is some kind of visual boundary that defines the community space; when interaction is continuous and not broken by formal coffee breaks or evening departures for sleeping in other quarters; and when the significant happenings

> in the community life occur in an area that is perceptually and physically central to the community. The community then takes form, flows, develops rhythms and patterns, assumes an identity, and is experienced by members as a living organism.[7]

The notion of living so close to people for any length of time does not appeal much in an individualistic culture, which treasures privacy. In an Eros culture, however, community is the highest value and the desire to be separate is perceived as wrong-headed or unhealthy.

Eros pathology readily appears when Eros is the only god being honored. If intimacy and openness are good, we might suppose that more intimacy and openness are better, and that still more openness and intimacy are better still. However, experience of closeness is not always as unambiguously positive as this. Sometimes, relationship maintains its intensity while reversing its meaning. Love turns to hatred or contempt. Sometimes the relationship-focused organization slides into self-indulgence and bitchiness. Sometimes people are simply so involved with relating to each other that they forget that the purpose of their organization was to do something. Unless Eros is accompanied by more responsible gods like Hera and Apollo, he may become destructive. Often enough, Eros' irresponsibility and lack of attention to the task lead to a takeover by Zeus.

Community organizations often have a strong Eros component, which is expressed in their behavior as well as in their ideology. Small issue-focused groups often develop a strong Eros culture, as the satisfactions of working with like-minded people become as strong an incentive to membership as the issues themselves. In Trompenaars' language, the culture is *equalitarian*, *communitarian*, *affective*, *particularist*, *diffuse*, and *inner-directed*. People do not want someone in authority making decisions for them; their focus is on what is good for the group rather than on what they can get out of it as individuals; they are more concerned with living up to their shared values than with worrying what the world outside thinks about them; and attending to people's needs is more important than following the rules. In Hofstede's language the Eros culture is *low power distance*, *collectivist*, and *feminine*. In Hall's language it is *high context* and *polychronic*.[8] People may be impatient (even insulted) when asked to spell out their principles, plans, and procedures, and they certainly don't insist on doing one thing at a time in a 'logical' order. It is difficult for large organizations to maintain a general culture in which the Eros-values are dominant, though sub-cultures within such an organization may be ruled by Eros values.

Eros made significant in-roads into organizational and community life in the seventies. Building on work done in the North Eastern United States at the National Training Laboratories, the Western world indulged Eros through the proliferation of encounter groups, T-groups, sensitivity training groups, and the like.[9] This burgeoning use of unstructured small group technology occurred in the shadow of the famous Hawthorne experiments that showed (simply) that if you take an interest in employees their productivity increases.[10] One of the hallmark characteristics of this work was the encouragement of a high level of self-disclosure combined with high levels of confrontation. The Western corporate world provided a context and permission at that time for this sort of work, and it was maintained until constrained by bad publicity surrounding some of its more extreme forms (e.g. the work of Werner Erhard and EST and its derivatives, for example) combined with the rise of the moral majority in the USA.

Prior to the withdrawal of widespread social permission, the rise in small group work in corporate settings was sowing Eros seeds in a corporate world that had conventionally placed little value on the interpersonal dimensions of leadership and management. It was (and still is) a world with little understanding of the power and value to be gained from enhancing the interpersonal functioning of individuals and improving the quality of their relationships. In Australia and other parts of the world, Eros used this work and the agency of trainers and consultants to insert himself into organizational life. The human relations fantasy took hold, namely the notion that investment in enhancing the quality of relationships among employees would be sufficient to engender higher levels of productivity.

Eros started to lose some of this influence in the corporate world in the early nineties. Somewhere in the period between mid 1993 and late 1995 – in North America (at least) – things changed dramatically. A number of forces combined under the influence of Apollo, Ares, and Hera to lower the level of social permission for work that sought to directly enhance the quality and functioning of relationships in the workplace.

Legal cases involving various groups and organizations offering personal development, e.g. the somewhat notorious cases surrounding EST and its derivatives such as Landmark and Forum, sowed strong seeds of doubt in the minds of many who were worried about sect-like behavior, control, and covert manipulation. Behaviorists (Prometheus) and cognitive psychologists (Apollo) rose into influential posts in major universities throughout the Western world. In a case that received widespread publicity, Charles Krohn was expelled from Pacific Gas and Electric for undertaking training that was alleged to be personal, confronting, values-driven, and (by definition) inappropriate in corporate settings.

Consequently we saw a tendency in corporate settings to dismiss (and label disparagingly) relational work with a psychological focus as a throwback to the 60s and 70s movement.

It is now apparent that in North America, the UK, and Europe there has been a sea change of socio-political ideology around these issues. Apollo, Prometheus, and Athena now hold sway more than ever. The Western world, we would venture to suggest, is now dominated in its espoused ideology by empiricist, rationalist, linear thinkers – more so than it ever was from the 60s and even up to the mid 80s. One of the consequences of this sea change has been a withdrawal of social permission for what could be construed as deep intrapersonal, psychologically-oriented training processes. Eros is no longer flavor of the month.

Paradoxically, at the same time we have witnessed in corporate life a growing realization of the importance of values, relationships, and spirituality in making for effective people, effective families, and effective organizations. This has two aspects to it. For some it is a genuine position that has led to deep, abiding, and positive gains to organizations. For others this rise in values and relational orientations is more superficial. When we scratch the surface we find people wanting to capitalize on the benefits of a relational orientation only in so far as it is in the service of greater productivity, and providing it is done within a rational and behaviorist fantasy.

The organization that authentically and congruently honors Eros may have become unfashionable, but it is to be treasured immensely. The organization that honors Eros is one in which people are valued. There is a common misconception that valuing people and valuing efficiency and product are antithetical. Peters and Waterman, in their study of successful companies,[11] showed that this is not the case at all. Gibb makes the same point: Eros is compatible with other gods:

> It is a compelling and seductive argument which insists that productivity comes from the emphasis upon product. At first blush this seems obvious. The problem is that organizations that focus on results, efficiency, and product tend to get lowered results and less product. It is a paradox that organizations which focus on giving freedom to the self-determining worker tend to out-perform those organizations that emphasize results and efficiency. What is forgotten is that it is people who make the product, who do the work that is the 'result', and who create their own efficiency. People who are engaged in activities they enjoy, who are turned on by what they are doing, who are proud of the products they are creating, who have a part in the total enterprise, and who are honored in the processes of work, tend to work hard and creatively. They produce.[12]

Gibb's comments here are as much about Dionysos' ideology of self-fulfillment as they are about Eros' ideology of relationship. The two are closely connected. Human experience tells us that we grow through relationship and that relationship is creative. Process thinkers since Alfred North Whitehead have been telling us for a long time to take our focus away from 'things' and look instead at the connections between them. Stop thinking of society as being made up of people, and see it rather as being made up of relationships. Complexity theorists like Ralph Stacey are now making the same point, and arguing that new forms and new ideas do not somehow unfold from what is already innate in us. They emerge rather through interaction. The future is constantly constructed 'through the detail of interactions between human bodies in the living present'.[13] Transformation into something new comes through relationship.

Eros is often associated with Aphrodite. He is often found in the company of the other 'young' gods, Hermes, Ares, and Dionysos; the climate engendered by good personal relationships is a climate in which communication, passion, and creativity are supported and encouraged. The presence of Eros makes life in any organization bearable; his absence can make life intolerable.

The consultant approaching an organization from the Eros perspective will hold for certain that an organization will only be truly effective if relationships are good. To improve the quality of relationships is to improve the quality of communication. Improved communication will lead to the more effective practice and greater productivity. Accordingly, the first task of the Eros-oriented change-agent will be to demolish the psychological and structural barriers to close relationships.

Crooked Hephaistos

Sing, O clear-voiced Muse, of Hephaistos renowned for skill
who along with gray-eyed Athena taught fine crafts
to men of this earth; indeed before that time
they used to live in mountain caves like wild beasts.
But now, thanks to Hephaistos, the famous craftsman,
they have learned crafts and easily for the full year
they lead a carefree existence in their own homes.
But have mercy on me, Hephaistos, and grant me virtue and happiness.[14]

Aphrodite and Hephaistos may have an uneasy relationship, but they are linked with each other for better or for worse.

Like Aphrodite, Hephaistos is an Asian god who was incorporated into the Greek religious culture. He was originally a fire-god, probably identified with the flaming emissions of natural gas that occurred in parts of Western Asia. With the discovery of the processes of metal manufacture and crafting, he became the god of the forge, and was imagined laboring in his workshop deep below the palace of the gods, making beautiful and useful objects for the other gods to enjoy.

Two things distinguish Hephaistos from the other gods. He is the only ugly god among the twelve Olympians. And he is the only god who works.

When he was born his mother, Hera, found him so repulsive that she hurled him from the sky down to earth, so that he was crippled by the fall. (Hera is certainly not a goddess of motherhood!) In another version of the myth, it was Zeus who threw him out, because he took Hera's side in an argument. In either case, there is evidence here of Hephaistos' connection with the old goddess cult, especially as Hera conceived him without any assistance from Zeus in order to show that she could do it by herself! Hephaistos is associated in the myths with a race of little people – pigmies, dwarves, or leprechauns – who live and work in caverns below the earth.

Hephaistos is obsessed by beauty. He slaves in his workshop making beautiful ornaments for Aphrodite, hoping by this means to win her love. She accepts them somewhat contemptuously and hops into bed with Ares. He has little understanding of relationships. He ineffectively tries to seduce or rape (it is not clear which) the goddess Athena, a goddess of crafting with whom he has much in common. To avoid the need to relate to real females, he surrounds himself with beautiful robot-girls made from precious metals, who care for him and do his bidding.

Hephaistos represents the paradoxical relationship that exists between pain and beauty. He personifies the agonies which people are willing to endure for beauty, the years of boring practice which go into seeking perfect form in any craft, the aching muscles and the calluses, and even the long-term physical injuries, which accompany the pursuit of beauty for the dancer, the athlete, the sculptor, and the musician. Yet, for all his sacrifices, he never quite manages to possess Aphrodite.

Hephaistos identified entirely with his work, but he does not seem to have been entirely happy in it. Many of his stories show him as resentful of the low status given him by the other gods, who actually regarded him as a bit of a joke. He got even with Hera for her treatment of him by sending her a throne as a gift; when she sat on it, she found herself trapped. None of the other gods could release her, and they had to send Dionysos to find Hephaistos and make him drunk in order to get the key from him. He constructed an invisible net to trap his wife Aphrodite making love with Ares.

It was Hephaistos who, on Zeus' orders, fashioned Pandora, the first woman – to punish Prometheus for helping mankind. He was carrying out Zeus' orders, also, when he further punished Prometheus by driving a metal stake through the Titan's chest to pin him to a cliff. It was Hephaistos, also, who relieved Zeus' splitting headache with his axe. He cut Zeus' head open and the goddess Athena sprang out.

Organizations with a strong Hephaistos culture believe in work for work's sake. Work is perceived to be a moral good. To get aches in your bones, blisters on your hands, sweat on your brow, and soot on your face (literally or metaphorically) gives you satisfaction and distinguishes you as a person of worth in the organization. The chief executive is proud of his or her trade or craft, still identifies with it, and enjoys the opportunity to show that he or she is still prepared to get engaged in the real work of the factory floor or professional practice. The Hephaistos enterprise is proud to produce tangible goods and services, has little interest in being slick and fashionable. Many organizations that worship other gods, have one or more Hephaistos sub-cultures within them. After all, somebody has to do the work while the other gods are off having a good time. An Hephaistos sub-culture can often be found in the filing room or the engine room, usually situated in the bowels of the building, in a group of workers who are simultaneously dedicated to their work and resentful that they are stuck with it. Looking for Hephaistos? Why not try the groups of highly trained professionals and technicians in government departments and other public service agencies. Not for them the hopelessness and apathy of Hades. Whilst they may feel unloved and under-valued they, nevertheless, seem to take extraordinary pride in the quality of their professional work or craft. We are thinking particularly of groups such as photographers, surveyors, engineers, and some IT professionals.

Organizations within service professions like teaching and nursing often have strong Hephaistos cultures, with their members convinced that they work inordinately hard, feeling resentful that no one really appreciates them, complaining about their oppression to any one who will listen, yet remaining dedicated to their task just the same. The Hephaistos culture is a task culture, not much interested in power or personal advancement.

Hephaistos' obsession with Aphrodite, the pursuit of beauty through work, is an aspect of organizational culture that is often overlooked. In some organizations both managers and workers approach their work as an aesthetic performance. This does not only apply to 'artistic' work. Any work can become art, and art cannot exist without work. When an organization allows people do their work with an eye to beauty and elegance and a consciousness of crafting, so that they get aesthetic satisfaction out of what they do, Hephaistos is being truly honored. Besides, people will often pursue aesthetic goals in their work irrespective of whether these goals are acknowledged by management, simply because human beings have a need for (or drive to) Beauty, which has to be satisfied somewhere. They are happy to work alone, and when they gather in organizations they develop a culture that, in Jung's language, is introverted, experiences the world through sensation rather than intuition, and evaluates experience through feeling rather than thinking.

In a study of the work culture of foundries (the original realm of Hephaistos), Kurt Dewhurst found that workers who brought an aesthetic sense and technical artistry to their work had special status among their peers. He quotes a foundry worker talking about his grandfather, a 'loose-work molder' who took pride in his mastery of technique and was recognized among his co-workers as someone who was especially creative and dedicated to his craft:

> He was the foreman – almost everywhere he worked he was the foreman. To a certain extent the foundries allowed people to make that sort of thing [art in the workplace] . . . Competition existed to see who could make the most complicated [work of art] . . . My grandfather was constantly battling to prove he was the best . . . There was a competition, a fellow cast a cup and saucer together, which requires about a five-part mold; you have to pull the center out, then the bottom, and sides come out at an angle [very difficult]. [Then] my grandfather cast a cup and saucer - with a spoon in it and two lumps of sugar on the spoon . . . they were always trying to best each other.[15]

Such behavior is characteristic of the Hephaistos organization.

Vikram Seth in *A Suitable Boy* gives us a picture of an organization driven by Hephaistos energy. He describes the Praha Shoe Company of Calcutta as a culture of hard work, craftsmanship, obsession with an ideal of beauty, and resentment.

> The Czechs for their part treated all Indians, with one exception, the same, whether they spoke Bengali or not, with contempt. Indians, they had decided from experience, were fond of talking, not working. The Czechs liked nothing better than to work: in order to increase production, quality, sales, profits, and the glory of the Praha Shoe Company. Talking usually put them at a disadvantage; by and large they did not speak or write good English, nor did they have a great deal of culture. It could be said of them that when anyone talked about culture they reached for their awl. People started out young in the Praha Shoe Company, whether in Czechoslovakia or in India; they began on the shop floor, there was no need for the niceties of a university education. The Czechs mistrusted on the one hand what they saw as an Indian glibness with words (union negotiators were the worst), and they resented on the other the fact that the British commercial establishment in Calcutta did not treat them, although they were fellow Europeans, as anything like their equals. The directors and heads of department and even covenanted assistants of the managing agency of Bentsen & Pryce, for example, would not dream of fraternizing with the Czechs of the Praha Shoe Company.
>
> The Czechs had transformed the face of the Indian footwear industry by rolling up their sleeves and creating a great factory and township on what had virtually been a swamp, by following this up with four smaller factories including the one at Brahmpur, and by running a tight network of shops throughout the country, not by hobnobbing over Scotch at the Calcutta Club. The Czech officers, including their Managing Director, had not been born to white collars. For them the Praha Shoe Company was their life and the Praha creed virtually their religion.[16]

Hephaistos cultures are not very good at looking at the big picture. It is Hephaistos who impels so many of the world's scientists to dedicate their lives to making weapons (actually one of Hephaistos' specialities). The character of 'Q' in the James Bond string of novels and movies reflects this side of Hephaistos. Hephaistos rightly resents the power of Zeus, but he carries out his orders without reflection. He does not dare stand up to the tyrant and his cohorts, but once he starts reflecting on his oppression he may not be averse to attempting a bit of sabotage. As the god of volcanoes he keeps his rage suppressed until it blows up and destroys the organization completely. He manages sometimes to make fools of those who think themselves his betters, but his rage prevents him from enjoying the spectacle.

The Hephaistos culture is introverted (Jung) yet outer-directed (Trompenaars). It is sensate and feeling (Jung), emotional (Trompenaars) and masculine (Hofstede), with low uncertainty avoidance and a long-term orientation (Hofstede). Status in an

Hephaistos organization is gained through achievement (Trompenaars), i.e. through hard work and skills, rather than given automatically on account of one's social class or family relationship.

Hephaistos is sometimes found with his wife, Aphrodite, but more often with Athena. He also has a lot in common with Prometheus, in spite of the injuries he inflicts on him. By disposition he is something of a loner, so he needs the influence of his mother, Hera, to maintain the bonds between people in an organization. When he is found working for Zeus, the combination can be enormously efficient and productive, but also potentially explosive. The main threat to a Hephaistos culture at present seems to come from Hermes, the god of the marketplace. Organizations which once prided themselves on their ability to build beautiful bridges, produce beautiful goods, or provide beautiful services, and which identified themselves with the excellence of their crafting, are under pressure to treat their products or services as commodities whose only value is their market value.

The consultant who brings an Hephaistos-perspective to her analysis of an organization will be interested in the work ethic of the organization. Do the members of the organization see themselves as engaged in a work worth doing and are they proud of their part in it? Does the organization actually produce what it is designed to produce? Is their work so designed that they can see it as craft rather than mindless slave-labor? Are they getting the satisfaction of seeing their crafting truly valued by the organization?

Hermes the Smooth Operator

Of Hermes sing, O Muse, the son of Zeus and Maia,
Lord of Kyllene and Arcadia abounding with sheep,
helpful messenger of the immortals, whom Maia bore,
the fair-tressed and well-loved nymph, when she mingled in love with Zeus.[17]

Hermes was the most popular of the gods. He was the god of travelers and messengers, heralds and liars, shepherds, thieves, merchants, and scholars. Like other Olympian gods, he was the amalgamation of several more ancient deities, but he appears in classical times as a very distinctive character. He is a very slippery god, an opportunist without any respect for conventional morality, a trickster, a con man, and a thief. He is also the messenger-god, who carries information between the gods and from gods to humans. He is the god of magic and the god of gambling. He flourishes in a climate of uncertainty. He is elusive, unpredictable, and mischievous, and cannot resist any opportunity to make a profit on a deal. He is also very charming, and known to be particularly friendly to human beings.

In a Hermes culture there is considerable emphasis on the free transmission of information, but not so much attention to whether that information is worth transmitting. Flexibility and mobility are greatly valued. There is a great deal of attention to image, but not much concern whether the image bears any relationship to reality. The Hermes organization is dominated by the image of the marketplace, so that the only value given to any activity (or any person) is its exchange value. Students, patients, audiences, prisoners, even the deceased, all become 'customers'. The Hermes organization is not very interested in actually producing anything. Its capacity to produce things is simply an asset to be bartered. Management is 'content-free'; there is no expectation that people in leadership positions have any knowledge and experience in the particular areas that the organization works in, as long as they can 'facilitate' the activities of others. It may be easier in such an organization to advance through smooth talking and a shiny résumé than through loyalty or hard work.

Hermes is a very friendly and charming god, but he is not really trustworthy. The pathology of the Hermes culture often appears in a total lack of ethical sense. For Hermes, there is no essential difference between truth and lies, between honest and dishonest dealing. A Hermes-dominated management may be pathologically slippery and elusive, not only with regard to moral principles, but also with regard to goals and practices and the treatment of employees. It is impossible to pin such people down, because they don't actually believe in anything. (Of course, this brings the advantage of infinite flexibility.) Their desire to see things from many perspectives and to keep all options open may make them incapable of making a decision. Their preference for image over substance may lead them to spend the organization's resources on creating the illusion that something is being done rather than actually doing something. It also leads them to an extensive use of euphemisms like 'right-sizing' and 'out-placing' to disguise reality. When something goes wrong, they devote their energy to 'damage control' (by which they mean maintaining the appearance that everything is all right) rather than remedying the situation. Hermes is inclined to be somewhat infatuated with his own cleverness, and Hermes-dominated organizations are, only too often, rather too clever for their own good. The organization taken over by Hermes will always be on the lookout for a magic solution: the last thing it is likely to be interested in is hard work. If it is not producing the results it wants it is likely to seek the solution in a 'restructure', and the pathology of Hermes is often seen in organizations which destabilize themselves by constant 'restructuring'. Hermes has no interest in the past and little in the future. All of his goals are short-term ones. At its best the Hermes culture is magical, exhilarating, constantly testing the limits of our inventiveness and flexibility; at its worst it is a culture of deception inhabited by amoral opportunists.

In her study of Lyndon Johnson, Doris Kearns portrays him as a Hermes figure, an opportunist who found great delight, as well as considerable advantage, in seducing and manipulating people:

> From facts, gossip, observation – a multitude of disparate elements – he shaped a composite mental picture of every senator: his strengths and his weaknesses; his place in the political spectrum; his aspirations in the Senate, and perhaps beyond the Senate; how far he could be pushed in what direction, and by what means; how he liked his liquor; how he felt about his wife and family; and, most importantly, how he felt about himself. For Johnson understood that the most important decision each senator made, often obscurely, was what kind of senator he wanted to be; whether he wanted to be a national leader in education, a regional leader in civil rights, a social magnate in Washington, an agent of the oil industry, a wheel horse of the party, a President of the United States. But his entrepreneurial spirit encompassed not simply the satisfaction of present needs, but the development of new and expanding ones. He would, for instance, explain to a senator that 'although five other senators are clamoring for this one remaining seat on the congressional delegation to Tokyo, I might just be able to swing it for you since I know how much you really want it . . . It'll be tough but let me see what I can do.' The joys of visiting Tokyo may never have occurred to

> the senator, but he was unlikely to deny Johnson's description of his desire – after all, it might be interesting, a relaxing change, even fun; and perhaps some of the businesses in his state had expressed concern about Japanese competition. By creating consumer needs in this fashion, and by then defining the terms of their realization, Johnson was able to expand the base of benefits upon which power could be built.[18]

For the god of the marketplace everything is a commodity, and everything is negotiable.

Hermes often takes the form of the trickster, the unpredictable figure who subverts every kind of order. Howard Hughes, the founder of Hughes Aircraft, was one such figure whose personal pathology deeply affected the culture of his company. The anecdotes about him celebrate his technical wizardry and inventiveness, his delight in the new, his knack for doing the unexpected, his constant destabilization of his own organization, his spectacular lack of sensitivity to people. In the oral history of the company, as recorded by Peter Tommerup:

> Hughes has been cast in the role of 'trickster', the quintessential embodiment of unresolved appetites and contradictions. He unavoidably alternates between being calculating and merely out of control. In every instance, he reduces order to chaos. Unlike Hyland [a later general manager], who helps to put events into perspective, Hughes scrambles them and places them out of focus.[19]

Tommerup argues that such stories, told and retold, (regardless of whether they are accurate historical records), contain the meanings that people derive from their participation in the organization.

As Hermes is the god of spies, it is not surprising to find intelligence organizations dominated by a Hermes consciousness. In *Spycatcher*, Peter Wright describes the culture of MI5 in Hermes terms.

> The profession of intelligence is a solitary one. There is camaraderie, of course, but in the end you are alone with your secrets. You live and work at a feverish

> pitch of excitement, dependent always on the help of your colleagues. But you always move on, whether to a new branch or department, or to a new operation. And when you move on, you inherit new secrets which subtly divorce you from those you have worked with before. Contacts, especially with the outside world, are casual, since the largest part of yourself cannot be shared. For this reason, intelligence services are great users of people. It is built into the very nature of the profession, and everyone who joins knows it.[20]

Many organizations in the advertising, marketing, and sales industries have strong Hermes cultures, as we would expect. We are likely also to find Hermes cultures, appropriately enough, in the media and travel industries. Yet when a Hermes culture becomes dominant in manufacturing or agriculture, the results can be disastrous. To see this at work, we need look no further than the deep pressure CEOs feel to respond to marketplace demands for certain styles of management, certain elements of strategic intent, and certain pathways of strategic direction. Gone are the days when a CEO was responsible to a Board alone for his/her performance. The marketplace, through the voices of analysts and financial journalists, now demands of CEOs a responsiveness to the market's short term imperatives for return on capital. This can place the corporate strategist in some very significant dilemmas, balancing long-term good against the need to keep the marketplace hounds from the door.

For the past two decades at least, political life has appeared to be dominated by Hermes personalities, and there is great pressure within institutions of all kinds to adopt Hermes culture. This is a source of great stress, as organizations traditionally dedicated to Demeter, Hera, Hephaistos, or Apollo are expected to suddenly abandon their focus on care, service, crafting, or research and become slick marketeers of these commodities.

An increasingly common and effective form of organization is the network. It is shaped by the Hermes images of unregulated communication, flexibility, and the subversion of central authority (Zeus) and hierarchical structures (Apollo). It does not have anyone in charge. It has no premises, no temple of its own, but is dispersed over a wide area, its activity constantly shifting from place to place according to where communication is taking place. It is constantly changing shape. In conventional organizational terms it is slippery and groundless and lacking in appropriate boundaries. It does not even have an established membership list.

The DuPont company is recognized as one of the corporate leaders in the application of networks.[21] They have cultivated, used, and enhanced the functioning of networks very extensively. Networks seem to perform well under conditions that require efficiency and flexibility together. They bring both know-how and information together in the one space, and the emergent synergy that seems to be associated with networks can be a strong source of motivation for employees. However, a network structure guarantees neither efficiency nor flexibility. A too common outcome is conformity, low-level energy and engagement. As with many of the gods there is often the subtle deception of one god masquerading as another. Much of the so called Hermes benefits of networks are veneer; the deeper reality is often Apollo in the background trying to bring order, stability, and systemization into what must be (of its very nature) a somewhat unpredictable and emergent phenomenon.

A key distinction between Apollo cultures and Hermes cultures lies in their attitude to uncertainty. Apollo cultures have little tolerance for uncertainty, and put a lot of energy into avoiding it. (Many of these ways consist of magical rituals disguised as rational administrative procedures.) Hermes cultures thrive on uncertainty. They love to live 'on the edge' and don't value anything enough to be committed to maintaining it. A Hermes initiative within an organization dominated by the Apollo values of order, hierarchy, and stability is likely to be perceived as a threat, and the guardians of Apollo values will make it their business to bring it into line, even while they talk the Hermes-talk.

Yet for all of this, the Hermes fantasy of emergent self-organizing networks of communications lies at the very heart of so much new science that is finding its way into organizational and management literature. Knowles,[22] Pensinger,[23] Capra,[24] Wheatley,[25] Stacey,[26] Kellner-Rogers,[27] and Kauffman[28] have all written at length about systems, including human systems, from a Hermes perspective.

> One of the ways in which self-organizing systems maintain this great capacity for growth and change is that they are the source. They don't have to wait for

> a leader. They are the source of these new structures and processes. But how do they do that? Well they do this because they are able to access the intelligence that's available throughout the whole system. So any living system is a network of communication pathways and the network of relationships. There is nothing in life that is not a network. It's one of the ways in which you – it's not the only way by any means – can define something as alive. But anything alive will always show up as a very messy network that works well because the network engages the intelligence of individuals and they share in a sense of what's important. So they share in the development of what's meaningful for them and they are absolutely connected[29]

The contempt of networks for command and control is evident in the dismay that the US Air Force Command experienced during the Vietnam War (known to the Vietnamese as the American War) in trying to locate the central command of the Viet Cong. The North Vietnamese had organized themselves into emergent networks of relationships without any core. This infuriated the senior officers in the US Air Force, for Zeus, Apollo, and Ares could not conceive of an army without a central command, so much so that they even suspected at times the loyalty of their own intelligence officers in their 'failure' to locate the Viet Cong central headquarters. This network arrangement allowed the Viet Cong extreme structural flexibility and high levels of efficiency in their responsiveness. They were able to manage massive structural re-organization of their military machine of 500,000 plus troops in a matter of weeks using nothing but highly-connected, dispersed communication channels. The mental models in use by US Air Force senior officers could not cope with such an idea.

The escalation of information technology has made it possible to entirely rethink our notions of organization in Hermes terms. The god of travelers is at particularly at home with the groundlessness of cyberspace and the motility of the information superhighway.

Peter Deusch's description of the Internet challenges conventional notions of organizational structure.

> No single person, company or government agency owns the Internet. No one person manages it, directs it, or otherwise is responsible for making it all work.

> While the truth of this statement is evident to anyone who has been exposed to the Internet for any length of time, the idea that something as large, complex, and successful as the Net could come into existence and keep itself growing at such an amazing rate, apparently without a single person or entity being empowered to maintain order, is a difficult concept for network novices to accept.
>
> Even if you assume that the many political issues required to build the Internet could be resolved through negotiations among hundreds of competing special interest groups, (unlikely, to say the least) it seems pretty far-fetched to assume that such an approach would be successful in resolving the thousands of technical conflicts that must arise while building something this complex.
>
> So who exactly is responsible for the technical decisions that shape the Internet? Who chooses the specific protocols and technologies that form the Net's core? Who sets priorities for development, makes decisions among competing approaches, and bangs heads together when disputes arise? What keeps the whole thing going if there's not some kind of king, emperor or despot around to chop off a few heads when the peasants get a little unruly?
>
> The answer, of course, is that this is all done by a collection of individual volunteers, people who access the Internet every day for their own work and who contribute something back to make it all work. These people work on the development and deployment of the Internet infrastructure through their participation in the Internet Engineering Task Force . . . This unique volunteer standards body offers a successful blend of participatory democracy and controlled anarchy that closely parallels the Internet itself.[30]

Deusch draws attention to the preference of networks for a pluralistic approach to problem solving. There is no assumption or convention of a 'best way' of dealing with technical problems. The idea that such decisions should be determined by 'managerial policy' is treated with complete contempt.

> Where there is legitimate disagreement among capable developers on the most suitable approach to take, multiple working groups are seen as one means of discovering the most suitable approach to take. It is generally expected that the best technical solution will become evident as the various working groups progress in their efforts. If this does not happen, then whenever possible it is left to the Internet user community to choose from among the proposed solutions.[31]

Deutsch wrote this in 1994. Since then we have seen an ongoing tension between the vision that he describes and the very different vision of those who want to own the net and control it in their own political or financial interests Zeus clearly has his eye on the internet. Whether he will manage to get control of it is yet to be seen. It may be that its very nature will prevent it from coming under centralized, hierarchical control.

Deusch's description of the IETF development community shows the values and energy of Hermes working quite compatibly with those of Prometheus and Athena. Hermes, being so charming, gets on well with all the gods. He gets on particularly well with Aphrodite. He can charm even Zeus and Hera, though everything he does is actually subversive of the authority and stability that they represent. He has great skill in disguise, and often pretends to be one of the other gods if it suits his self-interest.

The consultant who approaches an organization from the perspective of Hermes will be much more interested in process than content. How flexible and adaptable are the members of this organization? How open to change? How ready to improvise? Where are they 'stuck' and how can they be rescued from their 'stuckness'? How free is the flow of information? How well do they market themselves, and how skilled are they at persuading people to desire and buy what they produce?

Hermes seems to be the god whom consultants worship most enthusiastically. This theme is developed in Chapter 12 of this book, which focuses on Hermes as the god of the postmodern organization.

---

1. Hesiod, *Theogony*. Trans. A. Athanassakis (1983), p. 16.
2. Eros seems to have been originally a personification of what we now understand as the Earth's gravitational field. Eros was the force that draws the apple to the ground before he was the force that draws two lovers together.
3. The Story of Psyche and Amor (Eros) is known to us in a literary version by the Roman writer Lucius Apulius, who seems to have based it on a much earlier folk-tale. The simple mythical narrative has been transformed into sophisticated allegory.
4. Acts 2, 44 - 47. *The New Oxford Annotated Bible*, (1991), p. 164.
5. 1 John 4, 16 - 21, ibid., p. 353.
6. 1 Corinthians 13, 1-13. ibid., p. 243.
7. J Gibb, (1978) Trust, p. 214.
8. ET Hall (1981) in *The Dance of Life* discusses the monochromic/polychronic distinction. F Trompenaars and C Hampden-Turner (1998) in *Riding the Waves of Culture* discuss attitude to time as a distinguishing feature of cultures.

9. The origins and development of this work is well documented in A Kleiner (1996) *The Age of Heretics.*
10. For a discussion of the Hawthorne Effect see J Hughes (1976) *The Hawthorne Effect.*
11. T Peters & R Waterman (1982) *In Search of Excellence.*
12. J Gibb, op. cit., p. 197.
13. R Stacey (1996) *Complexity and Creativity in Organizations* , p. 6.
'Relating between diverse people in their local situations is understood as the process in which knowledge is perpetually reproduced and potentially transformed at the same time... It follows that knowledge is not stored but perpetually constructed. Knowledge is not shared as contents but perpetually arises in action. Knowledge is not transmitted from one mind to another but is the process of relating.'
14. A Athanassakis (1976) *The Homeric Hymns*, p. 63.
15. K Dewhurst. (1988) 'Art at Work: In Pursuit of Aesthetic Solutions', in M Jones, M Moore, & R Snyder, *Inside Organizations*, p. 247.
16. V Seth (1993) *A Suitable Boy*, p. 914.
17. Athanassakis, ibid., p. 31. Maia (mother) is another personification of Goddess Earth.
18. D Kearns (1976) *Lyndon Johnson and the American Dream*, p. 91.
19. P Tommerup (1988) 'From Trickster to Father Figure: Learning from the Mythologization of Top Management' in M Jones, M Moore, & R Snyder, *Inside Organization*, p. 329.
20. P Wright (1988) *Spycatcher*, p. 67.
21. For a discussion of networks at Du Pont, see PM Norling (1996) 'Network or Not Work: Harnessing Technology Networks', *DuPont*, Vol. 39, No. 1 p. 42.
22. R Knowles (1997) *Reaching New Ground* and (2002) *The Leadership Dance.*
23. W Pensinger, (1994) *Moon Over Hoa Binh.*
24. F Capra (1996) *The Web of Life.*
25. M Wheatley, (1992) *Leadership and the New Science.*
26. R Stacy, (1996) *Complexity and Creativity in Organizations.*
27. M Wheatley & M Kellner-Rogers (1996) *A Simpler Way.*
28. S Kauffman (1996) *At Home in the Universe.*
29. Transcript of talk given by Margaret Wheatley at a workshop in Brisbane, Australia, September, 1998.
30. P Deusch (1994) 'What is the IETF?' *Internet World*, p. 74.
31. ibid., p. 77.

10

THE POLYTHEISTIC ORGANIZATION

THE POLYTHEISTIC PERSPECTIVE

When the Greeks settled on the membership of their Olympian pantheon, they were making a statement about the archetypal patterns they experienced most powerfully in their lives. It is a statement about life that has had currency for nearly three thousand years. On the authority of that statement we may look for all of these gods in contemporary human behavior. If some of these gods appear to be missing, we may suspect that something untoward is going on.

It is our purpose in this book not only to examine what value the polytheistic perspective has in helping us to look at organizations, but also to suggest various ways in which this perspective might help us in working with organizations

We argue that organizational life functions through magical and mythical structures as well as rational ones. We suggest that even in an organization whose members pride themselves on their rational approach to problems and challenges, rationality functions largely at the mythical level.

The organization's story about itself is that decisions are made rationally, on the basis of the best information available. The reality is more likely to be that these 'rational' decisions are often made on the basis of managerial whim, prejudice, personal point-taking or personal loyalty, cowardice, denial, political maneuvering, impulse, panic, intuition, dreams, and visions – just as they are in 'irrational' organizations. The voice may be the voice of Apollo, but the actions are often the actions of Dionysos, Ares, Artemis, and the rest.

Alternative Narratives

When we come to explore the significance of shared narratives in organizations, we can learn a good deal from the practitioners of family therapy.

Theorists and practitioners of family therapy work extensively with a particular kind of dysfunctional organization. Many of them work within the 'narrative paradigm', arguing that people make sense of their world through the stories they tell themselves, and make their choices in accordance with these stories. They shape their lives and relationships by 'performing' these stories. However the story that they perform is often an inadequate one, which acts as a filter preventing them from perceiving anything that would disturb their assumptions and pre-suppositions. It becomes the task of the family therapist to call attention to whatever there is in the family's experience that challenges the 'dominant narrative'. The therapist challenges the illusion that the dominant story is the only story.

> The therapist raises to the foreground of the person's attention the alternative story which is endlessly present, drawn from the unremembered, neglected, minimized, or repudiated events in a person's life . . . to challenge the received text of life story and its constraining role. In this way the therapist engages in a collaborative role with the client as co-author.[1]

It requires little translation to present such ideas in the language of archetypal psychology. We are focusing in this discussion on what Gebser calls the mythical structure of consciousness, believing that the human capacity for story-making, story-telling and story-performing is an essential element in our experiencing of the world

– more basic than the human capacity to conceptualize. We have suggested that when individual consciousness gives way to group consciousness, magical and mythical thinking replace conceptualization altogether. What the archetypal perspective adds to this is the observation that the stories that groups and organizations tell themselves, and through which they filter and censor their experience, are variations on a limited number of 'old stories'.

Members of deliberately constructed organizations, like members of families, are recruited into the dominant narratives, the received mythology, of the organizations. Some organizations tend to have a unitary notion of truth, and membership of such organizations means accepting this truth about how the world is, how the organization is, and how each member ought to be, and shutting out any information that might challenge it. The change agent, like the family therapist, has to call the organization's attention to the things that do not 'fit' the dominant narrative, for these point to the neglected or suppressed 'alternative narratives', which carry the organization's potential for change.

Adopting the archetypal perspective puts a particular spin on this activity, because in attempting to see through an organization's ikons and behavior to the gods who govern it, we are calling on the history of Indo-European story-making to make some pre-suppositions about what these alternative narratives are likely to be.

In the approach we take here we have used the Greco-Roman pantheon as a template, both to guide us in our depiction of the dominant narratives of organizations and to point us to significant alternative narratives. In dealing with the unconscious dimensions of organizations we are not bound to use the template all the time, for we are well aware that some of the narratives of contemporary culture have no foundation in ancient Greece. Nevertheless, the test of this model is not in its theoretical purity but in its usefulness.

We recognize also that we are here enmeshed in our own story, which does its own filtering and censoring. So we must attempt to see through our assumptions and ideas to the archetypal image that dominates them. It will be clear enough from this discussion that the story in which we are enmeshed is a story about pluralism, flexibility, relativity, image, depth, liminality, and transformation. A fairly complex story perhaps, but one which we find widely told in our time.

If we accept the notion that the stories we keep telling ourselves are essentially the old stories, and test this particular story for fit against the template of the Greek pantheon, looking for the god who is being worshipped in this worship of complexity, flexibility, and plurality, we will find Hermes, the cowboy, the conman, the bringer of dreams, the guide to the underworld, the god of the in-between, the god who insists that all the gods must be worshipped. And also, we have to acknowledge, the god of subversion, thieving, deceit, and amoral opportunism. We need to be careful.

Some organizations see plurality and changeability as a problem to be addressed, and deal with it by strengthening the magical-mythical dimensions of group life. The wearing of uniforms, the chanting of slogans, the use of a 'secret language', the performance of induction rituals and 'rites of passage', the constant exposure to the wise sayings of the founder or the glorious history of the company are magical-mythical means of homogenizing the culture of the organization. To the same end, some companies and cults make a point of recruiting employees from among the least powerful groups in society, e.g. adolescents and ethnic minorities with a magical relationship to authority.

Other organizations see the diversity of their membership, with their diversity of gifts and points of view as a great asset that, more than anything else, gives them the capacity to respond in a flexible way to a constantly changing world. They don't find it uncomfortable that their organization does not worship at a single shrine. They are happy to worship many gods. They find polytheism liberating.

As individuals we have many values, many centers of worth. Most of us prefer to live in a society that respects plurality, rather than one that demands that we all hold the same beliefs and values. We are not as sure as our grandparents were about the absoluteness of any truth. The polytheistic organization is shaped in the same image as the flexible, multi-faceted individual and the flexible, multi-cultural society. It holds the same promise, feels the same tensions and meets the same contradictions.

The consultant who takes the perspective of Hermes will be faced with these same promises and tensions as he or she attempts to bring an organization's attention to its dominant and alternative narratives. In our own work, we find in the Greek pantheon not only an appropriate language for such an analysis, but a means of engaging people in an imaginal process that stimulates a creative engagement in the myths we live by. It also provides a map of possibilities, a guide to the discovery of hidden strengths and energies.

A Vision of Excellence

From their analysis of highly successful American companies in the eighties, Peters and Waterman came to the conclusion that excellence was associated with certain qualities:

> Our findings were a pleasant surprise. Our findings showed, more clearly than could have been hoped for, that the excellent companies were, above all, brilliant on the basics. Tools didn't substitute for thinking. Intellect didn't overpower wisdom. Analysis didn't impede action. Rather, these companies worked hard to keep things simple in a complex world. They persisted. They insisted on top quality. They fawned on their customers. They listened to their employees and treated them like adults. They allowed their innovative product and service 'champions' long tethers. They allowed some chaos in return for quick action and regular experimentation.[2]

What Peters and Waterman meant by 'excellence' was commercial success. They singled out eight attributes that seemed most characteristic of excellent companies. They are listed here with the gods that seem most closely connected with these attributes as Peters and Waterman describe them:

- a bias for action (Ares, Herakles)
- service to customers (Demeter, Hestia)
- autonomy and entrepreneurship (Herakles, Hermes)
- productivity through people (Eros, Athena)
- hands on, value driven (Apollo, Hephaistos)

- stick to the knitting (Hephaistos, Hestia)
- simple forms, lean staff (Apollo, Zeus)
- simultaneous loose-tight properties (Zeus, Dionysos, Hermes)

It is conventional to think that many of the qualities listed here are contradictory. Concentrating on productivity seems to be in conflict with concentrating on one's people. Giving attention to values and principles seems to be in conflict with simply getting on with the job. It does not seem to make sense to have an organization that is simultaneously 'loose' and 'tight'. Yet Peters and Waterman argued that the companies that qualified as excellent in their terms managed to carry all of these qualities.

If Peters and Waterman had used the language of mythology, they could have drawn on their evidence to conclude that the successful companies honored all the gods, that they were polytheistic rather than monotheistic. Nevertheless, their thinking was very much constrained by the conventional assumption that a good corporate culture will be 'strong', that is, a manifestation of a shared commitment to a particular set of attitudes and practices. It was axiomatic for them that all of these diverse qualities should be integrated in a cohesive and unitary culture. Evidence that some individuals and groups in these companies might be marching to a different drummer was likely to go unnoticed. Basing their analysis on the management view of what the company was about and how it operated made it even more likely that tensions and contradictions in the culture would go unremarked. From this perspective, Peters and Waterman developed a 'one size fits all' view of what makes for a good corporate culture, and suggested that companies that wanted to achieve similar success would do well to develop similar cultures. Of course, in this they were making the further assumption that corporate culture is controllable from the top down.

Several of the companies that Peters and Waterman selected as representing excellence have failed to maintain their commercial success in the years since. The reasons for this are obviously complex, and differ from case to case, but we can suggest that when a changing environment put a new crisis in their way, the particular attitudes and energy that might have enabled them to meet it were absent.

This is not to suggest that the ideal organization, commercial or otherwise, worships all the gods equally. Each organization is unique, just as every person is unique. The 'personality' of the organization reflects the particular gods that provide the energy, values, and perspectives of that organization. Yet, just as the healthy personality recognizes and attends to diverse human needs, the healthy organization attends to all the gods. While in some organizations alternative narratives and the energies that belong to them are suppressed, in others a plurality of perspectives is not only tolerated but supported. This is illustrated in Stern's account of the highly successful aerospace company, the Garrett Corporation, in which the 'personality' of the organization, while dominated by the Zeus image, also manifests the other gods of the pantheon.

Chairman Zeus

Stern's study of the Garrett Corporation[3] makes it clear that the firm's founder, Clifford Garrett, was a benevolent authoritarian who made great demands on his employees and treated them with loyalty and generosity. He expected managers and employees to give each other full support. The Garrett Corporation under Clifford Garrett's leadership was essentially a Zeus organization. There was no room for doubt about whose company it was, or who made the important decisions. Nevertheless, Garrett was aware that there were other needs to be addressed in human organizations besides those related to the exercise of power. His success as a benevolent Zeus-figure came from his concern that people's need for security, affection, respect, family, identity, achievement, and all the rest should be met as far as possible within their workplace. We can find in Stern's description evidence that the whole pantheon of gods was acknowledged. The following statements are taken from Stern's account:

> As a patron, Clifford Garrett hired, protected, and guided his employees in exchange for receiving their uncompromising loyalty. He ruled autocratically and made decisions unilaterally . . . [He] believed that his employees would do what he requested . . . [He] employed an open-door policy by which employees could bypass their immediate supervisors to voice grievances. (Zeus)
>
> Enormously compassionate to his employees, [Garrett] established humanistic industrial relations before other aerospace firms. His benevolence arose not only

from caring about the welfare of employees but also out of a desire to prevent unions from gaining a foothold. (Zeus, Demeter, Eros)

To support this natural flow of assistance, managers and employees established a framework for treating themselves as equals. Garrett insisted on removing the external trappings of rank and hierarchy. All offices had the same decor; no special decorations distinguished upper management. (Athena)

Employees frequently commented that the Garrett Corporation differed from other, more hierarchical, companies. As a section manager put it . . . 'There's just a great deal of communication between people here. There is no caste system here. Anybody can talk to anybody they want to in Garrett.' (Hermes, Athena)

'Throughout our company we try to remember that each man and women who works with us is an individual, intelligent, cooperative, and productive person' [from the industrial relations handbook]. (Athena)

[From a division manager] 'You can walk into any Garrett warehouse and you'll always find them squeaky clean. You don't find any cigarette butts on the floor. You won't find any old coffee cups in the corner, or paper, or dirt, or anything else.' (Aphrodite)

[His employees] relied on him to provide their essential needs. (Demeter)

Garrett wanted to be in complete control of selecting the benefits to be distributed. (Zeus, Demeter)

One of the [employees'] clubs most significant functions was to act as a benevolent society . . . Funds were allocated to bereaved employees who required emergency assistance upon the death of a close relative. (Hera. Eros)

[Quotation from a section manager] 'Garrett has been peopled through the years by people who just wouldn't give up. I can remember in the early days sitting next to a guy who came to work at eight o'clock in the morning, worked all the day, all that night, all the next day till 4:30 when he went home. Never got up from his desk. People do it because they want to, because they like what they are doing, and they want to see it get done. (Hephaistos)

Visible also are employees who participate in the decision-making process of the company. (Athena)

Employees are encouraged to tackle new problems whenever and wherever asked, even though they may no have expertise. Managers who have spent years filling a position may suddenly be requested to accept another one totally unrelated to the previous. (Hermes)

Engineers who were originally involved in designing a project may find themselves asked to solve problems resulting from their design years after the product has been on the market. (Prometheus, Herakles)

Employees strive to exceed the technical demands of the client. Garrett employees do not believe in cutting corners to produce a less than perfect product, even if they have to charge more for its superiority. (Prometheus, Apollo)

> Responsibility goes beyond internal company concerns to include consideration for the community at large. Employees seek to be recognized as 'corporate citizens'. Voluntary civic duties are vital to the organization's standing in the community. They include participation in cultural and civic affairs, in efforts to clean and beautify the environment, in programs to aid the disadvantaged and handicapped, and in activities to educate youth. (Hera, Artemis)
>
> At the Garrett Corporation, responsibility is measured by the degree of individual initiative taken in carrying out assignments. Employees are expected to accept challenges and solve problems creatively. (Herakles, Dionysos)
>
> Employees rely on management to provide for their personal well-being, for meaningful social contacts, and for career development. (Demeter)
>
> The innovative aspect of these products is reflected in the employees' pride at having been the 'first' to invent and produce them ... These 'firsts' were achieved, in part, because of the aggressive attitudes of the Garrett Corporation sales force – a fact well known in the industry. (Ares)
>
> By earning a reputation for major accomplishments, employees feel that they are contributing to the aerospace industry, and by implication, to society in general. (Prometheus, Herakles) [Garrett was able to balance this intensity by finding outlets for relaxation, a state of mind he encouraged others to achieve. (Hestia) Stern makes reference in this context to Garrett's own practice of meditation.]
>
> His secretary remembers how, when [Garrett] went into the shop he would publicly thank employees for their company involvement. He lavishly praised employees at social gatherings, too, making them feel important by calling them by their first names, and enquiring about the welfare of their families. (Hera)
>
> [Garrett's] belief in technical excellence was supported by a commitment to deal with others ethically. He refused to enter into shady deals and did not countenance unethical behavior among employees. (Apollo)[4]

This company, like Peters and Waterman's illustrative companies, had a clear identity based around a dominant value system (Zeus). It is not surprising that the benevolent patriarchy should provide a context for the kind of diversity illustrated here. It mimics the Olympian council of the gods, with Zeus presiding over a clutch of squabbling deities, giving them all a voice but setting firm limits on their behavior. It should be noted that in Greek mythology Zeus is not all-powerful. Each of the gods has his or her special domain, and Zeus cannot interfere in their business. In his relationships with the other gods he is not a tyrant, but instead 'first among equals'.

What is noticeable in the Garrett Corporation, or at least in Stern's description of it, is the relatively low profile of Hermes and Dionysos, the two gods who are actually subversive of the patriarchy, and the near invisibility of Artemis, a god who figures highly in current notions of corporate excellence.

In the sixties, under the leadership of Garrett, the company was enormously successful. However, when he came to describe this culture in the eighties, Stern found that the established Zeus-dominated Garrett culture was now proving to be a hindrance to success in a different commercial environment. It seems that the flexibility and inventiveness of Hermes and the creative energy of Dionysos were not available when they were needed. Like the corporations in Peters and Waterman's sample, which were thriving in the seventies yet failed in the eighties or nineties, the Garrett Corporation illustrates the principle that a strong and cohesive corporate culture, which ensures success in a stable environment, may prove to be a liability when the environment becomes unstable.

While the Stern account and Peters and Waterman's accounts of 'excellence' acknowledge the multiplicity of needs and values that must be addressed in a highly functioning organization, they minimize the tensions and contradictions that are inherent in any pluralistic organization. Most writers on organizational culture in the eighties were strongly inclined to think of culture as unitary. They wrote about the McDonalds culture or the Garrett culture as though all the organization's members shared essentially the same set of values and assumptions. They fashioned an image of the organization's common culture, rather than focusing on the culture's tensions and ambiguities. While this approach may have been plausible at the time, it seems increasingly clear that contemporary organizations are not so easily categorized. Organizations in the early twenty-first century are much less likely to be to be driven by a single definable set of objectives and hold a single definable set of values. They are more likely to reflect the ambiguity about values and objectives that characterizes contemporary society at large.

In any contemporary organization there are likely to be substantial contradictions between publicly avowed values and objectives and those privately held, between the values and objectives of 'the organization as a whole' and those of particular subcultures within it. Even the values and objectives of the individual members of the organization are likely to be somewhat unstable, and to shift according to time and context. An illustration of an organization experiencing the conflict between two archetypally constellated sub-cultures – one dominant and another struggling to maintain itself – is to be found in Tim Dalmau's 1991 study[5] of scientific communities in Antarctica.

The Gods and Goddesses of Antarctica

There appear to be significant differences in the ways in which men and women prefer to work in organizations. Women tend to operate more inclusively, more through relationships, more flexibly, and far more subtly than men. Their process may engender a more mutually satisfying result to the various people concerned than does men's process in the same context. Most organizations tend to rely on men's process - they tend to be far more exclusive in their dynamics, more competitive, less considerate and more political and when they achieve the results they seek they often do so at a social cost to the various people involved.

However, to make this crude distinction between 'men's process' and 'women's process' is to neglect a great deal of the complexity of human behavior. Many women find themselves frustrated by some of the aspects of 'women's process'; many men find themselves alienated by conventional 'men's process'. Even if we re-frame the distinction as 'feminine' and 'masculine' process, and argue, as Jung does, that the feminine in men and the masculine in women demand expression, we still underestimate the complexity of such distinctions. Neither masculinity nor femininity is uni-dimensional. One of the advantages of using the language of Greek polytheism is that it recognizes the many, apparently incompatible, dimensions of personality and behavior in a way that our simplistic polarity does not. Demeter, Hera, Athena, Artemis, Hestia, Aphrodite, and Persephone represent very different ways of being 'feminine', just as the male gods represent very different ways of being 'masculine'. Furthermore, Athena and Artemis clearly have characteristics that we would conventionally categorize as 'masculine', while Dionysos, Eros, Hephaistos, and Hermes have characteristics that we are conventionally inclined to label 'feminine'.

Within the Australian Antarctic communities, the male-female polarization has been critical. It is 'men's process' that is dominant. Work spaces are imagined as domains of rationality, objectivity, and impersonality. Antarctic history is a history of male-dominated domains. Indeed, only six countries of the nineteen who have wintering communities in Antarctica have had women in those communities in the last ten years. It is not the world of women, yet it is a world in which women do work and at some cost to themselves. In the world of engineering, science, and technology there seems little scope for understanding and appreciating gendered differences, let alone incorporating them into the day-to-day procedures and dynamics by which such organizations operate.

One of the most common cultural dynamics at work in any group of people is the one that seeks to preserve the group's unconscious corporate identity. Accordingly, it is predictable that we should find in much of the Antarctic literature and much of the experience of women who have been in Antarctica evidence of a strong cultural resistance to their presence. Where positions of authority are defined in instrumental or political terms rather than in supportive or collaborative terms, women are less likely to be interested in aspiring to them. These ways of describing an organization's authority structures help to exclude women from positions of authority.

This is not to say that what was past was wrong. Male cultures have their rightful place, and serve some very useful functions. For instance, we could speculate about the extent to which (at least at an unconscious level) men who went off to Antarctica did so as part of what Joseph Campbell calls their 'hero's journey': a time and passage in their lives where they set out on a great adventure, to confront dragons and seek their destiny in the company of other men - a physical journey with deep psychic functions. In modern, western industrialized nations the scope for physically enacting one's mythic journey is diminishing rapidly. For some, a posting in Antarctica offers such an opportunity.

One of the key stages in the hero's journey is the meeting with the goddess: the absent and unattainable, the punishing, the forbidden yet desired. It may be that women in Antarctic communities become unwitting repositories for the deeply unconscious and highly conflicted projections of their male colleagues as they go through their journey of transformation. If this is so, it is not surprising that they are often treated with hostility and ambiguous resentment and acceptance.

Neither is it surprising that, when thinking and talking about having women in Antarctic communities, those responsible for decision-making in this area should use a language that implies that they think of women as constituting 'a spectacularly different gender-specific management problem', as one returned female expeditioner once put it. This sort of language gives us loud and clear signals that their organizational 'masters' do indeed see women as the other and that the women themselves are caught up in the male culture that leads to this perception.

But the women themselves can complicate this unconscious dynamic. Women caught up in the myth of Artemis are pre-disposed to see male oppression and defend themselves against it by forming a coalition, which emphasizes their separateness and 'otherness'. There is nothing surprising in this, unless we really expect human behavior to be consistently rational. There are deep images and forces at work here. They are not amenable to change and resolution through rational discourse or process. It is as if we have two different tribal groups each living its own myth and each unable to appreciate the other for what it is. It has been conventional from time to time to talk in a simplistic way about a 'war of the sexes', as though such a conflict was pre-programmed in our genes and hormones on gender lines, but it is clearly more complex than this. At the surface level, the 'cultural split' in the Antarctic communities that was studied appears to be based on sex, but the old stories represented in these two distinguishable subcultures cross our socially constructed gender lines, and represent competing values in each individual as well as a dominant and alternative narrative in the group.

In the Antarctic communities we have on the one hand a sub-culture under the spell of Eros, Artemis, Hestia, and Demeter. The god Eros provides the perspective that the quality of a relationship really matters, that people should get on with one another, that trust and openness and mutual unconditional regard are important. The down side of Eros is that people under his spell have a tendency to become bitter if they find themselves in an environment that does not value such human concerns. They then can lose sight of strategy or goal and become defensive, passive, and resistant. Artemis helps them to experience a sense of 'at-oneness' with themselves and with nature. They tend to view people and evaluate their worth intuitively on who they are and what they do. They have an air of intactness about them, yet feel strongly about their causes and principles. They may also have a touch of paranoia. Hestia provides them with clarity in the midst of the confusing myriad of details, a sense of quiet tranquility in solitude that is 'detached', an ambiance of order and warmth. Sometimes, however, this goes too far and they come to feel alienated or isolated from their fellow workers and do not easily find recognition in a competitive workplace. The earth-mother goddess, Demeter seems to provide the fourth element of their energy source. She values emotional and psychological support, providing a solid and dependable place to be, with lots of nurturance and support.

Then we have the dominant sub-culture under the spell of Apollo, Prometheus, Herakles, and Ares. Apollo has them place a very high value on being rational, systematic, and orderly. Consequently, they value targets and goals that are visible to others, in an environment that fosters clear definitions, approaches the task 'scientifically', and prefers to look at the obvious rather than acknowledge the invisible. Apollo ensures they value order and harmony, thinking over feeling, distance over closeness, objective assessment over subjective intuition. But Apollo is joined in their sub-culture by Prometheus. He provides them with a pervasive belief that things will get better and better, that we gradually will get control of things and learn how to do everything and understand everything. People under his spell value the development of technology and systems to get control over whatever seems confusing or problematic. Herakles ensures that the most valued people are those who will fight for what they want. He encourages people to talk a lot about their own ambitions, to be tough, yet friendly. Problems are solved by facing them head-on, and they are unhappy unless they're energetic and ambitious for they don't like being pushed around. Finally, Ares ensures they are likely to have intense and instinctive reactions to issues, ideas, and each other. For him, the ideal environment is assertive and active. When riled, people under his spell can be physically abusive - they lack choice and are bundles of impulsive reactions. They have real difficulties 'going by the book'.

These two sub-cultures are driven by quite different perspectives, values, beliefs, and energies. They don't fall neatly into single-description categories and the sources of their respective differences do indeed seem to be archetypal. Each of these subcultures is itself pluralistic. The passion and impulse of Ares and the order and clarity of Apollo have nothing in common, but they live together in the sub-culture and in the individuals who comprise it. Likewise there is tension between the inward-looking Hestia and the outward-looking Eros, between the cozy dependence of Demeter and the idealistic independence of Artemis. But these differing energies come together, in tension, to give the sub-group a distinctive identity and 'personality'. And each sub-group defends its identity and its place in the world quite vigorously, indeed sometimes with stunning ferocity.

The tenacity with which an organizational culture or sub-culture will defend its identity in the face of information and experiences that would undermine it is illustrated in the following cases involving organizations embedded in the Hera narrative.

Family Life

Sometimes an organization espouses a mythology that is never publicly doubted but that is actually not compatible with the value systems of a significant number of its members. Arthur D. Colman and Georgia Lepper describe their work as consultants to organizations whose management was embedded in the Hera-Zeus mythology of 'the family', in spite of the dissonance between this mythology and the experience of staff and clients, and in spite of the inappropriateness of this myth for the organization's current context.

Colman's illustration is of the management group of a government agency concerned with conservation. The agency was in serious conflict with a well-organized citizen's group, which was opposed to the way the agency functioned. The consultant was employed to devise a way of approaching the problem.

> I met with the entire group for a weekend retreat. I soon discovered that the director was convinced of the 'goodness' of the way he and his management were performing. He said esprit was high and performance had improved in response to the current stress. He thought policy was well thought out and relevant to task. He was sure the agency was capable of changing its ideas and process if needed; that was not the problem; witness the successful incorporation of affirmative action hiring policies amply demonstrated by the women and minority present in the room. 'This group,' the director proudly told me, with affirming nods from

> the people in the room, 'is like a good American family. We care about our own, and we take care of our own. And we have tried and true family ways of changing things when they need changing'.
>
> Obviously a great deal was being left out. I have learned over many consulting efforts that whenever family metaphors are used to describe organizations, it is likely that the exclusion dynamic is particularly insidious. Hallowed family platitudes often hide a multitude of family sins, including incest, sexism, and 'black sheep' victimizations, to mention a few. Organizations are not families, and those that claim to be are usually profoundly afraid of their secrets and their differences. I listened sympathetically for a long time, considering how to intervene and discarding every intervention that came to mind. My silence was irritating to the group. They were paying me a good fee to be a non-contributor. They continued to speak about their coherence and shared values, their ability to integrate one and all into their 'family'. When and whether I would join was the unspoken question of the group.[6]

An organization embracing the Hera myth as its core myth, rationalizing its activity around the assumptions and images of this myth, is likely to be blind to the pathological aspects of this particular energy and perspective. Colman was employed as a consultant to help develop strategies to deal with a particular problem - attacks on the organization by a community-based group that was unhappy with its policies and practices. In true Hera style, the organization was closing ranks, accentuating the distinction between the cozy family within and the enemy aliens without, reverting to a magical clan-consciousness, in which all clan members think the same thoughts and chant the same slogans. On top of this, they were seeking to defend themselves against an unpredictable and inexplicable external world by employing a priest-magician-consultant who would lead them in a group ritual to ensure that they could remain the way they always were.

Colman's approach as consultant was to attempt to bring the inclusion-exclusion dynamic into awareness. He acted on the understanding that the inclusion-exclusion dynamic by which the organization so energetically distinguished itself from any one who attacked it, was likely to be the projection of an unconscious inclusion-exclusion dynamic operating within the 'cozy family' of the organization.

> 'If everything is so good,' I chided gently, 'then who are the public that seem to disagree with your policies? Why don't they feel part of your family? Who might they represent here? Is anybody feeling left out of the family here in this room, the way those citizens feel left out of your decision-making process and your decisions?'[7]

Predictably, this intervention received a hostile response, and the story of the 'big, happy family' was reiterated. However, the consultant's probing eventually prompted one participant to assert that 'I'm not part of this family. I've got my own family.' This led to similar assertions by others. People began to voice their doubts about the espoused myth. They mourned the loss of 'the good old days', but acknowledged that they might not have been as good as legend claimed. In the course of the retreat they came to accept the need to let in difference and to cease to defend against criticism and change.

Colman argues, as we do, that excluded or scapegoated elements of an organizational system carry its individuating potential the way the personal shadow carries that potential in an individual.

> It seemed likely to me that the outside group struck important unidentified views and feelings within the agency itself, whose 'family romance' effectively excluded criticism and difference in its members, let alone those it served – the public. The citizens' group could not be negotiated with effectively until this undercover dynamic within the agency was brought to light. Once the challenge to the family fantasy was out in the open, once the 'black sheep' were brought to light, the agency leadership would have a better chance to develop its leadership on more realistic grounds and find a new myth that better fit its present and future.[8]

Georgia Lepper gives us a further illustration of an organization embedded in the Hera myth and its response to a crisis. Her example is of a founder-managed family business, taken over by a holding company. The family company had operated profitably for three decades, in a specialist field. The holding company wanted greater profitability and better quality control, and blamed the inadequacies of its acquisition on poor management.

Assessment of the situation revealed that the managing director of the family company was in an impossible position, caught between the founder-chairman, who continued to demand full involvement in the running of the business, and the manager of the holding company, who could not leave him to manage. However, the problem was not restricted to the difficulties of decision-making. There was a clash between two very different cultures, two very different visions of effectiveness and excellence. The founder-chairman had presided over a mildly repressive, but essentially benevolent family organization, in which the values of loyalty and stability were pre-eminent, dependency was encouraged, initiative was suppressed and talent was inadequately rewarded. It was a 'cozy family' in which security and predictability were guaranteed. The archetypal pattern represented in the company's emotional life, its ikons and its dominant myth is the pattern we have labeled Hera. It was the Hera myth that framed employees' notions of meaning. On the other hand, when we look at the holding company, we find that the dominant images come from the myths of Apollo and Prometheus. The company was committed to a vision of rational management based on balance sheets, business plans and the utilization of new technologies. What was meaningful in one fantasy made no sense at all in the other.

Such a clash of cultures is common in organizational mergers and amalgamations. Lepper comments:

> Organizations throughout the public and private sectors are currently experiencing radical change, and this company provides an unusually clear example. Driven by technical change generally – telecommunications, internationalization, information technology – the organization with a clear boundary, a simple market, a clear sense of identity, is rapidly becoming a memory. Takeovers might be seen as a cause of this process – or as an effect of this process – or they might be seen as another aspect of psychoid processes operating at a deeper level within society. [9]

In its previous environment the family company's dominant narrative had been functional. It had given meaning to the activities of the organization's members and had enabled it to function effectively in its marketplace. In the new environment, this was no longer so. They found themselves in a condition of liminality, being pushed across the border between the comfortably known and the utterly unknown, where they could not even understand the behavior of people whom they had known and worked with for years. Their myth, which was their framework for constructing and interpreting meanings, was no longer available. Alternative myths, which might have sustained them at this time, had never had a chance to develop.

Under conditions of crisis we tend to become less rational, often regressing to infantile or childish behavior. When groups are in crisis we are likely to see a regression from a mental-rational to a magical-mythical structure of consciousness, with collective, instinctual reactions of panic, paranoia, rage, or impotence proving more powerful than whatever the quiet voices of reason might say, and group members putting their trust in magic rituals and the constant repetition of their undying truths. To intervene effectively in such a situation is very difficult. There is always a tendency for the consultant to be pulled into the very dynamic that she observes to be problematic - reinforcing a Zeus-Hera narrative by providing an alternative authority, strengthening an Apollo narrative by privileging 'logical' solutions, sustaining a Demeter narrative by taking on the mother role, amplifying a Hermes narrative through further destabilization, being 'taken over' by the panic, fear, or cynicism that is the collective emotional response to the organization's experience of liminality. Lepper summarizes the strategies she and her colleagues employed as follows:

> The intervention of the consultants (a program of executive coaching followed the initial period of assessment) resulted in a transformation of the perception of the managing director within the organization: seen to be effective, he became effective. Computerization of delivery and production was undertaken – an increase in the self-worth of managers led to a demand for and acceptance of change and training. The founder-chairman, through a series of counseling sessions, was helped to separate and begin the process of retirement. Understanding the meanings embedded in the complex was critical to the unlocking of the organization and the individuals within it, and the return to profitable activity.[10]

The image of unlocking is significant here. It was not a matter of importing into the company a set of values, perspectives, practices and procedures that were missing. What was necessary was to articulate the incongruence between the organization's dominant Zeus-Hera narrative and the member's current experience, to allow the alternative narratives to be felt, heard, and owned, and to find for these narratives an appropriate expression in practice and procedure.

The Fear of Actaeon

Sometimes an organization is 'stuck in a myth' without its members having any sense of what it is they are stuck in. They know there is something wrong, they are aware of some of its aspects, they have a felt sense of the whole of it, but it seems to defy any rational analysis. They can see that their current behavior is dysfunctional, but attempts to change seem to get them nowhere. If we by-pass rational analysis and attempt instead to see through the phenomenon to the archetypal pattern behind it, we may find a direct approach to grasping what is going on. This is illustrated in a series of events in a large Australian organization.

The organization concerned employs in excess of 4,000 people. It is an arm of one of Australia's state governments and its work, as an organization, requires a high level of technical expertise. Among its junior, middle, and senior management ranks there is a high proportion of scientists, engineers, and technical experts in the computing field.

The top executive team consists of the chief executive and his immediate six subordinates. Two of these subordinates were female; the minimum age was 35 years at the time of the intervention. One of the male members of the group came from the smaller technically-oriented department that had been amalgamated into the larger organization, and one of the two female representatives was the former chief executive of the clerically-oriented department that had also been amalgamated into the larger organization. In 'god-talk' we might say that the senior executive team of this organization has a history of being possessed by three gods in particular: Apollo, Prometheus, and Zeus.

Apollo has provided them with a perspective that places a very high value on being rational, systematic, and orderly. Consequently they have come to value targets and goals that are visible to others and an environment with clear definitions, which rewards intelligence and prefers to look at the surface of things rather than what underlies appearances. Apollo has also given them a shared instinct for order and form, and led them to feel quite uncomfortable with chaos and turbulence. He has ensured that they value order over disorder, thinking over feeling, distance over closeness, and objective assessment over subjective intuition.

Over the years Prometheus, on the other hand, has provided them with a trust in progress, a pervasive belief that they are making things better, that they can gradually get control over things, that they can learn how to do everything and understand everything. Under his spell they have come to value the development of technology and systems to get control over problematical elements in their organization or lives. They have come to see their role as somewhat revolutionary, that is, working towards a better new world order and changing society as a result. Unfortunately, Prometheus has also helped them down play intuition and feeling and any manifestation of the feminine. They have had little or no awareness of, or concern about, the long term social consequences of the technologies and systems they were using.

More than anything else, this group has a history of trying to mentally distance itself from the suffering of others. Thus, its members have been often out of touch with their own feelings. They think and express themselves verbally and logically with an inherent ability to focus on task. They are extremely comfortable with the written text and spoken word, and in some ways see themselves as heroes and heroines working toward a better world.

Zeus has had them under his spell also. He has ensured that the use of power and authority are quite visible. Enterprise and ambition have been held up to be desirable values among employees and loyalty has been highly prized. Zeus has led them to want to extend their boundaries and acquire more territory. Senior managers and executives have been inclined to down-play the importance of personal dilemmas and the problems and concerns of employees. They tend to devalue colleagues who have a strongly developed feeling function and consider their own perspectives superior. They have used networks extensively and shared power within what might be called a 'boys' club'.

This style of working has functioned reasonably well for over twenty years in this organization. New employees came to understand these things very quickly and accepted this as 'the way things are around here'. The previous Minister of the Crown to whom they reported for a long period was very careful to hold them in intellectual respect and keep his distance. Discussions between him and the senior executives were often about matters of principle, and a high value was placed on caring for the environmental implications of the organization's engineering programs and actions. Clearly Apollo and Artemis were productively involved in the relationship between the senior executives and their former Minister. Moreover, the top team in recent years had spent some effort in overcoming some of the difficulties both Apollo and Prometheus have with affect and the expression of feelings. They had increased significantly their level of awareness of how their own feelings are an important and significant part of their work together.

Eventually, the government of the day changed and a new Minister was appointed - this time a woman, and a person with a very different style of working. She seemed (to the men) unpredictable and punitive in her relating and managerial style. This relationship came to immobilize many of the senior executives, for the new Minister behaved as if she did not trust them, and eschewed their advice and consideration. Their experience of dealing with their new Minister was characterized by confrontation and tension. This was obviously a dilemma for the organization, which was able neither to change the Minister nor to overcome its own immobility.

'Rational' approaches to the dilemma would provide various complex strategies. Attempting to see through the phenomenon to its archetypal grounding provided a very simple one.

It appears to us that in many men there is a dynamic that we might label the 'fear of Actaeon' - a fear that women have the potential for violent retribution against men. To guard against this, men simply fail to engage with women on the issues that matter in the manner and style with which women wish to be so engaged. The fear is best illustrated through the story from the Greek classics of Artemis and Actaeon.[11] Artemis was one of the many daughters of Zeus. When she was an infant sitting on his knee he asked what gifts she would like. She responded by asking for eternal virginity, a bow and arrows, a saffron hunting tunic, sixty ocean nymphs to be maids of honor, twenty river nymphs to take care of her hounds, and all the mountains of the world. One day when she was bathing in a stream with her band of river nymphs at noon, young Actaeon, who was pursuing a deer, came upon her. He caught sight of her naked, and stayed to watch, captured by her beauty. This outraged Artemis and, lest he should boast to others that she had displayed herself naked to him, she changed him into a stag, whereupon his pack of fifty hounds tore him to pieces! In reflecting on this myth, Joseph Campbell was moved to say, 'What a blast of fear is contained in such symbols of the mind's and body's blocked desire.'[12]

It would seem as though Artemis was no longer at large in a healthy and productive manner in this organization. She had come to inflate the relationship between the executives and their Minister with a destructive energy.

In attempting to deal with their dilemma, the executives had become aware of their own feelings much more than in the past, and now became immobilized in their strategic decision-making and their ability to lead the organization in a corporate manner. It was somewhat ironic that the very thing they had worked so hard to develop (access to affect) had now become a disruptive force at work in the rational and Apollonian exercises of planning and decision-making. For months they believed they were successfully masking their frustration and fear from their subordinates, but it showed through nevertheless – far more visibly than they were able to acknowledge at the time.

The organization as a whole came to share the confusion of the senior executives. There was a sense of loss and bewilderment, and people said they no longer felt as though they owed the organization their loyalty. Confusion over goals became common in many forums and the overall systems and management functions started to deteriorate. In due course, the relationship between the Minister and the CEO became so dysfunctional that an outside facilitator was called in to assist them to talk to each other. As they came to acknowledge the incongruence between what they thought and how they felt, between what they said and how they behaved, and to appreciate and resolve some their differences, they found a new regard and respect for one another. With an increase in mutual trust came the possibility of exploring with one another ways in which they could build opportunities for creative self-expression. The simple telling of the Artemis story made a significant impact. The relationship between the Minister and the other senior executives began to alter for the better, and a new-found delight came to enter into their experience of her. This in turn filtered further down the organization.

From a depth perspective, this case illustrates how universal energies can manifest themselves in all levels of our organizational onion, i.e. their consequences are experienced at the level of identity and assumptions, values and purposes, beliefs and perspectives, and practices and procedures. From a life cycle perspective it also illustrates a typical liminal phase with its consequences again manifest at these four levels. As far as intervention practice is concerned it illustrates the value of coming to the organization as a facilitator rather than a diagnostician, to assist people first to see and own what is going on here, and then to see through the concrete phenomenon to the story that is being acted out and the god who is at work.

Care and Justice at Rivera High

One significant dimension of any organization's culture is the sense that people in the organization have of what constitutes right or wrong behavior.

In the early seventies Kohlberg published the results of his research into the ways people make moral decisions.[13] He argued that there are six stages of moral development. For some people, moral behavior consists simply in doing what they are told. For others it consists in doing what their community approves. According to Kohlberg the highest stage of moral development is what he calls 'morality with justice'. This consists in recognizing people's natural rights and treating every one fairly.

This seemed reasonable enough until Carol Gilligan pointed out that all Kohlberg's research subjects were men, and that if he had used women exclusively as his subjects he might have come to a different conclusion about the highest stage of moral development.[14] She suggested that men and women have different ways of judging right and wrong. Moral maturity among women is based on what she calls an 'ethic of care'. While men are inclined to see moral behavior in terms of universal principles of fairness and justice, women's morality is based on an understanding of responsibility and relationship to people. In their moral behavior men are sensitive to principles. In contrast, women are sensitive to people. Kohlberg had suggested that sensitivity to people was an inferior basis for morality than sensitivity to principles.[15]

We may argue with Gilligan's suggestion that the division between these ethical systems is firmly established on gender lines, and also with her suggestion that the two systems cannot be applied simultaneously. In observing the way organizations make moral decisions we see plenty of women arguing for fairness and plenty of men arguing for compassion, though we admit that the stereotypes are sometimes very much in evidence. We also see organizations working hard to handle the tension between the two systems, and doing so successfully.

When we talk the language of an ethic of justice, we are telling the story of Apollo. In this story there are universal principles of right behavior to be found if we apply our minds to it. Apollo is the god of truth and justice. Not arbitrary justice imposed at the whim of an autocrat (the domain of Zeus), but rational justice made clear by the light of Apollo the sun-god.[16]

When we talk the language of an ethic of care, we are telling the story of Demeter. The mother goddess gives us the energy to be sensitive to the needs of others and to take responsibility for looking after them. Eros is also involved. Eros also has a story of relationship, but Eros' story is about intimacy, not responsibility. It is Eros who connects us to people, but it is Demeter who enables us to feel concerned for others whether we like them or not, or even whether we know them or not.

Ernestine Enomoto studied the way the tensions between the two ethics were handled in a multiethnic, urban high school in the USA[17]. In particular she observed the ways that teachers, administrators, and office staff handled the problem of school non-attendance. She found a great deal of inconsistency in the ways that truancy and skipping classes were viewed and managed.

On the one hand, the school district had an explicit policy to ensure consistent action against truants, and the school was officially committed to following this policy. Accordingly, a number of systems and procedures were in place to ensure that the policy was carried out. Office staff and teachers had specific responsibilities for notifying the school administrators and parents, 'ticketing' offenders, carrying out disciplinary actions, keeping records. By carrying out these duties consistently, they could maintain fairness, justice, order, and stability.

In practice, however, things did not work this way. The attendance office was more inclined to display care than to mete out justice, usually interpreting the rules in favor of the students and allowing them to avoid punishment. Teachers generally interpreted the rules flexibly, doing whatever they found to work best for their students. However, they still had to do the paperwork, and the inconsistencies and contradictions between teachers' reports were a source of frustration. Of course, many students exercised their creativity to take advantage of the situation and skip class with impunity.

The principle that 'kids are more important than paperwork' had some negative consequences. Some teachers were frustrated that others did not follow the procedures. Others complained about those who did. Students complained that teachers showed favoritism in treating some students differently from others. They even complained that the failure of teachers to discipline them for skipping school or class showed that the teachers didn't really care about them! The consequence of this inconsistency was that for many teachers and students the school was perceived to be neither caring nor just.

What the school had failed to do was integrate justice concerns and care concerns into policy and procedures that expressed a general consensus about what was an appropriate way of managing this problem. There was no consensus that the attendance office should carry out its public function of administering discipline impartially to all students. Staff of the office felt comfortable in imposing rules on an ad hoc basis, and consequently there were complaints about some students getting preferential treatment. There was no consensus that staff should be sensitive to kids' special needs and problems and take these into account in imposing the rules. Teachers and administrators were inclined to follow one ethic or the other without acknowledging that each has its blind spots.

The worship of Apollo easily leads to inflexibility, bigotry, and an absence of compassion. The worship of Demeter and Eros can lead to a situation where it is impossible to impose any rules at all. However, as we have argued at length, a truly human life is polytheistic. The values of Apollo and the values of Demeter can be held in balance without diminishing them. It is not necessary to abandon the rule of law to exercise compassion, and we sometimes show our care for those who depend on us by insisting that they behave responsibly, and even by punishing them when this is appropriate. All three of these gods are necessary to good management and we need a polytheistic mentality to recognize them all and not pit them against each other.

Enomoto suggests that because there had never been a full and open discussion of these issues at Rivera High, to highlight the differences and find a way to integrate these ethics in practice, the school was unable to deliver either ethics or justice, in spite of the good intentions and deep concern of the staff.

Of course, from a polytheistic perspective, ethics involve more than care and justice. We can act by the ethics of Zeus and simply do what we are told by human or divine authority. Aphrodite, on the other hand, suggests that goodness is to be identified with beauty; many people object to child labor, slavery, or genital mutilation because they are not 'nice' rather than because they offend some universal and immutable law. The ethics of Hera guide our behavior according to our responsibility to our family or community. The behavior of the Mafia hoodlum may be criminal to mainstream society but perfectly ethical within his closed community. Dionysian ethics demand that we be true to ourselves and do nothing inconsistent with our growth into full human beings. The ethics of Hestia suggest that right behavior is found in service to others. The only god who gives us no ethical guidance is Hermes, unless we consider that opportunism and self-interest provide an adequate basis for morality. Unfortunately, the theorists of 'fast capitalism' appear to believe just that.

The One and the Many

As we have noted, Jung's attitude to groups and organizations was essentially negative. He saw them as hostile to individuation. Becoming a member of a group involves giving up some, at least, of our identity, with dire consequences.

> The bigger the group, the more the individuals composing it function as a collective entity, which is so powerful that it can reduce individual consciousness to the point of extinction, and it does this the more easily if the individual lacks spiritual possessions of his [sic] own with an individual stamp. The group and what belongs to it cover up the lack of genuine individuality, just as parents act as substitutes for everything lacking in their children. In this respect, the group exerts a seductive influence, for nothing is easier than a perseveration of infantile ways or a return to them.[18]

Jung's attitude towards groups and organizations was strongly influenced by his experience of social and political conditions in Europe in the thirties and forties, which he interpreted as the regression of both individuals and nations into infantile or primitive ways of being. What Gebser described as a retreat from rationality into the magical consciousness of the clan, Jung saw as group identification pulling the individual into the pre-rational consciousness of the infant. Where Gebser's interest was in culture, Jung's main concern was for what was happening to the individual.

Most psychoanalytic interpretations of group behavior still carry this sort of negative connotation. Bion, who is probably the most influential group theorist coming out of this perspective, saw our need to belong to a group as an expression of our unconscious desire to return to our infantile union with our mother, and our irrational behavior in groups as acting out this unconscious fantasy. In order to belong we give up part of our selfhood, part of our ability to think, part of our personal emotionality, part of our right to choose, part of our capacity to discriminate. It is certainly possible to make such sacrifices consciously, but generally we are not even aware that we are making them.

Following Bion we would see immersion in an organizational identity as regression to infancy, and see it negatively, distinct from the proper rational behavior that human beings are capable of in their better moments. However, this view is, in Gebser's language, perspectivist. It looks at the phenomenon from the perspective of rational consciousness and sees it as inferior to this rational consciousness with which it identifies. From the perspective we are taking in this book, it is not inferior, but simply different.

From our perspective, the privileging of the rational individual at the expense of the group is no less archetypally constellated than the privileging of the group at the expense of the individual, and is just as inclined to negative and destructive expression. Our sense of identification with the larger group is just as necessary for us as our ability to detach ourselves from it. The loss of our archaic identification with the earth and our species has had catastrophic consequences for our chances of survival, and the loss of our magical-mythical identification with clan and tribe leads to social calamity.

Greek mythology does not choose between our sense of being one with others and our sense of being individuals. Our archaic and infantile experience of unity and our need to hold on to it is told in the myth of the Great Mother. And the myth of the Hero tells not only of our species' successful clambering out of symbiotic union with the earth into individuality and reflection, but also of our private stories of separating ourselves from the mother who contained us and discovering ourselves as individuals.[19]

In Greek mythology the Hero and the Mother are usually in conflict. The organizations described in the above case studies were all immersed in a struggle between 'mother-stuff' and 'hero-stuff', but they are all different. The Greeks found that the primitive undifferentiated mother story did not adequately represent life as they found it, so the Great Goddess became differentiated into a number of goddesses, all carrying different aspects of the mother: Gaia, Rhea, Demeter, Themis, Maia, Aphrodite, Hera, Hekate, Artemis, Hestia, Cybele, Persephone. The mother's son-lover-hero became Dionysos, Apollo, Ares, Hermes, Herakles, Eros, Hephaistos, Adonis, Jason, Theseus, Prometheus, Achilles. Athena represents aspects of both. And, reflecting a political situation where sky-gods were more powerful than earth-goddesses and fathers were far more powerful than mothers, most of these heroes became sons of the Father also and transferred their allegiance to him. The triumphant Father-god himself was found to be too complex to have a single personality, and became the trinity of Zeus, Poseidon, and Hades and gained a genealogy in Uranus and Kronos.

Applying the template of the Greek pantheon to the contemporary organization enables us to be sensitive to such distinctions. Bion and the group relations theorists may be right in seeing the archetypal mother-image everywhere in group behavior, but she is not unidimensional. The hero story that is also carried collectively by organizations has to be acknowledged as equally 'irrational' at the level of image and emotion, and equally diverse in its expressions.

When we join an organization our unconscious is activated by its symbols, its myth, and the needs of its other members. We slip into an unconscious identification with some aspect of it, perhaps with a particular role that is constantly reinforced by the expectations of others. We become an actor in the organization's narratives. As Murray Stein suggests:

> The organization uses its individual members to act out roles as they become activated in the group's collective unconscious. The constellation and enactment of these archetypal roles forms the psychological underpinning for what is called the organization's 'culture'. A group's culture is made up of many such archetypally determined roles and enactments, most of them unconsciously motivated and shaped. Only the rare individual or organization has any insight at all into how this works or what the most crucial archetypes active in its midst are.[20]

The point of organizational consulting within an archetypal framework is to assist the members of an organization towards such insight. Not to replace myth and magic by awareness and reflection, but to bring awareness and reflection to the members' experience of their organization's myth and magic. As a consequence of such insight an organization may discover that it is entirely enmeshed in a particular myth that determines the way it relates to the world. It may decide that the myth in which it is enmeshed is inappropriate for its present circumstances, or it may become aware of alternative narratives, or it may realize that certain gods are being entirely neglected and decide do something about it. Or it may not wish to change. There is no archetypal formula for an effective organization. The perspective of this book is to emphasize plurality in the psyche of organizations and to suggest that organizations will be most effective if this plurality is acknowledged and honored.

The fantasy of the one and the fantasy of the many govern the way we behave and the way we think. On the one hand we have an inclination (which we can call archetypal) to seek unity, wholeness, or integration in our both personalities and our ideas. On the other hand we also have an inclination to split ourselves into bits and to hold on to contradictory ideas. Jung was one of the few psychologists of the past hundred years who fully acknowledged both the unity and the multiplicity of the individual personality. In a larger context he also acknowledged the ultimate oneness of all things and the primacy (and uniqueness) of the conscious individual. Much of Jung's psychological thinking was framed by the image of opposites in tension or balance – thinking and feeling, sensation and intuition, introversion and extraversion, ego and shadow, anima and animus, conscious and unconscious, good and evil. Jung emphasized the need to think of such opposites as polarities, not as dualities. If we see conscious/unconscious as a duality we define the conscious in terms of the absence of the unconscious and vice versa. Whatever is conscious is not unconscious. Jung suggests rather that conscious and unconscious are complementary; they are different aspects of the same reality and complete, rather than oppose, each other.[21]

We wish to bring the same perspective to our discussion of the polytheistic organization, except that we are dealing not with two apparent opposites at once but with sixteen. In a sense all of the gods in the pantheon are opposites of all the others. Apollo, for instance, is opposed to Aphrodite as spirituality is opposed to sensuality. He is opposed to Ares as reflection is to passion. To Artemis as brother sun is to sister moon. To Athena as higher wisdom is to practical common sense. To Demeter as independent hero is to containing mother. To Dionysos as intellect is to emotion. To Eros as formal structure is to human relationship. To Hades as light is to dark. To Hephaistos as abstract beauty is to concrete crafting. To Hera as self-promotion is to social responsibility. To Herakles as thought is to action. To Hermes as principle is to opportunism. To Hestia as purposeful movement is to stillness. To Prometheus as pure science is to applied science. To Zeus as law is to arbitrary power. To the whole squabbling pantheon as order is to chaos. In addition we can oppose the 'positive' Apollo (wisdom, rationality, order, clarity) to the 'negative' Apollo (dogmatism, rigidity, cold-heartedness).

In writing about what he called 'the functions of the psyche' Jung emphasized both their polar nature (thinking vs. feeling, sensation vs. intuition) and our need to integrate them in ourselves in order to become 'whole'. He does not suggest that they can be blended or lose their difference. He suggests, rather, that their 'oppositeness' can be transcended. Every energy, function, or image with which we identify has a polar opposite that we neglect or suppress, i.e. which becomes unconscious. Through what he calls our 'transcendent function'[22] we can bring our conscious one-sidedness into an encounter with our unconscious other-sidedness, not to substitute one for the other or to neutralize them, but to achieve greater balance and integration. The polarity remains, but now both functions are available to us. Andrew Samuels suggests in this regard that:

> What is involved is more than reaction formation or the crude combining of two possible attitudes. In individual analysis, the transcendent function mediates between a person as he or she is formed and the possibility of change. We see, not so much an answer, but the presentation of a choice or series of choices, with all the attendant risks. The 'opposites' were never as 'opposite' as they seemed.[23]

Logic cannot handle the task of facing in more than one direction at the same time, but imagery can. We can find images to link apparent opposites, and it is this property of images which induced Jung to put them at the center of his understanding of how we can transcend the opposites within us.

In our work with organizations we have regularly come up against ways of thinking that pit the gods against each other dualistically, as genuine opposites. If you want one, they say, you can't have the other.

- If you want to get the job done you can't afford to worry too much about people. (Prometheus vs. Eros)
- If you look after people too well they will never take responsibility for themselves. (Demeter vs. Herakles)
- You can't be an industrialist and a greenie at the same time. (Prometheus vs. Artemis)
- I can't manage effectively if I spend all my time consulting my staff. (Zeus vs. Athena)
- Staff here aren't paid to enjoy themselves. They're paid to do what they're told. (Zeus vs. Aphrodite.)
- If we abandon standard procedure in this instance we'll end in chaos. (Apollo vs. Dionysos)

- This is a very collaborative organization. If we raise this matter we'll have conflict and it will destroy our ability to work together. (Ares vs. Athena).

We do not want to minimize the real tensions suggested here, or to suggest that these statements are never true. Our point is that they do not have to be true. In fact, they are very often not true at all. The transcendent function enables us to think both/and instead of either/or. As Thomas Moore puts it:

> In genuine polytheism conflict can never be reduced to simple dualism, dialectic, or two-horned dilemma. A polytheistic perspective always opens out onto increased complexity and additional possibilities.[24]

There is a circularity in the relationship between individual and organization. The organization is made up of a collection of individuals, each with their own conscious/unconscious polarities, their own complexes, their own cluster of preferred and neglected gods. Interacting within specific structural and environmental parameters, these individual psyches comprise a collective, organizational psyche. This exerts constant influence on the individuals, both on long-term members whose psyches have been shaped for years by the organization's story, and on new members who are inducted into the roles to be enacted and the ways of thinking, imagining, and behaving that will enable them to belong. The members severally project on to the organization lost or neglected parts of their own personalities. The organization collectively projects onto individuals what cannot be consciously shared – and we see it in archetypal roles like father, mother, clown, scapegoat, guru, witch, bitch, golden boy, daddy's girl. And the individuals accept these projections, eagerly or resentfully, and act them out.

An organization's dominant myths are not simply carried in the vision statement, the CEO's pronouncements, the authorized history, the policy documents, the reward systems, the memos. They are also repeated in the formal and informal conversations between its members, and not only in their verbal conversations but in their non-verbal communications - even the unconscious ones. Most specifically they are constantly being 'performed' in their actions. Initiating a dialogue between the conscious organization and unconscious organization, necessarily entails opening up the same dialogue within individuals. If such a dialogue does not occur to some degree at least, the exercise at the organizational level will be either pointless or fraudulent.

Assisting an organization to transcend the polarities within its culture involves being able empathically to enter the experience of the organization and feel the enchantment of its dominant myths without being seduced by them. It means transcending the particular inside/outside, subjective/objective polarity that plagues scientific method. And it means abandoning our monotheistic perspective.

In discussing the necessity for a polytheistic perspective in organizations, Hillman cites the Greek tragedian Euripides:

> Each god makes a claim on us which we may pay only in the god's coin – this is an inescapable fact.

He goes on to argue that imagining a choice between the gods catches us in adversarial thinking, pitting one pattern against another and setting off a war between the gods. He suggests that the task is less one of choosing between styles than of appreciating diversity.

> Each situation that management must face will have a different configuration and will make its own peculiar demands which can be settled only in the coin of the mythical figure who shapes the situation at its source. Managerial skill becomes psychological perception, which in turn becomes mythological reflection – that is, a mythic sensibility regarding the roots of trouble. What 'coin' is now called for? 'Who' is now determining events? Which myth is now at work? Leadership entails learning the patterns, learning the ways of the gods, so that one does not fall prey to the monotheistic simplification of 'one size fits all'.[25]

Complexity theorists argue that it is only on the boundary between stability and instability (often referred to as 'the edge of chaos') that creative transformation is possible. We see organizations enmeshed in a dominant story that gives them both stability and identity, publicly acknowledging a need for change and even employing consultants to engineer it, but privately repeating the same comforting story over and over and rejecting the evidence that the story isn't true any more. To let go of this story is for them to descend into chaos. Without this myth they won't know who they are, and this is a terrifying prospect. A monotheistic organization may have to die in order to come back to life.

Throughout this discussion we have presented an ongoing image of the organization as a sort of collective person. This is not just an analogy. Complexity theory has turned our attention to the fractal nature of the universe. When we shift our level of analysis from species to tribe to group to individual we seem to find the same processes replicated. What interests us in particular is the way our notions of personal health and illness find ready application to health and illness in groups and organizations. Conventional European science has been monotheistic, just as conventional European religion has been. So we have had one truth to pursue, one god to worship, one civilization to cherish and impose on the rest of the world. Psychologists have pursued the notion that the healthy individual has a cohesive personality under the control of a strong ego. Management theorists have told us that the healthy organization is characterized by a cohesive culture marked by strong leadership. Now we find a new science, which has abandoned the notion of a single truth, religious people recognizing that 'oneness' and 'many-ness' are just different ways of imagining divinity. We find an increasing readiness to accept the legitimacy of diverse cultures. We find psychologists arguing that healthy people have multiple personalities and the management literature arguing that healthy organizations honor diversity.

To push this image of health and pathology a little further, the kind of pathology we call 'neurosis' in an individual consists of the endless repeating of the same internal conversations, the same internal role-plays. While the same conversation is being repeated over and over, there is not much chance of healing. It is only when complexity is introduced, when new internal and external voices are heard and the conversation gets a degree of variety and unpredictability, that there is any possibility of personal transformation. Sometimes this happens gradually, through changes in the person's environment and relationships. Sometimes it happens suddenly and painfully. Usually it needs the support of a trustworthy, non-judgmental friend, family member, or therapist.

We suggest that the same applies to organizations. As long as the pronouncements and conversations within an organization repeat a narrow range of themes, express a narrow range of values and manifest a narrowly defined identity, there is little possibility of transformation. As Stacey argues:

> When themes organizing experience, particularly those of gossip and fantasy, are reproduced in sparse, highly repetitive, habitual form with little variation, then there is very little possibility of creative transformation in either social or individual terms. However, when the themes organizing experience are rich in variety, reproduced with high levels of spontaneous variety, then the prospects for creative transformation are high.[26]

An individual or organization in a stable environment, where expectations do not vary and the future is already determined, can maintain the sense and appearance of health without much need for change. However, when the environment becomes unstable and the future becomes unpredictable, the definition of health changes. Now, staying healthy involves the capacity for change, the ability to respond spontaneously to new situations, a readiness to embrace one's 'alternative personalities'.

The change agent, like the therapist, has a clear role here, and it does not involve telling the client how to behave. Like the therapist, the change agent's first task is to listen, and to listen beyond the obviousness of what the client is saying and hear what is not being put into words but is there just the same. To hear the silent voices, the deviant voices, and the ironic voices. To hear the voices of all the gods. And then to help the client to hear them.

---

1. A Parry (1991) 'A Universe of Stories', in *Family Process*, 30, p. 28.
2. T Peters & J Waterman (1982) *In Search of Excellence*, p. 13.
3. S Stern (1988) 'Symbolic Representation of Organizational Identity', in M Jones, M Moore, and R Snyder, *Inside Organization*, p. 283f.
4. ibid., passim.
5. T Dalmau (1991)
6. AD Colman (1992) 'Depth Consultation', in M Stein and J Hollwitz, *Psyche at Work*, p. 100.
7. ibid., p. 101.

8. ibid., p. 103.
9. G Lepper (1992) 'The Complex in Human Affairs', in M Stein and J Hollwitz, *Psyche at Work*, p. 83.
10. ibid., p. 83. In Lepper's analysis she uses Jung's notion of the complex, which she defines in system terms as 'an emergent property of the living system, which includes the somatic, the psychic, the individual, and the collective as a series of emergent levels within a whole system (let us call it 'the human system')'. ibid., p. 74. The complex creates meaningful patterns through the interaction of archetype and experience. For a useful discussion of complex see EC Whitmont (1969) *The Symbolic Quest*, Chapter 4.
11. See Ovid, *Metamorphoses*. Trans M Innes (1955), p. 78.
12. J Campbell (1986) *The Power of Myth*, p. 111.
13. L Kohlberg (1973) *Essays on Moral Development*.
14. C Gilligan (1982) *In a Different Voice*.
15. This echoes the distinction made by Talcott Parsons between universalist and particularist orientations. See F Trompenaars & C Hampden-Turner (1998) *Riding the Waves of Culture*, Chapter 4.
16. Athena is also a goddess of justice, but she works in the framework of democratic decision-making rather than universal law.
17. EK Enomoto (1997) 'Negotiating the Ethics of Care and Justice', *Educational Administration Quarterly*, vol. 33 (3).
18. CJ Jung, (1964) *Collected Works* 10, 891.
19. See Jung (1951) *Collected Works 9*
'The 'child' is born out of the womb of the unconscious, begotten out of the depths of human nature, or rather out of living Nature herself. It is a personification of vital forces quite outside the limited range of our conscious mind; of ways and possibilities of which our one-sided conscious mind knows nothing; a wholeness which embraces the very depths of Nature.' Para. 289.
20. M Stein (1992) 'Organizational Life as Spiritual Practice' in M Stein & J Hollwitz, *Psyche at Work*, p. 10.
21. For Gebser, mental-rational consciousness is dualistic and mythical consciousness is polar. He interprets Jung's privileging of polar thinking as a 'conscious regression' into mythical thinking in order to break out of dualism and 'overcome the three-dimensional paternal world'. It is a move, 'not into a mythical two-dimensional, but into an integral four-dimensionality'. J Gebser, *Origin*, p. 398.
22. See CJ Jung (1961) *Collected Works* 8.
The term 'transcendent' is not here meant to have any metaphysical or spiritual connotation. It simply implies the ability to be detached from both terms of the polarity so that one is not favored over the other. Jung suggests that the emergence of a symbol representing a synthesis of the opposites releases creative energy that has been stuck in this phoney opposition and enables transformative shift in the individual.
23. A Samuels (1993) *The Political Psyche*, p. 63.
24. T Moore (1979) 'Artemis and the Puer', in J Hillman (ed.), *Puer Papers*, p. 199.
25. J Hillman (1995) *Revisioning Psychology*, p. 225.
26. R Stacey (2001) *Complex Responsive Processes in Organizations*, p. 160.

11
THE ARCHETYPOLOGY INDICATOR

Origins of the DNAI

When we first began to bring a Jungian perspective to our work with organizations, we found a need for a language that was precise enough and rich enough to label the various constellations of behaviors, emotions, perspectives, and assumptions which seemed apparent to us, and which we were inclined to label as 'archetypal'. Jung provides a language of archetype in his writings: anima, animus, persona, self, old man, trickster, shadow, and so on. This language is useful for many purposes, but we found it unsuitable for distinguishing the various dominant and alternative narratives we found shaping the lives of the organizations we dealt with. We needed a language that could cope with both creative and pathological forms of the patterns we detected. The metaphor of culture presented itself readily enough, and Jung himself had pointed to mythology as containing the imaginal forms of archetypal patterns. We found in the Greek pantheon a set of images and a language to distinguish the diverse narratives, and found in the notion of culture a framework for looking at the organizational phenomena that were of most interest to us.

Accordingly, we have drawn on the Greek pantheon to represent a number of recognizable and distinguishable cultures that we seemed to find in organizations.

Our model of key archetypal patterns was not logically derived. Unlike the Myers Briggs Type Indicator,[1] it is not a rational model based on polarities or dichotomies. It does not represent a closed system, as such logical models do. Neither is it empirically derived, like Hofstede's and Trompenaars' models of culture, which are based on polarities. The gods are innumerable and many-faceted and their complexity is unending. Indeed, the more closely we look at them the more complex they and their relationships appear. We can deal with them imaginally or mythically as distinct personalities, but when we try to deal with them rationally in the language of drives, needs, instincts, or perspectives, we find that they are not at all distinct and discrete. They overlap each other in many complex ways.

Rather than develop a classification based on abstract concepts or factor analysis, we started with a set of images that have been significant in European culture for three thousand years. We took the twelve Olympian gods, accepting the classical Greeks' ambivalence about precisely which twelve gods were actually the twelve. We translated divine image and narrative into specific attitudes and behaviors. Our experience in using the model in various organizations eventually led us to settle on sixteen god-images which seemed to us to represent sixteen specific constellations[2] of attitudes and behaviors which we found demonstrated in the organizations we studied.

There is certainly something arbitrary about stopping at the number sixteen. There are more than sixteen narratives dominant in contemporary organizations. There were more than sixteen gods worshipped by the classical Greeks. Nevertheless, we had to stop somewhere, even if it meant leaving out Poseidon, Persephone, Hekate, and Pan.

The selection of gods was determined by our experience in using the model. We ended up with six female and ten male gods, not because the goddesses are less influential than male gods in contemporary organizations, but because in our experience of working with organizations we have found the worship of the male gods more widespread. We have not come across organizations dominated by Persephone or Hekate, though they presumably exist. We could have introduced Gaia, or other personifications of the Great Mother, but we were able to represent her various aspects through Demeter, Artemis, and Hestia. Likewise Zeus, in his Senex (old man) aspect stands in for Kronos and Uranus.

In the instrument we have developed to explore organizational culture according to this model we have not attempted to represent specifically negative aspects of the gods. We do not have any items attributing to the organization the qualities of the devouring mother or the limb-tearing Dionysos. We have used neutral descriptive terms as far as we can, rather than give them a good/bad connotation. We might say that 'creative' is a 'good' word and 'treating people roughly' is bad, but this is Dionysos and Eros speaking. Ares does not think so highly of creativity and thinks rough treatment is perfectly appropriate. Likewise Aphrodite puts a positive value on 'sensual' and a negative value on 'systematic'. Apollo puts these the other way round. We try not to enter into this dispute.

We developed the Dalmau Neville Archetypology Indicator as an educational and consulting tool. We were suggesting that if people looked at their own organizations they would be able to detect certain specific patterns of assumptions, attitudes, and behaviors, and that these represented 'old stories'. We wanted to concretize these patterns to help people recognize them. Administering the DNAI was a means of getting people to become more aware of the ways they perceived their own organizations, to find patterns that they had not previously noticed, and to reflect on whether these patterns did indeed represent the 'old stories' that we were so interested in.

We had no intention at this stage of developing it as a research instrument. In this context, questions of 'validity' and 'reliability' did not really concern us. We were not interested in whether some one's responses to the questionnaire represented an 'objective truth' about the organization in question; we only wanted them to articulate their personal and subjective perception of the organization. It did not matter to us whether they would give the same answers to the questions on a different day; we only wanted to know how the organization seemed to them on this particular day.[3] If people within an organization gave widely varying responses on a particular item, or changed their responses from day to day, we accepted this as an additional piece of information about the organization's culture rather than as evidence of a lack of validity or reliability in the instrument.

In spite of our interest in the unconscious components of any organization's culture, we had to acknowledge that a questionnaire like this can explore only the perceptions and attitudes of which people are conscious.

Development of the DNAI was begun in 1991 and the task of refining it continues. The use of the instrument in workshops and consultancies has given us regular feedback about which gods are dominant in contemporary organizations and which items best represent their presence.

In spite of its origins as an educational tool, the DNAI seems to have some appeal as a diagnostic instrument. It is possible to use it in ways that seem to validate statements like: 'This is essentially an Eros organization'; 'The dominant narrative in this organization is the Promethean one'; 'Aphrodite is seriously neglected in this organization', to compare the profile of one organization with that of another, or to compare two sites within the one organization. When we administer the instrument to fifty managers in an organization and find that there is a great deal of consensus in the way they perceive and categorize their organization, we do have a sort of quasi-objectivity which enables us to make such statements. Of course, we have to keep in mind that the management perception of the organization is no more or less 'objective' than the perception of employees or clients.

While such quasi-objective statements may be made, and we might make them ourselves, we need to remember that the instrument is not constructed on the Apollonine fantasy of objective truth. It is constructed, rather, on the postmodern, Hermetic fantasy of shifting images. We present the instrument to any group in the hope that people will conscientiously record their awareness of the group's way of functioning and that this conscious awareness will give us adequate hints at the pattern which is operating both consciously and unconsciously in the life of the group.

In the meantime we can shift into the Promethean fantasy for a moment and argue that justification for the DNAI lies in whether it 'works' or not. Our experience has been that it is instrumentally useful, that it provides a handy technique for facilitating self-reflection and self-transformation in an organization. Whether we can also justify it in terms of intellectual rigor (within the Apollonine fantasy), elegance (within the Aphroditic fantasy), social value (Hera), or creativity (Dionysos) is not so clear!

The Archetypology Indicator

The DNAI is a 64-item questionnaire divided into two parts. Part 1 asks the respondent to rate 64 statements on a scale of 0–5 according to their accuracy as descriptors of their ideal organization, that is, the kind of organization which they would find it most satisfying to belong to. Part 2 asks them to rate the same items as descriptors of an actual organization. In the context of an organizational consultancy the questions are obviously related to 'the organization (or workplace) that would be ideal for me', and the actual organization (or workplace) that is being studied.

With each of the 16 items 4 descriptors are presented. These are separately rated. There are accordingly 64 descriptors in each of parts 1 and 2. Each descriptor represents a specific god. There are 4 descriptors for each of the 16 gods. Totaling these provides a score range of 0–20 for each of the 16 archetypal patterns. These can be graphed as a profile of the organizational culture.

While our interest is the unconscious dynamics of organizational culture, it is clear that a questionnaire cannot deal with these directly. The descriptors deal with group and individual behavior, perception, leadership, values, and emotionality, as they are observed by the members of the organization, on the understanding that these point to the core assumptions which lie at the deepest level of the organization's culture.

The four descriptors that represent the Aphrodite pattern in the current version are listed below for illustration. The full questionnaire is contained in Appendix 1.

- People in this organization expect a leader to make it a pleasant place to work.
- The most valued people in this organization are those who perform their tasks elegantly.
- People in this organization like to be surrounded by beautiful things.
- People in this organization like to have fun.

There are, as we would expect, high correlations between the scores on these descriptors. In the course of the development of the questionnaire, descriptors that are not positively correlated to the others have been rejected and replaced. There are also high correlations between some of these descriptors and the descriptors associated with certain other gods, notably Eros and Dionysos. This also is what we should expect. The archetypal patterns represented by the sixteen gods have significant overlap, and we have not attempted to make the patterns discrete by rejecting such 'redundant' items. If this were an evaluation instrument that was designed for sophisticated statistical analysis, we might be more concerned about its methodological purity. As it is, we are more concerned with the instrument's ability to raise the respondent's awareness of the presence or absence of certain patterns in the life of their organization, and in its ability to give us useful information about the organization's underlying story. The continuing development of the indicator has this aim in mind.

Using an Organizational Profile

The organizational profile contains a great deal of information about the culture of the organization. The following aspects may be usefully dealt with in discussion:

- The consensus or diversity in perceptions of the actual organization.
- The consensus or diversity in notions of the ideal organization.
- The sources of variation. Do the diverse assessments merely represent the perceptions of different individuals, or do they represent particular sub-groups within the organization?
- The gods which appear to be dominant in the organization. What basic assumptions shape the organization's thinking and actions? What needs are being satisfied?
- The possibility of inflation. Is the organization so dominated by a particular archetype that it carries its pathology as well as its constructive aspects?
- The gods that appear to be absent or ignored in the organization's view of itself. What needs are being neglected?
- Do the neglected gods represent the organization's 'alternative narratives'? What sources of creative action are being closed off by neglect of these narratives? Are there sub-cultures in the organization that keep these narratives alive?
- The nature of the organizational shadow. Do the neglected gods force themselves into consciousness through pathological behavior?

- The appropriateness of the organization's 'personality profile' to the professed purposes of the organization. Is the organization stuck in a story that no longer represents its experience?
- The comparison between the organization's profile and the organization's espoused theory of itself.
- The relationship between the dominant gods in the organization. Are the tensions between them utilized productively?
- Are the dominant gods associated with stability in the organization and are the neglected gods associated with threats to this stability?

Analysis of individual questionnaire items allows for further questions to be addressed.

- Which statements about the ideal and actual organization attract the highest scores and the greatest agreement?
- Which statements attract the lowest scores?
- Which statements attract the least agreement?
- Which statements show the greatest match between ideal and actual?
- Which statements show the greatest divergence between ideal and actual?

Such information provides an invaluable starting point for an organization's reflections on it own culture, its dominant and alternative narratives.

Three Case Studies[4]

The Community Organization

The DNAI was administered in the context of an investigation of the organizational culture of community learning centers in the state of Victoria. A qualitative study based on the study of documents and on interviews with both managers and clients in a sample of these centers had indicated that they possessed a common culture centered on values of participation, belongingness, and empowerment.[5] The DNAI was administered in a separate sample of centers to determine whether these conclusions could be confirmed by a more objective and quantitative methodology. Both samples included both urban and rural centers and represented both middle class and working class areas. The different centers are essentially autonomous but they perceive themselves to be linked as a network by shared values and vision. While the network operates a central office to deal with common administrative concerns and provide a common voice, this office intervenes very little in the operations of the centers.

The organizational profile depicted in Figure 11.1 essentially confirms the conclusions of the qualitative study. There are two high-scoring patterns – Athena and Eros – which represent the valuing of democracy/ participation/ power-sharing on the one hand and relationship/ community on the other. There is a group of moderate to high scoring patterns: Apollo, Artemis, Demeter, Dionysos, Hephaistos, Hera, Hermes, Hestia, and Prometheus. A lower scoring group includes the sensual and fun-loving goddess Aphrodite, on the one hand, and the decisively 'masculine' gods – Ares, Herakles, and Zeus – on the other. Hades scores very low.

Key Values

An indication of the key values in this culture may be found in the highest scoring items.

- The most valued people in this organization are those who can work cooperatively with others. (Athena)
- People at the top in this organization like to see themselves as providing a secure and supportive environment. (Demeter)
- The most valued people in this organization are those who understand their tasks and carry them out. (Apollo)
- People in this organization expect a leader to respect the contributions of all its members. (Athena)
- To really belong in this organization you should be interested in people. (Eros)
- Relationships in this organization are cooperative. (Athena)

A further indication of the nature of this organization's culture may be found in the rejection of the lowest scoring items.

- This organization treats its people roughly. (Ares)
- Relationships in this organization are dreary. (Hades)
- This organization manages its people by reward and punishment. (Zeus)
- People in this organization are focused on how hopeless it all is. (Hades)
- To really belong in this organization you should love technology. (Prometheus)

We would argue that a healthy organization will be pluralistic in its values. We would also argue that in a healthy organization goals and culture will be congruent. By both of these criteria, this organization appears to be healthy. There may be unrecognized drives to beauty (Aphrodite) conflict (Ares), heroism (Herakles), and power (Zeus), but most of the gods are honored. The extremely low score on the Hades dimension indicates that the organization is perceived to be very much alive.

It was necessary to address the question of whether these means were simply the averaging of diverse responses or did indeed represent a common culture, by comparing this profile with the separate profile of each of the nine centers included in this sample. All centers had essentially the same profile.[6]

Actual and Ideal

The profile (Figure 11.1) that represents respondents' description of 'the organization that would be ideal for me' gives us further information. We find that the Athena and Eros patterns are again dominant. The means as represented on this chart show the profile of the ideal organization to be almost identical with the actual organization, though analysis shows greater range and variation in responses to the ideal organization than to the actual. An item by item comparison reveals that for all eighty individual items no 'ideal' mean differs by more than one point from the 'actual' mean on the five point scale. Once again, there were no significant differences between the profiles of the individual centers. There seem to be no needs represented in this framework that the organization's members feel to be frustrated by the organization.

Figure 11.1

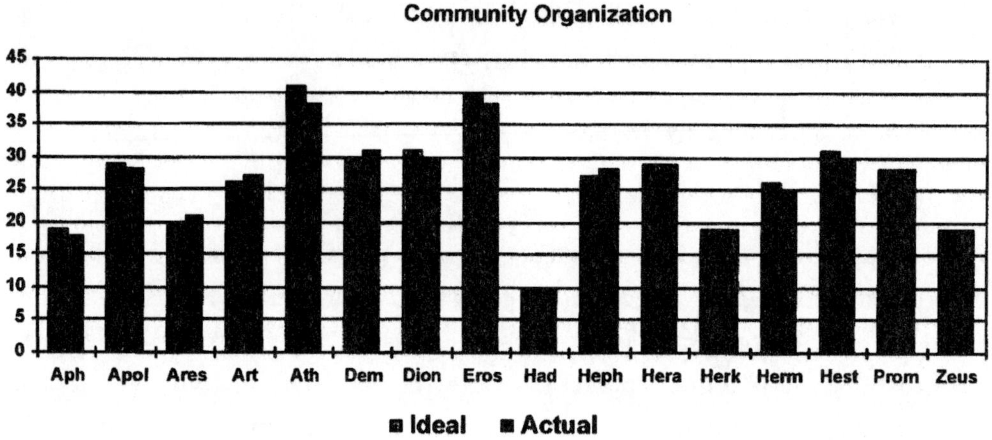

In this analysis, the greatest consensus (as represented by standard deviations) was found in the following high-scoring descriptors:

- The most valued people in this organization are those who can work cooperatively with others. (Actual and Ideal Athena)
- Relationships in this organization are cooperative. (Ideal Athena)
- People in this organization like each other. (Actual and Ideal Eros)
- The most valued people in this organization are those who understand their roles and carry them out. (Ideal Apollo)

There was similar consensus in strongly rejecting the following descriptors:

- Relationships in this organization are sensual. (Actual Aphrodite)
- People in this organization like to be stars. (Ideal Dionysos)
- Relationships in this organization are hierarchical. (Actual and Ideal Zeus)
- In this organization problems are dealt with by crashing through. (Ideal Ares)
- This organization treats people well or badly according to how likeable they are. (Actual Aphrodite)

The greatest disagreement was in regard to the following descriptors:

- People at the top in this organization like to see themselves as engaged in the same craft as those at the bottom. (Actual and Ideal Hephaistos)
- In this organization problems are dealt with by working on the problem cooperatively. (Ideal Athena)
- People in this organization don't like being pushed around. (Actual and Ideal Herakles)
- People in this organization are interested in producing the goods. (Actual Prometheus)
- People at the top in this organization like to see themselves as running a family. (Ideal Hera)

Conclusion

The picture which emerges is of a network organization which has a consistent culture across a range of locations. The culture is characterized by strongly held Athena values (cooperation, participative decision-making) and Eros values (intimacy, caring). There is no significant difference between members' description of the organization as they experience it and their description of the organization as they would like it to be. The analysis corroborates the evidence from interviews that the organization has a shared and distinct culture and that this culture is essentially compatible with the needs, aspirations and meaning-making of its individual members. There is a good deal of consensus about what sort of culture characterizes the centers, a good deal of consensus about what sort of culture people want, and a good deal of compatibility between the two.

The Mining and Resources Company

The context in this case was an investigation of the connections between organizational culture and safety in a multinational mining and resources company. The questionnaire was used to supplement the data collected through focus groups. The researchers met with work groups (including management teams) of between four and twenty people for a two to three hour workshop which comprised an initial discussion of how safety issues were handled in the plant, administration and scoring of the questionnaire, and feedback of the questionnaire results as a basis for further discussion. There were a total of 134 completed questionnaires, from nine sites in Australia and North America. The questionnaire was modified in this study to include a set of descriptors relating to safety.

Company Values

The organizational profile based on aggregated scores is represented in Figure 11.2. The profile for the actual organization is dominated by Apollo, Athena, Prometheus, and Zeus, as we might expect in a hierarchically structured resources company with a history of patriarchal, or at least paternalistic, management, and an espoused commitment to initiating more democratic structures. We might expect an historically successful company in this field to have a value system and mode of operating which are embedded in the myths of Apollinine rationality and order, Zeus-like centralization of power and Promethean progress and purposefulness. Athena, Zeus' loyal daughter, appeared in the group interviews to dominate both managers' and workers' espoused theories of best practice in management. The company illustrated in the graph is one where people (both managers and workers) would like to see more of the Athena, Demeter, Dionysos, and Eros dimensions of culture but are adequately satisfied as far as Apollo, Prometheus, and Zeus values are concerned.

Figure 11.2

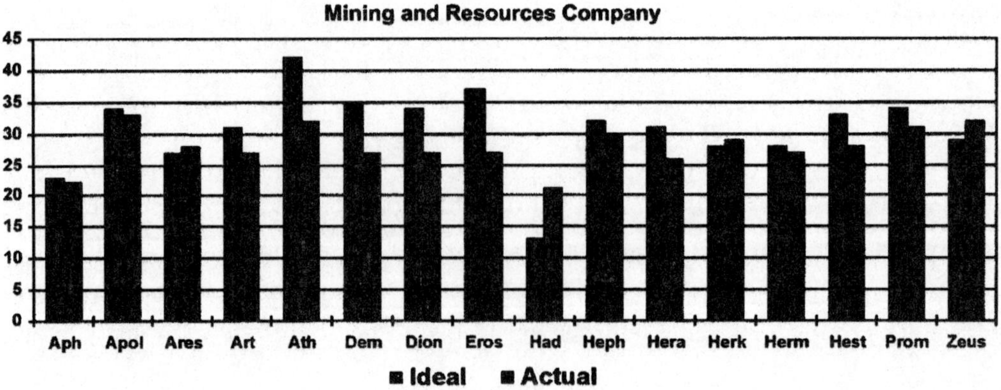

The highest scoring descriptors for the actual organization across the whole sample were:

- People in this plant expect a leader to keep the system functioning efficiently. (Apollo)
- People in this plant expect a leader to get things done. (Prometheus)
- People in this plant expect a leader to give clear directions. (Zeus)
- The most valued people in this plant are those who understand their roles and carry them out. (Apollo)
- People in this plant don't like being pushed around. (Herakles)

In the aggregated profile for the ideal workplace we find Athena prominent, ahead of Eros, Demeter, Apollo, Dionysos, and Prometheus. Athena received the highest mean score in every site visited. Eros was included in the top three scores in every plant but one. It should be noted that the desire for more Eros, Demeter, and Dionysos is not accompanied by a rejection of Prometheus and Zeus. Managers and workers appear to be generally satisfied with the degree to which the Zeus and Prometheus patterns are manifest in their workplaces. But they certainly fantasize an ideal workplace which is more cooperative and participative in its practices and procedures, and which does more to satisfy their needs for relationship, support, and creative action. The highest scoring descriptors of the ideal workplace indicate the kind of culture in which they believe they would like to work.

- People in my ideal workplace expect a leader to give clear directions. (Ideal Zeus)
- The most valued people in my workplace are those who can work cooperatively with others. (Ideal Athena)
- Relationships in my ideal workplace are cooperative. (Ideal Athena)
- People in my ideal workplace are interested in sharing their knowledge and expertise. (Ideal Athena)
- To really belong in my ideal workplace you should be dependable (Ideal Demeter)

It is noteworthy that Athena was prominent in the ideal profiles of the management teams as well as those of operators and maintenance crews. In interviews with management, we heard that they had a desire to adopt a more democratic management style and were attempting to do so, but were frustrated that the workers were unwilling to take on the responsibility that this entailed. In interviews with the operators, we heard that they wanted a more democratic plant and were ready to take it on, but management were unwilling to let go their power. In one plant with a previous history of autocratic and oppressive management, the leadership team complained that in spite of their good intentions they were finding it difficult to operate in a democratic manner because the workers did not trust them. In the same plant the workers complained that they were ready and able to take much greater responsibility for decision making in the plant but that management did not trust them.

Trust was a significant issue in the discussion of safety in all the plants. Management teams asserted that they made it clear to operators that safety was always to have priority over productivity. If the safety of operators was threatened in any way, the plant should be shut down until the problem was solved. In discussions with operators they agreed that this was what management told them. But in some plants the operators simply did not believe it. They were convinced that if they followed this instruction productivity would be affected and they would put their jobs in jeopardy. The lack of trust was reflected in low Eros scores in the profiles of these plants.

Closely associated with trust was the issue of honesty and deceit in communication between management and workers. In the plants where workers thought management were trying to deceive them about safety policy, they were themselves involved in a deceit about safety performance. They were expected to report every accident or incident involving safety, but they did not. In the context of threatened redundancies, they preferred to hide anything that might conceivably go on their record and jeopardize their prospects of future employment. Management knew this was happening but were inclined to collude in it because it improved the safety statistics of the plant. In deceit and collusion we have the shadow manifestation of Hermes. Hermes is not generally prominent in the profiles, either actual or ideal. The only place he has any prominence is in the 'ideal' profiles of the leadership teams in some of the plants, which may reflect frustration with the company's inflexibility and inability to change with a changing marketplace.

Culture and Safety

The comparison between two plants with similar work procedures and contrasting safety performance suggests a connection between work safety and particular aspects of organizational culture. Figure 11.3 shows the profiles of Plant A (poor safety performance) and Plant B (good safety performance).

The actual profile for Plant A is dominated by Apollo, Zeus, and Herakles/Ares, with Aphrodite and Eros representing the least significant patterns. The profile for Plant B is dominated by Athena, Apollo, and Prometheus, with Hades being least in evidence. (Apollo is actually the only god who appears among the three most dominant patterns in each of the nine plants, and in every sub-group except one.) While there are indications in both the group interview data and the DNAI data that plants with good safety records can be distinguished from plants with poor safety records on the basis of their organizational culture, the data does not lead to unambiguous conclusions. However, the comparison of Plants A and B illustrates the kind of pattern that appears to be associated with safety performance in this sample.

Figure 11.3

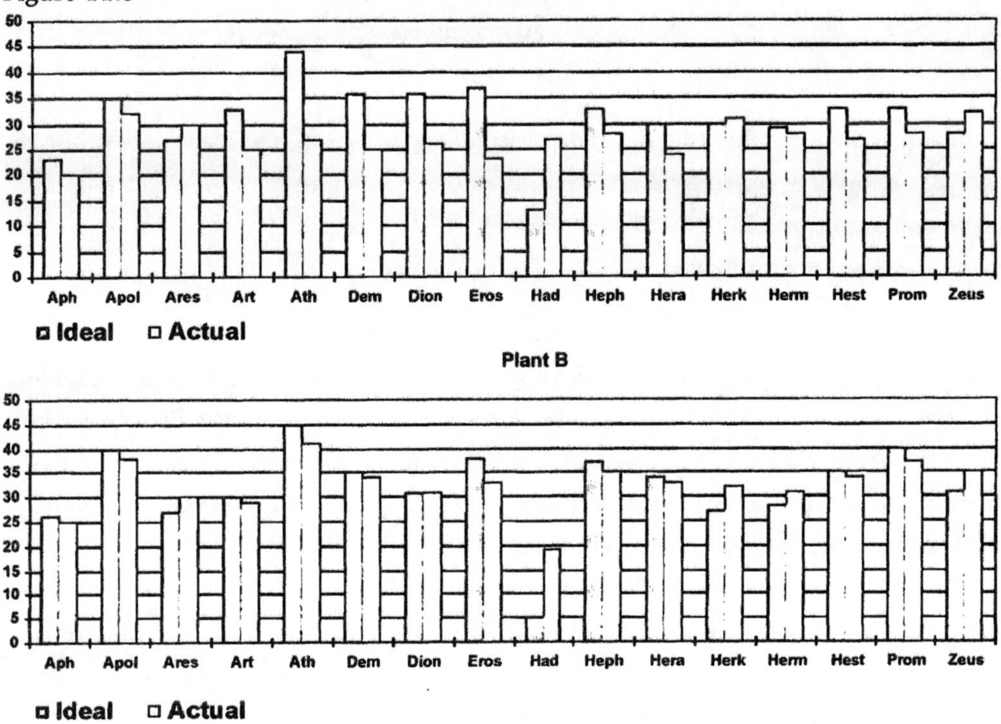

The profiles of these two plants differ in two distinct ways (Figure 11.3). In the first place, while order and clarity (Apollo) are significant in both profiles, Plant A, which has poor safety performance, is perceived by its workers to have a more autocratic management style (Zeus) and a more aggressive and individualistic work culture (Herakles/Ares). Plant B, which has excellent safety performance, is perceived to have a basically democratic management (Athena), and a commitment to efficiency and productivity (Prometheus). The Eros dimension is significant in Plant B and minimal in Plant A. The purposelessness of the Hades dimension is significant in Plant A and minimal in Plant B. (In the most accident-prone sub-group of employees in Plant A, Hades scores more highly than any other god in assessments of the actual organization.)

In the second place, the plant with good safety performance presents a very similar profile for the actual and ideal workplace (prominent Athena/ Apollo/ Prometheus) indicating that what people want and what they get are not in conflict. Workers in the plant with poor safety performance present a substantial contrast between their assessment of the actual plant (Apollo/ Zeus/ Herakles/ Ares) and their ideal (Athena/ Eros/ Dionysos/ Demeter). In the peculiarly accident-prone sub-group referred to, Eros' absence in the actual workplace and prominence in the ideal contrasts with the Hades' prominence in the actual and absence in the ideal.

In the third place, though this is not represented in the graph, the Plant A data shows more variation between individuals' scoring of the items than does the Plant B data. It seems that employees in Plant B have a more widely shared consensus with regard to their values and assumptions.

Fourthly, the mean scores for Plant B are higher than those for Plant A on every dimension except Hades. Even the distinguishing gods of Plant A – Zeus, Herakles, and Ares – are more strongly represented (albeit marginally so) in the Plant B profile. Plant B appears to be more energetically polytheistic in its culture. For instance, there appears to be no felt contradiction between wanting to participate in decision-making and wanting a leader who gives clear directions.

Conclusions

Whether or not a causal relationship can be established between safety performance and these four factors (separately or in association) is not clear[7]. Certainly, it is not possible to come to firm conclusions on the basis of this limited comparison. However, the interview data from all sites appears to support the same conclusion – that good safety performance in these plants can be construed to be related to:

- a privileging of teamwork and participative decision-making, associated with a sense of purpose and clear and unambiguous procedures
- a match between the kind of workplace culture people have and the kind of workplace culture people want
- a shared acceptance of and commitment to a set of cultural values and cultural practices
- the ability to acknowledge and address a full range of psychological, social and emotional needs.

If all four factors are necessary and sufficient conditions for optimal safety performance in this industry, we might expect to find such performance in plants where the workforce (not simply the management) is committed to full and intelligent involvement in decision-making with regard to safety issues and to providing and taking responsibility for clear and unambiguous safety procedures, within the framework of a pluralistic and inclusive system of values.

On the other hand, it may be that the strong Athena/Apollo culture in Plant B is just a particular case of a culture that is both cohesive and compatible with the workforce's needs. We might find that an efficient Zeus culture that meets a different set of psychological, social and emotional needs of a different workforce might also manifest excellent safety performance. We might find a family company where an efficient Hera culture meets the particular needs of a particular workforce, resulting in a high degree of workplace safety.

It is worth noting that the North American plant with outstanding safety performance produced a profile very similar to that of (the Australian) Plant B. Athena, Apollo and Prometheus are predominant, with the rest of the gods, apart from Hades, close behind. These two profiles may indeed point to best practice in this regard.

There is some support for this conclusion in the assessments of how safety would be handled in the ideal workplace. Highest scoring items aggregated across the whole sample are:

- Safety in my ideal workplace depends on people facing and overcoming safety problems. (Herakles)
- Safety in my ideal workplace depends on safety procedures being developed by the team. (Athena)
- Safety in my ideal workplace depends on people caring about each other. (Eros)
- Safety in my ideal workplace depends on having clearly understood safety procedures. (Apollo)

These items may be read as recommendations by the workers both to management and to themselves.

The Religious Community

The DNAI was administered in the context of a conference of a Catholic religious congregation that was meeting to review its activities and orientate itself to the future. All members of the congregation were invited to the four-day residential conference and twenty-nine (approximately one third) attended. The questionnaire was sent to the participants with their pre-conference information, and they were asked to complete and return it. The results were analyzed and were presented to the conference as a basis for discussion.

The conference was organized because there was a sense in the community that many of its members were experiencing difficulty in dealing with a world in which the traditional practices of the congregation were apparently not appropriate or effective. There was some tension between those who believed that the only way to survive was to reinforce traditional identity, priorities, and practices, and those who saw the need for a major reorientation.

In using the questionnaire in this group, the main interest was in the way the members wished to orient themselves towards the future. Accordingly, discussion focused on the profile for the ideal organization and the match or mismatch between actual and ideal.

Community Values

The profile of the community is represented in Figure 11.4.

Figure 11.4

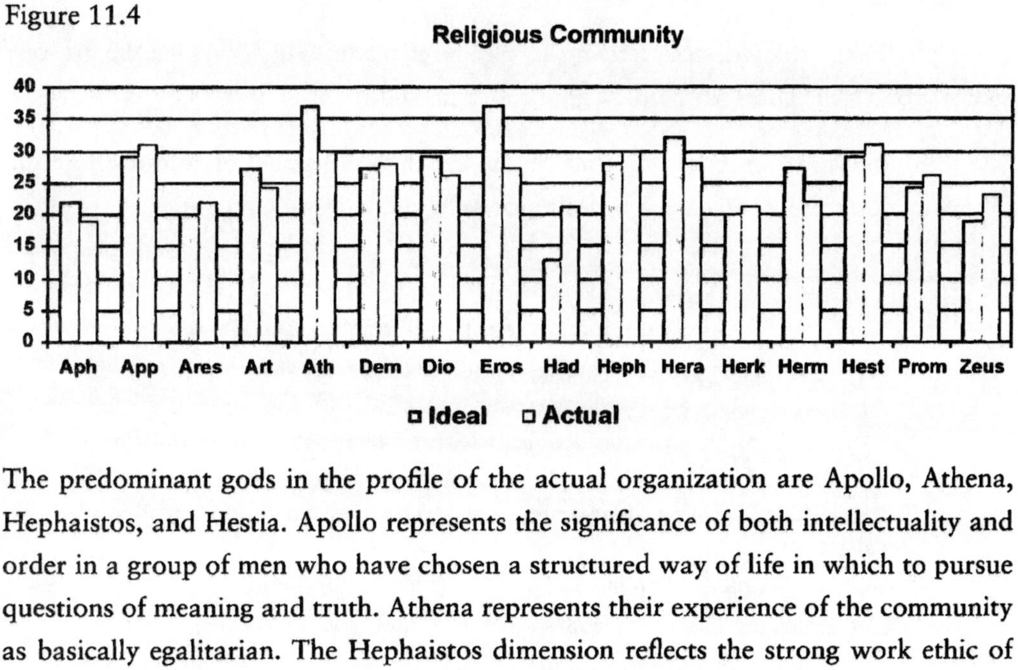

The predominant gods in the profile of the actual organization are Apollo, Athena, Hephaistos, and Hestia. Apollo represents the significance of both intellectuality and order in a group of men who have chosen a structured way of life in which to pursue questions of meaning and truth. Athena represents their experience of the community as basically egalitarian. The Hephaistos dimension reflects the strong work ethic of the group and their sense of themselves as being engaged in a craft. Hestia reflects the interiority of the culture, with its privileging of meditative practice.

The appearance of Hades as a fairly strong (though not predominant) dimension in the profile reflects the level of doubt in the community about the value and sustainability of its current activities. The ideal profile shows a strong desire for Athena – for a more participative and democratic organization – even though Athena is already prominent in the actual organization. It shows a strong desire for Eros – for a greater sense of community to combat a felt sense of fragmentation and alienation. It shows an ideal organization with minimal Hades in contrast to a somewhat demoralized organization represented in the score for actual Hades. It shows also a desire for a stronger presence of both Hera and Hermes – on the one hand more stability and shared commitment to the organization and, on the other, more flexibility and adaptability to counteract the current rigidity of Apollo. Finally, there is a desire for rather less of the paternalistic and hierarchical Zeus dimension.

Contrasts

These contrasts are made concrete in the specific items on which there is the greatest contrast between scores for actual and ideal organization.

The ideal organization scores significantly higher than the actual organization on the following descriptors, indicating a desire for an increase in these qualities:

- Relationships in this organization are strong and stable. (Ideal Hera)
- In this organization problems are dealt with through trust and openness. (Ideal Eros)
- In this organization problems are dealt with by facing them head on. (Ideal Herakles)
- To really belong in this organization you should be open to any possibility. (Ideal Hermes)
- People in this organization like to have fun. (Ideal Aphrodite)
- People in this organization are interested in community. (Ideal Eros)

The actual organization scores significantly higher than the ideal on the following, indicating a desire to decrease these qualities:

- People in this organization are lost and confused. (Actual Hades)
- People in this organization expect to be looked after. (Actual Demeter)
- People in this organization are preoccupied with how hopeless it all is. (Actual Hades)
- You will be comfortable in this organization if you are resigned to having things the way they are. (Actual Hades)
- Relationships in this organization are awkward. (Actual Hephaistos)
- Relationships in this organization are hierarchical. (Actual Zeus)

The validity of an instrument, broadly speaking, is its ability to tell you what you already know. In this case, the profile delivered by the DNAI did not represent new information for any of the participants. Indeed the conference was organized and attended because of a sense of incongruence between the congregation's traditional way of identifying itself both as a community and as an agent of change, and its current state of operational and ideological doubt. What was new information for the participants was the level of consensus in their assessment of the organizational culture and the ways in which the culture needed to change if it was to meet their needs. The level of consensus around the congregation's core values provided a sense of stability in which it was possible to confront present tensions and potential conflicts and to explore ways in which members might change their practices without threatening the values themselves.

Sites of Belongingness and Empowerment

These three organizations are very different in their purposes and this is reflected in their cultures. The mining and resources company would not be very effective in doing what it does if it developed the culture of the successful community organization, and vice versa. The religious community may be experiencing some tension between what it currently is and what it wants to be, but it cannot simply find an attractive culture somewhere else and copy it. If it is to survive it has to get in touch with its own 'formative tendency' and allow its own unique response to the new environment emerge out of its current experience of doubt. The descent into Hades as a prelude to resurrection is a powerful image within the Christian tradition.

The questionnaire on the ideal organization is included in the DNAI to give some clue of the emerging or frustrated energy in the organization. If we accept the validity of the organic metaphor and put our attempts at deliberate organizational change in the context of a living organism's ongoing self-organization, people's fantasies of the ideal organization may point to the kind of self-organization that is in process or potential.

It is worth noting in the three very different organizations presented here, the predominance of the Athena and Eros in the fantasy of the ideal organization. Horizontal power relations and an experience of community are idealized as essential attributes of the healthy organization. This gives some support to the notion that, whatever the express purpose of an organization, and the conscious purposes of those who become members of it, we find that there is a core, often unacknowledged, function of organizations and groups. They exist in order to be sites of belongingness and empowerment for their members. In a society where traditional sites of belongingness are disintegrating, this is not surprising.

The Multi-layered Organization

The DNAI can be used without reference to archetypal theory, simply to get information about the ways in people perceive an organization that they observe or belong to. It does not have to refer to any theory of archetype. If the particular groupings of items are useful it is because they represent particular patterns of thinking, valuing, and behaving in groups, and these particular patterns happen to be common enough and distinct enough to be a useful way of describing contemporary organizations. The gods may simply provide convenient and colorful ways of naming and distinguishing them. The god-image becomes a tool to help us in our thinking about organizations.

Nevertheless, we wish to take the gods more seriously. Not because we believe they somehow exist as transcendent, superhuman persons as pre-scientific peoples may have thought, but because we see them as root metaphors for particular, significant patterns of thinking, feeling, valuing, and acting, by which our consciousness and behavior seems to be structured. We cannot get away from them. Without them our behavior would disintegrate into meaningless fragments. Recognizing them not only gives richness and coherence to our lives. It prevents us from being stuck in particulars – in roles, in facts, in thoughts, or in the concrete necessities of our lives. When we cannot see them for what they are we become trapped in them – in obsessive ways of thinking or feeling which are blind to anything outside themselves. We cannot see another's point of view, because, as Hillman puts it, 'we are gripped by a particular vision'.

> Within and behind these ideas, making them so instinctually certain, so libidinally charged with excitement and endurance, so universally familiar, so few in number and repetitive in history, are the archetypes which form the structure of our consciousness with such force and such possession that we might, as we have in the past, call them gods.[8]

The gods and their stories are alive in the mythical structure, which is one layer of our multi-layered consciousness.

Pre-scientific peoples were enmeshed in the constantly repeated drama of the gods. They lived the myths from within, not being able to step outside them and subject them to scientific scrutiny and consider whether they made rational sense. This is not to suggest that they could not think, only that they may not have been able to distinguish between themselves and their thoughts. It was only with the development of mental consciousness that people became able to stand outside their thoughts and realize that these taken-for-granted thoughts, opinions, attitudes, and beliefs are something I have, not something I am. And it was only with this mutation to the mental structure of consciousness that people were able to stand outside their group culture for the first time and realize that these taken-for-granted thoughts, opinions, attitudes, and beliefs were actually borrowed from the group rather than the result of their own reflections. They became able to detach themselves from their world, look at it objectively and form their own conclusions about it.

When we look at the gods in organizations we may be able to detect the separate functions of the magic, mythical, and mental structures and the dynamic interplay between them. We may see the rituals and incantations of magic consciousness constantly working to keep things in control. We may see the myths being lived out without reflection and rationalized in a particular taken-for-granted set of beliefs and perspectives that represent the agreed truth about things. Or we may see individuals detaching themselves from this 'consensus reality' and trying to sort out the truth about the organization and its role by objective observation and reflection. It is often those who live on the margins of the organization who have the clearest notions of what is going on.

Robert Kegan has developed a model of human growth from infancy to adulthood, which roughly parallels Gebser's model of the evolution of consciousness in the species. He writes about the first order consciousness of the infant, the second order consciousness of the child, the third order consciousness which develops in late childhood, and the fourth order consciousness of late adolescence and adulthood. He is not concerned with emotion and imagination but confines himself to considering only the kind of thinking we are capable of at each stage. He argues that we move through a series of increasingly complex differentiations between subject (I) and object (It). In infancy (first order thinking) we were incapable of distinguishing between ourselves and our environment. In the second order thinking of childhood we make this distinction but identify with our physical experience. In third order thinking we perceive our physical experience as something we have and identify instead with the contents of our minds. In fourth order thinking we can disidentify from the contents of our minds and look critically at our own thoughts, opinions, and prejudices. Moreover, we can view with the same critical and tolerant mind the thoughts, opinions, and prejudices of others, on the assumption that it is possible by weighing and balancing all these ideas and their connections to arrive at the truth about things. We identify with our capacity to know in this systemic way. Kegan argues that living in the modern world demands that we be able to do this, but that only some of us succeed in doing it, and only for some of the time. This argument is reflected in the title of his book, In *Over Our Heads*.[9] Fourth order consciousness, as understood by Kegan, and mental-rational consciousness as understood by Gebser are more or less synonymous.

Both Gebser and Kegan go further than this. Gebser writes about the emergence in the twentieth century of a new, integral structure of consciousness. Kegan argues that the postmodern, post-industrial world (as opposed to the modern, industrial world) demands that we be capable of a new kind of thinking that he calls fifth order thinking. Gebser's notion of integral consciousness involves the ability to perceive the world aperspectivally, free from the limitations of time, space, and egocentricity, which characterize mental-rational consciousness. Kegan argues that fifth order thinking moves our fourth order systemic knowing from subject to object – that is to say, we cease to identify with our way of knowing, so that it becomes something we can reflect on. Our way of understanding and making meaning becomes one way of understanding and making meaning rather than the only way. In Gebser's understanding, integral, transegoic consciousness enables us to see reality as a whole without fragmenting it into bits as mental-rational consciousness does. In Kegan's theory, fifth order thinking enables us to incorporate diverse and contradictory perspectives, to assume their essential incompleteness without having to either choose between them or reconcile them, to see difference as an essential aspect of the way things are. Naturally, Kegan argues that if fourth order thinking is uncommon, fifth order thinking is even rarer, and not likely to be achieved before mid-life.

Be that as it may, for both Gebser and Kegan the new way of thinking is not just a matter of personal maturation. There is a major cultural shift in process, which both demands a new kind of consciousness and makes it possible. If we borrow Sheldrake's field theory for a moment, we can say that as more people find the capacity for integral or fifth order consciousness, a morphogenic field is established which makes it more and more likely that other people will make the same transition.[10]

We may usefully think of any organization as a cluster of organizations, all comprised of essentially the same people, inhabiting the same space but thinking in quite different ways. The magic organization does not think reflectively. It is aware of its experience but does not think about it. It experiences collective emotions – excitement, fear, anxiety – in response to events that happen to it. It engages in ritual acts to try to ensure that the things that happen to it are good. It keeps itself feeling secure by repeating slogans (or chanting incantations). If bad things happen it does magic to make the bad things go away. It clings obsessively to rituals that have worked for it in the past, and its decision-making is dominated by emotion.

The same people belong to a mythical organization that has a particular way of imagining the world and its place in it. It lives a story, which has a past and a present and a script for the future. Archetypal theory suggests that this particular story is a version of one of the big stories, the myths of the tribe, localized in time and place. Members of the organization may not perceive it as a story, for it is usually rationalized as a set of taken-for-granted ideas or beliefs, which members accept as a condition of their membership, but it is essentially a narrative of who we are, where we come from and where we are going. Decision-making in this mythical organization is shaped by this shared story, and it has limited flexibility in responding to unexpected events and changing circumstances.

The mental organization consists of all the individual members who are capable of distinguishing between themselves and the organization, of reflecting critically on the organization's beliefs, values, and behavior and of recognizing that these inherited beliefs don't necessarily represent the ultimate truth about things. They look at the evidence objectively and make rational decisions about appropriate courses of action.

The integral organization comprises all the members who can get a glimpse of the organization and its place in the world unconstrained by either the organization's notion of truth or their own prejudices and presuppositions. They can see through the particular phenomenon that is this organization to the whole human experience that is made concrete in it. They are not frightened by complexity, nor do they try to simplify it. They are able to act freely in complex situations. They glimpse many truths about the organization at once, and rather than try to resolve them they acknowledge the richness, diversity, and multiplicity of the organization and their relationship to it as the best bit of truth they are likely to get. They do not choose between the truth of Apollo and the truth of Dionysos or Hestia, nor do they believe that they must reconcile them or select particular bits of each of them in order to find the real truth. Rather they see the truth as including all of the incomplete truth of Apollo, all of the incomplete truth of Dionysos, all of the incomplete truth of Hestia and the other gods, and all of the tensions and contradictions between them.

It is easier to be in touch with our integral consciousness and welcome complexity when things are going well with us and our organization than when we are in crisis or under threat. A common human response to threat is to focus on the threat and ignore everything else. We develop tunnel vision and regress to simpler kinds of consciousness, responding to danger by running away, lashing out at any one in reach, or calling on magic to save us. It is when organizations are under threat that we are most likely to see rationality abandoned and magic embraced. There are usually shamans or gurus around in such circumstances to provide the magic incantations that are supposed to save us if we chant them long and loud enough – *downsizing* . . . *outsourcing* . . . *competition* . . . *re-engineering* . . . even *learning organization* and *archetype*. Magic still works in closed societies where every one believes in it. However, organizations nowadays are usually open societies and belief in a particular magic is not automatic. If an organization's response to threat is to be creative rather than reactive and regressive, the other layers of organizational consciousness must be brought into play.

Multi-layered Cultural Change

The challenge for us is to apply such thinking in working for change in organizations. We may use the DNAI or some other method to uncover the key pattern or patterns in the life of a particular organization, but what can we usefully do with the information? We are not dealing with a static structure here. Not only are the structures of organizational consciousness in dynamic interaction. So are the gods.

Let us suppose that we have an organization, say a manufacturing company, which is demonstrably stuck in a Prometheus/Zeus pattern. Management decides that current notions of good management practice and current commercial conditions dictate that the organization turn its back on Prometheus and Zeus and adopt a Hermes/Athena culture if it is to survive. Not an easy call. Cultural change is notoriously difficult and unpredictable.

We can work on the magic organization. The most extreme form of magic is to kill the organization and let another be born in its place. If the killing is humane, the ritual grieving is given its proper place, and the appropriate spells are cast at the birthing, the magic may work. This sort of magic is actually quite common, but often quite unsuccessful. Sacking and rehiring staff, moving head office to a new building with a different architecture, instituting an entirely new organizational structure, designing a new logo, paying a lot of money for a high profile consultant are all common forms of magic which certainly have the potential to work, but are often used ineptly. Magic works largely at an emotional level, and if the emotional dimensions of the proposed change are neglected the magic may turn against those who are using it. The dynamic potential of a new start is lost if staff have been demoralized or angered by the way the death and birth have been handled. The old culture will not just die on cue; we have to cease completely the rituals and incantations which sustain it, and replace them by the rituals of the new culture at the birth of the new organization.

For instance, a Prometheus culture can be sustained magically by the pride of place given to machines, the white coats worn by researchers or the symbols of status given to those most involved in the organization's mission of saving the world - whether they be engineers or missionaries. A Zeus culture is sustained by the symbols of hierarchical power – the lavish office, the high-backed chair, the paintings on the wall, the liquor cabinet, the particular forms of dress and address. An Athena culture requires symbols of an egalitarian ideology. The icons of a Hermes culture represent flexibility, inventiveness, and the free flow of information. The Athena/Hermes culture is sustained by such things as an open-door policy on the part of management, visibility and accessibility of all levels of management, egalitarian forms of address, high profile procedures for consultation, removal of the emblems of power and status, highly visible and widely available information technology to facilitate the crossing of internal and external boundaries, and a logo and incantation which represent the energy of Athena and Hermes.

All of these operate magically. They are capable of manipulating change without people being particularly conscious or intentional about the change they are involved in. Using the magic structure to initiate change generally appeals to management, because it believes it is in control of the process and does not even have to consult the people the magic is being used on. Many magic practices involve the spending of large amounts of money and using technology, both of which have intrinsic magic power. Using them enhances management's sense of itself as powerful.

However, magic alone is rarely enough, even when it is good magic. The mythical and mental organizations must also be dealt with.

This Zeus/Prometheus organization is embedded in a myth that upholds the values of patriarchal authority. It operates on the basic assumption that power comes from the top, that it is the role of management to govern and that of the workers to do what they are told. Even supposing that we are talking of a benevolent and paternalistic Zeus here rather than an oppressive and vengeful one, the boss's right to boss is not questioned. The story goes that if the boss gives wise and clear directions and employees carry them out conscientiously, everyone will live happily ever after. The story even includes the notion that the boss's commands are wise by definition. He (usually he) becomes wise the moment he becomes CEO. (Here we revert to magic.) Criticism of the boss is disloyal and subversive. According to this story, power is what life is all about, and workers are fortunate to be under the patronage of the powerful one. It is right that the structure of the company should support the power of the CEO and it is right that the giving and withholding of information should be an instrument of control.

This Zeus/Prometheus organization is also embedded in a story about progress. In this story, what life is essentially about is using technology to control nature and make a more prosperous world. If we run the company according to proper scientific principles (like a well oiled machine), if we take raw materials and turn them into the products which a civilized society needs, if we apply our minds intelligently to solving problems as they arise, if we set our minds on improving our processes and products, we will get rid of poverty, disease, and slavery and make ourselves more prosperous and the world generally a better place. In this story individuals are important, and the various constraints on their individuality are to be progressively demolished.

There is tension between these two stories. Prometheus would liberate people from the absolute power of Zeus. Zeus does not want to be constrained by any so-called scientific management principles in the exercise of his power. Zeus wants to maintain the stability of his universe; Prometheus believes in progress. What happens in the classical myth seems to be reflected in the solution found in many Zeus/Prometheus organizations. Zeus stops Prometheus interfering on behalf of humanity by nailing him to a rock in the far-off Caucasus until Prometheus submits to his power. Many organizations that honor Prometheus in their espoused theory actually marginalize and constrain him in their theory in action.

Let us suppose that the management of this particular Zeus/Prometheus organization is busy manipulating magic techniques to change its culture. What we may find is that it is attempting to do this without disowning or relativizing the assumptions that represent its taken-for-granted Zeus/Prometheus perspective.

Zeus is likely to be trying to impose an Athena culture and likely to be getting annoyed with people who resist his demand that they become more democratic. Prometheus is likely to be assuming that providing the information technology that research has shown to be most appropriate will automatically make people more Hermes-like in their relationship to the information they handle. At any rate there is likely to be a dissonance between the message being presented and the means of presenting it. This will interfere with the efficacy of the magic.

Manipulating culture through the mythical structure is essentially a matter of propaganda. The manipulators have no interest in having people reflect critically on the story they are presenting; they simply want the story to be accepted and become part of people's taken-for-granted truth. The mythical structure is so powerful in us, and the mass media exploit it so effectively, that we often think we have come to a rational decision based on evidence when we are really responding to the reiteration of an image. Television images or newspaper anecdotes that show our society becoming more violent, show youth out of control, or show our country being overrun by foreigners shape people's taken-for-granted truths about society regardless of what the available facts may be. However, mythical consciousness is conservative. It does not welcome a story that is entirely new. Propaganda only works when there is already a tendency, at least an unconscious one, to believe it.

If there is no emergent Athena/Hermes culture in the organization, attempts to invent one will be frustrated. However, if management is right in judging that the environment in which the company exists now demands the presence of Athena and Hermes, there is a good chance that Athena and Hermes are already stirring in the company in response to this demand. If management wants to nurture this different way of imagining the world and the company's place in it, it must find the Athena and Hermes elements in the current culture and enhance them.

What is valued in the Athena story is practical wisdom, the sharing of power and responsibility, mutual respect and a commitment to excellence. Hermes values a fluidity and freedom of action that comes from not being tied to any particular commitments. Athena's democratic process and Hermes' free flow of information are very compatible. Recognition and valuing of the cooperative activity and participative decision-making already going on in the company, and a demonstration of management's changed relationship to power might begin the revisioning of the company's collective story about itself. The Hermes story might be promoted by publicizing examples of inventiveness, flexibility, and good information flow. Once people begin to imagine the company, even tentatively, as a site of Athena/Hermes values and behavior, Athena and Hermes will find increasing public expression.

The most common obstacle to management-initiated cultural change is management's assumption that it can change the organization without changing itself. The stories and images of the desirable Athena/Hermes culture will have little impact if they are constantly contradicted by the stories and images of the Zeus management which has decided to impose a new culture, which expects to encourage the new organizational democracy without diminishing its own absolute power. If senior management wants the company to be more Athena-like and Hermes-like it has to change its own belief system. It has to stop taking for granted that it entirely owns the decision-making process, and that criticism of its decisions and challenges to its control are against the best interests of the company. It has to stop taking for granted that the company has a particular mission that defines its reason for existence and its way of operating. It cannot change in this way if it is itself embedded in the old organizational myth. Management must be capable of mental-rational, fourth order thinking, to stand outside its own myth and the rationalizations of its myth and observe them critically. Even if it is able and prepared to do this, it must somehow disentangle itself from this belief system without throwing the company into a downward spiral of doubt, distrust, and disorder.

If management's intervention for cultural change in the company employs only magical and mythical means we are acting as though management consists of rational people acting as self-conscious and reflective individuals while the majority of people in the company are stuck in a collective magical-mythical consciousness. If management and its consultants are the only people in the company capable of thinking reflectively and strategically, this might be appropriate. However, this is not likely to be the case. If the employees are denied the chance to use their reflective and strategic thinking to further the innovation, it is almost inevitable that they will use them to subvert or sabotage it.

In a mental-rational approach to cultural change all members of the organization will be invited to recognize the company's Zeus/Prometheus story and to discuss it critically. They will be invited to look critically at the prospect of cultural change and the reasons why management believes a particular cultural change is desirable. They will be given all the information necessary to engage in informed discussion. If they agree on the desirability or necessity of change they will be involved in developing the structures that will facilitate and maintain it. The process itself will be an elicitation of Athena and Hermes. Where mythical consciousness accepted the old mythology as representing the way we have to be, rational consciousness chooses the way we want to be, having decided on the evidence that this is the best way to be. There are clearly difficulties in initiating such a process in a large organization, and not all members of the organization will wish to be engaged in it. However, if this particular vision of change is really compatible with the emerging culture of the organization, these difficulties can be overcome. On the other hand, if the proposed changes go against the direction of the organization's self-organizing tendency, the attempt at cultural change will end in frustration and failure anyway.

An approach to cultural intervention that deals only with the rational organization will ignore or fail to recognize the magical and mythical dimensions of group culture. An integral approach will take full account of the magic and mythical as well as the rational, and it will do more. An integral approach to cultural change invites everyone to see the whole picture. It does not attempt to substitute Athena's beliefs, values, and assumptions for the beliefs, values, and assumptions of Zeus. It recognizes the incompleteness of the truth of both gods, and acknowledges the truth – and its incompleteness – of all the other gods as well. It does not try to reconcile the differences between the two perspectives, or let one overpower the other. The tensions and contradictions between the gods are as much aspects of the truth as the separate perspectives they offer. An integral view does not privilege as a matter of principle efficiency over relationship, cooperation over competition or order over creativity.

It looks for the richness and diversity in the company, its multiplicity of subcultures and its forgotten or suppressed stories. It is not constrained by the history of the company or its proclaimed identity to think that this is all the company can be. It invites difference to come forward and be honored. It encourages all of the company's capacities and potentials to declare themselves, so that they are all available to deal with whatever challenges the company may encounter. When it needs the energy of Zeus or Herakles, Zeus and Herakles will be available, as will Artemis and Dionysos and the rest when they are called on.

Such invitation and encouragement may not receive a very enthusiastic response. We seem to have a fairly tenuous hold on integral, and even rational, consciousness, and most of us slip back fairly readily into our personal and organizational fundamentalisms. There is some security in knowing that the way things are is the way they have to be, and we sometimes prefer to believe this rather than take the risky road to critical consciousness.

If cultural change is successfully achieved in this company it will be manifested at each layer of consciousness. The archaic organization holds the organization's culture in its instincts and rhythms – the way people walk, the way they use space, the group dance in which they are unconsciously engaged. The magic organization unreflectively maintains the Athena/Hermes culture through its ceremonies and icons. The mythical organization celebrates the Athena/Hermes story as 'the way things are'. The mental-rational organization consists of a group of individuals who, to varying degrees, are able to look at the company's current beliefs and values with a critical eye and keep a check on whether they are 'true'. The integral organization consists of those people in the company who can see a larger picture in which the proclaimed values of Athena and Hermes are only part of a pattern in the company, and the company is only part of a pattern in the greater scheme of things. They have a sense of the whole.

Many, even the majority, of the company's employees, management, board of directors, and shareholders may be uninterested in functioning at other than the magic or mythical level in that part of their lives which involves the company. Indeed, they may not be capable of the fourth or fifth order thinking which enable them to function at the mental-rational or integral levels of the company. They used to dwell comfortably enough in one company myth; this became uncomfortable and they substituted another, which they believe in with the same fervor. If this is the case there does not seem to be much chance of the company negotiating the first decades of the twenty-first century, unless the minority of rational and integral thinkers are extraordinarily clever and persuasive. We are surrounded by indications that fixed ideas are becoming an obstacle to survival, not just the survival of this company, which may not be terribly important, but the survival of our species and its planet, which we like to think is rather more significant.

---

1. The MBTI is based on four polarities theorized by Jung: introversion/extraversion, sensation/intuition, thinking/feeling, perception/judgment. Jung's conceptualization and the design of the MBTI refer to individual psychology, but it is possible to apply the resulting sixteen types (INFP, ESTJ etc) to the categorization organizational culture.

2. The metaphorical underpinning of the words 'constellation' and 'constellated' is worth spelling out. Constellations do not exist of themselves independently of an observer. It is the observer who 'constellates' a set of phenomena into a meaningful pattern. As far as the Pleiades, Orion, or the Southern Cross are concerned, the stars and galaxies that comprise them are thousands of light years apart. They only appear as a cluster because we observe them from a particular point in the universe. From another point in the universe the constellation will have an entirely different shape, or will disappear altogether.
   The 'archetypal' constellations of instincts, needs, behaviors, emotions, narratives, images, and ideas which we personify as Greek gods exist in the shape they do because we are choosing to perceive the raw elements of human experience from a particular point in human history and culture. Shift our vantage point slightly and we see the Hindu, Nordic, or Celtic gods. Shift it rather more and we see Rainbow Serpent or Coyote.
3. However, we did check the construct validity of the instrument by giving all the items, randomly sorted, to ten judges who had a thorough knowledge of the Greek pantheon. Only items that were attributed to the appropriate god by 90% of these judges were kept in the instrument.
4. Version 6 of the DNAI, which was used in these three studies, consisted of 80 items. Later versions have been reduced to 64 items.
5. See B Neville *Neighbourhood Houses: Twelve More Years*, in P Willis & B Neville (1996). The nine centers that responded to the questionnaire represent an independent random stratified sample. As it turned out there were in fact two centers that were included in both the qualitative study and the DNAI study. Each of the nine centers was sent a parcel of questionnaires and the convener/manager was asked to distribute them to a group including administrators, teachers, and students. Total number of completed questionnaires was 101.
6. Paired samples analysis (t-tests) comparing each center's profile with that of the entire sample indicated that there was no significant statistical difference between the profile of any one center and that of the population as a whole.
7. Managers of plants were invited to have their plants included in the study. No plants with notoriously bad safety records chose to be included. Accordingly, the sample did not include enough variation in safety performance to test these hypotheses statistically.
8. J Hillman (1977) *Revisioning Psychology*, p. 129.
9. See R Kegan (1995) *In Over Our Heads*.
10. See R Sheldrake (1988) *The Presence of the Past* for a discussion of morphogenic fields.

12

GOD OF THE CROSSROADS

A New Factor

In *The Ever Present Origin*, which was first published half a century ago, Jean Gebser introduces his theory of structures of consciousness by putting it in the context of an approaching planetary catastrophe.

> The crisis we are experiencing today is not just a European crisis, a crisis of morals, economics, ideologies, politics, or religion. It is not only prevalent in Europe and America but in Russia and the Far East as well. It is a crisis of the world and mankind such as has occurred previously only during pivotal junctures – junctures of decisive finality for life on earth and for the humanity subjected to them. The crisis of our times and of our world is in a process – at the moment autonomously – of complete transformation, and appears headed towards an event which, in our view, can only be described as 'global catastrophe'. This event, understood in any but anthropocentric terms, will necessarily come about as a new constellation of planetary extent.
>
> We must soberly face the fact that only a few decades separate us from that event. This span of time is determined by an increase in technological feasibility inversely proportional to man's sense of responsibility – that is, unless a new factor were to emerge which would effectively overcome this menacing correlation.[1]

Gebser was convinced that a 'new factor' was actually emerging, that human beings were becoming capable of a new way of thinking that might make them able to deal with the crisis, seeing that rational thinking appears to be incapable of doing so. He thought he could see both the disintegration of the rational structure of consciousness and the emergence of a new kind of thinking that was no longer bound by the constraints of quantified time and space, no longer stuck in either-or dichotomies, no longer forced to see the world from only one perspective at a time. Integral consciousness would enable us to see reality as a whole, from many directions at once, rather than in the fragmented way of our deficient rational consciousness.

The two decades in which Gebser's observations and insights developed into a theory of this emerging 'integrality' were not likely to give him romantic notions about humanity and its future. He had concrete experience of the dominance of a totalitarian ideology and a mass pathology, which appeared to him to represent a collapse of rationality and a regression to a primitive form of consciousness. (He fled from Germany to Spain in 1931, from Spain to France in 1936, and from France to Switzerland in 1939.) He does not present us with a romantic vision. What he does give us is documentation of an emerging 'possibility', and a theory of consciousness and culture that is consistent with it. In decades since he wrote this we have come considerably closer to catastrophe. But we can also find signs of a changing consciousness, which we may imagine as either contributing to the crisis or enabling us to negotiate it.

Gebser is not the only person to produce evidence that there was a major change in consciousness going on during the twentieth century. And he is not the only one to note that such leaps of awareness are generally fraught with anxiety.

The Story of Our Times

In the half century since Gebser wrote we have been hearing from various sources that human consciousness and culture is undergoing some sort of transformation.[2] The story we hear is sometimes the story of a collapsing civilization and an inevitable global catastrophe and sometimes a story of a coming bright new age, but the pessimistic and optimistic versions have certain themes in common when they address the nature of the contemporary world.

The story we hear is a story of complexity and chaos, of the dissolution of boundaries, of deceit, denial, and delusion, of the preference for image over substance, of the loss of familial and tribal bonds, of the deregulation of markets, ideas, and ethics, of an unwillingness of national leaders to confront reality and tell the truth, of the abandonment of rationality, of the proliferation of information, of a market-place so noisy that nothing can be clearly heard, of a world seen through a distorting lens, of an ever-tightening knot which we cannot unravel, or an ever-unraveling knot which we cannot tighten, of planetary dilemmas so profound that we cannot even think about them sensibly, let alone address them.

Gebser's own description of the state of the world echoes much of what we now associate with 'postmodernity'. We hear that time, space, matter, truth, logic have lost their stability and reliability. We hear that the collapse of our 'grand narratives' is an inevitable consequence of the information revolution. We hear that our society is maintained by a constant flow of information, to the extent that it no longer matters what the information is about as long as the flow continues. We hear that the information society is enmeshed in a fantasy of the marketplace, in which everything is a commodity, exchange is an end in itself and the only value is market value. We hear that the boundaries that used to separate individuals and nations are fast disappearing.

We hear that there are no longer any absolutes. Looking for universal truths is a waste of time and attempts to establish any universal truth are naïve and misguided. Whatever currently passes for truth is maintained as truth only because it supports the current power structure.

We hear that reality is essentially plural, that there is no principle by which we can decide that one truth, one form of life, one interpretation should be preferred over another. We hear that the boundaries between truth and fantasy, self and other, matter and spirit, good and evil are dissolving. We find ourselves surrounded by images, with no solid ground on which to stand.

There are elements in this story that we may find exciting and others that we may find frightening. Nevertheless it is a story that has been going around for some time, and there are elements of it that are so firmly embedded in our consciousness that they are no longer questioned.

The management literature has added its own contributions to this story. The gurus of the new capitalism[3] tell us that we are now living in a world where nothing is stable, where organizations must be constantly ready to make a flexible response to rapidly changing market conditions. They tell us that the market is actually the only reason that organizations exist. (In fact it's the only reason why human beings exist. We no longer belong to a nation, a society, a civilization, or a community but to an economy.) Their story is about flexibility, individuality, and diversity. It has its special magic words that are employed in incantations: *strategic management, just-in-time, managerial decentralization, devolution, deregulated environment, new work order,* even *enchanted workplace,* which point to a vision of a totally flexible organization without fixed boundaries and structures. One of its most popular variations is the happily-ever-after story of an emerging brave new world where the old hierarchical structures have dissolved and 'partners' collaborate in meaningful work and those who deserve prosperity get it. We have been telling our own version of this story in the preceding chapters.

This way of thinking often carries the label 'postmodern', though it is not really satisfactory to define a phenomenon by what it is not. However, whatever label we attach to it, it seems plausible to argue that there is something distinctive about contemporary Western consciousness and its institutions, which points to a specific sensibility, a specific way of dealing with the world. Some would argue that this is entirely new. We would suggest rather that it has been around for a long time, rooted in the magical-mythical foundations of our Western culture. Postmodernity is just the latest edition of an old story.

All About Hermes

The method of archetypal psychology is to attempt to see through this new story to the old story it is repeating and to the god whose myth it belongs to. Hillman suggests that we are always in one archetypal fantasy or another. We suggest that the archetypal fantasy that this story is enmeshed in is the fantasy of Hermes, the god who is both Trickster and Transformer.

The Homeric Hymn to Hermes tells us how, to avoid detection by the gods, Maia, the nymph who was Zeus' lover, dwelt in a deep cave where she bore a son,

> *who was a shrewd and coaxing schemer,*
> *a cattle-rustling robber, and a bringer of dreams,*
> *a watcher by night and a gate-keeper, soon destined*
> *to show forth glorious deeds among the immortal gods.*[4]

The hymn shows Hermes as a most precocious infant who, as he leaves the cave on the day he was born, comes across a tortoise. First he plays with it as any child might, then he kills it and makes a lyre out of its shell.[5] Accompanying himself on this instrument, he sings the very first song, which is about his parents' love-making.

Having joyfully and ironically sung of his parents' intercourse, he moves on to other things. He feels a craving for meat, so he leaves his lyre in his cradle and sets out to find some. For a rogue like Hermes, there is one utterly obvious way to obtain the meat he craves. He steals it. When twilight falls he seeks out the cattle of Apollo where they are grazing, and cuts fifty of them out of the herd.

To fool Apollo, he drives the cows backwards so they look as though they are walking the other way, and uses foliage to make the first pair of sandals, in order to disguise his own footprints.

Having invented stringed instruments and sandals, he now invents the fire-stick, and builds a fire. Next, he invents both cookery and religious sacrifice. He takes two of the cows he has stolen, slaughters and roasts them. By this time he has obviously forgotten about his hunger, for instead of making a banquet for himself, he takes the meat (which he stole from the gods in the first place) and offers it to the gods, making sure that he packages the carcasses in twelve equal pieces. Having performed the sacrifice, Hermes returns to his cradle, and lies gurgling and playing like any baby. His mother scolds him for his thieving, at which Hermes vigorously declares his intention of becoming the Prince of Robbers, so he can support the two of them in the manner they are entitled to.

The next day, Apollo arrives at the cave, having tracked the cows there, and angrily confronts his baby brother Hermes. Hermes lies shamelessly. He declares that he was only born yesterday, which is true enough, and then goes on to swear by the head of Zeus that he has never seen a cow in his life. Apollo won't accept this and picks up the baby Hermes to carry him to their father Zeus for judgment. Hermes' belly rumbles so loudly that Apollo drops him in disgust. Before the throne of Zeus, Hermes continues to lie, well knowing that nobody believes him, and eventually charms his way out of punishment by getting Zeus to laugh. Nevertheless, Zeus exacts from Hermes a promise not to lie to the gods again (though he need not necessarily tell the truth!) and sends his sons off together to find the cattle. Realizing Hermes' great strength, Apollo tries to bind his hands together, but Hermes the illusionist is far too slippery a character to be bound. As they sit together in the mouth of the cave, with Apollo continuing to accuse and Hermes continuing to deny, Hermes takes his lyre and begins to play. Apollo is charmed completely and begs to be given this wonderful instrument. Hermes willingly swaps it for the cattle and goes off to invent the Pan pipes.

So Apollo takes responsibility for music while Hermes becomes the god of herdsmen and shepherds (as well as cattle-rustlers), and of barter and negotiation (as well as stealing and deception). They become the best of friends. Hermes promises never to steal from Apollo again. He receives from Apollo his staff, or magic wand, for it is fitting that he should be a god of magic and illusion. Finally, he is designated messenger to Hades, the one who guides souls to the underworld.

God of the Crossroads

Hermes is ubiquitous in Greek mythology. He appears in the myth of every god. He is the shape-shifter with many names and many forms: the god of travelers, the god of boundaries and boundary-crossing, the god of cowboys, the god of merchants and markets, the god of persuasiveness, the trickster, the god of lies and deceit, the god of gamblers, the god of thieves, the god of illusions, the god of shamanic medicine, the god of the crossroads, the god of connections, of quicksilver, of fast footwork and smooth talking. He is slippery and seductive, the divine entrepreneur, a con man without ethics and without malice. He has no values of his own, no concern for substance. He slips into situations where he is not expected. He avoids confrontation; he has no interest in being a hero. He believes that everything is negotiable. He enjoys doing deals, being clever, playing the game. He is the herald of the gods, the connector, the carrier of information.

Hermes does not craft anything, like Hephaistos. He does not manage anything, like Zeus, or lead us to understanding, like Apollo, or ensure the smooth functioning of society, like Hera, or harvest and hoard, like Kronos. He does not fight, like Ares, or nourish, like Demeter, or protect the weak, like Artemis. He has no interest in good citizenship, like Athena, or ecstasy, like Dionysos. He does not wish to stay at home, like Hestia, but is constantly on the move. He loves paradox and process, trickery and risk. He is ambiguous and many-faced. He is everybody's mate. Yet,

> *Little is the profit he brings, and he beguiles endlessly*
> *the tribes of mortal men throughout the night.*[6]

The earliest image of Hermes is the stone-heap, which the ancient Greeks set up to mark crossroads and the boundaries of their land. From the first he is the god of liminality, the god of borders, and comes to represents everything that is borderline: the border between my country and yours, between night and day, between truth and falsehood, between life and death, between the world of humans and the world of the gods, between sanity and madness, between citizen and alien, between right and wrong, between human and divine and (in his child, Hermaphrodite) between male and female. Such distinctions belong to his brother Apollo. Hermes belongs on neither side of these boundaries, but transports us across them. He has no temples, but is worshipped at every crossroad.

As god of boundaries Hermes is also god of connections, an aspect that is manifested in his sexual enthusiasm. He spends a lot of his time chasing nymphs. He has casual and amiable sexual relationships with many goddesses, including even Artemis. He is the god of 'getting lucky' and the 'one night stand'.

There is nothing particularly original in applying the image of Hermes to our era. Jung, for one, was very conscious of the Hermetic in his own writing. New Age thinkers, particularly those with gnostic tendencies, are much inclined to the uncritical worship of Hermes. However, I want to suggest that we can also find the myth of Hermes in the abstractions of the so-called postmodern analysts of our culture, in the fantasies of the money market and the descriptions of the 'new work order' as surely as we can in the turgidities of Jung's alchemical writings.

For the last three or four hundred years, European consciousness has been dominated by other gods than Hermes. The Enlightenment and the birth of modern science were dominated by the image of Apollo, god of clarity, of light, of reason, of phallogocentric superiority. The industrial age from which we are emerging was dominated by the image of Prometheus. It is the failure of the Promethean fantasy that has precipitated us into the present age of uncertainty.

Prometheus, in Greek mythology, is the creator of men (though not of women), the superhuman hero who sacrifices himself by stealing fire from heaven, giving men light and heat and technology and thus freeing them from the domination of the gods and enabling them to become masters of the earth. The images of the Promethean myth – emancipation, technology, control, empowerment, progress - have shaped the guiding fantasy of the dominant (Western, masculine) consciousness for two hundred years or more.

European culture has dwelt, more or less uncritically, in a fantasy of progress, of liberating humanity from the power of 'Nature', of gaining control over the processes of life, of breaking free from poverty and ignorance and disease, and of doing all this through technology, through Prometheus' gift of fire and crafting. When one technology fails to deliver the paradise we switch our faith to another, within the same fantasy of inevitable progress.

This fantasy is at present wavering, as it becomes apparent that every solution provided by technology brings with it new problems, that our drive to master the planet has been taking us, perhaps irreversibly, towards the destruction of the planet and humanity, that technology manages to enslave more people than it emancipates, that heroic revolution does not inevitably bring freedom. We are losing our ability and, indeed, our will to reduce the world to simple cause and effect sequences that we have the cunning to manage. The Promethean vision is fading. Paradise is postponed. European civilization is shifting from an infatuation with Prometheus to an infatuation with Hermes.

However, though Apollinine and Promethean values are no longer so much a part of mainstream thinking that they are unchallengeable and assumed simply to reflect the truth about the world, we still find some resistance to letting them go. We are still inclined to think that we ought to be able to understand and control our world, and to feel some nostalgia for the days when we dwelt happily in the fantasy that one day we would be able to.

The Promethean myth and the Apollo myth are versions of the myth of the masculine, misogynist hero, combating the darkness and chaos, conquering the she-dragon, liberating man from the power of uncontrolled nature. They have their roots in a patriarchal politics, which Apollo clearly supports and Prometheus resists in the name of heroic individuality. However, human consciousness was not always dominated by hero stories. Before the hero story came the mother story, a story that emerged from the primal human sense of oneness with the nurturing and devouring earth. The emergence of the hero story in Greece in the second millennium B.C. coincides with a political and cultural conquest by which an indigenous, matristic, nature-worshipping culture was replaced by the culture of the invading warlords. In the old story, Nature is Mother and we are part of her. In the new story, Nature, still female, is darkness and chaos and monstrous strength, which Apollo, or Prometheus, or Herakles must overcome through the clear light of his masculine intelligence or the strength of his masculine arm.

In classical Greece, a polytheistic consciousness enabled both stories to be heard at once, and the classical pantheon and its mythology represent a meeting of these two very different versions of reality, albeit in a political context that was essentially patriarchal.

One place where we find the old story and the new story meeting is in the myth of Hermes, the smooth-tongued negotiator. It is Hermes who demonstrates that all the gods must be worshipped. Hermes is indeed the son of Zeus, but his primary connection is with Maia, the nymph whose name simply means 'old mother'. In the Homeric hymn of Apollo, we find that god announcing at his birth that his task is to 'prophesy the will of unerring Zeus',[7] then going off on his journey to establish the domination of reason over chaos by killing the she-dragon and taking over her shrine. Hermes' story has a similar structure, but Hermes is an anti-hero who is willing to subvert and destabilize the status quo and who announces to his mother that:

> *I shall be master of whatever skill is best*
> *to provide for you and me forever: we shall not suffer*
> *as you bid me, to stay right here and be*
> *the only two immortals not plied with gifts and prayers.*
> *. . . And if my father does not allow me this, I shall surely*
> *try to be, as I no doubt can, the chief of robbers.*[8]

Monotheistic societies do not have this ability to hold two stories in balance. Over the past two thousand years it has been the hero story that has generally represented orthodoxy, whether religious orthodoxy or scientific orthodoxy. The core assumptions of western civilization are anthropocentric and egocentric. The mother story has emerged from time to time, but proved unable to flourish in most political climates. Now we find the mother story emerging in the contemporary Hermes culture – in feminism, deep ecology, and nature mysticism. Hermes promises to subvert the patriarchy and see that Gaia/Maia gets the honor she deserves.

A Hermes consciousness delights in complexity. It trusts that what our rational minds perceive as chaos represents a higher level of order; it perceives a world at play where an Apollo consciousness sees a loss of control. The deceit and dishonesty, the opportunism, the entire lack of ethics, that characterize the infantile Hermes, are justified by him as destabilization of an oppressive system. 'Mother', he says, 'I'm only doing it for you.'

However, nothing is unambiguous in the Hermes myth. We find Hermes getting by very well in the patriarchy, in spite of his lack of commitment to it. Zeus makes him his messenger and he performs his task admirably, using his persuasive powers on Zeus' behalf. Hermes will do whatever suits his advantage, and as long as Zeus continues to hold the power he is content to be Zeus' man. Meanwhile, he continues his game of subversion and destabilization. Not even Zeus can really trust him.

Worshipping Hermes

It seems apparent that for a couple of decades our business culture has been worshipping the god of the marketplace with an excess of devotion. We still see an infatuation with the magic hand of the marketplace, enthusiastically supported by political leaders from both the right and the left. (Hermes is the god of disguises. He can disguise himself equally readily as a socialist or as a conservative). We have seen paper entrepreneurs become cultural heroes, twenty-three year old foreign exchange dealers (selected for their gambling instinct) become obscenely wealthy, educational institutions devoting their energies to pouring out a flood of economists and accountants, and rural and manufacturing industries brought to the edge of destruction.

The consequences have been catastrophic for national economies, for public morality, for countless unemployed, and for the political system. Nevertheless, the myth has not lost any of its power. It is rationalized into a belief that the unregulated marketplace is the source of growth, prosperity, freedom, and democracy. The fact that governments have been acting on this belief for a quarter of a century without any positive results to show for it does not inhibit their faith in it. Mythical consciousness is incapable of critical reflection.

Economists and moralists will have their own explanations as to why the infatuation with an unregulated marketplace should have had such consequences. We only want to point to the myth, where we see Zeus taking it on himself to control Hermes' infantile behavior, demanding that the young thief come to an accommodation with Apollo. It may be that the only societies able to avoid the catastrophic consequences of a Hermes inflation will be those where the intellectual and business culture is under the firm control of the Zeus, and where the enthusiasms of Hermes are balanced by those of his brother Apollo – reason and moderation. The Greeks were well aware of the dangers of monotheism, and could have warned us that Hermes, the inventor and trader, is not interested in producing and harvesting and hoarding. He is not even particularly interested in wealth. He gets his thrills out of doing deals and playing in the marketplace rather than in accumulating assets. Neither is he interested in ethics. If we want ethics (apart from the ethics of opportunism) we will have to look elsewhere – to Zeus for the ethics of absolute moral law and the ethics of traditional values, to Hera for the ethics of social bonds and social stability, to Demeter for the ethics of caring and nurturing, to Eros for the ethics of relationship, to Apollo for the ethics of rationality, to Hestia for the ethics of service, to Artemis for the ethics of earth-consciousness, to Aphrodite for an aesthetic ethics and to Athena for common sense and the ethics of citizenship. In the marketplace of a postmodern consciousness, ethics – like truth and relationship – has been deregulated.

However, it is not only the business and political cultures that are suffering a Hermes-inflation. Hermes has entered into areas such as education, health, and welfare, which once belonged to other gods. In education, for instance, we have seen the enduring notion of education as the transmission of culture (a Senex fantasy) and the pursuit of meaning (an Apollo fantasy), striving with some success to resist the fantasy of education as context for growth and relationship (Demeter, Dionysos, Eros), and a stronger challenge from a fantasy of education as skilling (Prometheus), only to be seduced by the charm of Hermes. Teachers and consultants have become 'knowledge workers', constructing knowledge and selling it to whoever can afford it. Educational institutions now happily take their wares into the marketplace and hawk them to whoever will buy. Debates about what is worth teaching have been replaced by debates about what will sell. Knowledge and skills are no longer imagined to be worth teaching for their own sake, but are justified only by their current market value. Areas of education that are hard to commodify (e.g. Humanities) are thought to have little value. Since the god of the marketplace is also the herald and messenger, the god of information exchange, there is plenty of attention given to communication and its technologies, but rather less to the notion of what is worth communicating. Substance has given way to image, and content has yielded to process and exchange.

The god of cheating and illusion has no interest in substance in any case. So we see the notion of essential substance disappearing from discourse as it has disappeared from physics. We find it disappearing from the world of finance, where the opulence of the gold bar and the tactility of the banknote have been replaced by the manipulation of a few molecules on a computer disk. We find it disappearing in the arts, also, where considerable effort and technical skill is expended in creating artworks that demonstrate only the pointlessness of creating artworks. We find the postmodern analysts of our culture engaged in discourse about the pointlessness of engaging in discourse, using an abstract, abstruse, pseudo-Apollonine logic to disguise the fact that they are saying nothing about nothingness. Hermes is, after all, the Trickster, the god of disguises. In following the convolutions of their thinking we might be reminded of Apollo, clarity and rationality personified, tracking his apparently backwards-walking cattle through the mountains and eventually finding not his herd but a baby playing in the dark.

Play is one Hermes image that is used by some postmodern writers to express (justify? romanticize? disguise? explore? hide?) the groundlessness to which their thinking leads. Hermes is quite happy with groundlessness, whether it is deconstruction or bootstrap theory or the Void or the two-dollar company. His winged feet never touch the ground anyway.

If we accept the notion that we are living through a particularly intense experience of the Hermes myth, we will not be surprised to encounter this language of 'play' and 'gaming' in a culture engaged in uncritical adulation of the entrepreneur and trapped in an addiction to gambling.

The pathology of Hermes is manifested in the paper entrepreneur, who grows nothing and manufactures nothing, but plays the market with skill and daring, sees no distinction between honest and dishonest dealing, and makes and loses paper fortunes with no concern (or even awareness) of the destruction of human hopes and human lives that this involves. It is manifested also in the image of the 'advertising man', surrounded by the Hermes images of mobility, communication, and fleeting satisfaction, in his Lear jet or sports car, setting up a 'deal', with one nymph on his arm and another on the phone. We find a similar shift away from substance in postmodern organizations and in the Hermes personalities that populate them.

The Hermes Organization

The Hermes-inflated organization is committed to nothing but doing deals and making money. Sometimes it is established just for this purpose. Sometimes it represents the subversion of an organization that was originally set up to produce goods or services, but where the takeover by a Hermes consciousness has turned the capacity to produce goods and services into a commodity to be bartered, just as another organization's capacity to create or analyze ideas becomes a commodity to be bartered. Hermes has no commitment to the music he enjoys so much. He happily trades it for a herd of cattle. Even outside media and advertising organizations, where the monotheistic worship of Hermes, the rogue and liar, is most obsessive, we find level upon level of management whose function is not production but information (or disinformation) exchange. People in such an organization do not need to have a commitment to the task itself. They need only know how to 'facilitate' it. Hermes the facile, the one who makes things easy, the smooth talker, is equally present in facilitation at its best and manipulation at its worst. In the Hermes-inflated organization it is easier to advance through smooth talking than through competence, loyalty, or hard work.

One reason why the Hermes-inflated people in an organization have no commitment to the substance of what they do is that they are all on the way to somewhere else. Hermes organizations are full of people whose only interest in their present position is as a steppingstone to somewhere else. Mr Black used to have a lowly position in the Department of Conservation, moved to a higher level in the Department of Education, and is looking forward to stepping up a further grade in the Department of Transport. He has no interest in Forestry, Education, or Transport, but plenty of interest in self-promotion. Ms Brown has taken a management position in the Health bureaucracy, not because Health is important to her or because she wants to learn something about it, but in order to make 'contacts' that will be financially useful to her when she returns to the private sector. Hermes is, after all, the god of travelers. We tend to take this situation for granted now, yet it is not long since promotion and preferment in corporations and State bureaucracies were determined by seniority (in the Zeus/Senex organization) or family relationship (in the Hera organization), or even administrative competence (in the Apollo organization), rather than by the extensiveness of one's networks and the glossiness of one's CV. We may have abandoned the Senex and Hera fantasies with relief, but the Hermes fantasy, in which promotion and preferment are decided by mateship, smooth talking, doing deals, developing an image, or conning a committee is hardly to be preferred.

The same fantasy defines the role of the chief executive of the postmodern organization, whose time and energies are spent networking, making contacts, traveling, persuading, massaging, and manipulating rather than having a hands-on role in the organization's daily business. It is seen in the blind faith in 'managerialism', which sees the management of organizations taken over completely by people with qualifications in the Hermes fields of commerce, finance, economics, and marketing, and does not notice the disappearance from management of those with experience and skills (or even interest) in the specific fields in which the organization is involved. The fantasy of 'content-free management' belongs to the world of Hermes. So does the mobility of the 'casualized' workforce, forced to be always on the move in a new work order that has no respect for notions of employer-employee loyalty (Hera), or for notions of employee security (Demeter), or for people's need to belong to place (Hestia) and people (Eros).

The arrival or emergence of a Hermes consciousness in an organization hitherto dominated by the Zeus image of patriarchal power, or the Promethean image of the machine may be greeted with relief or delight. At last, process is to be valued like power and product. We are all encouraged to see ourselves as entrepreneurs. As the Hermes inflation sets in, ungrounded 'facilitation' and unending exchange and negotiation take the place of decision-making and productivity, and simple visions and procedures get lost in an infinite complexification. The old certainties are undermined, the old roles and structures are destabilized. The delight fades. The ancient autocratic organization that everyone hated is transformed into a fantasy of 'the good old days', when the organization was purposive, when employees knew where they stood and had a sense of being looked after and achieving something.

A characteristic that many Hermes-inflated managers share is slipperiness. They are often charming people who skillfully disguise their lack of interest in substantive issues. Since they believe in nothing it is easy for them to avoid conflict and remain everybody's friend. They skillfully avoid making decisions where matters other than their self-interest are at stake; they avoid answering a direct question, or taking responsibility for anything, just as the infantile Hermes does. They are rogues and liars, but can be very inventive and engaging ones. Very often they have gained their position through disguise and deceit, adopting the Ares disguise in an organization looking for a leader committed to fighting passionately for its survival and prosperity, adopting the Apollo disguise in an organization seeking an executive committed to dealing rationally with its structures and procedures, adopting the Athena disguise in an organization committed to participation and democracy. In fact, Hermes-inflated managers are totally free of commitments to principles, products or people. They are always prepared to put their own interests ahead of those of the organization and will switch allegiances and ideologies whenever opportunity beckons. Loyalty is not a value they rate highly. They expect it neither of themselves nor of their subordinates.

In the Hermes-inflated organization, life is a game. There are no ultimate values, everything is negotiable, and the attitude towards conventional societal 'truths' is ironic or cynical. Roguery is more likely to be admired and rewarded than condemned. Yet rogues and liars have their own image of truth. From the Zeus perspective, truth is given, comes from God or the State or the Chief Executive. From the Apollo perspective, it is manifested through the clear light of the intellect. For Prometheus, it is enough to find out how things work. For Hermes, truth is a flash of beauty, glimpsed for the briefest of moments and always alluringly elusive, like the nymphs that ancient Greek travelers glimpsed for a moment in the forest, pursued, and lost; never sure that they had really seen anything. This image of truth is as present in the fantasies of postmodern science as it is in the fantasies of postmodern literature and postmodern politics. (It is not uncommon for the Hermes personality, male or female, to pursue the same fantasy in relationships.)

Hermes has his own way with language. When the literature of new capitalism speaks fondly of 'collaboration', 'participative decision-making', 'empowerment', 'communities of practice', and 'partnerships', it is Hermes the Trickster talking. Hermes happily disguises himself as Athena or Eros. If we understand such terms the way they are understandable in an Athena culture or an Eros culture we are likely to be deceived. While such words may be used to persuade us that the new work order is genuinely concerned with organizational democracy and empowerment, the ideology of new capitalism does not really permit workers to challenge its basic assumptions.

Organizational democracy may be a useful tool to meet the demands of the market, but it is often allowable only within a framework that believes with absolute faith that the market represents all that is worth valuing.[9]

We might reasonably expect that in an organization dominated by Hermes everything will be deregulated, including ideas, and that the core assumptions of the organization will be flexible and changeable. This is rarely the case. Hermes does not work alone. The power of Zeus permeates the wider culture, and has the capacity to turn Hermes' free marketplace into another absolutist ideology designed to maintain the power of those in charge. We have seen economic rationalism, which first emerged as a Hermes-like perspective, turn into a fundamentalist belief.[10] Where Athena and Eros are dominant in an organization, power-sharing and community are valued for their own sake, and Hermes plays a significant role in facilitating them. However, where we find organizational democracy being used to maintain the power of those in charge, we can recognize Hermes in his role of servant and messenger of Zeus.[11]

Yet the Hermes energy in an organization drives it towards greater mobility and flexibility. The Hermes organization relishes complex situations. People are not fussed by ambiguity, paradox, and risk. They are imaginative and inventive. They function freely and fluidly, unconstrained by the hierarchies and structures of the Zeus or Apollo organization. Their ambitions are not constrained by convention or tradition. They readily cross boundaries, both the boundaries that define the organization's goals and those that define its membership. Globalization, diversification, and multiculturalism are embraced with enthusiasm. The solid, material, and human assets of an organization are readily abandoned in favor of virtual property and virtual people. The Hermes organization does not think in terms of a mission. It is not interested in being heroic, in fighting for something it wants. It will always prefer to get what it wants by charm, seduction, or trickery. It is always on the move. Everything in the Hermes-inflated organization is 'fast'. To quote Tom Peters, one of the gurus of 'fast capitalism':

> I like the word 'ephemeral' almost as much as 'fashion' or 'fickle'. In fact I'm fond of speaking of the 'four ephemerals': ephemeral organizations . . . joined in ephemeral combinations . . . producing ephemeral products . . . for ephemeral markets . . . FAST.[12]

This privileging of the ephemeral, insubstantial, and transitory, which we somehow have come to accept as natural, belongs to the Age of Hermes. When we are asked to accept that this is the way it has to be, we need to reflect with some suspicion on whose good it serves to have everyone believe this. Myths do not necessarily reflect a deep and eternal wisdom about life. They reflect how life is experienced, not how it ought to be experienced. And sometimes they simply reflect the way those in power want us to experience life.

Trickery and Transformation

The Greeks had nothing in their mythology that approximates to Satan. The nasty or pathological aspects of behavior were shared out among all the gods. Hermes has his good side and his bad side. However, to make distinctions between positive and negative, healthy and pathological, we must adopt the perspective of Apollo. Hermes himself makes no such distinctions. From the perspective of Apollo (and Zeus, and Prometheus) the deceit, delusion, irresponsibility, and amorality apparent in many postmodern organizations are symptoms of a Hermes pathology. So are the boundary-crossing, the substitution of image for substance, the attack on rationality, the opportunism, the groundlessness of the winged god of illusion, the slipperiness of 'the unraveler' who cannot be pinned up or tied down, the restlessness of the god of travelers who never stays in one place.

Jung warned us that in every inflation we will find pathology, as the negative aspects of that complex/archetype get full expression. In the above account it is the pathological which predominates, for it is in our pathologies that we are most likely to become aware of the gods, at the social as well as the personal level. Yet we need a Hermes consciousness to escape the oppression of the old orthodoxies and to avoid new ones.

Hermes doesn't have an orthodoxy. He does not have a particular obsession or a particular perspective like the other gods. Even the perspective that values not having a perspective is relativized as only one perspective among many. As Rafael Lopez-Pedraza puts it:

> [The other gods] would seem to be the center of specific aspects of life to which they give their imprint. Whereas Hermes permeates the whole world because of his possibility of making connections, his commerce with, and constellation of the other gods from his borderline. He is the connection-maker and he is the Messenger of the gods . . . Hermes has no need to fight for his center; he does not have one.[13]

The development of a Hermes consciousness in the twentieth century provided a long awaited relief from the limitations of Apollonine consciousness and Promethean consciousness. The Enlightenment invited humankind to see the world clearly for the first time. The technological and industrial revolution invited us to break free from the domination of the gods and gain control of our world. Hermes is unfreezing the certainties of all these gods and destabilizing the structures that support them. He is inviting us to honor all the gods equally and to allow soul back into the world, and we can find him doing this even in human understandings and behaviors that we find destructive. It is consistent with Jungian theory to argue that it is the suppression of Hermes for so long that has led to this outbreak of Hermes-pathology, and that the best way of dealing with this is to acknowledge and value the positive manifestation of the god.

Among the gifts of Hermes that have been too rarely acknowledged in our organizations are imagination, flexibility, intuition, the sense of the sacred, playfulness, irony, delight in paradox, grace, magic, heterogeneity, complexity, multiplicity, luck, healing, and connection with the feminine. A healthy organization accepts such gifts with gratitude, while acknowledging that the giver is not entirely to be trusted. The Protector of Travelers sometimes guides us on our way and sometimes leads us astray.

All of the Olympian gods are complex in their manifestations, though none quite as complex as the god of complexity himself. It is Hermes the Rogue who provides the means to tell a sort of truth about the roguery and deception that seem to be epidemic in business, politics and the academy. It is Hermes the Trickster who undermines the oppressive, patriarchal structures that have been dominant in our organizational cultures, and allows the possibility of transformation. It is Hermes, the Bringer of Dreams, who provides the perspective of this book and insists that other perspectives be also honored. It is Hermes, Lord of the Road, who can guide us through the borderlands we now inhabit. And each time we arrive at a new crossroad, it is Hermes who enables us to choose which way to go.

The ancient Greeks could have warned us that when we give all our worship to one god, not only do we sentence ourselves to suffer the pathology of that god, but we find ourselves under attack from all the others. However, if we worship Hermes as one god among others, as his myth insists we do, we can find in a Hermes-consciousness the flexibility and inventiveness that may yet save us from the catastrophe to which our excessive faith in Apollo and Prometheus seems to have condemned us. The god of transformation, paradox, and ambiguity is unraveling a pattern of thinking and behavior that was, in its arrogant assertion of its own absolute truth, destroying the world. We have to be on the watch that the Trickster god does not lead us into a path that is just as destructive

Over the past century the taken-for-granted truths of the scientific-industrial age have been subjected to challenges they cannot answer, as we spiral down through operational doubt, ideological doubt, and ethical doubt towards absolute doubt in the core assumptions of our culture. The nihilism of some postmodern thinkers seems like a manifestation of absolute doubt. If we have no basis for valuing anything over anything else, they say, if we have no justification for arguing that one perspective is better than another, then nothing is to be valued or believed at all. We can avoid such nihilism by insisting that all values are to be valued, that truth is found in the aperspectival acknowledgement of all these limited perspectives, just as Hermes demonstrates that all the gods are to be worshipped.

Unfortunately, we have to learn again how to be polytheistic, how to acknowledge all the squabbling gods together rather than take sides and join in the fight. When the one god lets us down we tend to redirect all our worship to another. We must resist the impulse to return to a fundamentalist Zeus consciousness, or return to the monotheistic worship of Apollo or Prometheus, or even to the monotheistic worship of Gaia/Maia that the deep ecologists would promote; we must honestly worship all the gods together – Aphrodite and Athena, Ares and Eros, Demeter and Dionysos, Hera and Hestia, Persephone and Poseidon – to accept all their truths, to honor all their values, and to put up with their constant squabbling.

Guide to the Underworld

The notion of change consultancy that we have developed in this book is constructed and narrated within the fantasy of Hermes.

Hermes is probably the god whom consultants worship most devoutly. He is, of course, the god of transformation. He is the god who subverts the established order of things, who unfreezes what is frozen so as to make change possible. On top of that, he is the god who creates visions (and illusions), who insinuates himself into places (like smoke under the door), does his magic and leaves. He is, as the god of the free market, happy to sell himself to whoever wants to buy. He spends a lot of time and energy marketing himself. He thrives on images. He facilitates; he makes things easy. He gets a kick out of seduction. He is just passing through. The profession is solidly enmeshed in the health and pathology of the Hermes archetype.

Hermes' skills and inventiveness and his lack of concern for his own status and dignity made him in a particular way the god of servants. He was quite happy to act the servant, not only of Zeus but of all the Olympian gods. It is an image that sits well with the profession of a consultant. Consultants who are really interested in facilitating the process of their client organizations depend on a Hermes consciousness to do it. Consultants are rarely thrust into the role of heroes. If they were, they might well invoke Athena or Herakles to assist them. Sometimes, they are paid to be soothsayers, to proclaim the hitherto hidden truth. In matters of truth and prophecy, they need to invoke Apollo. Most often, however, they are contracted to guide an organization across a boundary (psychological, structural, or economic), without too much disturbing those who contracted them. If they wish to appear to be diligent servants they need to pray to Hermes for his gifts of plausibility, cunning, and luck, while pretending to be independent, logical, and knowledgeable in the advice they give.

The myth and personality of Hermes give us many images that we can develop in exploring the role of the organizational consultant or change agent. There is Hermes the Persuader, Hermes the Magician, Hermes the Bringer of Dreams, Hermes the Trickster, Hermes the Seducer, Hermes the Messenger, Hermes the Protector of Travelers, Hermes the Speedster, Hermes the Cowboy, Hermes the Energizer, Hermes the Transformer, Hermes the Connector, Hermes the Healer, Hermes the Spy, Hermes the Keeper of Secrets, Hermes the Border-crosser, Hermes the Inventor, not to mention Hermes the Confidence Man, and Hermes the Gambler. The particular Hermes image we want to amplify here is that of Guide to the Underworld.

In the model of organizational consulting and change agency that we have been expounding in this book, the consultant's task is to facilitate the organization's 'individuation' at whatever level this process is in motion. When we talk about levels of organizational consciousness in Gebser's language, or explore Lundberg's artifacts-perspectives-values-assumptions model of organizational culture or Sherwood's normative procedures-beliefs-myths model, or use Jung's or Freud's language to talk about the unconscious of the organization, we are imagining organizations via a metaphor of height and depth.[14]

Depth is where Hades dwells, and it is where the depth-oriented consultant takes the awareness of the organization and brings it back. Hermes is the only god who is able to visit Hades, the only god who can cross the border between light and darkness, between life and death.

There are a number of aspects of this visit to Hades (who in Greek mythology is both a person and a place) as far as the consultant and client are concerned.

One is the visit to Hades as the site of the unconscious dimensions of organizational life: the archaic undifferentiated belongingness that submerges the individual in a larger self and the instincts (such as fight and flight) that generate impulsive action; the magic rites ritually performed to keep the organization safe; the mythical narratives in which the organization's core assumptions about itself are enmeshed.

A second is the visit to Hades as the site of doubt – operational, ideological, ethical, or absolute – in the organization. Hades is the places where the organization is lost, confused, and depressed.

A third is the visit to Hades as the site of death and new life in the organization, to discover what in the organization is dying and what is about to be born. (Hades, the god of death, identified with Dionysos, the god of new life.)

Fourth is the visit to Hades as the shadow of the organization, all the aspects of the organization that contradict the organization's image of itself.

Fifth is the visit to Hades as the world on the 'other side', the hidden and unknown world outside the sunlit world of the organization's consensus reality, the secrets carried by the marginalized people in the organization.

All in all, visiting Hades is a risky business, but Hermes is the god of risk-taking. The point of the journey, of course, is to bring the client organization back from the Underworld and together examine what we have found in the clear light of Apollo's sun. But Hermes is only interested in the journey. The substance of what the organization finds and brings back is for other gods to bother about. It is not even wise to count on Hermes to bring the client back. He does not promise a two-way trip. His role is to guide the soul to Hades. He may be content to leave it there.

The consultant's Hermes-consciousness and Hermes-energy will take the process just so far: to put the organization in touch with the unconscious, imaginal, irrational, instinctual dimensions of its existence. If the client organization is to be supported in the process, if it is to understand and articulate what it has learned and take purposive and productive action, other gods have to be present.

Jung demonstrated in his writings that in the personal psyche there is drive towards 'individuation' – a dynamic that strives to resolve the polarity between the unconscious and conscious aspects of the self. Maslow's researches uncovered further evidence of an instinctual tendency towards what he called 'self-actualization'. Rogers became convinced through his research and practice as a therapist that our growth is shaped by a 'formative tendency'. The wide acceptance of the image of the organization as a living organism in recent management literature shows a growing conviction that organizations show the same sort of tendency. As long as people's observations of organizations were shaped by the metaphor of the machine, they simply did not detect this tendency, but it is now possible to see that organizations are self-organizing, nonlinear, open systems like plants and animals. Change is 'self-generating'. From within this different metaphor, it is obvious that organizations have within themselves an 'individuating', 'actualizing', 'self-organizing', or 'formative' tendency. They have, in Goldstein's words:

> . . . [their] own capacity for transformation, requiring only the right conditions for activation. That is, nonlinear systems have locked up within their nonlinearity a tendency towards change, growth, and development. This innate potential is similar to how an entire oak tree is contained in an acorn and only requires the right conditions to emerge. In fact, nonlinear systems are essentially evolving systems, transforming into greater and greater complexity.[15]

This is the metaphor of Maia/Gaia, where Hermes is most happily active. Hermes has many, many titles, but he does not appear anywhere to have the title of Teacher, Preacher, Carer, Director, Builder, Engineer, or Action Man, and he is no fan of hard work. The Hermes way to organizational transformation is more playful. If the images are activated, if the flow of information is not inhibited, if the connections are established, if nonlinear systems are unlocked, if the boundaries are explored, if power and role and status are set aside, if belief is relativized (including the belief that change is the only constant), if doubt is acknowledged (including doubt about the messages of Hermes), if ambiguity and paradox are welcomed, if the bonds are loosened, if marginal people are included and listened to, if delight is expressed, then something happens. What that something will be is unpredictable, but we can watch out for Hermes' trickery and count on Hermes' luck. And if we want that something to be productive, we will not let our infatuation with Hermes blind us to the need to worship all the gods, including the gods of rational structure, social stability, purposeful action, and inner focus.

Finally

We are currently in Hermes' territory, at the borderline of the unknown. There are several scenarios depicting the world we will find across that border.

One story is that nuclear weapons, exploding population, the irreversible pollution of our air and water and food, the greenhouse effect, the inevitable degradation of our soils, the regression to technologically enhanced tribalism, the proliferation of genetically mutated diseases and sundry other products of the Promethean Age will destroy us. If one of them does not get us, the others will.

There is another story about how globalization, a free market, and unregulated competition will eventually make everyone happy, healthy, and prosperous.

Another story is that genetic engineering, nanotechnology, information technology, and similar devices of Prometheus will save us from destruction and make the world a better place.

Another story is that we will be transformed by the insight that we are all cells of our mother Gaia, abandon our egocentric and anthropocentric assumptions, and learn to live in harmony with ourselves and Nature.

There is a story, too, about how an autocratic and totalitarian planetary government will be established as the only way to save us from ourselves.

Another story is that Zeus will decide that he has had enough of our sinful ways and smite us all with an asteroid.

Lastly there is the story that our species is being born into a higher order of consciousness, and that the current catastrophes which threaten us represent the pains of this new birth.

Our magical consciousness may have us casting spells to make us safe. Our mythical consciousness may have us accepting one or more of the above scripts as inexorably true and offering prayers to science or the market to ensure that it turns out well for us. Our rational consciousness will have us examining the evidence to see if it really supports any of these scenarios and setting out to solve the problems we have made for ourselves.

When Gebser tells us that while we are standing uneasily on this borderline between an unsatisfactory past and a threatening future, as rational consciousness disintegrates and a 'new factor' emerges which may enable us to avoid disaster, it sounds as though he is just telling us another story. In a sense he is. We cannot avoid being in one fantasy or another. Gebser's theory has its own mythical grounding; it is a way of imagining the universe – what it is, how it works, where we fit in it. Yet Gebser's story is about transcending the ways we imagine the world through our mythical consciousness and the incomplete truths we construct through our rational consciousness. If we can transcend these limited ways of experiencing, then reality will become transparent to us in its 'wholeness'.

The 'new factor' he writes about is the capacity to experience reality integrally, not framed in a particular story in the manner of Apollo and the other gods, but in all their stories, in the manner of Hermes. Gebser was very much aware of the limitations of the perspectival thinking which marks our various theories and histories of the future. What he claimed to detect is an emerging capacity to think aperspectivally, to see things from all directions at once, a capacity to experience the universe as whole, rather than through its various fragments. The story he is telling is different from the stories of modern science, as Hermes' world is different from the worlds of the other gods.

The capacity to think *aperspectivally*, *arationally*, and *wholistically* is not something we achieve through some sort of personal heroic struggle. Gebser argues that it is ever-present in the nature of things and is now emerging in the collective consciousness of the species. To use the language of the physicist, David Bohm, it is the 'implicate' order becoming 'explicate'.[16] The capacity for integral experience is not something to be achieved but something already there and waiting to be elicited.

Western culture both accepts and rejects the new reality, and in this tension there is a great deal of confusion and trauma. It is a hundred years since Planck and Einstein argued that we must abandon our notion that time is continuous and linear and quantifiable. It is almost as long since Bohr and Schrodinger articulated the principle that opposites are not contradictory but complementary, and since Whitehead argued that the Universe is made not of matter but of creativity. Long before people started to theorize about postmodernity, twentieth century science, art, literature, and film had begun to explore a reality that is not constrained by quantified space and time or by Apollinine notions of logic, a reality in which all our statements of truth are conditional and partial, and everything is connected. However, we keep returning to older and simpler ways of thinking. We know that our environment is permeated by toxic substances that our senses cannot detect, yet we are only stirred to act on this when we can see or smell them. We know that there are aspects of social life that cannot be directly seen or smelt or measured or costed – love, compassion, justice, altruism, and the rest – but we let our governments behave as though only those things that can be measured and costed exist. We know that humanity is not the center of the universe, nor even of the planet, yet we act as though everything exists only for our use. We have a great deal of trouble thinking in a proper rational manner which observes all the evidence critically, comes to logical conclusions, and acts accordingly. We uncritically go along with the consensus reality, immersed in trance, magic, and the myth that we are thinking and behaving rationally.

When we act collectively, we experience even greater difficulty in behaving truly rationally. We are generally able to set aside facts that would discredit the myth that gives our nation or organization its identity. Our myth tells us that we are entitled to a certain 'quality of life'; the evidence is that our lifestyle is creating conditions that will make life unlivable for our grandchildren. Even if we accept the evidence, we stick to our lifestyle, for our story still assures us that everything will turn out all right in the long run. The evidence may point to the conclusion that our company is involved in mining, manufacturing, or farming processes that add substantially to environmental degradation, yet our myth tells us that we are making a better world. We manage both to acknowledge the evidence and live by the myth. Our organizational myth may tell us that the specific work we do for public health, education, or welfare makes people healthier, happier, more powerful, or whatever. If the evidence shows that our activity does not make much difference, or may even make things worse, few of us will prefer to act on the evidence. In this often unacknowledged conflict between our mythical and rational knowing we are in a state of liminality, of 'in-betweenness', the domain of Hermes. This state of doubt – suspended, operational, or ideological - makes us both vulnerable to disintegration and open to transformation.

Whether or not Gebser is credible in his observations of the particular direction our consciousness evolution is going, some sort of transformation of our consciousness at the individual and collective level appears to be urgently necessary if we are to survive. Our organizations are key sites for such change.

1. J Gebser (1949) *The Ever Present Origin*, p. xxvii.
2. See for instance M McLuhan *Understanding Media* (1965); F Capra, (1982) *The Turning Point*; J Lyotard (1983) *The Postmodern Condition*; J. Gleick (1988) *Chaos: Making a New Science*; J R Saul (1992) *Voltaire's Children*; WI Thompson (1991) *Gaia 2*.
3. See for instance P Drucker (1993) *Post-capitalist Society*; C Handy (1989) *The Age of Unreason*; T Peters (1994) The *Tom Peters Seminar*; JH Boyett and H P Conn (1992) *Workplace* 2000.
4. A Athanassakis (trans. and ed.) *The Homeric Hymns*, p. 31: 13-16.
5. The first recorded instance of 'value-added production'?
6. A Athanassakis, ibid., p. 47: 576-8.
7. ibid., p. 19: 132.
8. ibid., p. 35: 166-175.
9. For a discussion of the use of language in 'fast capitalist' texts, see JP Gee & C Lankshear (1995) 'The New Work Order: Critical Language Awareness and "Fast Capitalism" Texts' in Discourse: *Studies in the Cultural Politics of Education*, 16(1).
10. We find the same phenomenon in the dogmatism of many poststructuralist writers.
11. It was Hermes who persuaded Prometheus that he could end his torture by giving Zeus the secret of how to maintain his power forever - by sharing it with the other gods.
12. T Peters (1992) *Liberation Management*, p. 15f.
13. R Lopez-Pedraza (1977) *Hermes and All His Children*, p. 8.
14. Gebser himself tries to avoid the metaphor of depth in discussing consciousness. He prefers the metaphor of intensity.
15. Goldstein (1994) *The Unshackled Organization*, p. 12.
16. See D Bohm (1980) *Wholeness and the Implicate Order*.

APPENDIX 1

A TOOLBOX FOR CHANGE AGENTS

INTERVENTIONS FOR CULTURAL TRANSFORMATION

In the first chapter of this book we outlined five guiding ideas that would frame our discussion of organizational culture:

> Contemporary organizations exist in a postmodern world.
> Organizational behavior has unconscious components.
> Patterns of behavior in organizations are archetypal.
> The whole organization is more than the sum of its parts.
> Intentional cultural change is unpredictable.

The same guiding ideas frame our discussion of the kind of interventions external consultants or in-house change agents might use for intentional cultural change in an organization. We hope that the interventions we describe here will not be read as recipes for successful intervention, however that is imagined. We certainly hope they will not be adopted as idiot-proof techniques. Idiot-proof techniques belong to magic consciousness, and magical techniques are of limited value in a modern organization, let alone a postmodern one. We believe that effective future-oriented intervention in the kind of organizational world we now inhabit not only demands a degree of integral consciousness in the change agent, but requires a style of intervention which invites the members of the organization individually and collectively to full engagement with the process.

The interventions described below are designed to seek what is unconscious in the organization and bring it into awareness so that it can be reflected on and integrated with thought and action. Some of these exercises will be confrontative, in that they will unfold aspects of the organizational culture that people don't particularly want to know about. People's response to them will sometimes be highly emotional. Such interventions are not likely to be productive unless there is an adequate level of trust in the group and adequately open communication. The change agent may need to do some work on trust and openness before leading the group into the underworld.

These interventions are based on our understanding that organizations are self-organizing systems. Self-organization is a process in which chance plays a major part. It is therefore unpredictable. We cannot anticipate the outcomes and, strictly speaking, cannot plan them. In the self-organizing model, planning is not something that takes place before an intervention, where we set out the desired outcomes and arrange the means to achieve them. Rather, planning has to set up the conditions for spontaneous adjustment to changing (and sometimes chance) conditions. The change comes from within the organization. Indeed, movement towards change is a basic property of a self-organizing system. The change agent's task is to disturb the energies that go into holding the organization in a false equilibrium – not to force or manipulate change but to provide freedom to change.

These interventions are structured to invite the participants to move from an embeddedness in image, narrative, and feeling and the third order thinking through which it is conceptualized, to critically-reflective, fourth order thinking. We are not implying in this structure that thought is superior to image and feeling, but that it is grounded in image and feeling. For us, the critically reflective thought that is a manifestation of the mental-rational structure of consciousness is not the endpoint of this process. We suggest that a full understanding does not come from leaving image, narrative, and feeling behind, but from integrating them with critical thought in a sense of the whole that does not stop at the assumed boundaries of the organization. Moving the organization onward demands image, narrative, and feeling at least as much as it demands rational analysis. Moving it onward in a direction that is sensitive to the larger world demands the aperspectival sense of the whole that comes with integral consciousness.

1. Working with Dreams

Dreams belong to the mythical structure of consciousness. If we want to learn how our unconscious mind is dealing with our experience, the exploration of our dreams is one way of doing this.

Both Freud and Jung worked hard to persuade people to take dreams seriously. Though there is a great deal in common in the way they approached their patients' dreams, there is one key difference. Freud believed that in dreams our unconscious mind is hiding behind images. Jung believed that in dreams our unconscious mind is revealing itself through images. As a result, Freud's approach was based on analysis and interpretation. The analyst is in the role of an expert who listens to the dream and then explains the meaning of its symbols. By contrast, Jung's approach was based on amplification. The analyst is in the role of a companion who joins the dreamer in exploring all the possible meanings of the dream until the dreamer finds a meaning that resonates strongly with her experience. For the Freudian analyst, dream symbols have specific and universal meanings, which the analyst knows and explains to the dreamer. For the Jungian analyst, the symbolism of a particular dream image will be different for each dreamer, though it will be grounded in culture and archetype. Accordingly, the 'real meaning' of the dream is what is felt by the dreamer in exploring the dream, not a meaning attributed to it by an analyst.

There is not space here for a full discussion of a theory of dreams, but it is necessary to say something of the kind of thinking behind our own work with dreams. There is an extensive literature on dreaming, which can be consulted by those interested in pursuing the subject.[1]

The conventional understanding of dreams is that they are personal and private. There is certainly a personal and private aspect of dreams, but there is also a collective one. The notion that dreams are our individual property is one that is widely shared in Western individualistic culture, but if we move outside the assumptions of this culture we find that in many other cultures dreams are understood very differently. Dreams are not something an individual 'has'; rather the dreamworld is a world that is there all the time, and which the individual occasionally enters. Dreams do not speak to the individual but to the tribe. It makes just as much sense to say that 'the world is dreaming' and that as individuals we become conscious of this dream in sleep, dressed in our own particular images, as it is to say that dreams are dreamed by separate, encapsulated individuals. Our sense of separate identity is a characteristic of our rational consciousness. In our magic-mythical consciousness we share a collective identity.

The collective nature of dreaming becomes apparent when dreamwork in done in groups which either have an ongoing connection or are currently sharing an intense group experience. It is apparent, for instance, when a group of people from an organization are spending a week together on retreat, focusing on issues critical to the organization. If a daily 'dream workshop' is included in the program, we find after a couple of days that not only are the participants dreaming and recalling their dreams, and not only do these dreams appear to be about issues confronting the group as a whole, but that the participants are beginning to 'share' dreams, finding common themes and even common images. At the level of our mythical consciousness we are more closely connected than we generally recognize.

Our approach to dreamwork follows Jung's lead rather than Freud's. It is also shaped by our need to work in groups in a way that involves the entire group as participants. We do not engage in 'dream analysis'. We prefer to follow Ullman's lead and call this kind of work 'dream appreciation'.[2] In the group we take the role of leader, but not the role of expert. As leader we focus on guiding the process of the group, but not the content. We want the participants to listen to each other; to respect each other's contributions to the discussion; to feel supported if they are fragile or anxious. We encourage clarification and deter argument; we acknowledge all contributions as potentially valuable; and we provide a clear structure for discussion and a clear expectation of an outcome. This structure may not be the best of all ways to run a dream workshop, but it is manageable and it demands neither magical skills nor exceptional wisdom. It is set out as a series of steps, but neither the number nor order of these steps is unchangeable.

Steps in Group Dream Appreciation

1. The dreamer tells the dream. It is best to do this in the present tense.

    I am walking down a road that seems familiar. My sister is walking beside me, but I cannot see her face. There is a bucket in the middle of the road . . .

2. Ask the dreamer to remain silent while each member of the group says in one word what they feel the dream is about.

    This is a dream about . . .

3. When the dreamer has heard all of these, ask him to say

    This is a dream about . . .

4. Ask the dreamer specific questions about the content of the dream..

    What sort of landscape does the road run through?
    How do you know it is your sister?
    How big is the bucket? Is there anything in it?

5. Invite the other members of the group to ask similar questions, relating only to what happens in the dream – not to what they think it might mean.

    How are you feeling as you walk beside your sister?
    Does the road run uphill or downhill?

6. Encourage the dreamer to explore the associations that the dream images have for him, i.e. the people, things or events that the dream images remind him of.

    Tell me about your sister?
    My sister is five years older than me. She is a very shy person . . .
    Tell me about the road?
    The road reminds me of the road to my aunt's place at Ballarat. We used to go there for holidays when we were little . . .

Tell me about the bucket?

It's like the bucket we used to use to feed the horse at my aunt's place . . .

7. Invite the other group members to explore their own associations for the dream images.

The sister reminds me of the painting in the foyer at head office.

The road reminds me about a song about a country road.

The bucket in the middle of the road reminds me of having to shift the kids' toys off the drive before I drove my car into the garage when I got home the other night.

8. Encourage the dreamer to explore the images as metaphors.

What might your sister be a metaphor for?

The feminine . . . relationship . . . shyness . . .

What might a road be a metaphor for?

Going somewhere . . . the journey of life . . . having a sense of direction . . .

What might a bucket be a metaphor for?

Containing something . . . carrying something . . . putting out fire . . .

9. Invite the other group members to explore the images as metaphors.

Walking beside your sister might represent the masculine and feminine aspects of your personality.

Your sister not having a face might represent that the feminine part of your personality is not able to show itself, not even to you.

The bucket might be connected with 'bucketing' someone or 'being bucketed'. It might be in the middle of the road because somehow this is standing in your way.

[The images have specific and personal meaning (It is your sister, a particular road), and also a collective meaning (sisters and roads have meaning which we all share). They may also have shared meanings in the culture of the organization. (A shared experience of 'bucketing', a particular focus on 'sisterhood', a reference to a particular corporate icon.) All the images are likely to have multiple meanings, and they may all be relevant to the dreamer. Dreams, like poems and paintings, are complex statements. You do not have to interpret the dream for the dreamer. If you keep amplifying the images (looking for more and more meanings rather than settling for one 'correct' meaning), the dreamer will find the meaning that 'feels right' and makes most sense.]

10. Ask about the context of the dream.

> *Can you remember what happened the day before you had this dream?*
> *What was going on in your life at the time you had this dream?*

[Assume that the dream will always contain something (in content or image) that refers to the previous day's experience.]

11. Invite the dreamer to narrate the dream again, telling it slowly in present time. Invite the other group members to imagine the dream along with the narrator, as if it is their dream and they are dreaming it.

12. Invite all the group members to put into words the feeling of the dream.

13. Examine the dream images as psychological projections of the dreamer.

> *What part of your personality might be represented by your sister? (the road? the bucket?)*
> *What is this part of you saying in the dream?*

[The dreamer's personality is represented by the whole dream. The 'I' in the dream is just that part of the personality that the dreamer finds it easiest to identify with.]

14. Invite the other group members to answer these same questions, as if it is their dream.

15. Help the dreamer to integrate the images of the dream by looking at how the images relate to each other.

> *What is your sister saying to you in the dream (whether she is actually talking or not)?*
> *What is the bucket saying to you, or doing to/for you?*
> *What is the road saying to your sister?*

16. Invite the other group members to answer similar questions as if it is their dream.

17. Come back to the dreamer's original sense of the dream, and check it against what the dreamer now feels the dream is about.

18. Explore whether the dream is making a general statement about life, and not merely a personal statement about the life of the dreamer. Remember that what the

dream says is essentially 'This is the way it is right now'. Or rather 'These are the ways it is right now'.

Is the dream saying something about the organization?

This whole process can be carried out without the facilitator making a single 'interpretation'. If the facilitator feels clever enough to suggest that particular images are grounded in particular archetypal patterns, or in the myth of a particular god, this is an option, but it is by no means necessary. The images don't have to 'stand for' anything, and we don't have to be eager to translate them into ideas. At the end of this process the dreamer and the group may have a strong sense of what the dream is saying without much ability to put it into words. It is important that the facilitator and participants do not succumb to the temptation to close off the dream with a single 'interpretation', and reduce it to a single meaning.

When a group is exploring dreams for the first time together, the dreams presented are likely to be personal. If a group meets regularly, the content and imagery of the dreams will become more of a shared experience, and people's dreams will begin to flow into each other. If the dreamwork is done within the context of an organization examining its own functioning, this will have a major influence on the content and imagery of the dreams presented. The associations participants find for the dream images will increasingly come from the organizational context

2. Exploring Incongruence

There is often a gap between what we think we believe and the ways we feel and behave. At the organizational level we talk about the clash between espoused theory and theory in use. At the personal level we call it incongruence or, if we are focusing on the belief level, we call it cognitive dissonance. We are inclined to view this sort of inconsistency as a 'bad thing' and accordingly we are reluctant to see it in ourselves and we get annoyed and defensive if someone tries to point it out to us. This is true of organizations as it is of individuals. We want it to stay unconscious. However, an exploration of incongruence or dissonance is an ideal starting point for personal or organizational transformation.

The following exercise is designed to bring into awareness the incongruence between people's espoused theories of leadership and their theories in use. It takes the form of a workbook, which the participants are required to complete prior to discussion. The structure and sequence of the questions they complete combined with the guided process of interaction which follows are designed to overcome one of the dilemmas associated with using processes of this sort. We are all programmed to avoid examining our theories in use. Moreover, we create group behavior patterns that reinforce this programming in ourselves and others, and we find ourselves locked in by our own behavior and the behavior of the group. This exercise begins with each participant reflecting in private on some occasion when she has been dissatisfied with her own performance, and documenting it. This critical reflection enables her to detach herself from the taken-for-grantedness of her theory in use and prepares her to hear feedback from her colleagues without defensiveness.

Inquiry into Effective Leadership: a Workbook[3]

The purpose of this exercise is to help you enquire into your ways of functioning as a leader, and the congruence between your theory of effective leadership and your actual behavior in a specific situation. With the help of the other members of your group you will articulate what you expect of yourself as a leader, and examine ways to make your experience of leadership more satisfying.

Individual Phase

Work through the following steps on your own.

1. Identify an incident in which your behavior as a leader was for some reason unsatisfying for you. It may be an incident in which you were unsure of your role, or when you experienced yourself as less effective than you might have been, or when you did something that you now perceive as unhelpful or inappropriate.

2. Write down some of the context of this incident. Describe the setting, who was involved, how you and your staff/colleagues behaved, what the outcome was.

3. Describe your intentions and objectives in the incident, and how you tried to achieve them.

4. In the two columns below, write a few paragraphs of the dialogue that took place. In the left hand column write down your interior dialogue, what was going on in your mind at the time: your thoughts, your feelings, your reactions. In the right hand column write down what you and the other person or people actually did and said.

INTERNAL DIALOGUE	EXTERNAL DIALOGUE

5. Read what you have written in these pages, then write down the assumptions you were apparently making in this incident about what makes for effective leadership. Try to look at what you have written as if you were a disinterested observer asking:

- What does all this say about this person's idea of effective leadership?
- What leadership principles does this person appear to be guided by?

Group Phase

With your group, work through the following steps.

Outline what you have written in steps 1–5. Other group members may ask questions for clarification. Do not get involved in debate or discussion about the content of the problem.

Listen without comment while the other members of your group act as consultants, discussing possible reasons for your perceived lack of effectiveness. In particular, they will address the following questions:

- What seem to be the main elements in this person's approach to leadership?
- What seem to be the consequences of such an approach in this instance?
- Consequences for the leader?
- Consequences for others?
- What values is the leader trying to uphold?
- How effective is the leader's behavior in upholding these values?
- Is there any incongruence between the values the leader seems to hold and his/her actual behavior?

Engage in dialogue with group members with the aim of clarifying for yourself what your theory of effective leadership is. This will involve reflecting on what you perceive as effective leadership, what values and principles this notion of leadership is founded on, and what you expect of yourself as a leader. It will also involve considering what kind of behavior would have been more satisfactory in this instance, and what skills you might need to develop in order to enhance the quality of your leadership. Write down your conclusions.

The quality of group functioning in this phase is crucial. The team is involved in a supportive and confronting dialogue with the enquirer, which seeks to help her to come to an understanding of the difference between her espoused theory and her theory in use. It does this in order to help the enquirer learn, to help her gain insight into the conditions under which her defenses and her theory in use inhibit her effectiveness and satisfaction. (The facilitator may have to intervene from time to time to coach the participants in the role of consultant.) This process of dialogue and support continues until the enquirer is satisfied that she has gained some insight into the incongruence between her behavior and ideals that has generated her dissatisfaction. The team is then encouraged to reflect on the experience of the enquirer and draw some generalized learnings from it. They are asked to review the process that they used to engage with the enquirer and find ways to improve it for the next person who takes on the enquirer role.

3. Art in the Service of Understanding

The visual and tactile arts provide an avenue to our unconscious. The following exercise employs crayons or pastels, but we could just as easily invite people to model with clay or plasticene, to cut and paste a collage, or to make a junk sculpture.[4]

Ask the group members to reflect briefly on questions like the following. (You might ask them to visualize a conversation with a curious anthropologist from another planet in which they hear and respond to these questions.)

- What is the purpose of this organization?
- What are the organization's greatest assets?
- How well does this organization do what it sets out to do?
- How does this organization treat its people?
- Who are the key people in this organization?
- Why do you remain a member of this organization?

- What tensions or contradictions do you see in this organization?
- How do you feel when you are thinking about the organization as you are doing now?

Distribute paper and pastels.

> Ask the participants to draw the organization in a way that expresses some of these thoughts and their feelings about them. Request them to do this without showing their drawing to anyone else or discussing it with anyone. Tell them that the group will have an opportunity to look at their drawing but they will not be identified.
>
> When the drawings are finished collect them and then distribute them randomly to the participants so that they each have a drawing in front of them.
>
> Ask them to imagine that they have drawn the particular drawing they have in front of them. Ask them to reflect on what they were thinking and feeling when they were doing this drawing.
>
> Each participant will now explain the meaning of the drawing as though it is their own work. They will maintain the role of the artist and answer any questions the group may ask about 'their' drawing.

In interpreting another person's drawing participants will tend to project their own beliefs and feelings into it, including beliefs and feeling which they are not inclined to admit to in themselves. It is much obviously much easier to be honest about perceptions and feelings about the organization when we are pretending to be some other anonymous person, especially if we have something critical or confrontative to say. However, this is not the only advantage to dealing with the drawings in this way. If the group members make a genuine attempt to identify empathically with the artist whose work they are claiming as their own, the exercise will serve to develop group consciousness and cohesion, and shared but unspoken assumptions about the organization and the participants' relation to it will emerge. If the artists listen to the interpretation of their drawings without rejecting notions that were not in their heads when they were drawing them, they may become aware of alternative voices within themselves.

4. Scanning[5]

Scanning involves using a stimulus word or phrase to evoke a series of images, without inhibiting the flow of images by reflecting on them or evaluating them. In the context of the exploration of an organization's culture, we might use the name of the organization as a stimulus word, or use such words and phrases as Things I like (don't like) about this company, Being frustrated, or Job satisfaction.

Scanning is best done with a partner, who undertakes to listen attentively without commenting.

- Ask the participants to sit in pairs facing each other, keeping eye contact as far as is possible. It is desirable that they hold hands or, if this is too uncomfortable for them, maintain some sort of minimal physical contact.
- Explain that scanning involves allowing images to emerge from our memory by using a stimulus, and waiting passively. It does not involve trying to produce images. And it does not involve thinking about them.
- Talk them through the exercise.

I want one of you to be the scanner; the other will listen with full attention, but will not comment until the scanning is completed.

The scanner should sit quietly . . . relax . . . let your mind go blank.

Now repeat the stimulus phrase **Things I like about this organization** aloud several times . . . Wait and see what images come up. When you get an image, tell your partner what it is. Then repeat the phrase again and wait for another image.

Do not TRY. Do not THINK. Do not EXPLAIN. Just report the images you get. The images do not have to make sense to you.

If no image comes up, just keep repeating the phrase and be receptive to whatever emerges.

After three minutes tell them to stop scanning and discuss with their partner whatever they feel needs explaining or expanding.

The partners then swap roles and repeat the procedure

Some people find it extremely difficult to relinquish control and adopt this passive and receptive attitude, but it is essential if we want to access our unconscious knowledge. As long as we are thinking in the conventional sense we are restricting ourselves to information that is already familiar to us. Scanning, by contrast, can surprise us with contents that we have forgotten or suppressed. However, to do it productively, we have to give up our habits of thinking – no words, no ideas, no analysis, no evaluation, only pictures. It may be necessary to give participants practice on an easier stimulus (e.g. Places I've been) before presenting them with more loaded stimulus phrases.

5. The Organizational Atom

This psychodramatic technique provides a way of looking at the relationships between elements of a person's organizational world.[6]

Explain that you wish to explore the organizational culture by examining one person's organizational world, through the image of the nucleus of an atom surrounded by electrons in energetic relationship to it. When you have a volunteer protagonist, ask her to stand in the middle of the room and reflect on what are the key elements of the organization as they affect her. They may be particular people, structural elements (Head Office, a particular department or branch) entities outside the organization (a funding body, an accrediting agency), even objects (a building, a corporate icon, a key document).

Facilitator: *Sally, imagine yourself at the center of this organizational world looking around at the people and things that have most impact on your life in this organization. You are going to select a number of these and examine the way you relate to them. Which one will we start with?*

Sally: *Head Office.*

Facilitator: *Look around this group and choose someone who can stand in for head office. (Jake is selected and comes forward.) Jake, you are now Head Office. Sally will give you your script. (Sally is asked what message she feels she gets from Head Office.)*

Sally: *We don't know you exist.*

(Jake, as Head Office, is asked to repeat this statement to Sally.)[7]

Jake: *We don't know you exist.*

Facilitator: *There's no need to reply to that now, Sally. What is another person or part of this organization that has a strong impact on the way you experience the organization?*

Sally: *Julie.*

Facilitator: *Select someone to stand in for Julie. (If Julie is present in the group it is better to select some one else to represent her.) Naomi is selected and comes forward.*

Sally, what message do you get from Julie, whether she actually says it in words or not?

Sally: *I enjoy working with you.*

(Naomi becomes Julie and repeats this line to Sally. This process continues until Sally is satisfied that the most important dynamics in her experience of the organization are represented and she is surrounded by a circle of group members in various roles.)

Facilitator: *Now I want you to look around this organization as you've represented it here. Move people around a bit. Place them closer to you or further from you according to how strongly they impact on your life in this organization.*

(Sally does this and returns to the center.)

Now they are all going to say something to you and I'd like you to reply to each one.

(Indicate when each is to speak, beginning at the person furthest from Sally and ending with the closest. Each repeats the statement given them by Sally.)

Head Office: *We don't know you exist.*

Sally: *That's a pity. It's your loss.*

Julie: I like working with you.

Sally: I like working with you to, but I'm worried that you're so stressed.

A key client: Why can't you people get your act together?

Sally: I'm just as frustrated as you are.

The corporate logo: I expect a bit more respect from you.

Sally: I think you're ridiculous.

After this exploration of Sally's organizational world the participants will need to be de-roled before beginning discussion. We suggest that after this kind of exercise discussion should be structured in four stages.

1. Sally sits silently while the other members of the group share what they find in common between their experience of the group and Sally's.

   - What elements in Sally's portrayal resonate most strongly with your experience of the organization?
   - The facilitator ensures that the discussion stays with the sharing of experience, and does not turn to analysis or critique.

2. Sally talks briefly about her own experience of engaging in this exercise.

   - Were there any surprises for you in what you found yourself saying? Do you feel you've left anything unfinished?

3. The other participants in turn talk about their experience of the exercise.

   - How did you experience yourself as Head Office in your brief conversation with Sally?

4. General group discussion.

- Does everyone experience the organization the way Sally does? What appears to be going on in this organization? What do you feel are the key unspoken issues in this organization? Does it have to be like this? Are there any self-fulfilling prophecies evident here? What would have to happen for it to change? How would the people in Head Office represent the organization if they were invited to do this exercise?

As time allows, this exercise should be conducted with several members of the group, so that shared consciousness can be acknowledged and alternative voices can be heard. This exercise, like other interventions in this chapter, is not designed to reduce diverse experiences to a single, static truth, but to uncover the complexities and contradictions that are hidden behind the organization's theory of itself. We suggest that change is impeded by simple truths and generated by complex ones.

6. The Council of the Gods[8]

This exercise is designed to raise people's awareness of alternative perspectives and alternative voices, which will be present, whether acknowledged or suppressed, in the organization's value system.

Introduce the exercise by speaking briefly about the gods as enduring, cross-cultural patterns of energy and behavior, which are personified in myths. Each god has his/her distinct energy, values, and ethics. In giving examples you may confine yourself to the Greek pantheon or call on other mythologies (Krishna, Wotan, Jahweh, Ahuramazda, Erishkigal, Coyote, the Rainbow Serpent).

Either ask each participant to select a god or distribute the names of gods at random. (Some participants may claim total ignorance of gods, but for the purpose of this exercise you can sum up the key concerns of each god in a couple of sentences.) The participants each make a name label with their god's name on it and sit in a circle, with an empty chair in the centre. They are asked to take on the role of that god, and to take on that god's particular wisdom and particular approach to reality.

After the gods have identified themselves, each participant in turn sits in the center chair and outlines a genuine problem they face in the organization. They then ask the circle of gods for advice on how to deal with it. The gods each answer in their own way, with full confidence in their own wisdom and full assurance that their solution to the problem represents the complete truth about what is important and how things should be done.

Sam: I have a problem with two members of my staff who have had some sort of fight and now seem to hate each other intensely. It's affecting relationships and efficiency in the whole department. What should I do?

Zeus: You're in charge. Tell them exactly what you expect of them and make it quite clear that you won't tolerate this behavior and its effect on the department. Let them know what consequences will follow for them if they continue to disrupt the work of the department.

Eros: Remember that it is love that makes the world go round. You can't let this sort of thing go on. You've got to find a way to bring them together. You should act as conciliator; get them to be open with each other and to trust each other again. If you are an adequate model of how people should treat each other with love and respect, you will find that their behavior will change and the whole department will become a more trusting environment.

Demeter: These people obviously need some tender loving care, and as head of this department it is your responsibility to give it to them – both personally and by making the department a safe and nurturing environment. When they feel personally secure, they won't need to defend themselves and attack each other.

Ares: Your problem is that you are worried about relationships when they are really irrelevant to the efficiency of your department. Set these two up to compete with each other so that the tension between them becomes an asset. If you forgot this lovey-dovey stuff and made the department properly competitive so that everyone was putting their energy into being more productive than everyone else, you'd find this problem would disappear.

Aphrodite: *You obviously don't have enough fun in your department. People are taking things too seriously, and forgetting to enjoy themselves. Forget about relationships and forget about efficiency. Stop putting pressure on people to perform. Let them enjoy the moment, encourage them to follow their bliss, and they'll find beauty in their activities and cease to be bothered with the trivialities you're so worried about.*

And so on. In general discussion after this exercise participants' recollection of the advice they have received from the gods is likely to be fairly selective. It may be useful to discuss what voices are most dominant in people's recollections after the exercise. Do these voices represent how the organization habitually deals with problems? Are there dominant voices in the organization that were not heard in this exercise? Are there voices heard in this exercise that are never heard in the organization? What gods appear to govern the ethics of this organization?

7. Focusing[9]

The technique of 'experiential focusing' is designed to get at our whole 'felt sense' of the world, or of a particular aspect of our world, at the present moment. While it has its origin in experiential psychotherapy it has proved to be a valuable tool for exploring organizational culture. The technique starts with bodily sensation (archaic structure), moves to awareness of felt sense (magic structure), translates this into image (mythical structure) and then into words and ideas (mental-rational structure). It aims to encompass the whole of an experience, keep these three modes of consciousness simultaneously in awareness and totally congruent with each other (integral structure).

Explain that you are going to explore participants' 'felt sense' of the organization or of a particular aspect of it. 'Felt sense' of the organization is different from thoughts about the organization or feelings about it. Our basic experience of the organization is felt in our bodies as something both vague (it is hard to put words to it) and precise (our vague felt sense of this organization is different from our vague felt sense of other organizations). Explain that this exercise requires participants to give up their usual ways of thinking, to avoid putting labels on feelings and to become passively receptive to images.

Ask the participants to get in touch with their sense of the whole organization: how they experience it in their body before they start labeling their feeling about it.

Talk them through the focusing exercise:

Go down into that part of you where you feel joy and anger and such things and get in touch with the way your body responds to the WHOLE of this organization (issue, experience) . . . a sort of vague, fuzzy feeling . . .

Don't do anything with that feeling . . . Just let it be and stay with it . . . the WHOLE of it . . . for a few moments, without giving it a name . . . Let it stay fuzzy . . .

Now, if you wait quietly, you will find that a picture will emerge out of that vague, fuzzy feeling . . . a picture that somehow represents something about that fuzzy feeling . . .

Don't be in a hurry . . . an image will come if you wait patiently . . . When you've got an image just rest with it for a moment . . .

Now go back and forth between that image and your felt sense to check whether they fit perfectly together . . . If they don't quite match, keep going between the image and the felt sense . . . let the image change until it fits just right . . . It doesn't have to make sense to you . . . It just needs to feel right.

When it fits perfectly you'll get a sort of mental 'click' and you'll know you've got it just right . . .

If you don't get the 'click' this time, don't worry. Maybe you'll get it next time.

Focus on the image you have and ask yourself the question 'What is it about this image?' and wait for a reply . . . Don't THINK about it . . . Just wait and you'll get a reply . . . It may be another image, or it may be a word . . .

Check back to the felt sense you feel in your body . . . Has it changed?

Have the participants reflect on this experience in pairs or triads before they join the larger group for discussion.

In discussion, move from the level of image and narrative, at which participants relate their experience and describe their image of the organization, to the level of concept, at which they reflect on these images and attempt to articulate their separate, personally experienced 'truths', to the level of holistic thinking at which they can combine all of these separate (and even contradictory) truths with a new 'felt sense' of the whole.

As with scanning, some participants will find it difficult to abandon the habitual ways of thinking which inhibit the flow of images from their unconscious. It may be necessary to discuss the notion that we know much more than generally comes into our awareness. This includes not only what we have been aware of and forgotten but also knowledge which we have experienced but never reflected on and been aware of 'knowing'. Much of what we know is stored in our brain as image, rather than as words or ideas; when we try to access it as words or ideas we may not be successful. If we allow it to emerge as image we can then translate it into words and ideas, though these may be unable to express all the complexity of meanings contained in the image.

8. Organizational Fairy Tales

This exercise represents an attempt to universalize participants' personal narratives of organizational life by accommodating them to the genre of myth or fairy tale.

If there are more than (say) twelve participants they should be divided into groups of four to six for this exercise.

Ask the participants to reflect for a moment on some incident or event in their experience of the organization that they feel shows something of what sort of organization this is. Suggest it is better to select an incident in which they have been personally involved rather than one that they have simply heard about. It does not need to be an important incident in the life of the organization, but it should have some significance for their own understanding of how the organization works and what it values.

Ask them to write a brief account of this incident. (The writing seems to increase the impact of this exercise.)

When all have finished they read their stories to the group.

Ask them to turn this account into a fairy tale and write it down. (Once again, the writing is important.) This will involve giving the story a setting far, far away and long, long ago. (It should begin with 'Once upon a time ...') It will also involve populating the story with the kind of characters we find in fairy tales: kings and queens, beautiful princesses and handsome princes, wizards and witches, trolls, goblins, elves, dragons, leprechauns, giants, talking trees etc. The story should end in a 'moral' that can be stated in a single sentence.

When they have finished their writing they read their fairy stories to each other.

If participants have been in small groups up to this point bring them together into a single large group to hear at least a number of these fairy stories and their 'morals' and to compare and contrast the perspectives represented.

The sharing of organizational fairy stories places people's personal experience not only in the context of other people's experience of the organization, but also in the context of the universal patterns of human behavior which are represented in the organizational culture. In discussion it is important to focus not only on the meanings which are common in the images presented, but also on the differences between people's experiences of the organization – not to set some images aside as not conforming to consensus reality, but to include them in the appreciation of the whole.

9. Listening to Deviant Voices[10]

Deviations from the status quo within systems can be the source of new beginnings. Management has to be primed to pick up weak signals from within the organization, signals that are often unnoticed because consensus reality is defensively maintained. In our view of organizational systems it is one of the responsibilities of management to foster deviant thinking in the organization and then to subject it to scrutiny so that the organization can experience new expressions of myth and belief and realize them in new directions and new ventures.

This exercise encourages the expression of 'heretical' thinking – thinking which challenges the taken-for-grantedness of the organization's myth and belief. It follows Sherwood's model of levels of doubt (See chapter 2.)

1. Lead the group in a discussion of the organization's self-image, goals, raison d'etre, and traditional way of operating. Use documents such as the organization's 'vision statement' if these are available. Do not be concerned with critiquing these 'official' statements of the organization's identity, but only with setting out participants' understanding of what it claims to be and how it operates. Encourage the group to offer truths at three levels:

- The operational level (This is what we do. This is how we behave.)
- The ideological level (This is what we think/believe. These are our objectives.)
- The ethical level (This is what we value. This is why we are here.)

[If the organization has reached the state of absolute doubt, it no longer holds any truths.]

2. Summarize on the whiteboard the organization's key truths about itself, using the above categories.

3. Ask participants to write down other truths about the organization that are never or rarely acknowledged because they conflict with the organization's story about itself. They do not have to be absolute and complete truths, but they must genuinely represent at least a partial truth as the participant sees it. Desirably, some of them will be truths that the participant has not before discussed with other people present. Encourage the participants to find heresies in all three categories.

4. Collect these lists of heresies and re-distribute them at random, so that each participant now has another (anonymous) person's list.

Each participant in turn reads out an item from their new list and offers it for discussion and verification (or falsification) by the rest of the group. Discuss operational truths first, then proceed to ideological and ethical truths. This process continues until the group has accumulated a list of 'deviant truths' on which they have some agreement.

5. Summarize the organization's key heresies on the whiteboard, using the same categories.

6. Explore the notion of a death/birth cycle in the organization. The status quo is maintained only by suppressing doubt. Change begins with doubt.

- Is the organization that represented the old truths now dying? Do these heresies represent a new organization, which is struggling to be born?
- Have all the old truths ceased to be true? Do the new truths contradict or complement them?
- If the old truths are already dead, how can we bury them?

Ask the participants to address the following questions in the light of the previous discussion:

- Who are we?
- What is our purpose?
- How will we achieve our goals?
- What practices and procedures are congruent with our identity and purpose?

We can distinguish between incremental and radical change in organizations. Problem-solving approaches address only incremental change, and incremental changes are designed to return the system to a state of suspended doubt. They are almost always new ways of expressing old purposes and goals. However, organizational change sometimes has to challenge the taken-for-granted truths that pervade the organization's collective sense of itself. Radical change is rooted in ideological and ethical doubt and oriented towards a new vision of the future.

We cannot impose new truths on an organization; we cannot teach an organization what it does not already know, though it may not know what it knows until we disturb its consensus reality. The aim of this exercise is to access the organization's 'silent knowledge' and to use it as a taking-off point towards the future.

This exercise highlights a commonly observed phenomenon in group dynamics. The members of a group share a collective experience of what the group is. The group is felt and imagined in a certain way; the members are caught up in its dynamics, which are often quite irrational. When people leave a group temporally for one reason or another they may reflect rationally on the group as an outsider and see irrational aspects of the group's behavior. They may even be critical of their own behavior in the group, which they perceive as stupid or self-destructive. When they go back to the group they find themselves caught up in the irrational dynamics of the group again and acting exactly as they did before. This can apply in organizations and committees just as it does in natural groups such as families.

In an organization we often find a certain view of reality dominant in the collective (mythical) thinking of the organization. There is an organizational narrative, which everyone believes in and acts on as long as they are within the organization. They don't feel the need to challenge it. However, when they go on leave, or even when they go home at night, they are freed from the organizational 'group-think' and may reflect on the organization rationally and critically as autonomous individuals. They may decide that the organization's taken-for-granted truths are simply false. Then they go back to the organization and find themselves once again going along with the organization's version of reality. Collective myths have enormous power to drag deviant thinkers into line. And they have great resistance to change.

10. Mapping the Organization's Narrative

Systematic attempts at organizational change will always meet with resistance. However, what is perceived as resistance by the change agent or the management that has hired him is perceived in much more positive terms by those who find the change interventions aimed at them. The old norms and practices meet their needs in one way or another, and must be protected.

If we view organizations as machines we will see equilibrium as a primary quality of an organization and change as something that occasionally occurs as a result of external pressure or intervention. On the other hand, if we view them as organic, self-organizing systems we will see change as a basic quality of organizations and equilibrium as an occasional interlude. In such a view, resistance can be seen as an attachment to the values and practices that characterize a particular state of equilibrium. This state of equilibrium may only exist in the imagination of those who claim to have experienced it.

The following exercise illustrates the notion that interventions for cultural change must take as much account of the imagined past as of the imagined future.

PHASE 1. PAST TO PRESENT

1. Invite the participants to tell stories about the past of the organization as they have experienced it and have heard other recollect it. Stories will include the official version of the organization's history as well as personal anecdotes and the legends of past heroes and villains. Invite participants to give each story a name.

2. Encourage participants to offer stories from the 'deep past' of the organization. It does not matter whether the stories are historically accurate, only that they represent the way the past is remembered.

3. Make a time-line on the whiteboard. As each story is told and named, write the story's name at the appropriate point on the line.

4. When the story-line from 'long, long ago' to the present time is complete, invite general discussion about what sort of organization this story-line appears to represent. Are there any important stories missing?

5. Have the group examine each story in turn with a view to labeling the values embedded in the story. A useful way to do this is to label the polarity or polarities inherent in each story, e.g. loyalty vs. disloyalty, obedience vs. insubordination, concern for employees vs. lack of concern, social responsibility vs. irresponsibility, opportunism vs. adherence to principle, focus on product vs. focus on people.

6. Invite the participants to list the key values of the organization as they have represented it. (It may be useful to have them do this privately then compare lists). Can any of these values be discarded? Are any of these values under challenge at the present time? Which of these values are essential to the integrity of the organization?

7. Put the idea that resistance to change can be understood as adherence to a value system that is under threat. This value system is often unconscious, in that it has never been thought through and articulated. Resistance is not just obstinacy, but is rather an affirmation of values.[11]

Phase 2. Present to Future

The second phase of this exercise takes the group from remembering the past to imagining the future.

1. Invite the group to discuss the future of the organization. In separate columns on the whiteboard list:

- What participants want to add to the organization
- What they want to keep
- What they want to get rid of.

2. Accept all items offered for these lists without discussing or evaluating them. Ask the participants to work in small groups in which they will accept for the purposes of the exercise that the organization is about to change in a significant way.

3. Develop a negative scenario for the organization, based on its current state.

4. Develop a positive scenario for the organization, based on its current state.

5. Share these scenarios in the large group. Refer to the lists on the whiteboard and add items if appropriate. Examine the procedures and practices on these lists and label the values that they express.

6. Explore with the group the notion that positive scenarios tend to maintain the organization's core values while changing the procedures and practices through which these values are expressed, while negative scenarios depict the loss of these core values.

7. Bring the discussion to an end by asking participants to reflect on the process of this exercise, particularly their experience of difference.

- What degree of consensus do you observe in this discussion?
- Do you personally share this consensus? Were you drawn into it? Did you challenge the consensus at any point?
- What sense of difference do you bring to the organization? What potential contribution does your difference make to the organization's process of change?

The organization as a collective is essentially irrational (not necessarily a pejorative term) and conservative. The magical and mythical structures of consciousness serve to maintain a repetitive pattern of behavior. Yet a traumatic change in environment may discredit the myth and force the organization to develop a new one. The most powerful members of the organization may be seduced by a new myth and impose it (or attempt to impose it) on the organization. Or the organization's members, as autonomous and rational individuals, may detach themselves from the collective myth and reflect on whether it is actually compatible with the information available. If they decide that this is the case, and that the organization nevertheless has a future, they can contribute their critique to the process of change. But a collection of autonomous individuals critically reflecting does not make an organization. Autonomous reflection does not provide collective energy and purpose; ideas have to be turned into action, and action is situated in story. Wherever we have collective action we have magic, myth, and the dynamics that are grounded in them.

11. Exploring Organizational Complexity

Organizations have both linear and non-linear aspects. In their linear aspects it is useful to think of them as behaving like machines, and we may intervene to modify or re-orientate or even 'fix' them and, if we are skilful enough, we may have some assurance that our interventions will have predictable results.

However, in their non-linear aspects they do not behave like machines and we invite disaster by attempting to treat them like machines. We have to find ways of dealing with complexity.

A useful way of thinking about the complexity of organizations and distinguishing their linear and non-linear aspects is provided by Stacey in his discussion of organizational complexity and creativity.[12] Stacey suggests that the different contexts for decision-making in organizations can be located on two axes representing the degree of certainty and the degree of agreement associated with them.

In any organization there may be areas of high certainty and high agreement (things people are sure about and which they concur in being sure about); areas of high certainty and low agreement (things people hold strong opinions on but disagree about); areas of low certainty but high agreement (things that people agree about but without much commitment); and areas of low certainty and low agreement (things that people are uncertain about and disagree in the ways they are uncertain about them.)

In the first of these areas (high certainty/high agreement) it is appropriate for management to think in linear ways; causes have predictable effects and planning can be logical and conventional strategies can be effective. In the high agreement/low certainty zone and the low agreement/high certainty zone relying on linear logic is also appropriate but can be risky. We cannot assume that we can accurately predict the consequences of our decisions. In the low agreement/low certainty zone we are always at the edge of chaos. Any event has complex and unpredictable causes and any decision has complex and unpredictable consequences.

The high agreement/high certainty zone is the zone in which the organization can claim a unitary and cohesive culture. The low agreement/low certainty zone represents divergent voices and multiple cultures.

Where there is high agreement and certainty, centralized control is effective. Where both are absent centralized control lacks the flexibility it needs. Power has to be devolved to managers who have the intuitive skills to respond quickly and flexibly to a constantly changing situation, and the personal stability to cope with the stress of doing so.

Clearly, organizations increasingly find themselves in a world where neither certainty nor agreement is possible in many areas of their operations.

The following exercise uses Stacey's model to raise awareness of the differences between the linear and complex elements of an organization's processes and activities, and to examine the most appropriate strategies to be employed in each area.

Individual Phase

Distribute the worksheet headed **Beliefs About The Organization** and ask them to write statements about the purposes, values, current state, and appropriate direction.

Worksheet: Beliefs About The Organization

Write something you believe about the aims and purposes of the organization and indicate as well as you can whether other people agree with you.

I believe that: ....
....
....
....
....

Almost everybody agrees with this statement ☐

A lot of people agree with this statement ☐

Hardly any one agrees with this statement ☐

Write something you believe about the values which are important in this organization and indicate as well as you can whether other people agree with you.

I believe that: ....
....
....
....
....

Almost everybody agrees with this statement ☐

A lot of people agree with this statement ☐

Hardly any one agrees with this statement ☐

Write something you believe about the way the organization currently functions and indicate as well as you can whether other people agree with you.

I believe that: ....
....
....
....
....

Almost everybody agrees with this statement ☐

A lot of people agree with this statement ☐

Hardly any one agrees with this statement ☐

Write something you believe about what the organization needs to do and indicate as well as you can whether other people agree with you.

I believe that: ....
....
....
....
....

Almost everybody agrees with this statement ☐

A lot of people agree with this statement ☐

Hardly any one agrees with this statement ☐

SMALL GROUP PHASE

1. Have the participants form groups of 4–6. Make each of these small groups as representative of the whole organization as is feasible.

2. Distribute the worksheet headed **Certainty and Agreement.**

3. Ask the groups to use the information on the previous worksheet as the basis for discussion on the degree of certainty and agreement about the aims, values, operations,

and directions of the organization. Ask them to write into each of the four quadrants one or more items that they consider to belong in that zone.

WORKSHEET: CERTAINTY AND AGREEMENT

Zone 2. Far from agreement Close to certainty	Zone 4. Far from agreement Far from certainty
Zone 1. Close to agreement Close to certainty	Zone 3. Close to agreement Far from certainty

Large Group Phase

1. When the participants have re-formed as a single group, discuss the small group process.

> Which quadrant attracted the most items?
>
> Which quadrant attracted the least items?
>
> Was there consensus in the small group with regard to what things members of the organization agree about?
>
> Was there consensus in the small group with regard to what things members of the organization are certain about?

2. Discuss the content of the quadrants, beginning with quadrant 1 and concluding with quadrant 4.

3. Discuss the organization's present strategies for dealing with matters in Zone 1. Contrast the low-change environment of Zone 1 with the high-change environment of Zone 4.

4. Discuss the organization's current and potential strategies for dealing with matters in Zone 2, 3, and 4. These may include both regressive strategies such as:

- Denial
- Censorship (including self-censorship)
- Scapegoating
- Fabrication
- Eliminating difference through staff selection

or constructive strategies such as:

- Unrestricted flow of information
- Genuine devolution of decision-making
- Recognition and reward for problem-solving at all levels
- Encouraging an experimental attitude
- Generating both trust and conflict

5. Discuss the balance in the organization's identity and operations between low-change and high-change zones.

- Does the particular distribution of items in these zones, as illustrated by the matrix, pose any threat to the organization's survival?
- Does the particular distribution of items in these zones offer any clues about the organization's potential future development?
- How can the organization best maintain the creative balance between stability and instability and avoid both ossification and disintegration?

12. Analyzing the Dynamics of Change

Phase 1

1. Introduce and discuss Lundberg's multi-layered model of organizational culture. (See chapter 2).

2. Distribute worksheet **Layers of Organizational Culture** and ask participants to use it to describe the culture of their organization.

3. Share and discuss this information.

   - Are there subcultures in the organization that would describe it differently?
   - Are there contradictory beliefs and values held by different groups or even within the same group?

Worksheet: Layers of Organizational Culture

Artifacts (The things we do and say; the things we make, the things we own; buildings; symbols; documents; organizational structures; and procedures)

***Perspectives** (What we believe; the ways we think about things)*
***Values** (What we hold most dear; what we feel strongly about)*
***Basic assumptions** (What we take completely for granted)*

PHASE 2

1. Ask participants to discuss in small groups the differences between the organization as they currently experience it and the organization as they would like it to be if everything was possible.

2. Ask them to focus on one specific change that they believe would make the organization better at doing what they want it to do.

3. Ask them to consider what factors (whether artifacts, perspectives, values, assumptions) in the organization's culture push it towards the change they want and what factors resist the change.

The worksheet **Cultural Change** can be used to organize this information.

WORKSHEET: CULTURAL CHANGE

Briefly describe a particular change you would like to see.

What artifacts (structures, icons, regular behaviors) in your organization encourage this change?

What artifacts (structures, icons, regular behaviors) in your organization will resist this change?

What perspectives and beliefs currently held in your organization will work towards this change?

What perspectives and beliefs currently held in the organization will work against this change?

What current values and attitudes would support this change?

What current values and attitudes would resist such a change?

What currently held assumptions would support this change?
What currently held assumptions would resist such a change?

Phase 3

1. Have each small group report on their discussion of the desirable change, the factors in the organization which incline it towards change, and the factors which are preventing the change occurring.

2. Suggest that the organization's status quo comes about because the forces for and against change are in balance. Change in one direction or the other can be achieved by either increasing the force on one side or lessening it on the other.

3. Have participants discuss in small groups the ways in which factors supporting the desired change can be strengthened or factors preventing change can be weakened. Suggest that they focus on lessening the resistance to the change. What needs are people trying to satisfy by resisting this change? Can these needs be satisfied in some other way?

4. Have groups report on their strategy for bringing about their desired change.

13. Creating a Chaordic Organization

Dee Hock, who created the credit card and the Visa Corporation, has used his experience to develop a process for creating the kind of flexible, humane organization which might flourish in the kind of business world which seems to be currently emerging. He suggests that rather than start with conventional practices and fit our purposes to them, decisions about practices, structures, and procedures need to come last. A lot of decisions need to be made before we decide on the shape of our organization. According to Hock, the issues need to be addressed in the following order, which can be used as the basis for structured discussion aimed at revitalizing an organization.[13]

Purposes: *If anything imaginable is possible, what would be the nature of our ideal organization? What would we wish to achieve?*

Principles: *What do we believe? What rules should guide our practice?*

People: *What community do we represent? What are our needs and resources?*

Concepts: *What is our idea of an organization which all may trust to be equitable, just, and effective? How would the people and structures relate to each other?*

Structure: *How can we embed our purpose and principles in the formal ways we organize ourselves?*

Practice: *How can all participants have an active, creative, and equitable role in deciding the best ways to achieve the purpose of our organization?*

14. Languages of Transformation

Robert Kegan and Lisa Lahey distinguish seven languages of the workplace, arguing that leaders are 'language leaders' and can choose between being thoughtful and intentional with regard to this aspect of their leadership or ratifying existing ways of communicating by simply doing nothing.

They suggest that if constructive organizational change is to be sustainable it must begin with a transformation of the 'language of complaint' to the 'language of commitment'. There are six transformations in all, from the language of complaint to:

The language of commitment
The language of competing commitments
The language of the assumptions we hold
The language of ongoing regard

The language of public agreement
The language of deconstructive criticism

The following exercise undertaken by a working group is a way of starting this process.[14] Each stage of the exercise consists of the following steps:

Writing individual responses to each question in the worksheet **Transforming Language.**
Sharing these in a small group, to explore what is common in the responses.
Sharing the small group responses in the whole group.
Mapping the 'big assumptions' of the group as they emerge.

By exploring their responses to these questions the working group first moves from what Kegan calls 'the language of the assumptions which hold us' to 'the language of the assumptions we hold'. Even small changes in the 'big assumptions' of the organization can lead to major changes in the organization's self-image and sense of possibilities.

It then moves through the three 'social languages' whose function is to maintain and upgrade these changes.

In discussing the 'social languages' Kegan and Lahey are careful to distinguish 'the language of ongoing regard' from 'the language of prizes and praising'. They make distinctions between 'the language of public agreement' and 'the language of rules and policies' and distinguish 'deconstructive criticism' from both 'destructive criticism' and 'constructive criticism'.

WORKSHEET: TRANSFORMING LANGUAGE

The language of complaint

What sorts of things – if they were to happen more frequently in your work setting – would you experience as being more supportive of your own ongoing development at work?

I could work more effectively if

....

....

The language of commitment

What commitments or convictions that you hold are implied in your earlier response?

I am committed to the value or the importance of

....

....

The language of competing commitments

What are you doing, or not doing, which is preventing your commitment from being fully realized?

....

....

What commitments or convictions that you hold are implied in this response?

I may also be committed to the value or the importance of

....

....

The language of the assumptions we hold

What assumptions underlie the behavior described in the previous statement?

I assume that if

....

....

The language of ongoing regard

What do you do or not do to express your appreciation of the work of colleagues?

I can recount the following recent occasions when I have demonstrated or failed to demonstrate that I value people's work

....

....

The language of public agreement

What publicly shared agreements are there about how people should relate to each other and to the tasks of the organization?

We all agree that ....

....

....

The language of deconstructive criticism

Am I able to hold negative evaluations of another's performance together with the possibility that there may be something for me to learn from the other person's perspective?

I can point to an occasion when I have used the experience of conflict to learn something of value from the other person?

....

....

15. The Magic Wand

Each of us carries an image of an ideal self. It is an image of the person that we would like to be, in more or less contrast to the person we experience ourselves to be. This image shapes our behavior to a large extent, even when we are behaving self-destructively. Organizations likewise carry an image of their ideal self. Sometimes it is described in their vision statement. Sometimes it is just a fantasy shared by the members of the organization. The image of the ideal organization, like the image of the ideal self, can be a source of discontent and frustration. It can also provide the energy and direction for change.

This exercise can be conducted as a visualization, it can take the form of a dialogue, or it can be acted out in a large or small group.

Imagine that you have a magic wand. It enables you to change anything you want to change.

I want you to explore this organization or workplace – its symbols, its structures, its people. Whenever you meet something that could be better, I want you to touch it with your magic wand. Whatever you touch changes the way you want to change it, and the organization or workplace becomes perfect for you.

Now describe the ideal organization or workplace.

When participants have shared and compared their visions of the ideal organization or workplace, have them reflect on their own behavior.

In what ways is your behavior reactive to the organization as it is?

In what ways is it proactive with the aim of constructing the organization as you would like it to be?

If we accept the idea that in complex systems very small changes can have a major impact, what might you do differently which could have a flow-on effect and significantly change the culture?

---

1. See R Bosnak (1998) *A Little Course in Dreams*; J Campbell (1974) *The Mythic Image*; P O'Connor (1987) *Dreams and the Search for Meaning*; J Sandford (1987) *Dreams: God's Forgotten Language*; M Ullman & C Limmer (1987) *The Variety of Dream Experience*.
2. The approach here is modeled on Montague Ullman's dream groupwork as described in *Dreams: A Group Approach* (1987).
3. For a fuller description and discussion of this exercise, see T Dalmau (1993).
4. This exercise is drawn from psychosynthesis, which is a theory and methodology originally designed for psychotherapy but adaptable to much broader use. For this particular exercise I am indebted to Glenda Lehmann. On psychosynthesis see R Assagioli (1970) *Psychosynthesis*; MY Brown (1983) *The Unfolding Self*; P Ferrucci (1982) *What We May Be*; B Neville (1992) *Educating Psyche*, chapter 4.
5. I was introduced to scanning by John Heron .
6. The techniques of psychodrama which were developed by Jacob Moreno are widely applied in therapy, less so in education and organizational development. See H Blatner (1973) *Acting In*; A Williams (1989) *The Passionate Technique* and (1991) *Forbidden Agendas*. See also Neville (1992), chap. 7.
7. The emotional impact of this exercise may be substantially increased by the use of the psychodramatic techniques of role reversal and doubling.
8. The idea behind this exercise comes from Jean Houston.
9. This is an adaptation of Eugene Gendlin's technique of 'experiential focusing' which was developed in a therapeutic context. See E Gendlin (1980) *Focusing*.
10. See J Sherwood (1977) *Leadership: The Responsible Exercise of Power*.
11. On dealing with resistance within a model of the self-organizing system, see Goldstein (1994) *The Unshackled Organization*, chapter 4. In an organization, resistance reflects employees' need to protect their sense of dignity, integrity, or ideals rather than their supposed primal inclinations to inertia. This need may be largely unconscious, and therefore, may appear as wilful obstinacy. Aggressively trying to overpower this resistance, then, is counterproductive in the long run because strategies of force are tantamount to threatening the dignity and integrity of the individuals involved. ibid., p. 56.
12. See R Stacey (1996) *Complexity and Creativity in Organizations*.
13. D Hock (1999) *Birth of the Chaordic Age*.
    Hock coined the word 'chaordic' to describe an organization that is at once chaotic and orderly. He eventually quit the Visa Corporation in frustration that his invention had become a credit card rather than a transaction device.
14. Adapted from Robert Kegan and Lisa Lahey (2001) *How The Way We Talk Can Change The Way We Work*. Kegan and Lahey provide a full explanation of the model and a number of exercises which may be utilized in helping participants to understand its implications.

APPENDIX 2
THE DNAI

The DNAI is a 32-item questionnaire divided into two parts. Part 1 asks the respondent to rate 32 statements on a scale of 0–5 according to their accuracy as descriptors of their ideal organization, that is, the kind of organization which they would find it most satisfying to belong to. Part 2 asks them to rate the same items as descriptors of an actual organization. In the context of an organizational consultancy the questions are obviously related to 'the organization (or workplace) that would be ideal for me', and the actual organization (or workplace) that is being studied.

With each of the 16 items 4 descriptors are presented. These are separately rated. There are accordingly 64 descriptors in each of parts 1 and 2. Each descriptor represents a specific god. There are 4 descriptors for each of the 16 gods. Totaling these provides a score range of 0–20 for each of the 16 archetypal patterns. These can be graphed as a profile of the organizational culture.

A detailed account of the development and features of the DNAI can be found in Chapter 11 – The Archetypology Indicator.

An electronic version of the DNAI may be accessed at:
www.learningextensions.com

If readers have questions regarding the DNAI, the authors may be contacted by email as follows:

Bernard Neville nevillebh@westnet.com.au
Tim Dalmau tim@dalmau.com

BIBLIOGRAPHY

Abt, T. *Progress Without Loss of Soul: Towards a Wholistic Approach to Modernization Planning*, Chiron Publications, Willmette, 1989.

Aischylos. *Prometheus Bound*. (trans D Grene), in Grene, D & Lattimore, R (eds.) *Greek Tragedies*, University of Chicago Press, 1960.

Alford, CF. *Group Psychology and Political Theory*, Yale University Press, New Haven, 1994.

Alvesson, M. 'Talking in Organizations: Managing Identity and Impressions in an Advertising Agency', *Organization Studies*, 15, 1994.

Argyris, C & Schon, D. *Organizational Learning: A Theory of Action Perspective*, McGraw Hill, New York 1974.

Assagioli, R. *Psychosynthesis*. Penguin, 1970.

Athanassakis, A. (trans. and ed.) *The Homeric Hymns*, John Hopkins University Press, Baltimore, 1976.

Bailey, G. *Mythologies of Change and Certainty in Late 20th Century Australia*, Australian Scholarly Publishing, Melbourne, 2000.

Bateson, G. *Steps to an Ecology of Mind*, Ballantine, London, 1972.

Bennis, WG, Benne, KD, & Chin, R. *The Planning of Change*, Holt, Rhinehart and Winston, 1961.

– *Changing Organizations: Essays on the Development and Evolution of Human Organization*, McGraw Hill, New York, 1966.

Bettelheim, B. *The Informed Heart*, Penguin, London, 1986.

Bion, W. *Experiences in Groups*, Tavistock, London, 1969.

Blatner, H. *Acting In*, Springer, New York, 1973.

Bohm, D. *Wholeness and the Implicate Order*, Routledge and Kegan Paul, London, 1980.

Boon, M. *The African Way*, Zebra Press, Sandton, 1996.

Bosco, D. 'The Great Mother's Work is Never Done: An Archetypal Perspective of the Matriarchal Mind at Work'. Paper presented to the International Symposium on Jung and Management, Omaha, NE. Oct 1994.

Bosnak, R. A *Little Course in Dreams*, Shambhala, Boston, 1988.

Bowles, MJ. 'Recognizing Deep Structures in Organizations', *Organization Studies*, 11(3), 1990.

Boyett, JH and Conn, HP. *Workplace 2000: The Revolution Shaping American Business*, Penguin, New York, 1992.

Bradbury, R. 'Management from Within', *New Management*, 1 (4), 1984.

Bridges, W. *Managing Transitions*, Addison-Wesley, Reading, MA, 1991.

Briggs Myers, E & Myers, P. *Gifts Differing: Understanding Personality Type*, Consulting Psychologists Press, 1995.

Brown, MY. *The Unfolding Self*, Psychosynthesis Press, San Francisco, 1983.

Brownwood, A. *It Takes All Types*, Baytree Publishing Co, Nicasio, 1999.

Bruck, C. *The Predators' Ball: How Michael Milken and his Junk Bond Machine Staked the Corporate Raider*, Simon and Schuster, New York, 1988.

Burns, T & Stalker, G. *The Management of Innovation*, Tavistock, London, 1961.

Buskirk, R. *The Frontal Attack*, John Wiley, New York, 1989.

Byatt, AS. *Babel Tower*, Chatto and Windus, London, 1966.

Campbell, J. *The Masks of God: Creative Mythology*, Viking, New York, 1968.

– *The Mythic Image*, Princeton University Press, 1974.

– *The Power of Myth*, Doubleday, New York, 1986.

Capra, F. *The Turning Point*, Simon and Schuster, New York, 1982.

– *The Web of Life: A New Scientific Understanding of Living Systems*, Anchor Books, 1996.

Colman, AD. 'Depth Consultation', in Stein, M & Stollwitz, J. *Psyche at Work*, Chiron Publications, Willmette, 1992.

Combs, A. *Radiance of Being: Complexity, Chaos and the Evolution of Consciousness*, Floris Books, Edinburgh, 1995.

Corlett, J & Pearson, C. *Mapping the Organizational Psyche*, Center for the Appreciation of Psychological Type, Gainsville, 2003.

Cunnington, B & Limerick, D. 'The Fourth Blueprint: Strategy, Structure and Culture in Australian Organizations'. Paper delivered to the Sixth Annual Strategic Management Conference, Singapore, October, 1986.

Dalmau, T & Dick B. *Promoting and Marketing Internal Consultancy Services*, Interchange, Brisbane, 1984.

Dalmau, T. 'Incongruence and Dissonance: Using Them Constructively to Improve the Effectiveness of Senior Executive Teams'. Conference Proceedings of the Fifth International Conference on Thinking, Townsville, Australia, July, 1993. 'The Gods and Goddesses of Antarctica'. Paper presented to the International Symposium on Jung and Management, Creighton University, Omaha, NE, October, 1994.

Dawkins, R. *The Selfish Gene*, Oxford University Press, 1990.

D'Cruz, JV and Steele, W. *Australia's Ambivalence towards Asia*, Monash Asia Institute, 2003.

De Geus, A. *The Living Company*, Harvard Business School Press, Boston, 1997.

Denhardt, DT. *In the Shadow of the Organization*, Regent, Kansas, 1981.

Deusch, P. 'What is the IETF?', *Internet World*, January, 1994.

Dewhurst, K. 'Art at Work: In Pursuit of Aesthetic Solutions', in Jones, M, Moore, M, & Snyder, R. *Inside Organizations*, Sage, Beverley Hills, 1988.

Donald, M. *The Origins of the Modern Mind*, Harvard University Press, Cambridge, 1991.

– *A Mind So Rare: The Evolution of Human Consciousness*, Norton, New York, 2001.

Drucker, P. *Post-capitalist Society*, Harper, New York, 1993.

Dunphy, D, Griffiths, A, & Benn, S. *Organizational Change for Corporate Sustainability*, Routledge, London, 2003.

Egan, K. *The Educated Mind*, University of Chicago Press, 1997.

Eisner, R. *The Road to Daulis*, Syracuse University Press, 1987.

Eliade, M. *The Myth of the Eternal Return: or Cosmos and History*, Princeton University Press, 1991 [1954].

Emery, F. & Trist, E. 'The Causal Texture of Organizational Environments', *Human Relations*, 18, 1965.

Enomoto, EK. 'Negotiating the Ethics of Care and Justice', *Educational Administration Quarterly*, vol. 33 (3), 1997.

Euripides, *Herakles*. Trans P. Vellacott, Penguin, New York, 1982.

Falcone, G. *Men of Honour: The Truth About the Mafia*, Fourth Estate, London, 1992.

Faulk, EH, Glickman, J, & Middleton, M. 'Low-cost Group Therapy: An Alternative to the Traditional Mental Health Delivery System', *Bulletin of the Meninger Clinic*, 52 (4), 1988.

Ferrucci, P. *What We May Be*, Tarcher, Los Angeles, 1982.

Feuerstein, G. *Structures of Consciousness*, Integral Publishing, Lower Lake, 1987.

Forrester, J. *Urban Dynamics*, Productivity Press, Portland, 1969.

Freud, S. *Civilization and its Discontents*, Penguin, London, 1985 [1929].

Gagliardi, P. 'The Creation and Change of Organizational Cultures', *Organization Studies*, 7, 2, 1986.

Gebser, J. *The Ever Present Origin*, Ohio University Press, Athens, 1985 [1949].

Gee, JP & Lankshear, C. 'The New Work Order: Critical Language Awareness and "Fast Capitalism" Texts' in *Discourse: Studies in the Cultural Politics of Education*, 16(1), 1995.

Geertz, C. *The Interpretation of Cultures*, Basic Books, New York. 1973.

Gendlin, E. *Focusing*, Bantam, New York, 1980.

Gibb, J. *Trust: A New View of Personal and Organizational Development*, Guild of Tutors, Los Angeles, 1978.

Gilligan, C. *In a Different Voice*, Harvard University Press, Cambridge, 1982.

Gleick, J. *Chaos: Making a New Science*, William Heinemann, London, 1988.

Goldstein, J. *The Unshackled Organization*, Productivity Pres, Portland, 1994.

Griffin, DR. 'Introduction to the SUNY Series on Constructive Postmodern Thought'. In Orr, DW. *Ecological Literacy: Education and the Transition to a Postmodern World*, SUNY Press, Albany, 1992.

Hall, ET. *Beyond Culture*, Anchor Books, New York, 1976.

– *The Dance of Life*, Anchor Books, New York, 1984.

Handy, C.*Understanding Organizations*, Penguin Books, 1976.

– *The Gods of Management*, Penguin Books, 1979.

– *The Age of Unreason*, Business Books, London, 1989.

Hawken, P, Lovins, A & Lovins, LH. *Natural Capitalism*, Back Bay Books, Boston, 1999.

Heller, J. *Catch 22*. Jonathan Cape, London, 1962.

Hellwige, J. *Hemispheric Asymmetry: What's Right and What's Left*, Harvard University Press, Cambridge, 1993.

Henderson, G. *Australian Answers*, Random House, Sydney, 1990.

Hesiod. *Theogony*, trans. A Athanassakis, Johns Hopkins University Press, Baltimore, 1983.

Hillman, J. *Revisioning Psychology*, Harper and Row, New York, 1977.

– *Archetypal Psychology*, Spring Publications, Dallas, 1983.

– *Kinds of Power: A Guide to its Intelligent Uses*, Doubleday, New York, 1995.

Hillman, J & Venturi M. *We've Had a Hundred Years of Psychotherapy and the World's Getting Worse*, Harper & Row, Los Angeles, 1992.

Hock, D. *Birth of the Chaordic Age*, Berrett-Koehler, San Francisco, 1999.

Hofstede, G. *Culture's Consequences: International Differences in Work-related Values*, Sage, Beverley Hills, 1980.

– *Cultures and Organizations: Software of the Mind*, McGraw Hill, New York, 1991.

Homer, *The Odyssey*, 11: 444.

House, R, Hanges, P, Javiden, M, Dorfman, W, & Gupta, V. *Culture, Leadership and Organizations: The GLOBE Study of 62 Societies*, Sage, Beverley Hills, 2004.

Hughes, J. *The Hawthorne Effect*, Nelson, London, 1976.

Huxley, A. *Brave New World*, Penguin, London, 1932.

Jaspers, K. (1953) *The Origin and Goal of History*, Yale University Press, New Haven, 1953.

Jaynes, J. *The Origin of Consciousness in the Breakdown of the Bicameral Brain*, Allan Lane, London, 1979.

Jung, CJ. *Collected Works*, Princeton University Press, 1953-63.

Kaufman, S. *At Home in the Universe: The Search for the Laws of Self-Organization and Complexity*, Oxford University Press, 1996.

Kearns, D. *Lyndon Johnson and the American Dream*, Harper and Row, Los Angeles, 1976.

Keen, S. *Hymns to an Unknown God*, Bantam, New York, 1994.

Kegan, R. *In Over Our Heads: The Mental Demands of Modern Life*, Harvard University Press, Cambridge, 1994.

Kennedy, M. *Office Warfare: Strategies for Getting Ahead in the Aggressive 80s*, MacMillan, London, 1985.

Kiersey, D & Bates, M. *Please Understand Me II: Temperament, Character, Intelligence*, Prometheus Nemesis, Del Mar, 1998.

Kleiner, A. *The Age of Heretics: Heroes, Outlaws, and the Forerunners of Corporate Change*, Doubleday, New York, 1996.

Kluckhohn, C *Mirror for Man*, New York, Fawcett, 1944.

Knowles, M. *Organizational Behaviour: Changing Concepts and Applications*, Harper and Row, Sydney, 1990.

Knowles, R. *Reaching New Ground*, San Francisco. Bay Area Organization Development Network, 1997.

– *The Leadership Dance*. Center for Self-Organizing Leadership. Niagara Falls, 2002.

Kohlberg, L. *Essays on Moral Development*, Harper and Row, San Francisco, 1973.

Knox, J. *Archetype, Attachment, Analysis: Jungian Psychology and the Emergent Mind.* Brunner-Routledge, New York, 2003.

Kramer, EM. 'Gebser and Culture', in Kramer, EM (ed.). *Consciousness and Culture: An Introduction to the Thought of Jean Gebser*, Greenwood Press, Westport, 1992.

Kriegler, RJ. *Working for the Company*, Oxford University Press, 1982.

Lauter, E & Rupprecht, CS (eds). *Feminist Archetypal Theory: Interdisciplinary Revisions of Jungian Thought*, University of Tennessee Press, Knoxville, 1985.

Layton, D. *Seductive Poison: A Jonestown Survivor's Story of Life and Death in the People's Temple*, Aurum Press, London, 1999.

Lepper, G. 'The Complex in Human Affairs', in Stein, M & Hollwitz, J. *Psyche at Work*, Chiron, Willmette, 1992.

Lewin, K. *Field Theory in Social Science*, Harper and Row, New York, 1951.

Lewis, R. *When Cultures Collide: Managing Successfully Across Cultures*, Nicholas Brierley, Naperville, 2000.

Linhart, R. *The Assembly Line*, John Calder, London, 1981.

Lopez-Pedraza, R. *Hermes and All His Children*, Spring Publications, Dallas, 1977.

Louis, M. 'Organizations as Culture-bearing Milieux', in Pondy, L, Frost, P, Louis, M, Morgan, G, & Dandridge, T. *Organizational Symbolism*, JAI Press, London, 1983.

– 'An Investigator's Guide to Workplace Culture', in Frost, PJ (ed.). *Organizational Culture*, Sage Publications, Beverley Hills, 1985.

Lovelock, J. *The Ages of Gaia: A Biography of Our Living Earth*, Oxford University Press, 1988.

– *Gaia: A New Look at Life on Earth*, Oxford University Press, 1979.

Lundberg, CC. 'On the Feasibility of Cultural Interventions in Organizations', in Frost, PJ, Moore, LF, Louis, MR, Lundberg, CC, & Martin, J. *Organizational Culture*, Sage, Beverley Hills, 1985.

Lyotard, J. *The Postmodern Condition*, University of Manchester Press, 1983.

McCnaimhan, B. *The Centre*, Mercury Press, Melbourne, 1994.

MacLean, P. *The Triune Brain in Evolution*, Springer, New York, 1990.

McLuhan, M. *Understanding Media: The Extensions of Man*. McGraw Hill, New York, 1965.

Marais, E. *The Soul of the White Ant*, Penguin, London, 1973.

Margulis, L, Sagan, D & Morrison, P. *Slanted Truths: Essays on Gaia, Symbiosis and Evolution*, Copernicus Books, London, 1997.

Maturana, H & Varela, F. *The Tree of Knowledge: The Biological Roots of Human Understanding*, Shambhala Publications, Boston, rev. 1998.

Mernissi, F. *The Harem Within: Tales of a Moroccan Girlhood*, Bantam, New York, 1994.

Merton, T. *Contemplation in a World of Action*, George Allen and Unwin, London, 1968.

Meyerson, D & Martin, J. 'Cultural Change: an Integration of Three Different Views', *Journal of Management Studies*, 24, 1987.

Mintzberg, H. *Structure in Fives: Designing Effective Organizations*, Prentice-Hall, Englewood Cliffs, 1983.

Mitroff, I. *Stakeholders of the Organizational Mind*, Jossey-Bass, New York, 1983.

Moore, T. 'Artemis and the Puer', in Hillman, J (ed.). *Puer Papers*, Spring Publications, Dallas, 1979.

Morgan, G. *Images of Organization*, Sage, Beverley Hills, 1986.

Murphy, J & Jung, M. 'Jean Gebser, The Commonweal and the Politics of Difference', in Kramer, EM (ed.). *Consciousness and Culture: An Introduction to the Thought of Jean Gebser*, Greenwood Press, Westport, 1992.

Neumann, E. *The Origins and History of Consciousness*, Princeton University Press, 1955.

Neville, B. *Educating Psyche: Emotion, Imagination and the Unconscious in Learning*, 3rd ed. Flat Chat Press, Melbourne, 2005.

– 'Neighbourhood Houses: Twelve More Years', in Willis, P & Neville, B. *Qualitative Research Methods in Adult Education*, David Lovell Publishing, Melbourne, 1996.

The New Oxford Annotated Bible, Oxford University Press, 1991.

Nijsmans, M. 'A Dionysian Way to Organizational Effectiveness', in Stein, M and Hollwitz, J. *Psyche at Work*, Chiron Publications, Willmette, 1992.

Norling, PM. 'Network or Not Work: Harnessing Technology Networks', *DuPont*, Vol. 39, No. 1, 1996.

O'Connor, P. *Dreams and the Search for Meaning*, Paulist Press, New York, 1987.

– *Beyond the Mist*, Allen and Unwin, London, 2001.

O'Flaherty, WD. *Dreams, Illusions and Other Realities*, University of Chicago Press, 1984.

Ovid. *Metamorphoses*, (trans M. Innes) Penguin Classics, 1955.

Parsons, T. *The Social System*, Free Press, New York, 1951.

Parry, A. 'A Universe of Stories', in *Family Process*, 30, 1991.

Pensinger, W. *Moon Over Hoa Binh*, Foundation Autopoy, 1994.

Peters, T. *Liberation Management: Necessary Disorganization for the Nanosecond Nineties*, Fawcett, New York, 1992.

– *The Tom Peters Seminar: Crazy Times for Crazy Organizations*, Vintage Books, New York, 1994.

Peters, T & Waterman, J. *In Search of Excellence: Lessons from America's Best-run Companies*, Harper and Row, Los Angeles, 1982.

Plutarch. 'The Life of Licurgus' in Talbot, R (ed. and trans.). *Plutarch on Sparta*, Penguin Classics, 1988.

Price, L. *The Dialogues of Alfred North* Whitehead, Godine, Boston, 2001.

Raspa, R. 'The Ocean World Paradox: Managing Nature as Carnival'. Paper presented to the 8th International Standing Conference on Organizational Symbolism, Copenhagen, June, 1991.

Roberts, W. *Leadership Secrets of Attila the Hun*, Warner, New York, 1989.

Robertson, R & Combs, A (eds.) *Chaos Theory in Psychology and the Life Sciences*. Hove, Maurice Erlbaum Associates, Hove, 1995.

Roddick, A. *Business as Unusual*, Thorsons, London, 2000.

Rogers, CR. *On Becoming a Person*. London: Constable, London, 1961.

– *A Way of Being*, Houghton Mifflin, Boston, 1980.

Rousseau, D. 'The Construction of Climate in Organizational Research', in Cooper, C & Robertson, I. *International Review of Industrial and Organizational Psychology*, Wiley, New York, 1988.

Royko, M. *Boss: Richard J. Daley of Chicago*, Dutton, New York, 1971.

Sampson, IS. *The Sovereign State: The Secret History of International Telephone and Telegraph*, Stein and Day, New York, 1973.

Samuels, A. *The Political Psyche*, Routledge, London, 1993.

Sandford, J. *Dreams: God's Forgotten Language*, Harper and Row, San Francisco, 1989.

Saul, JR. *Voltaire's Children*, Penguin, London, 1992.

Schaffer, R & Thomson, H. 'Successful Change Programs Begin with Results', *Harvard Business Review*. Jan – Feb, 1992.

Schein, E. *Process Consultation: Its Role in Organizational Development*, Addison-Wesley, Reading, 1969.

– *Organizational Psychology*, 2nd ed., Prentice Hall, Englewood Cliffs, 1970.

– *Organizational Culture and Leadership: A Dynamic View*, Jossey Bass, San Francisco, 1985.

– 'The Role of the Founder', in Frost, PJ et al. *Reframing Organizational Culture*, Sage, 1991.

– *The Corporate Culture Survival Guide*, Jossey-Bass Publishers, San Francisco, 1999.

– *Process Consultation Revisited: Revisioning the Helping Relationship*, Addison-Wesley, Reading, 1999b.

Seel, R. 'Culture and Complexity: New Insights on Organizational Change', *Organizations and People*, 7, 2, May 2000.

Semler, R. *Maverick: The Story of the World's Most Unusual Workplace*, Warner Books, Los Angeles, 1995.

Senge, P. *The Fifth Discipline: The Art and Practice of the Learning Organization*, Doubleday, New York, 1990.

Seth, V. *A Suitable Boy*, Phoenix House, London, 1993.

Singer, J & Loomis, M. *Singer Loomis Type Development Profile*, Moving Boundaries, Gresham, 1996.

Sharp, D. *Personality Types: Jung's Model of Typology*, City Books, Toronto, 1987.

Sheldrake, R. *A New Science of Life: The Hypothesis of Formative Causation*, Blond and Briggs, London, 1981.

– *The Presence of the Past: Morphic Resonance and the Habits of Nature*, Times Books, New York, 1988.

– *The Rebirth of Nature: New Science and the Revival of Animism*, Rider, London, 1993.

Sherwood, J. *Leadership: The Responsible Exercise of Power*, Management Design Inc, Cincinnati, 1977.

Slattery, P. *Nunawading North Neighbourhood Centre*, Hildegard Press, Melbourne, 1983.

Stacey, R. *Complexity and Creativity in Organizations*, Berrett-Koehler, San Francisco, 1996.

– *Strategic Management and Organizational Dynamics: The Challenge of Complexity*, Pearson Education, London, 2000.

– *Complex Responsive Processes in Organizations*, Routledge, New York, 2001.

Stein, M. *In Midlife*, Spring Publications, Dallas, 1983.

– 'Organizational Life as Spiritual Practice' in Stein, M & Hollwitz, J. *Psyche at Work*, Chiron Publications, Wilmette, 1992.

Stern, S. 'Symbolic Representation of Organizational Identity', in Jones, M, Moore, M, and Snyder, R. *Inside Organization*, Sage, Beverley Hills, 1988.

Stevens, A, *Ariadne's Clue*, Princeton University Press, New Jersey, 1998.

Szvent-Gyeorgy, A. 'The Drive in Living Matter to Perfect Itself', *Synthesis*, Spring, 1974.

Tacey, D. *Remaking Men: The Revolution in Masculinity*, Viking, New York, 1997.

Taylor, F. *Scientific Management*, Harper and Row, New York, 1947.

Thompson, WI. *Gaia 2: Emergence: The New Science of Becoming*, Lindisfarne Books, 1991.

Thucydides. *The Peloponnesian War* (trans. Rex Warner), Penguin Classics, 1975.

Tommerup, P. 'From Trickster to Father Figure: Learning from the Mythologization of Top Management' in Jones, M, Moore, M, & Snyder, R. *Inside Organization*, Sage, Beverley Hills, 1988.

Trompenaars, F & Hampden-Turner, C. *Riding the Waves of Culture: Understanding Diversity in Global Business*, McGraw-Hill, New York, 1998.

Turner, V. *The Forest of Symbols*, Cornell University Press, 1970.

Ullman, M. *Dreams; A Group Approach*, Sage Publications, London, 1987.

Ullman, M & Limmer, C. *The Variety of Dream Experience*, Continuum, New York, 1987

Van Maanen, J. 'The Smile Factory: Work at Disneyland', in Frost, PJ, Moore, LF, Louis, MR, Lundberg, CC, & Martin, J (eds.). *Reframing Organizational Culture*, Sage, London, 1991.

Vickers, G. *Towards a Sociology of Management*, Chapman and Hall, London, 1967.

Volk, T. *Gaia's Body: Towards a Physiology of Earth*, Copernicus Books, 1992.

Waldrop, M. *Complexity: The New Science at the Edge of Order and Chaos*, Touchstone Books, 1992.

Weber, M. *The Theory of Social and Economic Organization* (trans. A Henderson & T Parsons), Oxford University Press, 1947.

Wheatley, M. *Leadership and the New Science*, Berrett-Koehler, San Francisco, 1999.

Wheatley, M & Kellner-Rogers, M. *A Simpler Way*, Berrett-Koehler, San Francisco, 1996.

White OF & McSwain, CJ. 'Transformational Theory and Organizational Analysis', in Morgan, G. *Beyond Method: Strategies for Social Research*, Sage, Beverley Hills, 1983.

Whitehead, AN. *Modes of Thought*, Macmillan, New York, 1938.

Process and Reality: Corrected Edition, The Free Press, New York, 1978.

Whitmont, EC. *The Symbolic Quest: Basic Concepts of Analytical Psychology*, Princeton University Press, 1969.

Wilber, K. *The Atman Project*, Quest, Wheaton, 1980.

– *Up From Eden*, Doubleday New York, 1981.

– *A Brief History of Everything*, Shambhala, Boston, 1996.

Williams, A. *The Passionate Technique*, Routledge, London, 1989.

– *Forbidden Agendas*, Routledge, London, 1991.

Willis, P & Neville, B. *Qualitative Research Methods in Adult Education*, David Lovell Publishing, Melbourne, 1996.

Wolfe, T. *The Right Stuff*, Farrar, Strauss, and Giroux, New York, 1979.

Wright, P. *Spycatcher*, William Heinemann Australia, Sydney, 1988.

INDEX

A

B

C

D

E

F

G

H

I

J

K

L

M

N

O

P

R

S

T

U

V

W

Z